War and State Formation in Ancient China and Early Modern Europe

The Eurocentric conventional wisdom holds that the West is unique in having a multistate system in international relations and liberal democracy in state-society relations. At the same time, the Sinocentric perspective maintains that China is destined to have authoritarian rule under a unified empire. In fact, China in the Spring and Autumn and Warring States periods (656–221 BC) was a system of sovereign territorial states similar to Europe in the early modern period. In both cases this formative period witnessed the prevalence of war, formation of alliances, development of centralized bureaucracy, emergence of citizenship rights, and expansion of international trade. This book examines why China and Europe shared similar processes but experienced opposite outcomes. This historical comparison of China and Europe challenges the presumption that Europe was destined to enjoy checks and balances while China was preordained to suffer under a coercive universal empire.

Victoria Tin-bor Hui is a visiting Assistant Professor in Political Science at the University of Notre Dame. She was an Assistant Professor in Political Science at the University of Illinois. She received a Ph.D. from Columbia University and has received fellowships from the John M. Olin Institute for Strategic Studies at Harvard University, the Center for International Security and Cooperation at Stanford University, the Helen Kellogg Institute for International Studies at the University of Notre Dame, the Harry Frank Guggenheim Foundation, and the Institute for the Study of World Politics.

War and State Formation in Ancient China and Early Modern Europe

VICTORIA TIN-BOR HUI

University of Notre Dame

CAMBRIDGE
UNIVERSITY PRESS

CAMBRIDGE UNIVERSITY PRESS
Cambridge, New York, Melbourne, Madrid, Cape Town, Singapore, São Paulo

Cambridge University Press
40 West 20th Street, New York, NY 10011-4211, USA

www.cambridge.org
Information on this title: www.cambridge.org/9780521819725

First published 2005

Printed in the United States of America

A catalog record for this publication is available from the British Library.

Library of Congress Cataloging in Publication Data

Hui, Victoria Tin-bor, 1967–
War and state formation in ancient China and early modern Europe /
Victoria Tin-bor Hui.
    p.   cm.
Includes bibliographical references.
ISBN 0-521-81972-5 (hardback) – ISBN 0-521-52576-4 (pbk.)
    1. World politics.   2. China – Politics and government – To 221 B.C.   3. Europe – Politics
and government.   4. State, The.   5. War.   I. Title.
D32.H85   2005
931 – dc22
2004024989

ISBN-13   978-0-521-81972-5 hardback
ISBN-10   0-521-81972-5 hardback

ISBN-13   978-0-521-52576-3 paperback
ISBN-10   0-521-52576-4 paperback

To Mike and Mom, who give me unconditional support
To Hana Meihan, who grows up with this project

Contents

Contents

Tables and Maps

Tables

Maps

Acknowledgments

I have become heavily indebted in the course of writing this book. First of all, I must thank my dissertation advisers, who guided me through the difficult dissertation writing process. Jack Snyder, in particular, was responsible for inspiring me to embark on a comparison of ancient China and early modern Europe. In the initial stage, most professors thought that my topic was a crazy one – because no one would care about ancient China, because there could not possibly be enough sources to work with, or because it would not be possible to write a dissertation on two civilizations. Sinologists further believed that any work on pre-1949 China belonged to the history department rather than the political science department. There were many moments when I felt discouraged, but Jack gave me unswerving support. This research would not have been possible without him. While Jack inspired me to analyze the balance of power in ancient China, Ira Katznelson stimulated my interest in state-society relations. His graduate seminar "The State" in spring 1996 was so stimulating that I remain nostalgic about it to this day. Moreover, I want to thank Thomas Bernstein for agreeing to risk his reputation on my research and for keeping me aware of the expectations of China specialists. In this spirit, Andrew Nathan likewise challenged me to face various sinological assumptions.

My intellectual debts can also be traced to Charles Tilly, Robert Jervis, and Jon Elster. Chuck's theory of state formation forms the backbone of this book. Chuck is not just a master in his own work but also a legendary mentor for graduate students. He was just as heavily and directly involved with my dissertation as my advisers. He would share with me his manuscripts and offer speedy (sometimes overnight) comments on my multiple drafts. In addition, I borrow heavily from Robert Jervis's systems theory, Jon Elster's brand of rational choice theory, and Julian Franklin's take on classical and modern political theories. Jon Elster also deeply influenced my thinking and writing styles. It was a most embarrassing and enlightening experience when such a senior professor took more than two hours to explain to me (a then-second-year graduate student) why my draft class paper was completely incoherent. This book represents my efforts at blending the best teaching on international relations, comparative politics, and political theory, which I am happy to say is all available at Columbia University.

I have equally fond memories of my short stays at the John M. Olin Institute for Strategic Studies at Harvard University in 2000–2001 and the Center for International Security and Cooperation at Stanford University in 2001–2002. In addition to support from the Harry Frank Guggenheim Foundation and the Institute for the Study of World Politics, these two fellowships provided the necessary resources for my earlier research. Most of all, faculty members and Fellows provided valuable comments as well as moral support. I specifically thank Fiona Adamson, Robert Art, Bear Braumoeller, Lars-Erik Cederman, Thomas Christensen, Charles Cogan, Lynn Eden, Taylor Fravel, Stacey Goddard, Iain Johnston, Andrew Kydd, Gregory Mitrovitch, Alex Montgomery, Daniel Nexon, Stephen Rosen, Scott Sagan, Mark Sheetz, Monica Toft, Benjamin Valentino, and Erik Voeten. Moreover, Scott Mainwaring provided a "home" for me at the Helen Kellogg Institute for International Studies at the University of Notre Dame when the manuscript entered the final production stage.

I should also express my gratitude to other colleagues. Participants at the Dartmouth Workshop "Hierarchy and Balance in International Systems," including William Wohlforth, William Brenner, Daniel Deudney, Arthur Eckstein, David Kang, Stuart Kaufman, Richard Little, and Charles Jones, offered helpful suggestions. In addition, Gary Bass, Daniel Bell, Joseph Chan, Claudio Cioffi-Revilla, Michael Freeman, Robert Goodin, John Ikenberry, Lionel Jensen, Edward Kolodziej, Jack Levy, Marc Plattner, Samuel Popkin, Sidney Rittenberg, Richard Rosecrance, Peter Rutland, Richard Snyder, Harrison Wagner, Yu Xingzhong, Zhao Dingxin, and participants at various presentations and conferences provided criticisms of different aspects of my argument.[1] Moreover, I am thankful to Chang Wejen of the Academia Sinica for hosting my research

---

[1] Chinese names follow the Chinese convention by beginning with surnames.

trip to Taipei in September 1997, and to Zhu Feng of Peking University for hosting my research trip to Beijing in November 1997.

For a book that bridges political science and history, I extend my special thanks to historians. Political scientists in general and realist scholars in particular are often criticized for abusing history. For this reason, I have been very mindful not to distort history – especially Chinese history – myself. So Kee-long provided informal suggestions on historical sources. Mark Lewis and Bin Wong gave me precious comments on my dissertation. Ralph Sawyer and Douglas Henderson examined the revised draft. Bruce Brooks scrutinized my draft Chapter Two in excruciating detail and answered innumerable questions on different aspects of ancient Chinese history. I am also indebted to members of the Warring States Working Group and the China/Greece Colloquium listservs for sharing their opinions. I benefited immensely, in particular, from Stephen Angle, Thomas Bartlett, Christopher Beckwith, Taeko Brooks, Chow Kai-wing, Steve Farmer, Paul Goldin, Andrew Huxley, Whalen Lai, Victor Mair, John Major, Yuri Pines, Moss Roberts, Steven Sage, David Schaberg, Raphael Sealey, and Adam Smith. As Chinese records are extremely controversial, I do not always follow the suggestions of historians. Bruce Brooks, for instance, fiercely argues that classical texts except the *Chunqiu* (Spring and Autumn Annals) involve retrospective reconstruction and should not be used as historical sources at face value. I share Bruce's view that historical records are inevitably products of political struggles. But if that is true, then I am skeptical of his efforts to establish *the* truth about ancient Chinese history. It is difficult enough to establish truths in contentious politics even in our own time – witness the arduous tasks faced by various truth commissions and war crimes tribunals.

As this book potentially challenges mainstream theories in political science and conventional wisdoms about two civilizations, I have taken too long to sharpen the theoretical arguments and substantiate the historical details. I am exceptionally grateful to Cambridge University Press for the advance contract and various editors for their patience and assistance. The one person I cannot possibly thank enough is my husband, Michael Davis. As a professor of comparative constitutionalism, international law, and human rights, he first convinced me to attend graduate school and then encouraged me to "follow my heart" in tracking my own path in my research. Although many people thought that my topic was tantamount to "a kiss of death," Mike gave me unyielding moral and financial support. While I was writing this book, he had to tolerate many obscure discussions (such as comparison of the Mencians and the Huguenots) at the dinner table. His inputs are everywhere in the text. Moreover, I must also thank my mom, who supports whatever I do even though she does not know what my scholarly work is about. Furthermore, I owe my little girl, Hana, all the lost time she could not spend with her mommy.

I

A Dynamic Theory of World Politics

This book originates from a peculiar puzzle: Why is it that political scientists and Europeanists take for granted checks and balances in European politics, while Chinese and sinologists take for granted a coercive universal empire in China? This research question is not as odd as it appears because China in the Spring and Autumn and Warring States periods (656–221 BC) was a multistate system that closely resembled Europe in the early modern period (AD 1495–1815). Although it is often presumed that China or Zhongguo refers to the "Middle Kingdom," this term originally referred to "central states": *zhong* means "central" and *guo* means "states."[1] As the early modern European system did, the Zhongguo system experienced disintegration of feudal hierarchy, prevalence of war, conditions of international anarchy, emergence of sovereign territorial states, configuration of the balance of power, development of the centralized bureaucracy, birth of state-society bargains, expansion of international trade, and other familiar phenomena of international and domestic politics. If the balance of power prevailed in international politics and the constitutional state triumphed in state-society relations in Europe, then why did the opposite outcomes occur in ancient China? Is it because China was destined to have authoritarian rule under a unified empire as taught in standard Chinese history books? Alternatively, is it possible that the European trajectory was far more contingent than is presumed by the Eurocentric perspective?

To understand two historical trajectories as what they are, I have been driven to work out a dynamic theory of world politics that blends Eurocentric and Sinocentric perspectives, connects the ancient and the

---

[1] Chen 1941, 643; Loewe 1999, 993–994; Ye 1992, 89–135.

modern, reconciles alternative trajectories and opposite outcomes, and incorporates persistent continuity and endogenous transformation. To achieve these goals, the proposed theory examines the mutual constitution of international competition and state formation, the simultaneity of competing causal mechanisms, the strategic interaction of actors, the conjuncture of motivation and capability, the interaction of agency and structure, and the coexistence of institutional stasis and innovations. Scholars of international politics and state-society relations generally presume that attempts at domination are necessarily checked by countervailing mechanisms. This mainstream perspective is not inaccurate, but it is one-sided. A dynamic theory should examine coercive mechanisms and strategies which *facilitate* domination as well as countervailing mechanisms and strategies which *check* attempts at domination. A dynamic theory should also view politics – both international and domestic – as processes of strategic interaction between domination-seekers and targets of domination who employ competing strategies and who are simultaneously facilitated and burdened by competing causal mechanisms. As strategic interactions generate multiple equilibria, it is then possible to see how strategies and mechanisms are transcendent across time and space while outcomes are sensitive to historically contingent conditions. By accounting for both similarity in processes and divergence in outcomes, this dynamic framework also highlights in what ways Chinese history could have followed the European pattern and at what moments European history could have followed the Chinese pattern.

Given the unusual comparison of China and Europe, I introduce the unfamiliar ancient Chinese system in the first section and discuss the "uncommon foundations" method in the second section. The building blocks of a dynamic theory are outlined in the third section. Although the proposed theory is meant to integrate the dynamics of international politics and the dynamics of state formation, the two spheres are discussed separately in the fourth and fifth sections. The initial and environmental conditions that shape the competition of opposite mechanisms and strategies are addressed in the sixth section, and some common "alternative explanations" are clarified in the last.

1.1   Cases

Chang Kwang-chih suggested two decades ago that

[i]t is time to consider the possibility that theories of history could be built on the development of other civilizations. . . . Chinese history is as formidable and massive

as Western history, but it has not been analyzed in the same way.... Chinese records will make an important contribution to historical theory: they will confirm it through substantial data, or they will modify it to some degree, resulting in generalizations of ever wider applicability and validity.[2]

In the same spirit, Kenneth Waltz recommends that scholars "look farther afield . . . to the China of the [W]arring [S]tates era . . . and see that where political entities of whatever sort compete freely, substantive and stylistic characteristics are similar."[3] Indeed, of all historical systems in world history, the ancient Chinese system most closely resembles the stereotypical anarchical international system because it is composed of sovereign territorial states while other systems are constituted by nonstate entities (such as city-states) or dissimilar units (that is, the coexistence of territorial states, city-states, city-leagues, city-empires). Not surprisingly, the few scholars who have accepted the challenge to compare China and Europe have produced very interesting findings.[4] Richard Walker has identified many "obvious" and "unbelievably precise" parallels between ancient China and modern Europe.[5] Bin Wong discovers that many "[i]deas and institutions that are specifically 'modern' in the West are simply not 'modern' in China."[6]

Similarly to the early modern European system, the ancient Chinese system emerged from the ruins of the prior feudal order. Zhou established a feudal hierarchy after conquering Shang around 1045 BC.[7] The Zhou king directly ruled vast areas that he could effectively control. At the same time, the king enfeoffed his sons, relatives, and high officials (who had made significant contributions in the takeover) to defend distant strategic points from the conquered Shang people and their former allies.[8] Each

---

[2] Chang 1983, 128–129. Following the Chinese convention, Chinese names begin with surnames unless the scholars in question go by English names.

[3] Waltz 1986, 329–330. Among political scientists, scholars of international relations who aspire to universal theories across time and space are the most sympathetic to a comparison with ancient China. A number of them have introduced the ancient Chinese system to students of international relations (IR). See Bau 1986; Chan 1999; Chen 1941; Holsti 1995, 34–49; 1999, 284–286; Johnston 1995; Walker 1953. Other IR scholars have also alluded to the ancient Chinese system. See Cusack and Stoll 1990, 5–8, 16; Jervis 1997, 133; Levy 1983, 10; van Evera 1998, 36–37; 1999, 179–182.

[4] However, it is important for adventuresome social scientists to learn from historians of China. Otherwise, scholars may well produce misleading accounts.

[5] Walker 1953, xi.   [6] Wong 1997, 101.

[7] There is no agreement on when the Zhou era began. I adopt Sawyer's dating. Sawyer 1993, 380, fn. 10. Some historians use 1122 BC. Dating of any events before 841 BC can only be based on rough estimates.

[8] Zhou feudalism is called *fengjian*. This term literally means to "enfeof [nobles] and construct [the state]." Hook 1991, 169.

enfeoffed lord would move to the designated area with his whole lineage and build a garrisoned city-state called *guo*. In the beginning, the Zhou king's authority was buttressed by both his position as the head of an extended lineage and his control over far superior economic resources and military strength. Over time, however, blood ties between the Zhou king and feudal lords became distant. At the same time, the balance of capabilities gradually shifted in favor of *guo* because the centrally located Zhou court had little room for expansion while feudal units could expand into uncharted surrounding areas.

The Zhou hierarchy eventually crumbled in 770 BC, when a disastrous "barbarian"[9] attack forced the Zhou court to move eastward from Hao to Loyang. This incident "marked the definitive end of the political and military dominance of the royal house."[10] The court's resource base was dramatically reduced after losing Hao to "barbarians" and granting additional lands to various powerful *guo* as rewards for their assistance during the crisis. In the subsequent Spring and Autumn period (770–453 BC) and Warring States period (453–221 BC),[11] *guo* were independent of the Zhou court. As an assertion of this new reality, the Lu *guo* began to keep its own court chronicle, the *Chunqiu* or *Spring and Autumn Annals*, in 722 BC. The Zheng *guo*, which bordered Zhou, even repeatedly seized harvests from the royal domain. To "punish" Zheng, Zhou declared war in 707 BC but suffered a humiliating defeat. Henceforth, Zhou sank further to "the level of her formal vassals."[12] In diplomatic meetings, all heads of *guo* treated one another as equals despite their differences in feudal ranks.

Historians of ancient China typically date the beginning of the multi-state era in 770 BC. However, the disintegration of feudal hierarchy is not the only criterion for dating the onset of system formation.[13] Jack Levy

---

[9] Descendants of the Zhou lineage generally viewed non-Zhou peoples as "barbarians," even though the latter could be just as civilized as the former.

[10] Lewis 1990, 47. The Zhou era before the move is thus called "Western Zhou" and the era afterward "Eastern Zhou." But some historians object to the term "Eastern Zhou" as it carries the problematic implication that the Zhou court still exercised authority over *guo*. While the court most likely maintained some moral and ceremonial authority, effective authority was a different matter.

[11] The Spring and Autumn period was named after the Lu chronicle *Chunqiu* (Spring and Autumn Annals). The Warring States period was named after *Zhanguo ce* (Stratagems of the Warring States), which was written in the Han Dynasty. Historians have no agreement on the year that divides the two periods. I use 453 BC, when Jin was split into Han, Wei, and Zhao.

[12] Hsu 1965a, 5. Zhou was eventually exterminated by Qin in 256 BC.

[13] Borrowing from the state formation literature, I use the term "system formation" to refer to the formation of an international system.

argues that an international system is composed of "states characterized by the centralization of political power within a given territory, independent from any higher secular authority and interacting in an interdependent system of security relations."[14] Barry Buzan and Richard Little highlight the third element, arguing that "a set of states that cannot pose each other military threat fail to constitute an international system."[15] The ability of states to form interdependent relations is a function of "interaction capacity," that is, "the amount of transportation, communication, and organizational capability" in a system.[16] Levy suggests that "the French invasion of Italy at the end of 1494 and the Treaty of Venice in March of 1495 mark the coalescence of the major European states into a truly interdependent system of behavior" in Europe.[17] In ancient China, military and diplomatic contacts remained bilateral and regional rather than systemic in scope for a century after 770 BC. Bruce Brooks observes from Lu's *Spring and Autumn Annals* that it was not until around 659 BC that *guo* developed sufficient contacts to acquire systemwide mutual awareness.[18] Coincidentally, Chu repeatedly attacked Zheng from 659 to 653 BC and Qi responded by mobilizing a northern alliance, which invaded Chu's territory in 656 BC. I thus date the onset of the ancient Chinese system in 656 BC. The ancient Chinese system ended at the establishment of a universal empire in 221 BC, whereas the early modern European system ended at the conclusion of the Napoleonic Wars in 1815.[19]

In the multistate era, *guo* waged wars against one another, made and broke alliances as they saw fit, and set up diplomatic offices to handle matters of war and peace. In this environment, ancient China developed the art of war and the markers of territorial sovereignty light years before Western practices.[20] The *zhongguo* or central states in ancient China

---

[14] Levy 1983, 21.   [15] Buzan and Little 2000, 80.   [16] Ibid.

[17] Levy 1983, 21. Some scholars of international relations date the onset of the modern European system in 1648. See Philpott 2001; Gross 1968. However, as Gross points out, "The Peace of Westphalia did no more than legalize a condition of things already in existence." Gross 1968, 60; also Krasner 1999. Moreover, historians tend to use either the French invasion of Italy or the convenient century marker of 1500.

[18] I thank Bruce Brooks for this crucial point. Personal communication, June 2 and November 7, 2002.

[19] From then on, many modern phenomena such as the industrial revolution, laissez-faire capitalism, and liberal democracy would make the comparison with ancient China more problematic. But I will discuss the post-1815 world in Chapter Five, Conclusion and Implications.

[20] Ancient Chinese diplomacy was mission-based. Thus, it may be said that diplomacy was not as developed in ancient China as in Renaissance Italy. However, at the onset of the early modern period, diplomacy in the rest of Europe was also less institutionalized than

were similar to European states: they were territorial in that they defined their rule as "exclusive authority over a fixed territorial space" and were sovereign in that they "claim[ed] final authority and recognize[d] no higher source of jurisdiction."[21] Although *guo* were originally city-states sparsely located throughout the Yellow River valley, they became larger and larger territorial units as the more powerful pacified surrounding areas and conquered weaker neighbors. In the Spring and Autumn period, buffer zones were gradually taken over and noncontiguous pieces of territory were sometimes peacefully exchanged. With more continuous territory, boundaries became increasingly hardened with checkpoints established along borders. Envoys who wished to cross a third state to their destinations had to seek permission or risk seizure and death. In the Warring States period, the territorial aspect of sovereign states was increasingly "marked by the building of chains of watch stations and forts at strategic points, and ultimately the creation of large defensive walls along the boundaries of the various states."[22] In the late multistate era, travelers were even required to carry identification documents or what we in the modern era call "passports."[23]

Ancient China resembled early modern Europe not just in interstate relations, but also in state-society relations. The sovereign territorial states in ancient China developed centralized authority with bureaucratized administration, monopolized coercion, and nationalized taxation. It is often presumed that the centralized bureaucracy is modern and Western. However, Herrlee Creel highlights that "[t]he most surprising and perhaps the most illuminating similarities appear when comparison is made between China's government as it existed two thousand years ago and the highly centralized bureaucratic administration of modern states."[24] The distinction of the state from the reigning ruler, the separation of public offices from officeholders, the selection and promotion of officials on the basis of objective and meritocratic criteria, the universality and impartiality of publicly promulgated laws, the registration and enumeration

---

in Italy. Moreover, in ancient China, there were such recurrent occasions to arrange alliances, declare war, or make peace that there were almost constant diplomatic exchanges between the *guo*.

[21] Spruyt 1994, 34.   [22] Lewis 1999, 629.

[23] Such documents were inscribed on bronze, wood, or other materials and were designed to give official permission to let the bearer through government checkpoints. Yates 1980, 26.

[24] Creel 1970a, 3; see also 1970b, 124. Creel refers to the early Han Dynasty. But the administrative technologies listed here were developed in the Warring States period and then adopted by the Qin and Han Dynasties.

of populations, the central budgeting of revenues and expenditures, the amassing of statistics and reports, the capacity for direct rule, and other administrative techniques were developed in China two thousand years ahead of Europe. Moreover, as I shall elaborate later, state-society bargains in terms of legal rights, enlightened thoughts, and welfare policies indigenously emerged on Chinese soil long before they blossomed on European soil. In short, ancient China shared striking similarities with early modern Europe in many crucial respects.

Before I proceed further, I should underscore that this book does not provide a complete account of interstate and state-society relations in two historical systems which together span 757 years. No single analysis can do such a daunting task. As Charles Tilly says about his macrohistory of the second millennium, "I must deal with historical facts like a rock skipping water...I do not know all the history one would need to write this book fully."[25] Nor do I know enough about the ancient Middle East, classical Greece, pre-Mauryan India, classical Maya, Renaissance Italy, Samguk Korea, and Tokugawa Japan to claim that this China-Europe comparison is generalizable to other historical systems.[26] I hope only to take the first step toward broad comparisons of whole systems.

1.2 Method

If ancient China resembled early modern Europe in both international and domestic politics, then why is it that a coercive universal empire triumphed in the former but checks and balances predominated in the latter? Is it simply because ancient China and early modern Europe are not comparable cases? After all, the two systems represent extreme ends of East and West in terms of culture; they are located on opposite sides of the Eurasian continent in terms of space; and they are separated by more than two millennia of time. As such, these two systems are not amenable to the principle of maximizing underlying commonalities, which requires the researcher to "test the validity of propositions by making comparisons between two situations that are identical except for one variable."[27] However, historically grounded social scientists have observed that the ceteris paribus assumption almost never holds in comparative

[25] Tilly 1992 [1990], 35.
[26] See Buzan and Little 2000; Kaufman 1997; Watson 1992; and Wohlforth et al. 2005.
[27] Jervis 1997, 73.

history.[28] If scholars were to follow this principle strictly, then comparative studies would be confined to mostly neighboring countries.

To break out of this unnecessary restraint, more and more scholars have
set aside universal theories, which make invariable propositions irrespective of contexts, and focused on causal mechanisms, which have varying
effects, depending on contexts.[29] As Jon Elster puts it, "The distinctive
feature of a mechanism is not that it can be universally applied to predict
and control social events, but that it embodies a causal chain that is sufficiently general and precise to enable us to locate it in widely different
settings."[30] Douglas McAdam, Sidney Tarrow, and Charles Tilly even unambiguously abandon the "common foundations" method and advocate
the "uncommon foundations" method.[31] They use "paired comparisons
of uncommon cases" to find out how recurrent causal mechanisms combine differently with varying initial and environmental conditions to produce radically different outcomes.[32] I adopt this historical-institutionalist
approach and pay special attention to initial and environmental conditions, timing, and path dependence.[33] At the same time, I also follow the
structural approach common in international politics and examine how
the pressure of war compelled similar causal mechanisms across time and
space. As Tilly neatly captures it, "Europe shared many political processes
with China, but put them together in different sequences, combinations,
and environments, with dramatically different consequences."[34]

When we focus on causal mechanisms instead of universal laws, it
is also possible to refrain from examining ancient China through the
lenses of the European trajectory. Edgar Kiser and Yong Cai study Qin
China as "an empirical outlier and a theoretical anomaly" for theories of
bureaucratization.[35] Many colleagues in international relations have likewise expected me to address the question "Why did the balance of power

---

[28] Jervis even speaks of "the perils of using the *ceteris paribus* assumption" because this
approach makes it impossible to analyze systemic processes such as feedback effects and
the interaction of units and system. Jervis 1997, 76.
[29] Skocpol claims to follow the standard comparative method in her analysis of the French,
Russian, and Chinese Revolutions. However, as Goldstone points out, Skocpol does
not comply with the standard comparative method and presents no "law" of revolutions. Her argument in fact "delineates a specific historical set of conditions that occurred in similar fashion in several places." Goldstone 1991, 56–57; Skocpol 1979,
40–41.
[30] Elster 1993, 5.   [31] McAdam, Tarrow, and Tilly 2001, 81–84.   [32] Ibid., 83.
[33] Collier and Collier 1991; Katznelson 2003; Mahoney 2000; Mahoney and Rueschemeyer
2003; North 1990; Pierson 2000; Thelen 1999; 2003.
[34] Tilly 1998, 7.   [35] Kiser and Cai 2003, 518.

fail in the ancient Chinese system?"[36] As Bin Wong observes, when we take the European experience as the norm and non-Western experiences as abnormal, we are led "to search for what went wrong in other parts of the world."[37] Another problem with the "Why not?" question is that it presumes "a unidirectionality of social development"[38] and so makes understanding alternative trajectories difficult. Charles Tilly suggests that we should consider "the possibility that the Western experience was a lucky shot, an aberration, a dead end, or simply one among many paths."[39] Hence, I treat ancient China as "a significant case that must be integrally explained by any theory that is to be considered adequate," rather than a "deviant case" that diverges from the European norm.[40]

At the same time, I do not think that Eurocentric theories are necessarily inapplicable to non-European contexts.[41] As Wong points out, "Eurocentric views of the world are inadequate, but they are not necessarily more wrong (or right) than comparisons made from other vantage points."[42] The Sinocentric claim to Chinese uniqueness is particularly problematic. While it is wrong for Europeanists to presume that checks and balance represent the norm, it is also wrong for sinologists to assume that the universal empire and the authoritarian tradition represent the inevitable course of Chinese history. Both views make the mistake of studying history retrospectively by looking at political phenomena at the present and working backward for their causes. Such an approach produces a "certainty of hindsight bias" that blinds us to various "suppressed historical alternatives" or paths not taken.[43] It also buries the "hundreds of states that once flourished but then disappeared."[44] A better approach is to work prospectively by beginning at formative stages in history and searching forward for alternative paths and outcomes.[45]

In tracing Chinese and European histories as they unfold, I also follow Bin Wong's "symmetric perspectives" by evaluating China from the

---

[36] Chi Hsi-sheng, who examines the "Chinese warlord system" of 1916–1928, follows the "Why not?" approach. He applies Morton Kaplan's balance-of-power theory and asks why various warlords violated many of the essential behavioral rules necessary for system stability. Chi 1968; Kaplan 1979.

[37] Wong 1999, 210; see also Blue and Brook 1999; Sivin 1982.

[38] Kohli and Shue 1994, 310.   [39] Tilly 1975, 4.

[40] Blue and Brook 1999, 8. As Arthur Stinchombe puts it, "One does not apply theory to history; rather, one uses history to develop theory." Cited in Goldstone 1991, 39.

[41] Some mainland Chinese scholars have tried to develop an international relations theory "with Chinese characteristics." See Chan 1998.

[42] Wong 1997, 7.   [43] Lebow 2000, 559; Mahoney 2000, 530.

[44] Tilly 1992 [1990], 9.   [45] Tilly 1975, 14–15; 1992 [1990], 33.

European perspective *and* evaluating Europe from the Chinese perspective.[46] This approach is tantamount to using early modern Europe as a real "counterfactual China" and ancient China as a real "counterfactual Europe." In the standard counterfactual thought experiment, the analyst asks what would have happened if a hypothesized cause had been absent.[47] But this imaginary counterfactual method is of little use to systems analyses or macrohistorical studies because interrelated phenomena "cannot change one at a time."[48] This difficulty, however, can be solved by using real cases to anchor the counterfactual.[49] In the historical analysis, I examine first ancient China in light of Eurocentric theories and then early modern Europe in light of the ancient Chinese experience.

1.3   Building Blocks for a Dynamic Theory of World Politics

To examine ancient China and early modern Europe as what they are, the research questions should be phrased in a value-free manner: If the two historical cases shared similar processes of interstate and state-society relations, then why did they witness diametrically opposite outcomes? What accounts for the early convergence but eventual divergence of the ancient Chinese and early modern European trajectories? What accounts for the early stability of checks and balances but eventual triumph of domination

---

[46] Wong 1997, 93.   [47] Fearon 1991, 1996; Lebow 2000.   [48] Jervis 1997, 73.

[49] Tilly uses imperial China to construct a "counterfactual Europe" to find out under what conditions and by what processes post-Westphalian Europe would have moved closer to Chinese forms of politics, such as "domination by a single encompassing state" and "exclusion of the bulk of the population from direct participation in public politics." Tilly 1998, 5. "To do this counterfactual work," Tilly notes that "we must reverse the Westphalian process, and therefore perhaps the course of the Thirty Years War.... We must construct a Holy Roman Empire that emerged from the war not only dominant within its scattered lands but territorially contiguous and formidable along its frontiers. We must conjure up a sufficiently forceful Habsburg monarch – Philip IV, Ferdinand III, or perhaps even Maximilian I of Bavaria – to ally with the pope in uniting Catholic Europe and reconstructing the empire as its bulwark. We must manage more defeats for Gustavus Adolphus and more victories for Wallenstein as well as my non-ancestor Tilly." Tilly 1998, 6–7. Such a scenario of a hegemonic Europe is analogous to what Lebow calls a "miracle counterfactual." Lebow 2000, 565–566. By conjuncturally altering so many historical events in one counterfactual exercise, Tilly would have overstretched the human imagination. But he solves the problem by using a concrete Chinese case to anchor his counterfactual. In addition to historical narratives, computer simulation allows one to "rerun history." See Axelrod 1997; Cederman 1996, 1997; Cusack and Stoll 1990. It is interesting to note that initial conditions are as important in computer simulation as in comparative history. Even when decision rules are held constant, computer simulation generates different results, which are due to random differences in the initial wealth of significant actors and in the order in which actors become active. Axelrod 1997, 139–140.

TABLE 1. *A Dynamic Framework of Competing Logics*

The Logic of Balancing	The Logic of Domination
Balance of Power or Resistance	Counterbalancing Strategy (Divide-and-Rule or Divide-and-Conquer)
	Ruthless Stratagems
Rising Costs of Expansion or Administration	Self-Strengthening Reforms

in ancient China? I propose a dynamic theory of world politics which not only integrates Eurocentric and Sinocentric perspectives, but also accommodates both balancing and domination. An important theme in the study of politics is power. Yet, political scientists rarely study the full spectrum of power politics and often bracket the *problematique* of domination. Scholars of both international relations and state-society relations argue that attempts at domination are invariably checked by the mechanism of balance of power or resistance and that of rising costs of expansion or administration. I argue that we have to examine not just what power seekers *cannot* do, but also what they *can* do. Domination-seekers can overcome resistance and costs by pursuing counterbalancing strategies, ruthless stratagems, and self-strengthening reforms. As a shorthand, I use the "logic of balancing" in referring to countervailing mechanisms and the "logic of domination" in referring to coercive mechanisms. To understand the simultaneous interplay of domination and balancing, we should see politics as strategic interaction between domination-seekers and targets of domination who employ competing strategies and who are simultaneously assisted and obstructed by competing causal mechanisms. This theoretical framework is summarized in Table 1. Before I discuss how the logic of balancing and the logic of domination operate in international politics and domestic politics, I shall spell out three interrelated building blocks which are essential to a theory of change: strategic interaction of strategies and mechanisms, heterogeneous motivations of human behaviors, and integration of agency and structure. While these building blocks are not at all new, they are often misspecified in mainstream political science theories – especially international relations theories.

Strategic Interaction of Strategies and Mechanisms

A dynamic theory should consider politics as a process of strategic interaction between competing strategies and mechanisms rather than a parametric constant. The idea that political changes "arise as the result of the action and interaction of individuals" is quite established in political science.[50] In game theory, analysts underscore the fact that the ability of any actor to achieve his/her goal depends on the actions of others. In comparative politics, Charles Tilly and other scholars of state-society relations examine "the pattern of tactical moves and countermoves between regime and challengers."[51] In international relations, Ivan Arreguín-Toft argues that "every strategy has an ideal counterstrategy."[52] Although Kenneth Waltz explicitly dismisses strategies, he in fact employs the language of strategic interaction in his discussion of power: "Whether A, in applying its capabilities, gains the wanted compliance of B depends on A's capabilities and strategy, on B's capabilities and counter-strategy, and on all these factors as they are affected by the situation at hand."[53] Waltz even defines the supposedly structural mechanism of "external balancing" as "*moves* to strengthen and enlarge one's own alliance or to weaken and shrink an opposing one," and "internal balancing" as "*moves* to increase economic capability, to increase military strength, to develop clever strategies."[54] Chinese military classics share this strategic-interactive perspective. They highlight that the key to victory lies in "the matching of opposites and complementaries one against the other" – the challenge of the astute commander is to match the adversary's capability and strategy with the appropriate counterstrategy.[55]

Politics involves strategic interaction between not just actors and their strategies, but also causal mechanisms. This view may be contrary to the standard positivist approach, which prohibits hypotheses that say, "If x, then y and not-y." However, "contradictory processes" are often at work in political phenomena.[56] In electoral politics, Elster observes that some voters tend to "favor the candidate tipped to win (the 'bandwagon effect')" while others tend to "identify with the one tipped to lose (the 'underdog effect')."[57] In international politics, both power politics and normative concerns are real forces. As Edward Carr argues, international politics "will, to the end of history, be an area . . . where the ethical and coercive factors of human life will inter-penetrate and work out their tentative and uneasy compromises."[58] John Owen similarly suggests that

---

[50] Elster 1989b, 13; also Schelling 1960.   [51] Goldstone and Tilly 2001, 181.
[52] Arreguín-Toft 2001, 104.   [53] Waltz 1979, 191–192.
[54] Ibid., 118 (emphasis added).
[55] Lewis 1990, 118. Note that Arreguín-Toft's view is based on Mao Zedong's military thought.
[56] Hirschman 1992, 139; also Katznelson 1997, 100–101.
[57] Elster 1993, 3.   [58] Carr 1964, 100.

because "*realpolitik* pushes policy into one direction and liberalism in another," the "combined effect conceals two strong mechanisms working at cross purposes."[59] While the interaction of normative and coercive mechanisms typically operates on negative feedback, both sets of forces on their own may operate on positive feedback. When negative feedback is at work, any change automatically sets in motion countervailing forces to reestablish the equilibrium. When positive feedback operates, a change in one direction sets in motion reinforcing pressures that produce further change in the same direction.[60] The simultaneity of positive and negative feedbacks explains why human history has witnessed both stability and change. Moreover, because the interactions of both actors and mechanisms produce multiple equilibria, outcomes are inherently unpredictable a priori.

Heterogeneous Motivations of Human Behaviors

A dynamic theory of world politics should also pay attention to the heterogeneity of human motivations. Human behaviors are driven by not just the cold-blooded calculation of costs and benefits, but also the normative concern for the common good.[61] Interest is not the primary – or even the only – motivation in a wide range of political phenomena. However, it is legitimate to treat interest as the beginning point of analysis and see how far we can go before we must concede to norms. As Elster points out, "self-interest is more fundamental than altruism" in the sense that "[i]f nobody had first-order, selfish pleasures, nobody could have higher-order, altruistic motives either."[62] If we proceed by treating individuals as self-interested egoists, what logical implications should we expect? To put it briefly, the relentless pursuit of narrow self-interest unconstrained by norms should lead to a world of opportunism in which actors pursue gain-maximizing behaviors and have difficulty effecting cooperation.[63] Such a scenario is conducive to coercion and domination rather than checks and balances.

---

[59] Owen 1994, 122.

[60] Arthur 1989; 1990; Jervis 1997, ch. 4; Pierson 2000. Positive feedback is analogous to the concept of "increasing returns" in economics.

[61] Human behaviors are also driven by passions and emotions, for example, fear, hope, anger, shame, honor, envy, and vanity. Although classical thinkers such as Machiavelli and Hobbes emphasized both passions and interests, modern social scientists tend to ignore the former and focus on the latter. For exceptions, see Crawford 2000; Elster 1989b, ch. 7; 1999; Hirschman 1977.

[62] Elster 1989b, 53–54.   [63] Elster 1989b, 60; Williamson 1985, 30.

In international relations, realist thinkers – from Niccolò Machiavelli
and Thomas Hobbes through Hans Morgenthau to Robert Gilpin and
John Mearsheimer – have argued that self-interested rulers pursue opportunistic expansion, which provides the driving force for realpolitik
competition.[64] Kenneth Waltz, however, revises classical insights and suggests that rational states should seek to maximize security rather than
power because "security is the highest end" and "power is a means not
an end."[65] Other Waltzian realists – whether they are of the offensive or
defensive variant – follow suit.[66] In doing so, Waltzian realists miss the
dynamism in the oft-cited maxim that states "at a minimum, seek their
own preservation and, at a maximum, drive for universal domination."[67]
It is true that self-interested states desire survival above all else and that
they are not blind expanders. But self-interested states should logically
pursue opportunistic expansion, that is, "incremental, repeated, and localized efforts to expand power," when the prospective benefits outweigh
the prospective costs.[68] Eric Labs argues that "decisive military victory
is the most common form of opportunity" because it "emboldens the
victorious state to pursue war aims much greater than it had originally
planned."[69] In addition to military victories, ambitious states may also
create windows of opportunity by diplomatic maneuvers and internal
mobilization.[70] Moreover, when earlier attempts are successful, over time
self-interested states should steadily upgrade their expansionist goals, ultimately culminating in attempts at universal domination. Opportunistic
expansion is thus a dynamic mechanism that facilitates endogenous and
coercive transformation in international politics.

If we follow through the logical implications of the self-interest assumption, we should also expect actors to pursue gain maximization
with guile. As Elster points out, "Acting according to self-interest means
never telling the truth or keeping one's promise unless it pays to do so;
stealing and cheating if one can get away with it or, more generally, if
the expected value of doing so is larger than the expected value of the

---

[64] *The Prince*, ch. 3; *Leviathan*, pt. 2, ch. 29; Morgenthau 1973, 35; Gilpin 1981, 23;
     Mearsheimer 2001, 168–170, 238. See also Kydd 1997, 116; Schweller 1996, 100; Wendt
     1992, 408.
[65] Waltz 1979, 126.
[66] In general, defensive realism argues that "states attempt to expand when expansion in-
     creases their security," and offensive realism argues that "a state's capabilities shape
     its intentions: it will expand when it can." Lynn-Jones 1998, 160, 163. Note that even
     Mearsheimer, the strongest advocate of offensive realism, emphasizes that the fundamen-
     tal motive driving state behavior is survival. Mearsheimer 2001, 34.
[67] Waltz 1979, 118.   [68] Labs 1997, 12.   [69] Ibid., 19.   [70] Van Evera 1999, 70–71.

alternative."[71] In the international arena where the costs of measurement are high and enforcement is difficult, the benefits from cheating and reneging easily exceed the benefits from cooperative behavior. It is thus not surprising that Niccolò Machiavelli observed that "those rulers who have not thought it important to keep their word have achieved great things . . . [and] have been able to overcome those who have placed store in integrity."[72]

A world of self-interested actors is a world of dog-eat-dog competition not just in interstate relations, but also in state-society relations. If a ruler betrays his allies and breaks his word in the international realm, he is likely also to subjugate his citizens in the domestic realm. It is no coincidence that the public choice literature generally treats the state as the predatory Mafia.[73] Moreover, since even the most powerful ruler cannot govern by himself, we should expect self-interested officials similarly to engage in cheating, shirking, power struggles, and court intrigues. Realist theorists of international relations typically presume that the state is a unitary actor with coherent preferences, well-grounded beliefs, and a centralized capacity to act on decisions.[74] However, an honest rational account must follow methodological individualism, which views "the individual human action as the basic building block of aggregate social phenomena."[75] The analyst has the burden to show how any particular society can establish efficient institutions that channel individual interests to serve the national interest. Douglas North believes that "it is hard – maybe impossible – to model such a polity with wealth-maximizing actors unconstrained by other considerations."[76] Indeed, even rulers may place their personal interests in tenure and autonomy above the national interest of international competitiveness.[77] As we shall see in subsequent chapters, innumerable rulers and officials in both ancient China and early modern Europe sacrificed the public interest for private gains.

Opportunism is conducive to coercive transformation not only because the strong seek power maximization, but also because the weak face the

---

[71] Elster 1989a, 264; also North 1990, 55.   [72] *The Prince*, ch. 18, in Wootton 1994, 53.

[73] North 1990, 140.

[74] For critiques of this IR assumption, see Elster 1989b, 177; 2000, 692–693; Jervis 1998, 988; Kahler 1998, 930–940; Milner 1998.

[75] Elster 1989a, 8–9.

[76] North 1990, 140; North and Thomas 1973, 1–2. Similarly, Elster argues that it is "plain wrong" for social scientists to believe that it is possible to design institutions that "make it in people's rational interest to speak the truth, keep their promises and help others." Elster 1989b, 52.

[77] Rosenthal 1998, 101.

collective-action problem. Resistance to domination is a form of public good that entails costs to participating individuals. This means that although all targets of domination would benefit from successful resistance and suffer from successful domination, those who pursue short-term self-interest will free-ride on others' contribution.[78] As Robert Putnam observes of the "uncivic community" in southern Italy, a general atmosphere of "defection, distrust, shirking, exploitation, isolation, disorder, and stagnation" can lead to "the Hobbesian, hierarchical solution to dilemmas of collective action – coercion, exploitation, and dependence."[79] By the same logic, Alexander Wendt believes that collective action is "nearly impossible" in a Hobbesian international system because each state must constantly fear being stabbed in the back.[80] When targets of domination exist in competitive isolation from one another, it should not be very difficult for power seekers to subjugate them one after another.

It may be argued that self-interested actors can engage in voluntary cooperation if they play the tit-for-tat strategy as in the game of the Prisoners' Dilemma. The tit-for-tat strategy prescribes that players always cooperate in the first game, and that they cooperate in each subsequent game if the other player cooperated in the previous game.[81] However, Robert Axelrod, an ardent proponent of this strategy, emphasizes that "[a]mong self-interested egoists, the 'always defect' strategy is always stable" while the "tit-for-tat is collectively stable if and only if the discount parameter w is large enough."[82] Moreover, the straightforward extension of the two-person Prisoners' Dilemma to an n-person version "will not sustain cooperation very well because the players have no way of focusing their punishment on someone in the group who has failed to cooperate."[83] Follow-up analyses of Axelrod's model show that "a population motivated only by material self-interest continues to degenerate systematically into an all-defect equilibrium."[84] As Elster explains, "The conditions under which people will cooperate out of self-interest are quite stringent. The individuals must not be too myopic.... The gains from universal cooperation must be substantial; the gain from unilateral noncooperation not too large; and the loss from unilateral cooperation small."[85] Such assumptions are hardly realistic in the real world. In international politics where survival is at stake, the loss from unilateral cooperation can be loss of sovereignty while the gain from unilateral noncooperation can be

---

[78] Olson 1965.   [79] Putnam 1993, 177.   [80] Wendt 1992, 400.
[81] Elster 1989a, 43.   [82] Axelrod 1984, 63, 59.   [83] Axelrod 1997, 7.
[84] van der Veen 2001, 27.   [85] Elster 1989a, 132.

territorial expansion at the expense of potential allies. Under the shadow of war, states also tend to adopt a foreshortened time horizon. Thus, although the gain from universal cooperation is survival for all, states that are always tempted to take advantage of one another will prefer defection to cooperation.[86]

Waltzian realists are not concerned about such deleterious implications of the self-interest assumption because they believe that self-interest can check self-interest in a way similar to the operation of the "invisible hand" in economics. As Kenneth Waltz argues, when each state "seeks its own good," the systemic effect "transcends the motives and the aims of the separate units."[87] However, Karl Polanyi pointed out long ago that unrestrained capitalism would ultimately destroy itself.[88] In a similar vein, Hans Morgenthau believed that power competition would produce self-destructive conflicts unless it could be ameliorated by a "silent compact" among states.[89] As Robert Jervis observes, if "economic liberalism must be embedded in broader societal norms," then the pursuit of self-interest "can yield stability and a modicum of productive peace only if it is bounded by normative conceptions that limit predatory behavior."[90]

Indeed, many self-proclaimed rational accounts are based on *benign* or *enlightened* self-interest rather than unconstrained self-interest. But the idea of enlightened self-interest, which is "alive to the interests of others,"[91] in fact concedes to norms. As Elster points out, why should actors refrain from preying on one another "unless it is out of respect for a moral or social norm?"[92] Scholars of collective actions have highlighted that the ultimate decentralized solution to the collective-action problem rests with shared norms.[93] When actors share norms about what they should and should not do to one another, they can develop mutual trust,

---

[86] Keohane uses the Prisoners' Dilemma to illustrate that cooperation is possible in international anarchy. Keohane 1984. For critiques, see Grieco 1988; Powell 1994, 327–328.
[87] Waltz 1979, 90. [88] Polanyi 1944.
[89] Morgenthau 1973, 174, 219; see also Buzan and Little 2000, 46.
[90] Jervis 1997, 137. [91] Putnam 1993, 88.
[92] Elster 1989a, 264; see also North 1990, 30, 35, 55, 110.
[93] Axelrod 1997, 7; Elster 1989b, 186–87; Green and Shapiro 1994; Tarrow 1998, 10; Scott 1990, 151–152. Decentralized solutions are more basic than hierarchical ones because the formation of a central institution to impose cooperative solutions itself involves collective action. Elster 1989b, 131. In fact, even Hobbes's Leviathan involves a mutual contract, which in turn is based on the shared "law of the Gospel: whatsoever you require that others should do to you, that do ye to them." *Leviathan*, pt. 1, ch. 14, in Morgan 1992, 624. But such a hypothetical contract is so unrealistic that most scholars use the "Hobbesian solution" to refer to the top-down imposition of order and cooperation.

which then allows them to overcome opportunism.[94] In the Prisoners' Dilemma, the tit-for-tat strategy is based on the norm of reciprocity or fairness.[95] In domestic politics, the democratic norms of trust and compromise mean that politicians who win greater electoral support in regular and free elections will not jail their challengers and that momentary losers will not pick up weapons to challenge electoral results. While these norms are taken for granted in consolidated democracies, they are very weak in fragile democracies, especially those that have experienced civil wars. In international politics, norms refer to, first, the respect for the mutual coexistence of great powers and the independence of smaller and weaker states; and, second, the concern for the normative conduct of war and diplomacy. The first norm leads to the voluntary restraint from pursuing opportunistic expansion and the willingness to participate in costly balancing or resistance efforts. The second norm leads to the voluntary restraint from using cunning stratagems and barbaric tactics in order to seek advantage over rivals. When such norms are routinely followed, the system may be said to have undergone peaceful transformation from a "system of states," where states are driven by gain maximization, to a "society of states," where actors "have some recognition of common interests in maintaining the system."[96] As I shall illustrate, such a norm-based system did not exist in either ancient China or early modern Europe.

Cultural relativists may argue that rationality is a product of Western culture and is not applicable to non-Western societies. Roland Bleiker believes that "the very concept of an anarchical international system is virtually absent from the Chinese philosophical tradition."[97] But China's history is in fact one of almost incessant warfare from antiquity on. Gu Jiegang, a first-generation critical historian, suggested that the *Zuo zhuan* (Zuo's Tradition), a Chinese classic from the ancient era, "should be renamed 'book of mutual attacks.'"[98] Sinologists also point out that Confucianism does not conceive of the rational individual who engages in cost-benefit calculation of material interests.[99] However, as we shall see in subsequent chapters, Chinese history would have turned out differently if Confucianism had had more than cosmetic influence on politics. The Chinese tradition is more accurately characterized by Legalism, which is single-mindedly concerned with how to preserve and strengthen the state.

---

[94] Fukuyama 1995, 26; Putnam 1993, 89.   [95] Elster 1989b, 133.
[96] Holsti 1999, 284; see also Bull 1977; Osiander 2001.
[97] Bleiker 2001, 191.   [98] Gu 1982 [1926], 3.   [99] Nuyen 2002, 135.

Legalist classics such as the *Shang jun shu* and *Han Feizi* argue that human beings are naturally self-seeking and so the wise ruler should use liberal rewards and stringent punishments in order to motivate the people to serve the state.[100] In military affairs, *Sunzi bingfa* (Sunzi's Art of War) advises in the very first chapter that the ruler should calculate relative power before launching a campaign.[101] The *Sunzi* also advocates the principle of *quanbian* – *bian* refers to changes in the circumstances and *quan* means "to judge or assess the balance of forces and the dynamic tendencies in a given situation at a given moment and to select the appropriate action."[102] As Iain Johnston points out, this principle represents "an explicit admonition to strategists to act rationally in the expected-utility sense of rationality."[103] Since both ancient China and early modern Europe were full of rational actors who engaged in cost-benefit calculation and who preyed on the weaker, I treat rationality as an "as-is" fact rather than merely as an "as-if" assumption.[104]

Integration of Agency and Structure

The third building block of a dynamic theory is an interactive view of agency – what actors choose to do and what they can do – and structure – what actors are compelled to do and what they cannot do. It is hardly novel to say that a theory of change requires more attention to agency, but political science theories have a tendency to sink agency into structure. It is quite understandable why Waltzian realism, which strives for a theory that "explains continuities, . . . recurrences and repetitions, not change,"[105] emphasizes how "structures limit and mold agents."[106] Constructivists, in contrast, are concerned with change and have therefore advocated the mutual constitution of structure (defined as the international system) and agency (defined as states or other constituent units). Yet, because many constructivists reject methodological

---

[100] *Han Feizi*, ch. 45; *Shang jun shu*, chs. 5.23 and 2.6.
[101] The five indicators of relative power are the degree of harmony between rulers and their people, the correctness of the season, the advantages of terrain, the skills of the commanders, and the degree of military discipline. *Sunzi bingfa*, ch. 1; Lewis 1990, 115. Some historians argue that Sunzi was not a historical figure. See Brooks 1994, 59; Lewis 1999, 604. I thus refer to the *Sunzi bingfa* as a text but not to Sunzi as a person.
[102] Lewis 1990, 118.   [103] Johnston 1995, 152.
[104] For discussions of rationality and history, see Bates et al. 1998; Elster 2000; Mahoney and Rueschemeyer 2003.
[105] Waltz 1979, 69. Layne also argues that international politics is essentially "unchanging (and probably unchangeable)." Layne 1994, 10–11; see also Morgenthau 1973, 10.
[106] Waltz 1979, 74.

individualism and insist that individuals are embedded with their social environment and collectively shared systems of meanings, they in fact highlight the constraints of shared norms.[107] Scholars of comparative politics equally privilege structure over agency. Theda Skocpol flatly denies the role of agency when she proclaims, "Revolutions are not made; they come."[108] Historical institutionalists typically treat institutions as determining constraints.[109] Even the rational choice approach provides no better solution. For instance, Margaret Levi makes a special plea for "bringing people back into the state,"[110] but she underscores that rulers are "subject to *determinant constraints* on their behavior"[111] and that "[t]he real action...does not...come from the internal considerations of the actor but from the constraints on her behavior."[112] This position is hardly distinguishable from structural realism, which also argues that states make policy choices "subject to the constraints they face."[113] As Elster points out, by conceptualizing rational choice as "choice under constraints," rational choice scholars "are led, paradoxically, to argue that choice almost does not matter because any variations in behavior must be explained by variations in opportunities (or cost-benefit calculations)."[114]

While rational choice analysts and constructivists aspire to restore agency but fail, Waltz aspires to a structural theory but provides some hints at an interactive view of states and system. On the surface, Waltz explicitly dismisses "reductionist" analyses that try to understand an international system "by knowing the attributes and the interactions of its parts."[115] However, he also argues that the aim of a systems theory is to show "how the structure of the system affects the interacting units and how they in turn affect the structure."[116] He adds that "[i]f one's approach allows for the handling of both unit-level and systems-level causes, then it can cope with both the changes and the continuities that occur in a system."[117] Thus, it is not entirely correct to criticize Waltz's theory for having "only a reproductive logic but no transformational logic."[118] To understand how an international system and its constituent units interact,

---

[107] Checkel 1998, 342; Risse 2000, 5.   [108] Skocpol 1979, 17.

[109] A notable exception is North, who suggests that institutions should be understood as "the humanly devised constraints that shape human interaction." North 1990, 3.

[110] Levi 1988, 185.   [111] Ibid., 9 (emphasis added).

[112] Levi 1997, 25.   [113] Glaser and Kaufman 1998/99, 201.

[114] Elster 1989b, 15. Almond similarly criticizes such "a definition of choice that denies the existence of choice!" Almond 1990, 49.

[115] Waltz 1979, 18.   [116] Ibid., 40.   [117] Ibid., 68, 122.   [118] Ruggie 1986, 152.

a dynamic theory should see international and domestic politics as an integrated whole. Robert Gilpin and other scholars have argued that "every theory of international relations requires a theory of the state."[119] Interestingly, just as Waltz has a latent theory of the mutual constitution of states and system, Barry Buzan and Richard Little observe that Waltz's balance of power theory contains "a hidden theory of the state" which suggests that "because the internal structure of the state impinges upon its power, the internal structures of states will converge."[120] As we shall see, a theory of state structures can provide a powerful mechanism for endogenous transformation.

An interactive view of agency and structure should also regard politics as presenting opportunities as well as constraints. John Hobson highlights that the political structure is simultaneously a "realm of opportunity" and a "realm of constraint."[121] As Peter Gourevitch aptly captures it, international politics provides not just the threats of "being conquered, occupied, annihilated or made subservient," but also the opportunities of "power, dominion, empire, glory, 'total' security."[122] Similarly, domestic politics presents not just "hurdles to mobilization"[123] or "obstacles to be overcome,"[124] but also "a resource pool into which states dip."[125] It is true that the most efficient means of mobilization typically involve erosion of entrenched privileges, and so we may safely expect vested interests to resist policy changes. However, there are moments of "punctuations" (in the punctuated equilibrium framework) or "critical junctures" (in the path dependence framework) when fundamental reforms are most

[119] Gilpin 1981, 15. Similarly, liberalism highlights the centrality of state-society relations to world politics. See Moravcsik 1997.

[120] Buzan and Little 1996, 410. Buzan, Jones, and Little continue: "Although Waltz does not explore the issue, it is likely that he would agree that states without a central government will be unable to compete successfully with states possessing centralized government." Buzan, Jones and Little 1993, 146.

[121] Hobson 2002, 77, 75; also Gilpin 1981, 26. Similarly, Elster argues that institutions are simultaneously "enabling" and "restricting." Elster 1989b, 150.

[122] Gourevitch 1978, 896.

[123] Christensen introduces the concept of "national political power," defined as "the ability of state leaders to mobilize their nation's human and material resources behind security policy initiatives." But he quickly subverts this concept by operationalizing it as "hurdles to mobilization" or "the degree to which state-society relations distort leaders' preferred policies." Christensen 1996, 11.

[124] Skocpol argues that dominant-class members who were "in a position to obstruct monarchical undertakings" were "obstacles to be overcome" in social revolutions. Skocpol 1979, 49.

[125] Hobson 2002, 77.

likely.[126] How do such unusual moments come about? Robert Gilpin argues that "the principal mechanism of change throughout history has been war."[127] As Roberto Unger observes, "War – even limited war – brings instability as nothing else can. For each successful or failed military adventure, there are some elites in the contending countries that are gaining and others that are losing, in riches, power, and honor."[128] Military defeat, in particular, is a common marker of rising opportunity because it facilitates the questioning of the established order and opens minds to institutional innovations.[129] Thus, the pressure of war does not just impose constraints which reproduce continuities, but also generates opportunities which facilitate changes.

Even when we are dealing with obvious constraints rather than opportunities, we should refrain from seeing politics as merely the art of the possible – a framework which is similar to the idea of "choice under constraints." As captured by Vaclav Havel's *The Art of the Impossible*,[130] politics is also the art of turning the seemingly impossible into the possible. Gabriel Almond cautions against treating "human behavior as simply reactive" because constraints "exhibit varying degrees of manipulability."[131] As Niccolò Machiavelli pointed out, "[T]he truly virtuoso prince should know when to seize his chances and will recognize what needs to be done. He will identify opportunities where others see only difficulties, and recognize necessity where others believe they have freedom of choice."[132] Again, despite Waltz's explicit dismissal of agential efforts, he quietly agrees with Machiavelli on this point:

Systems change, or are transformed, depending on the resources and aims of their units and on the fates that befall them.... Structures shape and shove. They do

---

[126] The two frameworks are similar. IR scholars tend to refer to punctuations and equilibria while comparativists tend to refer to critical junctures and path dependence. "Critical junctures are characterized by the adoption of a particular institutional arrangement from among two or more alternatives. These junctures are 'critical' because once a particular option is selected it becomes progressively more difficult to return to the initial point when multiple alternatives were still available." Mahoney 2000, 513; also Collier and Collier 1991, 29; Katznelson 2003, 283; Thelen 2003. In a parallel manner, in the punctuated equilibrium framework, stages of equilibrium or relative tranquility are interrupted by punctuations or sudden and dramatic changes. Spruyt 1994, 24–25; Krasner 1984. Most scholars treat critical junctures or punctuations brought on by war as exogenous. However, if we can explain war and military defeats, then we may develop an endogenous theory of change.

[127] Gilpin 1981, 15. Gilpin also argues that war is "the only available mechanism for change." Gilpin 1981, 6.

[128] Unger 1987, 147.   [129] Avant 2000, 48–49; Goldstone and Tilly 2001, 183.

[130] Havel 1997.   [131] Almond 1990, 35–36.   [132] Wootton 1994, xxix–xxx.

not determine behaviors and outcomes, not only because unit-level and structural causes interact, but also because the shaping and shoving of structures may be successfully resisted . . . [w]ith skill and determination. . . . Virtuosos transcend the limits of their instruments and break the constraints of systems that bind lesser performers.[133]

In addition to skillful diplomacy, asymmetrical warfare, guerrilla warfare, and the nonviolent strategy of resistance are examples of how political actors can create opportunities and overcome constraints.

While I emphasize creativity and intentionality, I make no assumption that agency involves prescience or omnipotence. As Kalevi Holsti argues, a rational, agent-based account "does not preclude folly, misjudgment, wishful thinking, poor prediction, unanticipated consequences, and other foibles and shortcomings."[134] In both China and Europe, countless actors failed to respond to international pressure and thus left very few traces in historical records. Even virtuosos such as Napoléon could make blunders. Strategic mistakes, if made by the most powerful actors at critical moments or collectively by a significant cluster of actors, could fundamentally alter the trajectory of a whole system.

The ensuing analysis uses the framework of the dynamics of competing logics to weave together agency and structure in two senses – the mutual constitution of system and states and the interaction of structural pressures and agential strategies. First, the mechanism of self-strengthening reforms provides a theory of the state which connects the unit level and the system level. Second, all five mechanisms embody both agency and structure. Self-strengthening reforms are structural to the extent that they are compelled by international competition, but they are also agential in that their successful pursuit requires institutional innovations. Ruthless stratagems and counterbalancing strategies may appear to be strictly strategic, but they are also compelled by international competition. Although the mechanism of balance of power or resistance is often taken to be structural, it is also agential in that successful resistance requires special efforts to overcome the collective-action problem. By the same token, the mechanism of rising costs of expansion or administration is structural to the extent that it is shaped by the law of diminishing returns, but the costs and benefits that go into the calculus are subject to agential manipulation.

---

[133] Waltz 1986, 342–344.   [134] Holsti 1991, 16–17.

1.4   Dynamics of International Politics

The Logic of Balancing in International Politics

Let me now use the building blocks to formulate a dynamic theory of world politics, beginning with Eurocentric perspectives of international politics.[135] According to realist theories, "the logic of world politics"[136] should be characterized by checks and balances. They argue that attempts at domination are necessarily blocked by "two of the most powerful regularities in international politics: the balance of power and the rising costs of expansion."[137] The first countervailing mechanism is most notably represented by Kenneth Waltz, who argues that the instinct for survival in international anarchy "stimulates states to behave in ways that tend toward the creation of balance of power."[138] He is not concerned about opportunistic expansion because he believes that "balances of power tend to form whether some or all states consciously aim to establish and maintain a balance, or whether some or all states aim for universal domination."[139] Waltz insists that the balance of power should prevail "wherever two, and only two, requirements are met: that the order be anarchic and that it be populated by units wishing to survive."[140] As Jack Levy elaborates, "[T]he balancing mechanism almost always works successfully to avoid hegemony" because "[s]tates with expansionist ambitions are either deterred by the anticipation of blocking coalitions or beaten back by the formation of such coalitions."[141]

The second checking mechanism is associated with Robert Gilpin, who argues that "large-scale territorial conquest and empire building [are] prohibitively expensive."[142] This is because "as a state increases its control over an international system, it begins at some point to encounter both increasing costs of further expansion and diminishing returns from further expansion."[143] Beyond the point where marginal costs exceed marginal

---

[135] An earlier version of this argument was published in *International Organization* in 2004 as "Toward a Dynamic Theory of International Politics: Insights from Comparing the Ancient Chinese and Early modern European Systems," vol. 58, no. 1, pp. 175–205, reprinted with the permission of Cambridge University Press.

[136] Snyder 1991, 125.   [137] Ibid., 6.

[138] Waltz 1979, 118. Walt revises Waltz's balance of power to the balance of threat. Walt 1987. If powerful states always seek opportunistic expansion, then power is directly translated into threat and there is no need to differentiate between the two.

[139] Waltz 1979, 119; also Waltz 1986, 334.

[140] Waltz 1979, 121.   [141] Levy 2003, 131, 133.

[142] Gilpin 1981, 121. Theorists of the offense-defense balance share this argument. See Glaser and Kaufman 1998; van Evera 1998.

[143] Ibid., 106–107; also Mearsheimer 2001, 37.

benefits, expansion will become overexpansion and the conquering state will bring about its own ruin. Among various costs of expansion, the most central is the "loss-of-strength gradient," or the degree to which a state's military and political power diminishes as the state attempts to influence other states and events farther away from its home base.[144] This gradient essentially means that long-distance campaigns – which attempts at universal domination necessarily involve – are almost always bad moves. Territorial expansion also involves administration of conquered territories and subjugation of resistant populations. As even successful conquests can become millstones and drain the conqueror's economy, Gilpin speaks of "the law of the optimum size of organization due to the increasing cost of administration."[145]

Realists believe not only that universal domination is next to impossible, but also that the unipolar hegemonic status – the necessary step toward universal domination – is elusive. As Waltz argues, "In international politics, success leads to failure. The excessive accumulation of power by one state or coalition of states elicits the opposition of others."[146] Although Gilpin believes that hegemonic states commonly rise, he also argues that they normally fall as a result of differential rates of growth, costs of overexpansion, and development of domestic interests that distract from international competition.[147]

Although realists disagree over the relative importance of the balance of power and the costs of expansion, they share the view that negative feedback is the norm in international politics. As Waltz emphasizes, "[A] balance, once disrupted, will be restored in one way or another."[148] Although Gilpin writes of *War and Change*, he also believes in the restoration of equilibrium.[149] It is curious that realists claim the permanence of power politics but rule out the possibility of domination by fiat. But is the world so wonderfully designed that any deviation from equilibrium is unmistakably self-corrected? Unlike his fellow realists, Morgenthau recognized that equilibria in power relations were "essentially unstable" and "precarious."[150] Jervis suggests that disruptions to equilibria are not always corrected because international politics is characterized by positive feedback as well as negative feedback.[151] Although international relations scholars tend to slight positive feedback, theorists of the state have amply

[144] Boulding 1963, 245. See also Herbst 2000, 23.   [145] Gilpin 1981, 148.
[146] Waltz 1989, 49; also Layne 1993.   [147] Gilpin 1981.
[148] Waltz 1979, 128; also Morgenthau 1973, 168.   [149] Gilpin 1981, 13.
[150] Morgenthau 1973, 161–162.   [151] Jervis 1997, ch. 4.

demonstrated that small differences in power distribution can be exacerbated through path dependence over time.[152] While negative feedback reproduces system maintenance, positive feedback generates endogenous transformation which may well culminate in a single winner over time.

Contra realists, constructivists and liberals think that politics is transformable. However, they have a normative bias in their tendency to "consider only ethically good norms"[153] and bracket "norms and ideas that are both revolutionary and evil."[154] Although Alexander Wendt cautions that "institutions may be cooperative or conflictual,"[155] he presumes that competitive systems should mature into cooperative systems and that "'[m]ature' anarchies are less likely than 'immature' ones to be reduced by predation to a Hobbesian condition."[156] Marred by such a one-sided view, constructivism provides few clues to the triumph of a coercive universal empire in ancient China; the emergence of evil geniuses such as Napoléon, Hitler, and Stalin in modern history; or the surge of ethnic violence and international terrorism in the post–cold war era. To understand the full spectrum of international politics, it is necessary to pay attention to "constructivism with coercive characteristics."[157]

The Logic of Domination in International Politics

To examine the dynamism of both coercive and normative transformation of world politics, I argue that the logic of world politics should be understood as the dynamics of competing logics. That is to say, it is necessary to study the relative weaknesses and strengths of the logic of balancing and the logic of domination. First, how reliable is the balance-of-power mechanism? Is it true that the desire for survival in anarchy is sufficient to generate the balance of power, in terms of both balanc*ing* as a strategy and balanc*es* as outcomes?[158] Is it true that states always join the weaker side against attempts at domination and that it would be foolish for any states to pursue power maximization?

If we follow realists' assumption that states are driven by narrow self-interest, then the puzzle is not why balancing failed in some systems, but, as Ethan Kapstein puts it, "why . . . alliances ever form at all."[159] Critics

---

[152] Mahoney 2000; Pierson 2000.   [153] Checkel 1998, 339.
[154] Jervis 1998, 974.   [155] Wendt 1992, 399.   [156] Ibid., 409.
[157] Jackson and Krebs 2003, 2. Moravcsik argues that liberalism – when it is understood as a positive theory rather than an ideology – can address both conflictual and cooperative international relations. Moravcsik 1997.
[158] For the two concepts of the balance of power, see Levy 2003.
[159] Kapstein 1995, 761.

of balance-of-power theories have pointed out that effective balancing involves the collective-action problem.[160] Although all states want to survive, the expected level of cooperation is pitifully low. Self-interested states not only have difficulty staging effective balancing which checks attempts at domination, they may even pursue other strategies which facilitate domination. The repertoire of such strategies includes distancing (staying away from targets of domination), declaring neutrality, buck passing (free-riding on the balancing efforts of other states), bandwagoning (allying with the domination-seeker), appeasement, and even submission.[161] Weak states, in particular, tend to ally with the stronger side "because they lack the capabilities to stand alone, and because a defensive alliance may operate too slowly to do them much good."[162] Moreover, even when some states do engage in balancing, weak balanc*ing* as a strategy may fail to bring about balanc*es* as outcomes. If only a few states engage in balancing, they can be easily outnumbered and will conclude that balancing is futile. As Jervis explains this self-fulfilling or tipping dynamics, "If an actor thinks the regime will disintegrate – or thinks others hold this view – he will be more likely to defect from the cooperative coalition himself."[163] It is noteworthy that while balancing generates negative feedback and helps to preserve an international system, bandwagoning and other strategies generate positive feedback and facilitate coercive transformation.[164] Even Waltz acknowledges that "[i]f states wished to maximize power, they would join the stronger side, and we would see not balances forming but a world hegemony forged."[165]

The inherently weak balance-of-power mechanism can be further weakened by the divide-and-conquer strategy. Jervis suggests that "when faced with a hostile alliance a state can choose either to win over some of its members or to isolate and weaken them."[166] Randall Schweller observes that revisionist states tend to isolate weaker victims.[167] Even Waltz speaks of moves to "weaken and shrink" opposing alliances.[168] Indeed,

---

[160] Jervis 1997, 111; Rosecrance 2003; Schweller 1996; Wohlforth 1999. Grieco argues that states should fail to cooperate not just against joint threats, but also for joint gains. In a brutish world where today's friends may become tomorrow's enemies, states are more concerned about relative gains than absolute gains and so would forgo any benefits from cooperation if their partners may gain relatively more. Grieco 1988, 500.

[161] See Christensen and Snyder 1990; Jervis 1997; Rosecrance and Lo 1996; Schroeder 1994b; Schweller 1994; 1996.

[162] Walt 1987, 31; see also Handel 1990; Lab 1992.

[163] Jervis 1982, 366; also 1997, 150–152.   [164] Schweller 1994, 92–93, 107; 1998, 77.

[165] Waltz 1979, 126.   [166] Jervis 1997, 238.

[167] Schweller 1998, 195.   [168] Waltz 1979, 118.

domination-seeking states may forestall formation of alliances and break up existing ones. They may also approach opportunistic expansion in a piecemeal and gradual fashion by isolating prime targets and making tactical peace with secondary targets. If domination-seekers follow this course of action, they can minimize the likelihood of having to fight concerted balancing alliances as well as multifront wars with unallied enemies.

To facilitate the divide-and-conquer strategy, domination-seeking states may resort to ruthless stratagems. In Niccolò Machiavelli's view, international competition is a game of fraud and treachery. To maintain the state and to achieve glory, he advised the prince to "pay no attention to what is just or what is unjust, or to what is kind or cruel, or to what is praiseworthy or shameful."[169] This realpolitik view is widely shared in Chinese military classics which argue that deviance from morality is necessary for "the survival of a higher virtue."[170] Most notably, the *Sunzi bingfa* proclaims, "Warfare is the Way of deception."[171] To seek victory, the *Sunzi* recommends "unorthodox" tactics or techniques of surprise and deceit.[172] The ideal commander should be "a master of maneuver, illusion, and deception" who is able "to disguise his intentions while penetrating the schemes of his adversary and to manipulate appearances so that the enemy would march to its doom."[173] The ideal diplomat should similarly be an "archetypal figure of the realm of stratagem and cunning."[174] Deceptive tactics work best if targets of domination share the domination-seeker's gain-maximizing ambitions and can be readily tempted by promises of material gains. As the *Sunzi* suggests, "if [the enemy] seeks benefit then tempt him."[175] In addition to deception, domination-seekers may engage in brutality. As *The Prince* explains, "If you do [people] minor damage they will get their revenge; but if you cripple them there is nothing they can do."[176] Such cunning and brutal tactics are useful not just in

---

[169] *The Discourses*, bk. 3, ch. 41, in Wootton 1994, 215.   [170] Lewis 1990, 128.

[171] *Sunzi bingfa*, ch. 1. Similarly, "[T]he army is established by deceit." *Sunzi*, ch. 7, trans. Sawyer 1994, 168, 198. Sunzi and Han Fei are sometimes called China's Machiavelli. But one may also call Machiavelli Europe's Sunzi. Bloodworth and Bloodworth argue that Machiavelli's dictums are so "Chinese" that Machiavelli would have spoken approvingly of various theories and practices in Chinese history. Bloodworth and Bloodworth 1976, ch. 31.

[172] *Sunzi bingfa*, ch. 5, trans. Sawyer 1994, 187.   [173] Lewis 1999, 632.   [174] Ibid.

[175] *Sunzi bingfa*, ch. 1, trans. Lewis 1990, 124. *The Prince* also suggests that "people are so simple-minded and so preoccupied with their immediate concerns that if you set out to deceive them, you will always find plenty of them who will let themselves be deceived." *The Prince*, ch. 18, in Wootton 1994, 54.

[176] *The Prince*, ch. 3, in Wootton 1994, 9–10.

counteracting balancing, but also in reducing the costs of war. As testi-fied by the *Sunzi*'s wisdom that "to bring the enemy's army to submit without combat is the highest skill,"[177] it is significantly cheaper to win wars with "unorthodox" tactics than to engage in direct confrontation. It is even less costly to undermine the enemy's ability to wage war by "sowing doubts and rumors, bribing and corrupting officials, and exe-cuting estrangement techniques."[178] It should be noted that, while the advice in *The Prince* and the *Sunzi bingfa* may be timeless, the concrete moves that win the game should be tailored to the specific characteristics of domination-seekers and targets and the particular circumstances in question.

The second countervailing mechanism of rising costs of expansion is based on the law of diminishing returns – that continued expansion of any organization should eventually face increasing marginal costs and decreas-ing marginal benefits.[179] As implied by the term "law," this mechanism is often regarded as immutable. However, the point at which marginal costs intersect with marginal benefits is an empirical question that varies with contexts. As agriculture is subject to diminishing returns, territo-rial conquest should expand the supply of arable lands and so the costs of war may be seen as high-yield investment.[180] This is particularly the case if the population-to-land ratio is high so that control of resistant populations is not very difficult.[181] In such circumstances, successful war should yield "additional land and the associated labor force that [add] directly to both economic and political power."[182] Thus, expansionist states may well enjoy economies of scale – which operate on positive feedback – before they suffer from diseconomies of scale – which operate on negative feedback.

To a significant extent, the costs and benefits of war are shaped by the pursuit of "self-strengthening reforms." This term is adopted from not just the Chinese concepts of *fuguo qiangbing* (rich country and strong army) and *ziqiang yundong* (self-strengthening movement), but also Machiavelli's view that "no method of defense is good, certain, and

---

[177] *Sunzi bingfa*, ch. 3, trans. Lewis 1990, 116.
[178] Sawyer 1998, 4. See, in particular, *Liu Tao* (Six Secret Teachings).
[179] Gilpin 1981, 106–107.
[180] Arthur 1990, 93; Gilpin 1981, 79–81; Mearsheimer 2001, 212.
[181] In contrast, in premodern Africa where lands were abundant and populations were sparsely distributed, the primary objective of war was to capture people and treasures rather than to seize territory. Herbst 2000, 13–15; also Scott 1998, 185.
[182] Kaysen 1990, 49.

lasting that does not depend on . . . your own strength."[183] This concept
also has close affinity with the Waltzian concept of "self-help" which
means that "states must help themselves . . . by providing for their own
security."[184] Waltz argues that states should do so by taking "moves to
increase economic capability, to increase military strength, to develop
clever strategies."[185] As Waltz presumes that states seek only security and
invariably balance against attempts at domination, he uses the label "internal balancing" to refer to such moves.[186] While this may be true for
status quo states,[187] ambitious ones may take advantage of their superior
military strengths, higher economic capabilities, and cleverer strategies
to pursue opportunistic expansion and even to establish domination. I
thus prefer the more dynamic term "self-strengthening reforms" to the
one-sided term "internal balancing moves."

The mechanism of self-strengthening reforms also provides a theory
of the state necessary for a dynamic theory of international politics.
Although Waltz believes that "[o]ne cannot infer the condition of international politics from the internal composition of states,"[188] internal
balancing efforts inevitably involve mobilization of human and material
resources in the domestic realm. Neoclassical realists have observed that
a state's relative capability is not a simple function of available national
resources, but of the government's ability to extract the wherewithal of
war and to command support from society.[189] To understand this process
better, scholars of international relations may turn to theorists of state
formation who study precisely this subject matter. According to Charles
Tilly, war and preparation for war involve rulers in extracting the wherewithal of war, which then creates the central organizational structures of
states.[190] The crucial processes of state formation are monopolization of
the means of coercion, nationalization of taxation, and bureaucratization

---

[183] *The Prince*, ch. 24, in Wootton 1994, 74.
[184] Waltz 1988, 624.   [185] Waltz 1979, 118.
[186] Waltz tends to equate "self-help" with "balancing." As he puts it, because "[t]hose who
do not help themselves or who do so less effectively will fail to prosper and lay themselves
to attacks," states are stimulated to "behave in ways that tend toward the creation of
balances of power." Waltz 1979, 118; also 91. Moreover, because he privileges external
balancing over internal balancing, the term "self-help" is sometimes used as a synonym
for external balancing, which means reliance on allies rather than reliance on one's own
efforts.
[187] As Schweller argues, Waltzian realism has a status quo bias. Schweller 1996.
[188] Waltz 1979, 64.
[189] Christensen 1996, 11; Rose 1998, 161–162; Zakaria 1998, 35–41.
[190] Tilly 1992 [1990], 14–15.

TABLE 2. *Mutual Constitution of International Competition and State Formation Through Self-Strengthening Reforms*

Internal Balancing Moves (Improvement of Relative Capability)	Self-Strengthening Reforms (Mobilization of Resources by Improving Administrative Capacity)	State Formation Processes (Centralization of Authority)
"Increase Military Strength"	Establishment of a Standing Army by National Conscription	Monopolization of the Means of Coercion
"Increase Economic Capability"	Imposition of Direct and Indirect Taxes; Promotion of Economic Productivity	Nationalization of Taxation
"Develop Clever Strategies"	Replacement of Aristocracy by Meritocracy	Bureaucratization of Administration

of administration. If states seek to "increase military strength" by building national armies, "increase economic capability" by rationalizing and nationalizing taxation, and "develop clever strategies" by establishing meritocratic administration, then they can simultaneously strengthen the state's administrative and extractive capacity. As such, internal balancing moves and state formation processes are mutually constituted through self-strengthening reforms. This argument is summarized in Table 2.

State capacity in state-society relations is a critical component of relative capability in interstate relations. First, military reforms enhance fighting capabilities and chances of victory. Second, fiscal and economic reforms generate more resources to finance the costs of expansion. Third, administrative reforms allow a state to raise and manage larger armies, mobilize more national resources for war, and alleviate logistical problems in long-distance campaigns. When a self-strengthened state develops the capacity for direct rule – that is, the ability of the ruling court to penetrate the society down to the village level without reliance on intermediate power holders such as regional magnates and local landlords – it can even engage in total mobilization for war. Fourth, administrative capacity facilitates consolidation of control over conquered territories and extraction of additional resources from subjugated populations. When scholars of international politics argue that conquest does not pay, they do not mean that conquered territories do not possess resources for extraction; rather, they are uncertain whether the conqueror possesses the administrative capacity to extract resources from conquered populations.[191] Fifth, administrative reforms are also conducive to the development of clever strategies because innovative ideas are more likely to be implemented under meritocracy than under aristocracy. Sixth, a self-strengthened state has less need for allies and does not have to share the spoils of victory. And when a self-strengthened state does desire allies, it will find that strength attracts. As Machiavelli put it, "auxiliaries" or allied troops are generally "useless and dangerous,"[192] but "if you have a good army, you will always find your allies reliable."[193] All these processes, in turn, intensify opportunistic expansion. As Robert Gilpin observes, "The critical significance of the differential growth of power among states is that it alters the cost of changing the international system and therefore the incentives for changing the international system."[194] Compared with the static concept of internal balancing moves, the dynamic concept of self-strengthening reforms thus makes it possible to understand the endogenous and coercive transformation of international politics.

The concept of self-strengthening reforms also differs from internal balancing in that it provides room for human creativity and historical contingency. Although international competition compels states to take "moves to increase economic capability, to increase military strength, to develop clever strategies,"[195] international competition does not dictate *how* states meet such daunting challenges. If states mobilize additional wherewithal of war by building up administrative capacity, then they are engaged in self-strengthening reforms. As states are differently structured, some states may develop higher extractive capacity, thereby enjoying a competitive edge over others with lower capacity. It is also possible that states take the easier course of relying on intermediate resource holders rather than the harder course of building up administrative capacity. For instance, states may turn to military entrepreneurs to build mercenary

[191] Glaser and Kaufman 1998, 68; Hopf 1991, 477–478; Kaufman 1997, 174, 183; Liberman 1993; van Evera 1999, 99–106.
[192] *The Prince*, ch. 12, in Wootton 1994, 38.
[193] *The Prince*, ch. 19, in Wootton 1994, 56.
[194] Gilpin 1981, 95. Neoclassical realists also argue that "an increase in relative material power will lead eventually to a corresponding expansion in the ambition and scope of a country's foreign policy activity – and that a decrease in such power will lead eventually to a corresponding contraction." Rose 1998, 167; also Christensen 1996; Schweller 1998; Zakaria 1998.
[195] Waltz 1979, 118.

armies, tax farmers to collect direct and indirect taxes, international financiers to provide loans and credits, and venal officials to fill administrative positions. While such measures can bring about larger armies and higher revenues for immediate campaigns, they erode central authority, strain fiscal resources, and even damage fighting capability in the long term. Realists may believe that the pressure of international competition should always discipline states to adopt or emulate self-strengthening measures.[196] Although I argue that war makes institutional innovations possible, there is no guarantee that war always generates changes. As Douglass North and Robert Thomas point out, political leaders may adopt inefficient institutions rather than efficient institutions because the establishment of efficient institutions involves much higher transaction costs in the short-term.[197] To make matters worse, inefficient institutions can be immensely persistent because they create powerful vested interests that resist reforms[198] and produce a widening "ingenuity gap."[199] I. A. A. Thompson labels various inefficient practices "self-destructive . . . expedients."[200] Accordingly, I use the term "self-weakening expedients" to refer to internal balancing moves that mobilize resources by relying on intermediate resource holders. The differences between self-strengthening reforms and self-weakening expedients are summarized in Table 3.

Overall, international politics should be seen as processes of strategic interaction between domination-seekers and targets of domination. Domination-seekers do face the logic of balancing – the balance of power and the rising costs of expansion. But they may overcome the constraints by pursuing the logic of domination – or an aggressive grand strategy combining self-strengthening reforms, divide-and-conquer strategies, and ruthless tactics.[201] In this competition, the logic of domination is naturally advantaged over the logic of balancing. Because the balance-of-power mechanism involves the daunting collective-action problem, it is quite questionable whether targets of domination can pursue effective

---

[196] Gilpin 1981, 176; Waltz 1979, 118.

[197] North and Thomas 1973, 7, 100. Kahler points out that military technologies diffuse far more easily than political and economic institutions. Kahler 1998, 195.

[198] Arthur 1989, 116–117; Mahoney 2000, 521; North 1990, 52, 99.

[199] Homer-Dixon 2000, 288.

[200] Thompson 1995, 291. Kennedy also calls such practices "expedients, easy in the short term but disastrous for the long-term good of the country." Kennedy 1987, 54.

[201] A grand strategy is defined as "the full package of domestic and international policies designed to increase national power and security." Christensen 1996, 7.

TABLE 3. *Self-Strengthening Reforms Versus Self-Weakening Expedients*

Internal Balancing Moves (Improvement of Relative Capability)	Self-Strengthening Reforms (Mobilization of Resources by Improving Administrative Capacity)	Self-Weakening Expedients (Mobilization of Resources by Relying on Intermediate Resource Holders)
"Increase Military Strength"	Establishment of a Standing Army by National Conscription	Establishment of a Standing Army by Military Entrepreneurs and Mercenary Troops
"Increase Economic Capability"	Imposition of Direct and Indirect Taxes; Promotion of Economic Productivity	Tax Farming for Ordinary Taxes; Loans and Credits for Extraordinary Revenues
"Develop Clever Strategies"	Replacement of Aristocracy by Meritocracy	Sale of Public Offices to Private Capital Holders

balancing. At the same time, self-strengthening reforms, divide-and-conquer strategies, and ruthless stratagems significantly enhance coercive capabilities and reduce the costs of war. If domination-seeking states build up military and economic capabilities, maneuver to fight targets seriatim, score victory on the battlefields, and make war pay for war, then opportunistic expansion may well snowball all the way to universal domination. Conversely, if domination-seekers adopt self-weakening expedients instead of self-strengthening reforms, and do not ruthlessly pursue divide-and-conquer strategies and Machiavellian tactics, then conquest will be difficult and system maintenance will be more likely. Nevertheless, it is important to keep in mind that processes of strategic interaction generate multiple equilibria which are unpredictable a priori.[202] While the advantaged side has a better chance of winning, international competition is also a trial of skills, strategies, and determination. Ultimately, the actual outcomes are dependent on the strategic interplay between domination-seekers and targets, and between coercive mechanisms and countervailing mechanisms. This is another way to say that we should examine historical contexts.

---

[202] It is certainly possible – though not likely – for self-strengthened states to maintain the balance of power. See Wagner 1986.

Dynamics of International Politics in Ancient China (656–221 BC) and Early Modern Europe (AD 1495–1815)

In both ancient China and early modern Europe, ambitious rulers pursued opportunistic expansion by building stronger armies and raising more revenues.[203] As indicated in Chapter Two, ancient Chinese rulers generally understood that if they wanted to survive and conquer other states, they would be required to develop a substantial material base, establish administrative organizations, and undermine the enemy's strength. As various states embarked on self-strengthening reforms, divide-and-conquer strategies, and nasty and brutish tactics, international competition was relatively intense throughout the multistate era. At the same time, the Eurocentric mechanisms of balance of power and rising costs of expansion also operated to block attempts at domination. Contrary to the Sinocentric view that China was destined to become a unified empire, the ancient multistate system was in fact reasonably stable for more than three centuries. The situation changed in the second half of the fourth century BC, when various great powers deepened their self-strengthening reforms and introduced universal military conscription. The scale of war surged, medium-sized states were conquered, and territorial transfers among great powers became commonplace. Although alliances were formed, states routinely switched sides and abandoned allies. Against this backdrop, the state of Qin ultimately achieved universal domination by pursuing the most comprehensive self-strengthening reforms and the most ruthless strategies and tactics.

While Chapter Two involves a within-case comparison of why the state of Qin succeeded while other states in the ancient Chinese system failed, Chapter Three provides both a within-case comparison of various hegemony seekers in early modern Europe and a cross-case comparison of early modern Europe and ancient China. In light of the ancient Chinese trajectory, I argue that European domination-seekers failed largely because they did not employ the whole repertoire of the logic of domination. As Bin Wong points out, "The comparative historical perspective reveals an element of contingency that reflects the *incompleteness* of European patterns of . . . change."[204] Niccolò Machiavelli advised at the onset of the early modern period that the ambitious prince lay down "good laws and good armies"[205] and combine the strength of the lion with the

---

[203] For a concise version of this comparison, see Hui 2004.
[204] Wong 1997, 87 (emphasis added).   [205] *The Prince*, ch. 12, in Wootton 1994, 38.

wit of the fox.[206] Apparently, few European kings and princes heeded his words. Although European powers pursued opportunistic expansion and practiced counterbalancing strategies, they rarely employed cunning and ruthless tactics against one another (though they did apply such tactics against "uncivilized" populations) as was common in the ancient Chinese system.

More importantly, the earliest domination-seekers, Valois France and the United Habsburgs, adopted self-weakening expedients rather than self-strengthening reforms. In ancient China, domination-seekers increased military strengths by building national armies, increased economic capabilities by rationalizing national taxation, and developed clever strategies by establishing meritocratic administration. In contrast, their counterparts in early modern Europe increased military strengths by using mercenary armies and increased economic capabilities by contracting loans and selling public offices. The use of mercenary troops instead of national armies was the source of various problems. First, mercenaries were extremely expensive. While war making should theoretically be a labor-intensive activity in the preindustrial age, the contraction of military service effectively turned it into a capital-intensive venture at increasing marginal costs. According to military historians, "the great bulk of the increase in military expenditure [could] be attributed directly to the growth of military manpower – not to tactical or technological changes related to the general adoption of gunpowder weapons."[207] As European rulers could not pay for war by ordinary tax receipts, they became increasingly reliant on self-weakening fiscal expedients for extraordinary revenues. Second, mercenary forces had lower fighting capabilities. As Machiavelli observed, mercenaries exhibited "cowardice"[208] and were "useless for they have no reason to stand firm apart from the little bit of pay that you give them.[209] With the adoption of self-weakening expedients, therefore, wars were often indecisive, territorial conquest was difficult, and the independence of weaker states was rarely at stake.

The situation changed at the turn of the eighteenth century when a significant cluster of states embarked on self-strengthening reforms one after another. As in the second half of the fourth century BC in ancient

---

[206] *The Prince*, ch. 18, in Wootton 1994, 54.   [207] Rogers 1995, 7.

[208] *The Prince*, ch. 13, in Wootton 1994, 43.

[209] *Discourses*, bk. 1, ch. 43, in Wootton 1994, 140. Machiavelli also denounced mercenaries as "factious, ambitious, ill-disciplined," "unreliable, treacherous, and ... worthless." He believed that a wise ruler "would rather lose with his own troops than win with someone else's." *The Prince*, chs. 12, 13, in Wootton 1994, 38, 43.

China, the scale of war escalated and territorial conquest became more common. International competition was further intensified after Revolutionary France underwent the most comprehensive self-strengthening reforms Europe had ever seen. With a logic of domination that more closely resembled that in ancient China, the Napoleonic empire was able to sweep through the European continent, conquer weaker states, and make conquest pay. At the height of that empire, Europe was on the verge of following the ancient Chinese coercive trajectory. Nevertheless, France suffered from the shadow of a self-weakened past. The late timing in the pursuit of self-strengthening reforms and the early adoption of self-weakening expedients in early modern Europe stacked the odds against the Napoleonic empire. Revolutionary and Napoleonic France inherited crippling national debts from the ancien regime. Unable to build an empire on its own national resources, France was heavily reliant on allies for the wherewithal of war and thus vulnerable to their defection. At the same time, the problem of runaway war costs had led France's chief rival, Britain, to develop the public credit system. Paradoxically, then, Europe was deflected from the logic of domination by the use of the cowardly and costly mercenaries and unreliable allied troops condemned by Machiavelli.

Rethinking the Hobbesian Metaphor for International Politics

Realists often use the Hobbesian state of nature as a metaphor for international politics. They somehow do not realize that this metaphor is conducive to coercive transformation. Thomas Hobbes argued in *Leviathan* that "the condition of mere nature" is "the condition of war," and "such a war . . . is of every man against every man."[210] If we transpose this image onto international politics, the Hobbesian metaphor "describes international relations as a state of war of all against all, an arena of struggle in which each state is pitted against every other."[211] If the state of nature nurtures the emergence of the Leviathan, then incessant international competition should generate the triumph of the universal Leviathan rather than the maintenance of international anarchy.[212]

---

[210] *Leviathan*, pt. 1, ch. 13, in Morgan 1992, 621. As did Hobbes, ancient Chinese thinkers articulated a "natural philosophy of violence" – that violence was inherent to human nature and that a sage king was necessary to provide order. Lewis 1990, ch. 6.

[211] Bull 1977, 24–25. For an analysis of the Hobbesian metaphor for international politics, see Williams 1996.

[212] There is also an "ineluctable tendency toward universal empire" in computer simulation. Cusack and Stoll 1990, 191; also Cederman 1996, 264; Kaplan 1979, 36.

Alexander Wendt and other constructivists argue that anarchy should be conceptualized as a historical variable rather than a constant.[213] In the same manner, we may problematize the Hobbesian state of nature as a historical variable. In this reformulated Hobbesian logic, the self-interested motivation for opportunistic expansion should provide the driving force for coercive transformation, and the logic of domination should provide the necessary capability. In ancient China, the early pursuit of self-strengthening reforms brought about intense international competition. As the stakes of war were high, states were compelled constantly to upgrade their self-strengthening reforms and to pursue dirty stratagems and brutal tactics. It was in such an increasingly Hobbesian-cum-Machiavellian world that Qin, the most nasty and brutish state, could make life solitary and short for others. In early modern Europe, in comparison, the early pursuit of self-weakening expedients significantly tempered international competition for most of the early modern period. In such a less-than-Hobbesian world, even the self-strengthened and highly innovative Revolutionary and Napoleonic France could not amass sufficient coercive capability. As the ancient Chinese system was more Hobbesian than the early modern European system, it is not surprising that the universal Leviathan triumphed in the former but not in the latter. To complement this theoretical and historical analysis, Chapter Three includes some crude quantitative indicators in terms of frequency of war, battle deaths, and death rates of sovereign territorial states.

1.5   Dynamics of State Formation

As Hobbes and Machiavelli understood it, the struggle for power shapes not only the international realm, but also the domestic realm.[214] Compelled by the pressure of war, rulers who wished to maintain survival, recover losses, or establish hegemony would have to strive to increase their military and economic capabilities. In mobilizing the wherewithal

[213] Wendt 1992; 1999; also Jervis 1997, 109; Powell 1994, 337. This is analogous to the idea of "stateness" as a historical variable. Nettl 1968.

[214] An earlier version of this argument was published in *Journal of Political Philosophy* in 2001 as "The Emergence and Demise of Nascent Constitutional Rights: Comparing Ancient China and Early Modern Europe," vol. 9, no. 4, pp. 372–402, © 2001 Blackwell Publishers; used with permission. I used the term "constitutional rights" in 2001. But the term "citizenship rights" is more appropriate for this historical analysis because it is less loaded with the modern connotation of parliamentary oversight of executive acts. I thank Charles Tilly and Bruce Brooks for their suggestions.

of war, rulers created not just larger armies, but also a range of administrative, fiscal, and policing organizations. As Charles Tilly succinctly states:

The building of an effective military machine imposed a heavy burden on the population involved: taxes, conscription, requisitions, and more. The very act of building it – when it worked – produced arrangements which could deliver resources to the government for other purposes....It produced the means of enforcing the government's will over stiff resistance: the army. It tended, indeed, to promote territorial consolidation, centralization, differentiation of the instruments of government and monopolization of the means of coercion, all the fundamental state-making processes. War made the state, and the state made war.[215]

More specifically, war made the state by destroying feudal, parcelized authority and creating centralized, rationalized authority through the processes of monopolization of the means of coercion, nationalization of taxation, and bureaucratization of administration.[216]

Europeanists often believe that such state formation processes are uniquely European and modern. But the same dynamics had once prevailed in the system of *zhongguo* or central states in ancient China. As Mark Lewis observes,

In the competition to mobilize ever larger bodies of men, various states began to claim the services of the populations of their rural hinterlands and the lower social classes, which had hitherto played no political role. These reforms involved the allocation of land...in exchange for the payment of taxes and the provision of labor and military service. The process was progressively extended in various states, until it culminated in the reforms of Shang Yang in Qin state, where the entire adult, male population was registered, ranked, and allocated land on the basis of military service.[217]

Although war created state structures in both China and Europe, war did not produce the same regime types in the two systems. Indeed, it is quite ambiguous which regime types war produced even in the European context. Tilly observes that there is a paradox in European state formation: Militarization goes with civilianization, and centralization goes with constitutionalism.[218] James Scott similarly depicts the state as "the vexed institution that is the ground of both our freedoms and our

---

[215] Tilly 1975, 73.
[216] Bean 1973; Brewer 1989; Downing 1992; Ertman 1997; Giddens 1987; Mann 1988; Nettl 1968; Poggi 1990; Porter 1994; Rasler and Thompson 1989; Tilly 1975, 1992 [1990]; Weber 1958.
[217] Lewis 1990, 9.   [218] Tilly 1992 [1990], 122, 206.

unfreedoms."[219] As Bin Wong vividly captures it, the European experience embraced "two narratives – the cheerful story of parliamentary institutions and democratic ideology and the drama of aggressive centralization of power by growing national bureaucracies that increased their claims on social resources through fiscal extraction and engagement in war. Indeed, the two processes proceeded in uneasy tension as much as they complemented each other."[220] Of course, political philosophers have debated for centuries whether the modern state is inherently coercive or fundamentally consensual, with the princely perspective of Niccolò Machiavelli, Jean Bodin, and Thomas Hobbes on one side, and the social-contract theory of John Locke and other liberals on the other.

Despite this recognition of contradictory processes, many theorists of the state have taken a unilinear view of state formation. In the first round of scholarship to "bring the state back in,"[221] the state is seen as coercive. As Karen Barkey and Sunita Parikh write, "State-makers who were ultimately successful at building centralized, differentiated organizations with a monopoly of coercion over a defined territory were those who undid and then redid the structure of society according to their own agendas....It is in the process of asserting control that the state restructures, imposes order upon, and sets the boundaries around society."[222] Although this view has persisted in the literature, other scholars of state-society relations have moved toward a strategic-interactive approach that examines both top-down and bottom-up processes.[223] Nevertheless, whereas earlier works often push society out, current analyses have a tendency to overprivilege society. In their efforts to restore bottom-up processes, scholars of state-society relations come quite close to arguing that state domination necessarily generates societal resistance. Joel Migdal, for example, believes that "attempts at domination are invariably met with opposition...by those trying to avoid domination."[224] James Scott also argues that "the logic of a pattern of domination...encounters a reciprocal resistance from below."[225] Anthony Giddens likewise argues that "[t]he more effectively states seek to 'govern,' the more there is likelihood of counter-balance in the form of polyarchic involvement."[226] Although Tilly specifically examines both the top-down "logic of coercion" and the bottom-up "logic of capital,"[227] his account is fundamentally

---

[219] Scott 1998, 7.   [220] Wong 1997, 158.
[221] This is the title of an edited volume by Evans, Rueschemeyer, and Skocpol 1985.
[222] Barkey and Parikh 1991, 527–528.   [223] See Tilly 1999.   [224] Migdal 1994, 21.
[225] Scott 1990, 128.   [226] Giddens 1987, 341.   [227] Tilly 1992 [1990], 127.

society-centered: "The organization of major social classes within a state's territory, and their relations to the state, significantly affected the strategies rulers employed to extract resources, the resistance they met, the struggle that resulted, the sorts of durable organization that extraction and struggle laid down, and therefore the efficiency of resource extraction."[228] In short, theorists of the state resemble scholars of international politics in focusing on the logic of balancing, that is, the mechanism of balance of power or resistance and the mechanism of rising costs of administration.

The Logic of Balancing in State Formation

The logic of balancing underlies the "military basis of citizenship and democratization."[229] Scholars of state formation point out that citizenship rights and democratic representation emerged because rulers were compelled to share power as the price for the wherewithal of war. They observed that when kings and princes encroached on the society for human and material resources, they met resistance from resource holders. Faced with resistance, rulers could use brute force to seize the needed men, money, or grain. But the use of force itself would require resource mobilization and might stimulate rebellions. Few rulers could compete successfully in international politics if they simultaneously faced challenges at home. As Niccolò Machiavelli understood it, even the most power-hungry prince "must serve the interests of his subjects" "in order to maximize his own power."[230] Thus, despite their preference for the contrary, European kings and princes were forced to bargain with societal actors. Out of bargaining then "emerged increased involvement of subjects in national affairs...and enforceable claims on the state so extensive we can begin to speak of citizenship rights – even, in some cases, of democracy."[231] This observation can be traced quite far back in history. In the medieval period, the pressure of war already produced the birth of representative bodies – *cortes* in Spain, *parlements* in France, parliament in England, and estates in other parts of Latin Europe. In the early modern period, the intensification of international competition led to more extensive citizenship rights. In the age of universal military conscription, ordinary male adults acquired the franchise because military

---

[228] Ibid., 15. [229] Downing 1992, 25; also Kant 1970 [1795], 104.

[230] Wootton 1994, xxxvi.

[231] Tilly 1992, 708, 711. Citizenship rights do not necessarily mean democratic representation. Some scholars argue that only democracies have citizens. Schmitter and Karl 1996, 51. But such an understanding is inapplicable to early modern Europe.

service involved "reciprocal obligation, rights, and freedoms."[232] In the age of total war in the twentieth century, the franchise was extended to women, and, ultimately, to eighteen-year-old youths.

The logic of balancing in state formation also involves the mechanism of rising costs of administration, which overlaps with that of rising costs of expansion in international competition. The costs of administration involve the recruitment of officials to carry out central orders, measurement of available resources, monitoring of compliance, punishment of noncompliance, and other costs of running any government.[233] Although the state can use brute force to compel compliance, coercive control itself is costly. As Joe Migdal puts it, "It is simply impossible for a state to achieve tractability by relying exclusively on its judges and jailers. No matter how vaunted the bureaucracy, police, and military, officers of the state cannot stand on every corner ensuring that each person stop at the red light, drive on the right side of the road, cross at the crosswalk, refrain from stealing and drug dealing, and so on."[234] As the problem of costs converges with that of resistance, scholars generally argue that effective rule should rest on some kind of consent. And consent is supposed to be best achieved by democratic representation.

The Logic of Domination in State Formation

Similarly to scholars of international politics, theorists of state formation significantly underestimate the logic of domination. If the state is a set of administrative and coercive institutions, then "state power is in the last analysis coercive power."[235] State-society bargaining should not be understood as a simple function of "the extent to which others control resources on which rulers depend and the extent to which rulers control resources on which others depend."[236] Domestic politics is not divorced from power struggles. If the logic of balancing in interstate competition can be overcome by the logic of domination, then the checking mechanisms of resistance and costs in state-society relations can be similarly overcome by self-strengthening reforms, the divide-and-rule strategy, and insidious ruling tactics.

As self-strengthening reforms and state formation processes are mutually constituted, the "self" in self-strengthening reforms refers to not just the domination-seeking state vis-à-vis other states in international competition, but also the state vis-à-vis the society in state formation. Each of

---

[232] Downing 1992, 204, 138.   [233] Kiser and Cai 2003; Levi 1988, 23.
[234] Migdal 1997, 223.   [235] Geuss 2001, 14.   [236] Levi 1988, 17.

the three key elements of self-strengthening reforms should significantly enhance rulers' coercive capability vis-à-vis societal actors. First, military reforms typically involve the formation of a standing army. An army established for interstate competition can be easily deployed to suppress internal resistance. Although disgruntled populations may rebel, they can be readily crushed by the state's overwhelming military force. As Tilly acknowledges, bargaining is "obviously asymmetrical: at the showdown, cannon versus staves."[237] When the asymmetry is compounded by state monopolization of the means of coercion, then even much hated regimes can be invulnerable to mass-based rebellions unless important segments of the state's own armed forces choose to defect.[238] Second, economic reforms involve nationalization and rationalization of taxation. When rulers enjoy higher and more steady flows of revenues, they can build mightier military and police forces. When taxation reaches the general populations beyond narrow groups of resource holders, moreover, rulers can increase their relative autonomy from society. Third, both military and economic reforms require improvement of administrative capacity. The resulting centralized bureaucracy "marks a decisive turning point in the history of the state"[239] because it has helped simultaneously to reduce administrative costs, compel taxation and conscription, maximize surveillance, and prevent resistance. It is true that coercive apparatuses are expensive to set up, but the administrative capacity to assess taxation based on wealth or output and to remit revenues from the point of collection to the state treasury has simultaneously reduced the costs of resource extraction and increased the amount of revenues.[240] Moreover, when the state develops the means to measure and collect taxes, it can also detect and punish nonpayment. Similarly, when the state develops the capacity to register young men and prevent evasion, it can enforce compliance to conscription. In addition, when the state develops the capacity for direct rule and penetrates local communities with centrally appointed officials, it can establish powerful instruments of surveillance. The creation of population registers and cadastral surveys, in particular, has facilitated "a policy of rounding up undesirable minorities."[241] As Bruce Porter concludes, the centralizing tendency of war making can easily lead to "a

---

[237] Tilly 1992 [1990], 102.

[238] This is the phenomenon of "regime defection," defined as "a sustained process by which significant elements of a previously stable ruling coalition align with the action programs of revolutionary or other opposition groups." It is the key mechanism for regime change both now and then. McAdam, Tarrow, and Tilly 2001, 196.

[239] Watkins 1934, 36.   [240] Brewer 1989, 182.   [241] Scott 1998, 4.

TABLE 4. *Self-Strengthening Reforms and the Simultaneous Enhancement of the Logic of Domination in Both International Competition and State Formation*

Self-Strengthening Reforms	Enhancement of the Logic of Domination in International Competition	Enhancement of the Logic of Domination in State Formation
Establishment of a Standing Army by National Conscription	Standing Armies and National Armies Are More Effective Than Feudal Levies in Fighting Wars	Standing Armies Are More Effective in Internal Suppression; Monopolization of the Means of Coercion Renders Unarmed Resistance Ineffective
Imposition of Direct and Indirect Taxes; Promotion of Economic Productivity	Higher and More Steady Flows of Revenues Help to Finance Wars	More Resources Help to Finance Internal Coercion; Wider Tax Bases Accord Rulers Relative Autonomy
Replacement of Aristocracy by Meritocracy	Bureaucratization Facilitates Mobilization of Resources and Consolidation of Conquered Territories	Bureaucratization of Administration Facilitates Surveillance of Society and Prevention of Resistance

triumph of raw power" and "a disaster for human liberty and rights."[242] These arguments are summarized in Table 4.

What of the checking mechanism of resistance central to theories of state formation? To a considerable extent, scholars believe that resource extraction necessarily stimulates resistance because private properties are involved. Since resource holders are not expected to give up their private possessions voluntarily, analysts are naturally led to focus on resistance. As Tilly argues, "War and preparation for war involved rulers in extracting the means of war from others who held the essential resources – men, arms, supplies, or money to buy them – and who were reluctant to surrender them without strong pressure or compensation."[243] This argument is deeply rooted in classical philosophy, both classical liberalism and classical realism. John Locke most clearly articulated the liberal doctrine

[242] Porter 1994, xv.   [243] Tilly 1992 [1990], 15.

that the arbitrary seizure of property – not just life and liberty – constituted tyranny.[244] American revolutionaries put this doctrine into practice when they proclaimed "no representation, no taxation." Even Machiavelli advised the prince that while he should make himself "feared," he should not make himself "hateful" by seizing properties from subjects or imposing crushing taxes on them.[245] Similarly, although Jean Bodin advocated absolute sovereignty, he also believed that "there is no prince in all the world who has the power to levy taxes on the people at his pleasure any more than he has the power to take another's goods."[246] If the king could not legitimately claim the subjects' private properties, then it is understandable why property rights provided the foundation for citizenship rights. However, property rights have never been absolute. Hobbes already denounced the principle "that every subject hath of a propriety in his lands and goods exclusive of the sovereign's right to the use of the same" because it "tendeth to the dissolution of a commonwealth."[247] In places where the Crown theoretically owns all the lands, subjects have little justification for resistance. Moreover, the nationalization and routinization of extraction can generate "habitual consent"[248] as subjects become accustomed to "fixed duties laid down by the state, to taxation and military service."[249] The homogenizing logic of direct and uniform rule may further nurture "state-led nationalism" which indoctrinates subjects to place obligations to the state above all other obligations.[250]

This does not mean that domination-seeking states can abandon all forms of state-society bargains. State formation scholars presume that concessions must take the forms of citizenship rights and democratic representation. But concessions may also take the form of paternalistic material welfare. As Joel Migdal points out, "What have modern states done to ensure that each subject toes the line, even without a police officer at every corner? ... Those same weighty code books that spell out the dos and don'ts for individuals also implicitly address people's needs."[251] As testified by modern authoritarian regimes, socioeconomic rights such as the rights to subsistence and development can serve as substitutes for

---

[244] *Second Treatise*, par. 222.   [245] *The Prince*, chs. 16 and 17, in Wootton 1994, 50, 52.
[246] *Commonwealth*, bk. 1, ch. 8, in Franklin 1992, 41.
[247] *Leviathan*, pt. 2, ch. 29, in Morgan 1992, 707, 710.
[248] "Habitual consent" is defined as "customary obedience [as] a consequence of tradition [and] habits of obedience." Levi 1997, 29; also Migdal 1997, 225.
[249] Hintze 1975a, 175.   [250] Tilly 1992, 709.   [251] Migdal 1997, 223.

political rights and civil liberties.[252] While political rights empower resource holders and reinforce checks and balances, economic rights make societal actors dependent on the state and reinforce state domination over society. If the former constitutes the liberal social contract, the latter may be termed the "invidious social contract."[253] Postwar communist regimes have practiced even more insidious exchanges, convincing the selected minority to act as informants for the secret police "in return for modest perquisites, such as access to western currency, the right to purchase a new car, or simply the chance to amplify their own sense of self-importance."[254]

Even when subjugated populations have the motivation for resistance, it is important to examine whether they have some organized capacity for collective action against the state. Unlike scholars of international relations, theorists of state-society relations are very much aware of the collective-action problem. They have observed that discontents are rarely coalesced into mass-based resistance movements unless several stringent conditions are met: (1) People who have shared grievances are connected by durable social ties, (2) ordinary people have powerful allies inside or outside the state, and (3) the state's coercive forces are either diverted by external threats or divided by internal disputes.[255] Nevertheless, there is a tendency to think that the collective-action problem is overblown. As Sydney Tarrow puts it, "That puzzle is a puzzle – and not a sociological law – because, in so many situations and against so many odds, collective action does occur, often on the part of people with few resources and little permanent power."[256] This view overlooks that rulers may pursue the divide-and-rule strategy to decapacitate societies. If the solution to the collective-action problem rests with shared norms which, according to Tarrow, "depend on shared understandings, on dense social networks and connective structures,"[257] then "the logic of a pattern of domination is to bring about the complete atomization and surveillance of subordinates."[258] The Hobbesian-Machiavellian conception of

---

[252] Liu Huaqiu, head of China's delegation to the United Nations World Conference on Human Rights in Vienna in June 1993, argued that "for the vast number of developing countries, to respect and protect human rights is first and foremost to ensure the full realization of the rights to subsistence and development." Cited in Angle 2002, 242.

[253] This term is from Richard Schroder, a theologian from the former German Democratic Republic. Cited in McAdams 2001, 13.

[254] McAdams 2001, 15.   [255] Tilly 1992 [1990], 99, 100–101; also Skocpol 1979, 115.

[256] Tarrow 1998, 7.   [257] Ibid., 10.   [258] Scott 1990, 128.

atomistic individuals driven by scarcity and ambition may seem extreme, but it is not at all unrealistic in many parts of the world. If trust is what enables any community to overcome the problem of opportunism, then the instillation of mutual distrust by a network of informers can reduce subjects to a situation of mutual predation.[259] Even the seemingly innocuous policy of simplifying communal land use into individual freehold tenure makes it possible for the state to "break the hold of the community over the individual household."[260] If all factors of production can also be bought and sold and the poorest families can lose out altogether, then families have incentives to maneuver to acquire more than their neighbors.[261]

On balance, then, the logic of domination enjoys the upper hand over the logic of balancing in state formation as in international competition. State formation processes allow the state simultaneously to accumulate coercive power and demobilize the society. In such circumstances, the alternatives for subjugated populations are not resistance versus acquiescence, but guaranteed repression versus grudging submission. As Jack Goldstone and Charles Tilly argue, it is important to examine not just the threat of domination if actors do not engage in resistance, but also the threat of repression if they do.[262] Thus, the more likely outcome of the war-makes-state process should be the absolute state with rulers above the law, rather than the constitutional state with rulers subject to the law. Viewed in this light, it is understandable that Harold Lasswell was once worried that the age of total war could lead to "a world of garrison states" in which "specialists on violence" would erode all democratic practices and control every aspect of social life.[263]

Dynamics of State Formation in Ancient China and Early Modern Europe

The triumph of domination and coercion was, of course, what happened in ancient China. However, the military foundations for citizenship had

---

[259] Fukuyama 1995, 26; Putnam 1993, 89; Scott 1990, 128–129.
[260] Scott 1998, 41.   [261] Skocpol 1979, 149.
[262] Goldstone and Tilly distinguish between "current threat" (as harms under the existing regime) and "repressive threat" (as costs of repression if protest is undertaken) in resistance movements. Goldstone and Tilly 2001, 184–185. They argue that scholars of resistance movements have focused on repressive threats but overlooked current threats. Interestingly, scholars of state formation and international relations have tended to ignore repressive threats.
[263] Lasswell 1941, 309.

once existed in ancient China as in early modern Europe. The need to mobilize popular support for war generated three major sets of citizenship rights: legal protection, freedom of expression, and material welfare. Unfortunately, the early development of self-strengthening reforms or state formation allowed rulers to amass coercive capabilities and even to erode earlier state-society bargains. The capacity for direct rule, in particular, facilitated the institutions of household registration, mutual surveillance, and collective responsibility. The Qin state would atomize the people by holding individuals collectively responsible for crimes committed by relatives and neighbors and by encouraging them to report on one another with handsome rewards. By destroying the fabrics of family and society, the Qin state could dominate the society with little recourse to the actual use of force.

But success at preventing and suppressing resistance did not rule out the need for state-society bargaining. Qin's rulers wanted to excel in international competition and so needed to command the active support of peasant-soldiers who fought wars, paid taxes, and cultivated food. Although the Qin state stifled freedom of expression, it strengthened the bargain of material welfare. In exchange for the hard labor of fighting and farming, peasant-soldiers received the right to subsistence through land grants, farm tools, technical assistance, and a countercyclical policy to regulate grain prices. To encourage military distinctions further, the state of Qin handsomely rewarded contributions to victory by lands, money, honors, and servants, on the one hand, and severely punished losses and surrender in war by confiscation of properties, imprisonment, and even death, on the other. Moreover, although Qin's rulers imposed harsh punishments for noncompliance, they maintained the bargain of justice by consistently and universally applying rewards and punishments to all social classes. Qin's use of carrots and sticks proved to be extremely effective in pushing forward the logic of domination – they not only served as substitutes for constitutional bargains, which weakened the logic of balancing in state formation, but also created enthusiastic support for expansionism, which enhanced the logic of domination in international competition.

In light of the ancient Chinese trajectory, the logic of balancing could be consolidated in early modern Europe because domination-seekers adopted self-weakening expedients rather than self-strengthening reforms. Self-weakening expedients weakened the state not only vis-à-vis other states in international competition, but also vis-à-vis societal actors in state-society struggles. Specifically, the use of military entrepreneurs negated efforts at monopolizing the means of coercion

TABLE 5. *Mutual Constitution of Self-Weakening Expedients and State* Deformation

Internal Balancing Moves (Improvement of Relative Capability)	Self-Weakening Expedients (Mobilization of Resources by Relying on Intermediate Resource Holders)	State Deformation Processes (Erosion of Central Authority by Intermediate Power Holders)
"Increase Military Strength"	Establishment of a Standing Army by Military Entrepreneurs and Mercenary Troops	Monopolization of the Means of Coercion Impossible
"Increase Economic Capability"	Tax Farming for Ordinary Taxes; Loans and Credits for Extraordinary Revenues	Rationalization and Nationalization of Taxation Derailed
"Develop Clever Strategies"	Sale of Offices to Private Capital Holders	Bureaucratization of Administration Negated

and centralizing military command; the contraction of loans and credits negated efforts at rationalizing and nationalizing taxation; and the sale of offices negated efforts at bureaucratizing the administration. Even more ominously, when European rulers auctioned out the state's administrative and coercive apparatuses to quasi-independent venal administrators, military entrepreneurs, and private financiers, they also empowered potential competitors to use state institutions for their personal ambitions. Thus, whereas war made the state through self-strengthening reforms in ancient China, war in fact *deformed* the state through self-weakening expedients in early modern Europe.[264] As Jean-Laurent Rosenthal points out, "The evolution from absolutism to parliamentarianism" represented "not an equilibrium phenomenon . . . [in] a bargaining nexus but a fundamental shift in the distribution of power."[265] It was because European rulers commanded so little control over the state's inherent coercive capacity that they were compelled to make extensive concessions. The mutual constitution of self-weakening expedients and state *de*formation is summarized in Table 5.

[264] Although most scholars of state formation presume that war made the state, Ertman and Thompson have highlighted that war in fact weakened a number of early modern European states. Ertman 1997; Thompson 1976; 1995; see also Brewer 1989, 138; Kaiser 1990, 20.
[265] Rosenthal 1998, 97–98.

Nevertheless, when Prussian, Russian, and French rulers eventually embarked on ancient-Chinese-style self-strengthening reforms, they were able to amass coercive capabilities quickly. However, the early use of mercenaries also led Britain to develop a fiscally focused self-strengthening model, the public credit system, which required guarantees by the Parliament. As thorough administrative reforms facilitated state domination while parliamentary oversight enhanced constitutional checks and balances, the British state thus embodied a rough balance between the logic of domination and the logic of balancing. As other European states followed the British model in the ensuing Pax Britannica, they also reflected the "paradox of European state formation" discussed earlier. Interestingly, it was the quintessential Weberian state, rather than the Chinese state, that successfully achieved the Confucian ideal of the Mean (*zhongyong*) in its ability to maintain harmony between two opposing forces without leaning too much in either direction.[266] I discuss these processes of state formation in Chapter Four.

1.6 Self-Strengthening Reforms Versus Self-Weakening Expedients: Other Things Are Rarely Equal in Comparative History

Overall, the mechanism of self-strengthening reforms is the most critical in shaping the competition between the logic of balancing and the logic of domination in both interstate and state-society relations. It is also the key to understanding endogenous transformation and alternative trajectories in ancient China and early modern Europe. In ancient China, self-strengthening reforms provided the fuel for the coercive transformation of both international competition and state formation, culminating in the triumph of the universal Leviathan. In early modern Europe, the early adoption of self-weakening expedients weakened the logic of domination, allowing the logic of balancing to maintain rough parity in both the international and domestic realms.

If international competition should compel self-strengthening reforms and self-strengthening reforms should enhance coercive capabilities and minimize costs, then why did the earliest domination-seekers in early modern Europe pursue self-weakening expedients? If we follow the ceteris paribus assumption in standard comparative analyses – that all things except the designated causal variable(s) are equal – then it would be difficult

---

[266] *Zhongyong*, see Editorial Department of the "Complete Works of Confucian Culture" 1992.

to tackle this question without resort to untheoretical historical contingencies. As noted earlier, scholars of state formation and comparative history often find this assumption unrealistic. The solution is to follow the historical-institutionalist approach, which places initial and environmental conditions, timing, and path dependence at the center of theoretical comparisons. I argue that the ancient Chinese system began with a more or less clean slate whereas the early modern European system was confounded by initial and environmental conditions.[267] While political life is supposed to be poor in the Hobbesian state of nature, early modern Europe was relatively wealthy as a result of the expansion of international trade and the influx of bullion. The higher level of monetization then made it *possible* for the earliest domination-seekers to rely on intermediate resource holders rather than to improve their extractive capacity. In ancient China, international trade existed but began to expand only after the onset of system formation. With a low level of monetarization, which more closely resembled poverty in the state of nature, the earliest domination-seekers had no easy recourse. The only way they could build larger armies and raise higher revenues was to build up their administrative capacity. As the adoption of self-strengthening reforms versus self-weakening expedients significantly shaped relative capabilities and war costs, ancient China followed the coercive trajectory while early modern Europe was derailed from it. The relative openness of the early modern European system further compounded the initial differences by providing outlets for territorial competition and ruthless stratagems.

In ensuing chapters, I examine, first, how international competition compelled similar mechanisms and strategies in both ancient China and early modern Europe; second, how differences in initial and environmental conditions shaped the timing in the adoption of self-strengthening reforms, which, through path dependence over the course of several centuries, brought about two increasingly divergent trajectories of system transformation and state transformation; and third, how international competition continued to compel convergence of the two historical

---

[267] It is noteworthy that various assumptions used in computer simulation, in which political dynamics literally begin with a clean slate, are more descriptively accurate of ancient China than of early modern Europe. First, at the onset of system formation in ancient China, units are relatively small and their geographical distribution is relatively concentrated. Second, land warfare predominates and naval warfare is insignificant. Third, opportunistic expansion provides the driving force for international dynamics, balancing is weak, conquest pays, and territorial consolidation is achieved through piecemeal encroachment. See Cederman 1997; Cusack and Stoll 1990.

trajectories but initial and environmental differences continued to set them apart.

1.7   "Alternative" Explanations

Overall, the framework of dynamics of competing logics is designed to integrate seemingly incompatible Eurocentric and Sinocentric perspectives, international politics and domestic politics, the realist view of power politics and the liberal-constructivist view of normative transformation, the Waltzian balance-of-power theory and the Gilpinian hegemonic cycle theory, and other divergent views of world politics. As such, I do not discuss how this framework fares in comparison with alternative explanations. In positivist social sciences, theories are expected not only to explain the issues and cases on hand, but also to explain them better than alternative explanations. Such an exercise essentially reduces alternative explanations to a Hobbesian world of zero-sum competition. It is my personal conviction that scholars should work toward "peaceful coexistence" among "alternative" explanations.[268] As Ira Katznelson suggests, when we "bring [alternative explanations] together, transcend the question of which one is right," we may see that "they compose a coherent...tableau."[269]

It may be argued that this conjunctural analysis of competing mechanisms and strategies is unnecessarily complex. Stephen van Evera, for example, argues that conquest was simply easier in ancient China and harder in Europe.[270] If the offense-defense balance is defined in terms of "the cost ratio of offense to defense,"[271] I think we can subsume it under the mechanism of rising costs of expansion. Geography and technology are addressed as "alternative explanations" in Chapter Three and analyzed under the mechanism of rising costs in Chapter Two. It may also be argued that the differential outcomes in the two historical cases can be easily explained by cultural homogeneity in China and cultural heterogeneity

---

[268] A number of IR colleagues have wondered whether I am a realist, liberal, or constructivist. I am a realist in the sense that I emphasize the centrality of power. I am a liberal in the sense that I underscore the importance of state-society relations. And I am a constructivist in the sense that I study the mutual constitution of international competition and state-society relations. On the whole, I am a political scientist who integrates international relations, comparative politics, and political theory.

[269] Katznelson 1997, 100.   [270] Van Evera 1998, 36–37; 1999, 179–182.

[271] Glaser and Kaufman define the offense-defense balance as "the ratio of the cost of the forces the attacker requires to take territory to the cost of the forces the defender has deployed." Glaser and Kaufman 1998, 50.

in Europe. Again, I would prefer to treat this issue in terms of case comparability, but I reluctantly address it as an "alternative explanation" in Chapter Three. Of all the factors that are supposed to make Europe unique in conventional accounts, religion is the only phenomenon that existed in early modern Europe but not in ancient China. But I treat religion as an environmental condition that shapes the interaction of causal mechanisms and strategies, rather than an "alternative explanation," in Chapter Four.[272]

---

[272] However, I can only briefly touch on religion in Chapter Four. The role of religion deserves another book-length project. For more on this subject, see Nexon 2003; Philpott 2001.

2

The Dynamics of International Politics in Ancient China

Kenneth Waltz expects "substantive and stylistic characteristics" in ancient China to be similar to those in early modern Europe.[1] He is correct. The Eurocentric logic of balancing – which encompasses the mechanisms of balance of power and rising costs of expansion – was predominant from the onset of system formation in 656 BC to the turn of the third century BC. For more than three centuries, attempts at domination were made and checked, ambitious hegemons rose and fell, balancing as a foreign policy was pursued, and balances as roughly equal distribution of relative capabilities occurred at various times. The length of this period of sustained stability was comparable to the whole span of the early modern period. However, from the midfourth century BC on, the Warring States system became increasingly unstable. States one after another intensified their pursuit of the logic of domination – self-strengthening reforms, divide-and-conquer strategies, and cunning and brutish stratagems. Most notably, the state of Qin developed the capacity for direct rule and moved toward total mobilization for war. Qin also shrewdly complemented its increased relative capability with ruthless strategies and stratagems on both the diplomatic and military fronts. From 356 to the third century BC, Qin gradually rose from relative weakness to hegemony and then to domination. Qin eventually achieved universal domination in the ancient Chinese world in 221 BC.

As Qin succeeded at the supposedly impossible task of universal domination, scholars of international politics may conjecture that the Warring States must be uniquely incapable of balancing or that conquest must be

---

[1] Waltz 1979, 329–330.

uniquely easy in the ancient Chinese system. While it is factually accurate to say that Qin's victims failed at balancing against domination, we should not take the a priori assumption that the balance of power should normally succeed. As argued earlier, if we follow the realist assumption that states are motivated by self-interest, then effective balancing is very difficult. This chapter illustrates how the motivation of self-interest facilitated coercive transformation in the ancient Chinese system. This does not mean that Qin's drive for domination was easy. Qin faced not just the balance of power and the rising costs of expansion, but also the barriers of geography and the difficulty of consolidation of conquests. However, Qin managed to overcome them with both strength and wit. Before I examine how Qin overcame multiple layers of seemingly insurmountable countervailing mechanisms, I first briefly outline relative checks and balances in the system from 656 to 284 BC.

2.1   Early Triumph of the Logic of Balancing (656–284 BC)

From the onset of the multistate era to the turn of the third century BC, the rise and decline of Chu, Qi (in two different eras), Jin, Wu, and Wei provide textbook cases for Waltzian balance of power and Gilpinian costs of expansion.[2] These domination-seeking states rose to preeminence as a result of uneven rates of growth, but they all declined as a result of the checking mechanisms of balance of power and rising costs of expansion.[3]

Chu was the first powerful *guo* to be reckoned with in the *zhongguo* (central states) system. It was located in the Dan River, Huai River, and

---

[2] I discuss only great powers. The great powers in ancient China with their dates of entry and exit are as follows: Qi (656–284 BC), Chu (656–278 BC), Qin (632–221 BC), Jin (632–453 BC), Wu (584–475 BC), Yue (482–335 BC), Wei (408–293 BC), Han (404–293 BC), Zhao (404–260 BC), and Yan (284–279 BC). See Appendix II for the list of wars involving great powers in the ancient Chinese system. See Appendix III for the operational criteria in identifying great powers and in compiling wars involving great powers.

[3] For sources on warfare in ancient China, see Blakeley 1999a; Brooks and Brooks, http://www.umass.edu/wsp; Chan 1999; Chen 1941; Chen 1991; Creel 1970a; Ding and Wu 1993; Gao 1992, 1995; Gao 1998; Ge 1989; Guo 1994; Guofangbu 1989; Hong 1975; Hsu 1965a, 1997, 1999; Lao 1985; Lewis 1990, 1999; Lin 1992; Mu and Wu 1992; Sawyer 1994, 1998; Sanjun daxue 1976; Sun 1999; Tian and Zang 1996; Walker 1953; Wu 1995; Xie 1995; Xing 1987; Yang 1977, 1986; Yates 1980, 1982; Zhang and Liu 1988; "*Zhongguo lidai zhanzheng nianbiao*" editorial board 2003. In general, English sources are more careful than Chinese sources in checking transmitted texts against archaeological evidence. Note also that the dates of some major events may be one year off in different sources because each state employed its own calendar and no uniform time scheme existed. Lin 1992, 8–9, 466, 473.

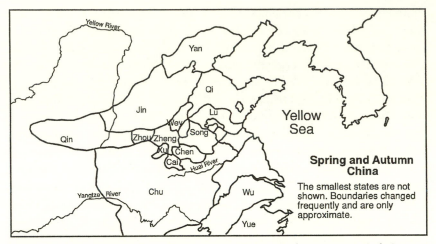

MAP I. Ancient China in the Middle to Late Spring and Autumn Period. *Source:* Reprinted from Herrlee Creel (1970), *The Origins of Statecraft in China* (Chicago: University of Chicago Press), 204, © 1970 Herrlee G. Creel, with the permission of the University of Chicago Press; reprinted from Victoria Tin-bor Hui, "Toward a Dynamic Theory of International Politics: Insights from Comparing the Ancient Chinese and Early Modern European Systems," *International Organization*, 58 (1): 186, with the permission of Cambridge University Press.

Yangtze River regions – south of the Yellow River valleys where central *guo* were clustered. Such a geographical location means that Chu had vast uncharted areas to expand and rich resources to exploit. Through most of the multistate era (until it was taken over by Qin after 316 BC), Chu enjoyed the largest territorial size and the richest natural resources. Moreover, because Chu was a non-Sinitic *guo* and was not directly influenced by Zhou feudalism, it developed protobureaucratic administration ahead of various Zhou *guo*. As Barry Blakeley points out, "Chu governance – in the critical respect of centralization of power – lay on the cutting edge of developments throughout much of Eastern Zhou times."[4] Although Chu's chief ministers were aristocrats as in other *guo*, official positions were not hereditary but selected on the basis of ability, character, and experience.[5] Most notably, Chu was the first *guo* to rule newly conquered territories by centrally appointed officials as *xian* or dependent territories, rather than by hereditary nobles as fiefs.[6] This policy allowed Chu to consolidate conquests and facilitated its rise to power. Chu also

---

[4] Blakeley 1999b, 57; also Creel 1970b, 153.
[5] Creel 1970b, 149–150.   [6] Ibid., 144.

collected rudimentary statistics on its population and resources early on.[7] Commanding both the availability of resources and the capacity to exploit them, Chu posed a menacing threat to the Zhou court as early as the Western Zhou period. After the Zhou court declined in the Spring and Autumn period, Chu set its ambition on Zhou *guo* in the heart of the Yellow River plain, in particular, Zheng, Chen, Cai, and Song. To deal with Chu's aggression, various Zhou states formed an alliance under the leadership of Qi's Duke Huan in 656 BC (which marked the onset of the ancient Chinese system).[8] With overwhelming allied forces encamped in its territory, Chu made peace with the alliance and turned its ambitions to the Huai River valley.

After the death of the energetic Duke Huan in 643 BC, the northern alliance lost its leader and Chu reemerged as a dominant power. But Chu's supremacy was soon checked by Jin, another Zhou *guo* in the middle of the Yellow River valley. In 645 BC, Jin suffered a devastating defeat by Qin in which a large number of Jin's aristocratic warriors were annihilated.

---

[7] The survey was probably conducted in 548 BC. Ibid., 152.

[8] Duke Huan began to organize anti-Chu alliances in the early years of his reign. But the alliance formed in 656 BC was the first Qi-led alliance that invaded Chu's territory in response to Chu's aggression against Zhou states. Note that there is an intense controversy over whether Duke Huan pursued nascent military, economic, and administrative reforms. Mainstream historical analyses typically discuss such reforms. Brooks, a critical historian, disputes this view. He points out that Qi's reforms are recorded in the *Zuo zhuan* (Zuo's Tradition), which was retrospectively written in the Warring States period, but not the *Chunqiu* (Spring and Autumn Annals), the only text undisputedly written in the Spring and Autumn period. Brooks, Warring States Workgroup (hereafter WSWG) communication, September 27, 2002. Some historians also express doubts about the historicity of Guan Zhong, who was supposed to be Duke Huan's chief strategist and administrator. See Rosen 1976. Other historians argue that it is not practical to rely on the extremely terse *Chunqiu* and disregard other available texts. While the analyst may feel less certain about particular events if they do not appear in the *Chunqiu*, it is a big jump to say that developments that appear in the *Zuo zhuan* but not in the *Chunqiu* did not happen at all. Yuri Pines suggests that the compilers of the *Chunqiu* selected events on the basis of their ritual significance to the Lu court, but not on their political significance. For instance, the defeat of Yue by Wu in 494 BC is not recorded. Pines 2002, 250–251, fn. 10. Brooks himself acknowledges that the *Chunqiu* omits some important developments, especially those in western states. For example, the Qin-Jin wars and the general growth of interstate trade are not recorded. It is not the job of a political scientist to resolve acrimonious debates among historians. Nevertheless, as Qi was weaker than Chu, I am skeptical that Qi could have taken on the mighty Chu had it not pursued some nascent self-strengthening measures. Brooks argues that if Qi indeed pursued reforms, then Qi would not have needed allies and Qi's power would not have declined immediately after Duke Huan's death. However, as we shall see in Chapter Three, even Napoleonic France needed allies. Moreover, as we shall see later and in the next chapter, the institutionalization of self-strengthening reforms was extremely difficult in both ancient China and early modern Europe.

Faced with a crisis, the Jin rulership sought to extend its resource base from *guoren*, citizens residing within the walled city-state, to *yeren*, subject populations in the hinterland. Jin provided land grants to *yeren* and required land taxes and military service in return.[9] This policy allowed Jin to recover quickly to face a subsequent Qin attack in 644 BC. The succeeding ruler Duke Wen, who had spent some years in exile in Chu, further expanded Jin's army strength on the model of his predecessor and reformed Jin's government on the model of Chu's nascent bureaucracy.[10] In 632 BC, Jin defeated Chu and claimed leadership of the central states.

With rough parity in their relative capabilities, the Chu and Jin camps in their protracted hegemonic struggles produced only momentary victories and losses. To divert Jin's forces, Chu sought the friendship of Jin's western neighbor, Qin. Similarly, to put Chu in the position of fighting two-front wars, Jin introduced the knowledge of chariot warfare (which was commonly practiced on the central plain) to Chu's southeastern neighbor, Wu. In response, Chu sought to break the Jin-Wu communications line, while Jin tried to break the Qin-Chu alliance and courted Qi's friendship. In 546 BC, several secondary states, which were sandwiched between the two great powers and became battlefields in the century-long rivalry, initiated a peace conference. As Jin and Chu were unable to subjugate each other, they grudgingly agreed to a formal peace treaty. The efforts of Jin and Chu to balance and counterbalance each other thus produced a classic scenario of the balance of power whereby ambitions were checked by ambitions. Jin and Chu also left the important legacy of *fuguo qiangbing* (rich country and strong army) reforms that was to shape the dynamics of international competition for centuries.

The Jin-Chu equilibrium did not last long. The emerging Wu soon pursued a policy to "defeat Chu in the West, intimidate Qi and Jin in the North, and subjugate Yue in the South."[11] Wu, which was originally a small and weak non-Sinitic state located in the peripheral southeast, managed to increase its relative capability with Jin's assistance from 584 BC. Wu also imitated Jin's self-strengthening measures to build larger

---

[9] Lewis 1990, 56–58; Tian and Zang 1996, 106–108. This is another controversial issue. As Jin's reforms – as are Qi's reforms – are based on the *Zuo zhuan* rather than the *Chunqiu*, Brooks argues that they did not happen. Brooks, WSWG communication, May 20–28, 2002. I find Brooks's argument less convincing for Jin than for Qi. Most notably, while Qi under Duke Huan did not engage in any direct confrontation with Chu (Qi and Chu attacked only the lesser states sandwiched between them), Jin had to fight Chu and managed to sustain the rivalry with Chu for a century.

[10] Creel 1970b, 155–157.   [11] Mu and Wu 1992, vol. 1, 80.

armies and raise higher revenues.[12] To fight the significantly more powerful Chu, Wu designed an indirect strategy by splitting its armies into
three divisions and periodically sending one division to launch hit-and-
run attacks on different areas of Chu. As Chu had to stay alert at all
times while Wu only needed to use a portion of its military strength, Chu
became exhausted over time. Moreover, Wu made secret alliances with
Chu's minor allies, who resented Chu's domination in the Yangtze River
region, thus acquiring valuable logistical support, local guides, and field
intelligence. After decades of efforts to build up national strength, Wu
launched a surprise attack and captured Chu's capital in 506 BC. However, Wu's king became self-indulgent with the luxuries in Chu's capital
and failed to cripple Chu's military strength immediately.[13] Chu thus had
a breathing chance to ask for assistance from Qin and soon drove away
the conquerors. Despite this setback, Wu took over Chu's regional domination in the south and became emboldened to compete for systemic
hegemony. Wu defeated Qi in 484 BC and successfully forced Jin to give
up the leadership role at an international meeting in 482 BC.

Wu's ambition, in turn, was blocked by the countervailing mechanisms
of rising costs of expansion and balance of power. Wu had to commit huge
resources not just to build a strong army, but also to construct a canal
system to provide logistical support for its long-distance expeditions to
the north. At the same time, Chu – as Jin had previously – encouraged
the rise of Wu's southeastern neighbor, Yue. Wu inflicted a devastating
defeat on Yue in 494 BC. To prevent an imminent conquest, Yue bribed a
high minister in Wu, who convinced Wu's king to allow Yue to continue
survival as a dependent. Yue's ruler then feigned loyalty to Wu but secretly
increased army strength, improved agricultural productivity, and made
alliances with Jin, Qi, and Chu.[14] Yue also lured Wu into the trap of
exhaustion by encouraging Wu to seek hegemony in the north and to
engage in massive construction projects. A golden opportunity occurred
in 482 BC, when Wu's core forces were competing for systemic hegemony

[12] The conventional view holds that Wu solicited the service of a military genius, Sun Wu,
the putative author of the *Sunzi bingfa*. See Sawyer 1994, 151–157. For disputes of this
view, see Brooks 1994, 59; Lewis 1990, 68; 1999, 604.
[13] Machiavelli provided a nice explanation: Conquests that are "full of delights" can inflict
"revenge on their conquerors without a fight and without bloodshed, for [the delights]
infect them with their wicked habits and leave them ready to be defeated by the first
attacker." *Discourses*, bk. 2, ch. 19, in Wootton 1994, 182.
[14] As van Evera argues, the weaker could feign docility, conceal capability, hide grievances,
and keep military plans secret so as to prevent preemptive attacks and wait for the ripe
moment to launch a surprise attack. Van Evera 1999, 43–48, 78.

in the north. Yue captured Wu's capital and reversed the balance of relative capabilities. Yue eventually eliminated Wu in 473 BC. This was the first time a great power was successfully conquered in the ancient Chinese system. This precedent – as were other pace-setting developments in the system – was to be followed by other expansionist states.

Before the next phase of mutual annihilation arrived, however, there was relative calm in great-power competition at the interval between the Spring and Autumn period and the Warring States period in the midfifth century BC. While Chu, Yue, and Yan continued to annex weak neighbors, Jin, Qin, and Qi successively fell into internal power struggles. Such domestic conflicts resulted in the demise of old ruling houses, which might still cling onto some feudal vestiges, and the rise of new rulers, who were more inclined to take any actions in order to excel in international competition. In Jin, a prolonged civil war which began in 497 BC eventually resulted in the partition of the state by the noble clans of Han, Zhao, and Wei in 453 BC. As the successor states of Jin soon kicked off a new era of self-strengthening reforms, I use the year of partition as the dividing line between the Spring and Autumn and Warring States periods.[15]

Compared with Han and Zhao, Wei inherited the most strategic pieces of territory along the Yellow River. Wei's Marquis Wen (445–396 BC) was an ambitious ruler who sought to restore Jin's glory. He issued a decree to invite talents from all over the ancient Chinese world in order, in Waltzian terms, to "develop clever strategies."[16] To "increase military strength," Wei's reformers rationalized earlier conscription measures, developed larger peasant armies, and introduced professional crack troops. To encourage military valor at all ranks, Wei's commanders offered generous rewards for contributions to victories. To "increase economic capability," Wei's administrators built on previous land grants and land taxes,

---

[15] The development of self-strengthening reforms may be seen as a process of "punctuated equilibrium," as discussed in Chapter One. The process witnessed incremental changes in the Spring and Autumn period and then experienced a "punctuation" or revolution at the interval between the Spring and Autumn and Warring States periods. During the early centuries, the pressure of war already compelled various great powers to gradually expand their army size, promote population growth, stimulate agricultural production, and hire talents of more humble origins. In the fifth century BC, the civil war that carved up Jin also accelerated various reform measures that had been slowly developing earlier. The process experienced another "punctuation" when Qin introduced universal conscription in 356 BC. In Europe, there was a similar process of incremental changes in the early modern period and punctuations during the revolutionary era. On related "punctuations" in the development of state capacity, see Chapter Four.

[16] Recall that Waltz defines "internal balancing" as "moves to increase economic capability, to increase military strength, to develop clever strategies." Waltz 1979, 118.

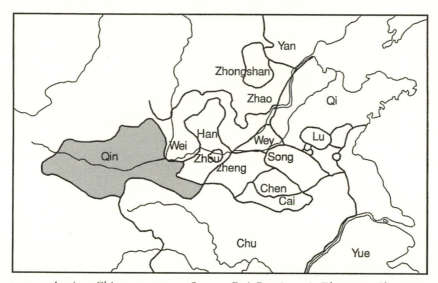

MAP 2. Ancient China ca. 450 BC. *Source:* Rui Gao (1995), *Zhongguo Shanaggu Junshishi* (Beijing: Academy of Military Sciences), map 20. Reprinted from Victoria Tin-bor Hui, "Toward a Dynamic Theory of International Politics: Insights from Comparing the Ancient Chinese and Early Modern European Systems," *International Organization*, 58 (1): 187, with the permission of Cambridge University Press.

posited a standard size of landholding for all households, and formalized a system of "small-scale peasant freehold worked by a single family as the basic unit of production."[17] To maximize extractions without destroying peasants' livelihood, Wei's reformers also took steps to improve agricultural productivity. To promote intensive farming, the Wei state not only maintained the Spring and Autumn practices of opening up forests and wastelands, encouraging double and multiple crops, and developing hybrid seeds, but also pioneered large-scale irrigation projects. Such efforts were significantly facilitated by iron implements, which came into general use in the fifth century BC.[18] Wei's economists further innovated the "ever-normal granary" policy to protect peasants against inevitable annual fluctuations by buying and storing grains in good years and selling them at low prices in bad years.[19] To minimize evasion from military

[17] Li Kui, who was in charge of Wei's economic policies, was the first to articulate "a theory of the state based on revenue from small-scale farming." Lewis 1999, 605.

[18] Brooks and Brooks 1998, 3; Sawyer 1994, 53; Yates 1982, 409.

[19] France introduced this policy in the Revolutionary era. Moore 1966, 83. The United States introduced this policy under the same name in 1938. Creel 1970a, 27. In the Warring

service and land tax, Wei's ministers also proceeded to register households. With various measures to improve national productivity and to mobilize previously untapped human and material resources, Wei reached a new height of power and wealth.

In the second half of the fifth century BC, when other states were still suffering from weak central authority or even civil war, Wei's ascendance in relative capability was remarkable. In his quest for hegemony, Marquis Wen was careful to cultivate an alliance with other successor states of Jin, that is, Han and Zhao. The "three Jin" alliance scored numerous victories over other great powers, Qi, Qin, and Chu. Wei took from Qin large tracts of strategic territory along the west bank of the Yellow River in the period 413–385 BC. Wei also seized cities and counties from Chu in 391 BC, from Zheng in 393 BC, and from Song in 391 BC. Wei further conquered Zhongshan, a medium-sized state, in 406 BC. Wei thus achieved the hegemonic status (being the most powerful in the system) that had eluded previous aspirants.

However, Wei's hegemony was precarious. The three Jin alliance broke down when Wei and Zhao fought over Wey in 383 BC. As former allies became enemies and former enemies became allies (Zhao sought help from Chu) in this war, the old pattern of wars based on the dominance of Jin and its successors gave way to a new pattern of fluid alliances.[20] Wei managed to maintain hegemony on its own when other great powers continued to suffer from weak leadership. But the situation changed in the midfourth century BC, when internal power struggles in Qin and Qi were concluding. Compelled by Wei, new rulers of both states soon introduced their own *fuguo qiangbing* reforms. When Wei attempted to subjugate Zhao in 354–352 BC and Han 344–340 BC, both targets sought Qi's intervention. Qi severely defeated Wei on each occasion. Although Wei quickly recovered from the first defeat, its core forces were annihilated in the second defeat. Wei thus lost the hegemony to Qi in 341 BC.[21] At the same time, Qin took advantage of Wei's preoccupation with Qi to recover lost territory on the west bank of the Yellow River. In ensuing decades, Wei suffered more defeats and lost more territory. In 293 BC, Wei – along with Han – further lost the great-power status after 240,000 allied troops were annihilated

States period, Chu also provided relief loans for peasants to purchase seed grains. Weld 1999, 85.

[20] Lewis 1999, 617.

[21] The two instances are also known as the battle of Guiling in 353 BC and the battle of Maling in 341 BC.

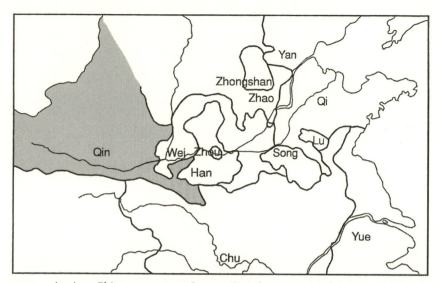

MAP 3. Ancient China ca. 350 BC. *Source:* Rui Gao (1995), *Zhongguo Shanaggu Junshishi* (Beijing: Academy of Military Sciences), map 23. Reprinted from Victoria Tin-bor Hui, "Toward a Dynamic Theory of International Politics: Insights from Comparing the Ancient Chinese and Early Modern European Systems," *International Organization*, 58 (1): 188, with the permission of Cambridge University Press.

by Qin. Thereafter, Wei and Han became Qin's prime targets of territorial encroachment.

Wei's experience of rise and decline was to be repeated by Qi. Similarly to Jin and Qin, Qi went through protracted internal power struggles at the interval between the Spring and Autumn and Warring States periods. Conflicts finally ended when the Tian clan usurped the legitimate ruling house. To mobilize popular support and to deal with heightening international competition, King Wei (356–320 BC) reformed Qi's government and appointed meritocratic administrators, strategists, and generals. With the assistance of a famous military strategist, Sun Bin,[22] Qi devastated Wei in two major wars and seized the hegemony in 341 BC. The succeeding rulers King Huan (319–301 BC) and King Min (300–284 BC) were eager to exploit Qi's hegemonic status and sought further territorial expansion. In 314 BC, Qi attacked Yan, a medium-sized neighbor in its northwest, and turned it into a dependent. Qi also defeated other great powers: Chu in

---

[22] Sun Bin is often taken to be the author of the *Sunbin bingfa*. But this conventional view is disputed.

303–302 BC and Qin in 298–296 BC. Qi reached the height of its relative capability in 286 BC, when it conquered Song; that conquest allowed Qi to expand its territorial size by 50 percent and to take over the prosperous capital city, Dingtao. In the same year, Qi launched additional attacks on Chu, Han, Wei, and Zhao.

As was the fate of all previous domination-seekers, however, Qi soon experienced a decline in power. Other states were jealous of Qi's conquest of Song. Qin, which was recognized by Qi as a co-hegemon in 288 BC (when both kings jointly proclaimed the title *di* or emperor),[23] was eager to weaken this formidable rival. Yan, which Qi had subdued since 314 BC, had been secretly planning a revenge. Yan seized the opportunity of widespread resentment and mobilized an anti-Qi alliance of Yan, Zhao, Qin, Han, and Wei in 284 BC. As Qi's defense along the Qi-Yan border was very weak, Yan's army easily marched into Qi's heartland. At the same time, the armies of Qin, Han, Wei, and Zhao attacked from the west. With the combined forces of five states, Qi's armies were annihilated, the king was slain, and the entire state was occupied, with the exception of two fortified cities, Ju and Jimo. Although Qi eventually regained independence in 279 BC, it was never to recover its previous glory.

Overall, the rise and decline of domination-seeking states in the ancient Chinese system provide ample support for the Eurocentric perspective that the mechanisms of balance of power and rising costs of expansion should always operate to check attempts at domination. Contrary to the Sinocentric wisdom that the multistate era represented only an interregnum destined to be unified, the *zhongguo* system was reasonably stable for three and a half centuries. It was certainly not obvious to statesmen in the late fourth century BC that the system would be rolled up a century later.

2.2   Qin's Rise from Relative Weakness to Universal Domination (356–221 BC)

There was also no sign that Qin was preordained to become the ultimate unifier of the ancient Chinese system. During the early centuries, Qin consistently pursued a defensive foreign policy. From 656 to 357 BC, Qin initiated only 11 (or 7 percent) of 160 "wars involving great powers" (wars characterized by the participation of at least one great power on

---

[23] However, both emperors soon dropped this title under pressure from other states.

either side).[24] In the Spring and Autumn period, it may be said that Qin performed the role of "the balancer": Qin was courted by both Jin and Chu during their prolonged rivalry from 632 to 546 BC; Qin also saved Chu from Wu's conquest in 505 BC. At the height of Wei's hegemony, Qin suffered from protracted succession struggles and lost to Wei large tracts of strategic territory on the west bank of the Yellow River. Blocked from the central plain by the mighty Yellow River, Qin was "a minor factor in interstate wars."[25]

The situation started to change after Duke Xian (384–362 BC) staged a successful coup in 385 BC. Duke Xian had spent some years in exile in Wei. Upon his accession to the throne, he introduced Wei's household registration system to increase mobilization of human and material resources. From 366 to 361 BC, Qin took advantage of Wei's preoccupation in the east and recovered some important lost territory on the west bank of the Yellow River. Duke Xian's successor, Duke Xiao (361–338 BC), was similarly committed to building up Qin's power and wealth. As Wei's Marquis Wen did, Duke Xiao issued a decree to invite the best minds from all over the Chinese world to help him. Shang Yang, whose talents were not appreciated in Wei, went to Qin. From 356 BC, Shang Yang launched the most comprehensive self-strengthening reforms known in ancient Chinese history. Shang Yang also took advantage of Wei's two major defeats by Qi and recovered more lost territory in the Qin-Wei wars of 354–351 BC and 341–339 BC.[26]

The original motive of Duke Xian and Duke Xiao was probably only defensive; that is, they wanted to enhance Qin's security against Wei and restore Qin's place among great powers. As Qin's relative capability improved, however, Duke Xiao and his successors switched to an aggressive policy of opportunistic expansion. From 356 to 221 BC, Qin initiated fifty-two of a total of ninety-six "wars involving great powers" (or 54 percent). Qin scored forty-eight victories in those fifty-two wars (or 92 percent). Qin further won three of five wars in which it was the target. As a result, Qin pushed Wei out of the west bank of the Yellow River by 328 BC. Qin also proceeded to seize territory on the east bank of the Yellow River from its

---

[24] See Appendix II. Wars in which Qin was the target are not counted among these eleven wars. The definition of "wars involving great powers" follows Levy. Levy 1983, 74.

[25] Lewis 1999, 618.

[26] Qin won some decisive victories over Wei in 354–351 BC, when Wei was preoccupied with Qi and Zhao. After Wei secured its eastern flank and turned its attention to Qin, Qin decided to make a strategic retreat. In 350 BC, Qin made peace with Wei by returning some pieces of territory. Yang 1977, 45–48. For the war of 341–339 BC, see later discussion.

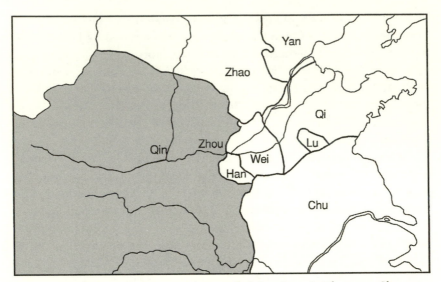

MAP 4. Ancient China ca. 257 BC. *Source:* Rui Gao (1995), *Zhongguo Shanaggu Junshishi* (Beijing: Academy of Military Sciences), map 26. Reprinted from Victoria Tin-bor Hui, "Toward a Dynamic Theory of International Politics: Insights from Comparing the Ancient Chinese and Early Modern European Systems," *International Organization*, 58 (1): 192, with the permission of Cambridge University Press.

immediate neighbors, Wei, Han, and Chu. Qin decisively defeated Chu in the wars of 312–311 BC and 301–298 BC. Qin then annihilated the core forces of Wei and Han and knocked them out of great-power status in 293 BC. Qin's ascendance to hegemony was formally recognized by Qi (which became the strongest power after devastating Wei in 341 BC) in 288 BC, when rulers from both states jointly assumed the title of emperor. Qin soon ascended further, from bipolar hegemony to unipolar hegemony, after Qi was decimated by an anti-Qi alliance in 284 BC. Qin moved on to deal severe blows to the remaining two great powers, Chu in 280–276 BC and Zhao in 262–257 BC. In 257 BC, all other states had lost great-power status. Qin further crossed the threshold of controlling about half of the territory in the system. (Compare Maps 3 and 4.) By 241 BC, Qin had taken so much territory in the central plain that it encircled Han and Wei and shared borders with Qi. Qin launched the final wars of unification in 236 BC and established the Qin dynasty – the first universal empire in the Chinese world – in 221 BC.

Why did Qin succeed at universal domination while all previous domination-seeking states were effectively checked by the logic of balancing? Why did Qin's relative capability only rise and snowball but not decline? Why was there not another rising power to check Qin? Did Qin's targets pursue self-strengthening reforms and form balancing alliances? Did Qin face rising costs of expansion? Why was Qin able to consolidate conquests of whole, sovereign territorial states? During Qin's rise to domination, the countervailing mechanisms of balance of power and rising costs of expansion continued to operate. In fact, Qin was weaker than other great powers during the early decades of its ascendance. However, Qin relentlessly pursued self-strengthening reforms, divide-and-conquer strategies, and ruthless stratagems. To bridge seemingly insurmountable gaps in relative capabilities and to preclude the prospect of fighting concerted alliances, Qin would not hesitate to resort to "unorthodox" measures such as lying and cheating, bribing corrupt kings and officials, and sowing dissensions between kings and commanders. Let us examine how Qin achieved the seemingly impossible.

2.3 Overcoming the Balance of Power

As scholars of international relations would expect, when Qin's relative capability rose and became increasingly threatening to its neighbors, other states responded with the balance-of-power strategy. However, it is often overlooked that the balance-of-power strategy may be countered by its opposite – the divide-and-conquer strategy. In the ancient Chinese system, the critical period from the late fourth to the midthird century BC was the age of *hezong* and *lianheng* strategies.[27] The *hezong* strategy followed the rationale of the balance of power by calling for the uniting of weaker states to resist the strongest. At the same time, Qin also developed the *lianheng* strategy, which sought to forestall and break up *hezong* alliances

---

[27] Lewis 1999, 632–641. Accounts of *hezong* and *lianheng* alliances are based on the *Zhanguo ce* (Intrigues of the Warring States) and the *Shi ji* (Records of History). Crump believes that the *Zhanguo ce* was written as a training menu for persuasion and thus mixed fictional dialogues with historical events. Crump 1964, ch. 6; 1996, 36–40. The *Shi ji*, in turn, relied on the *Zhanguo ce*. Thus, historians have doubted the historicity of these two texts. Given the paucity of historical records, many historians continue to refer to these texts but exercise caution. See Lewis 1999; Sawyer 1998; and various Chinese historians. In addition, because both texts were written in the early Han Dynasty, the terms *hezong* and *lianheng* were probably anachronistic. However, from the IR perspective, the important issue is whether ancient Chinese states formed alliances with and against Qin. Crump indeed agrees that "[t]here must have been constant and chaotic alignments and realignments among the Zhou states against each other and with each other against the continually threatening state of Qin." Crump 1964, 91.

by playing off the various states against one another with threats and bribes, and then marshalling overwhelming force to conquer them seriatim. The terms *lianheng* and *hezong* were based on the geographical locations of the major states. (See Map 3.) As Qin was located to the far west of the ancient Chinese system, the ideal alliance pattern to balance against Qin's eastward advance was to form a vertical bulwark linking Yan and Zhao in the north, Han and Wei in the center, and Chu in the south, hence *hezong* or vertical. To break up this north-south axis, Qin's strategy was to form *lianheng* or horizontal alliances with Han, Wei, and Qi.

In the competition between the *hezong* and *lianheng* strategies, the former suffered a dismal record in terms of both the formation of balancing alliances and the defeat of Qin. Qin's fifty-two expansionist wars from 356 to 221 BC met only eight allied responses.[28] Five of the anti-Qin alliances were defeated by Qin's forces or dissolved by Qin's *lianheng* strategy. Although Qin was defeated by the other three alliances, the defeats were not decisive and could not block Qin's rise to domination. Events surrounding the first *hezong* alliance of 318 BC already boded ill for the balance-of-power mechanism. First, the alliance was formed very slowly and reluctantly. After losing the hegemonic status in 341 BC, Wei tried to form an alliance against Qin as early as 334 BC. But other states were suspicious of the once-expansionist Wei. Wei itself wavered between balancing and bandwagoning. Second, when the alliance was finally formed, it was not composed of all the six states which Qin eventually conquered. Qi, the then-hegemonic power, probably did not regard the less powerful Qin as a threat and so did not participate. Chu and Yan joined the alliance but did not contribute troops. While Chu was less powerful than Qi, it was on par with – if not more powerful than – Qin at the time. Yan was located in the peripheral northeast and probably did not think that the distant Qin presented any serious threat. Third, allied forces did not have unified command. While the armies of Han, Wei, and Zhao still outnumbered those of Qin, allied forces fought separately, thus giving Qin the opportunity to divide and defeat them one by one. Fourth, the alliance disintegrated quickly. After a speedy defeat, Wei unilaterally left

---

[28] Traditional accounts typically list five *hezong* alliances which are proclaimed as such in the *Zhanguo ce*: alliances in 318 BC, 298–296 BC, 287 BC, 247 BC, and 241 BC. I include other allied efforts to resist Qin. Half of the balancing alliances were formed specifically to check Qin's rise to domination (in 318–317 BC, 298–296 BC, 287 BC, 241 BC), while the other half were direct responses to Qin's attacks (in 294–286 BC, 276–274 BC, 259–257 BC, 247 BC).

the alliance and made peace with Qin in 317 BC. Moreover, Qi took advantage of Wei's and Zhao's defeat by Qin and attacked them in the hope of making easy territorial gains.

After repeated onslaughts by Qin, Han and Wei joined forces in 294–286 BC and 276–274 BC. In both cases, however, the uncoordinated armies of Han and Wei were divided and defeated. In between these two attempts, the badly embattled Han and Wei sought an alliance with Qi, Zhao, and Yan in 287 BC. But the conflicts of interests among allies allowed Qin to dissolve the alliance before it even set off.[29] By 241 BC, Qin had seized so many areas of territory that it shared borders with Qi. But Qi still refused to participate in an alliance with Zhao, Chu, Han, Wei, and Yan. Moreover, allied forces continued to have no unified command. Worse, after Qin launched a surprise attack on Chu's camp at night, Chu left the battlefield without notifying its allies. As it was hopeless to fight Qin without Chu, the rest of the allied forces also retreated.

Anti-Qin alliances managed to win three times. Unfortunately, in each of these instances, allies failed to hold together to defeat Qin decisively. In 298–296 BC, the allied forces of Qi, Han, and Wei forced their way to the strategic Hangu Pass (which provided an easy passage to cross the Yellow River) and compelled Qin to return some territory to Han and Wei. But Qi, the strongest power at the time, was discontented because it contributed the most efforts but gained nothing. Qi soon made peace with Qin so as to seek its own territorial ambitions. In 259–257 BC, Chu and Wei helped to relieve Qin's siege of Zhao's capital, Handan. However, allied forces had become very fearful of Qin and did not pursue Qin's retreating army. Against such a backdrop of dismal balancing, the alliance of 247 BC was uncharacteristically promising and had a respectable chance of checking Qin's seemingly ineluctable rise to domination. When Qin laid siege to Wei's capital, Daliang, Wei secured assistance from Chu, Han, Yan, and Zhao. Remarkably, allies placed their forces under the unified command of a Wei general who had lifted Qin's siege of Zhao in 259–257 BC. Moreover, the commander in chief pursued Qin's retreating army to the east bank of the Yellow River. Faced with unified resistance, Qin resorted to a *lijian* or estrangement tactic: Qin bribed Wei's high officials to spread the rumor that the commander, a brother of the king, had ambitions to assume the throne. After Wei's king dismissed the commander in 246 BC, the prospect for effective balancing vanished.

---

[29] Alliances that failed to take military actions do not count as wars.

The *hezong* alliance of 247 BC illustrates the importance of examining not just the weakness of balancing efforts, but also the strength of Qin's divide-and-conquer strategy and the ruthlessness of Qin's stratagems. Qin actively sought to overcome the balance of power by forestalling the formation of *hezong* alliances and by breaking up already formed ones. To achieve this goal, Qin "was never reluctant to lie in diplomatic meetings, to acquire information on other states by espionage, and to bribe key figures in the courts of other states into collaboration."[30] As Ralph Sawyer puts it, Qin rolled up other states "partly by aggressively subverting state governments through the stimulation of disaffection and by fomenting political wrangling among the remaining states."[31] As Qin's rise to domination was successively resisted by Wei, Qi, and Zhao, it is instructive to examine in greater detail how Qin divided and then conquered these once-hegemonic and great powers.

In 344 BC, Qin had scored some important victories over Wei by taking advantage of Wei's preoccupation on the eastern fronts. But Wei remained the strongest power and planned an allied preventive campaign against its rising neighbor.[32] To avert this potentially devastating attack, Qin's Shang Yang requested an audience with Wei's ruler, Marquis Hui. Shang Yang suggested that as the hegemon of the ancient Chinese world, the marquis should, first, seize the title "king" which had hitherto been reserved for the Zhou king,[33] and, second, subdue the more worthy targets Qi and Chu rather than the weaker Qin. Marquis Hui soon convened an international meeting and proclaimed himself "King Hui." However, except Qin, which feigned support, other great powers boycotted Wei's move. The enraged King Hui thus attacked Han, the weakest among great powers. When Qi intervened on Han's behalf, Wei was so devastated that it lost the hegemonic status to Qi in 341 BC.

Shang Yang seized this golden opportunity and invaded Wei in 340 BC. But he was not confident that Qin could win against such a formidable power in a direct confrontation. It happened that Wei's army was commanded by Prince Ang, an old friend during Shang Yang's stay in Wei. Shang Yang pretended to offer a peace agreement and invited Prince Ang to Qin's camp to negotiate the terms. But Shang Yang's hidden plan was to capture Prince Ang. Without a commander, Wei's army was easily

---

[30] Hsu 1997, 5.   [31] Sawyer 1998, 116.

[32] A preventive war is one initiated by a stronger state against a rising rival. It is analytically distinguished from a preemptive war, whereby a rising power initiates the conflict.

[33] Except in the non-Zhou states Chu and Yue, rulers with Zhou lineage retained their feudal titles such as "marquis" and "duke" at that time.

defeated and Wei was forced to cede territory. By resorting to a dirty stratagem which exploited friendship and trust, Shang Yang achieved the unimaginable reversal of the Qin-Wei balance of relative capabilities. It is remarkable that Shang Yang's cunning stratagem would later be justified "on grounds of *raison d'etat.*"[34] In the following decades, Qin inflicted defeat after defeat on Wei.

With the fall of Wei, the most formidable obstacles to Qin's eastward advance in the late fourth century BC became Chu in the south and Qi in the east. Among various great powers in the early Warring States period, Chu had the largest territory (which was twice the size of Qin ca. 350 BC) and the richest natural resources. Even worse for Qin, Chu was allied with Qi, which became the strongest power after 341 BC. To defeat these formidable rivals, Qin proceeded to break up the Chu-Qi alliance. In 312 BC, Qin's chief minister, Zhang Yi, promised Chu's King Huai (328–299 BC) six hundred *li* of territory (in the Shangyu area, which Chu previously forfeited to Qin) if Chu would break the alliance with Qi.[35] Chu took the offer but Qin ceded only six *li*. The infuriated King Huai launched two poorly planned campaigns against Qin but was severely defeated. As a result, Chu not only did not receive the promised territory, but also lost six hundred *li* plus two cities in the strategic Hanzhong area, which gave Qin a critical opening to the central plain. Later, in another war from 300 to 298 BC, Qin reapplied the same plot it had earlier used on Wei: In 299 BC, Qin's King Zhao (306–251 BC) invited Chu's King Huai to the Qin court to conclude a peace agreement, but Qin soon took Chu's king hostage to extort territorial concessions. As Chu refused to cede territory, Qin returned to the use of force. In 280–276 BC, Qin made a surprise invasion into Chu's heartland and seized the western half of Chu's core territory, including the capital, Ying. Henceforth, Chu lost its great-power status. Fortunately, as Chu had conquered Yue in 306 BC (and was to conquer Lu in 249 BC), it could survive adequately in the eastern part of its former territory.

Qin was also astoundingly successful at playing off its immediate neighbors, Chu, Han, and Wei, against one another. At the turn of the third century BC, these three states had started on the road of decline but remained

---

[34] Li 1977, xxvi. As the *Shi ji* remarks, Shang Yang "deceived his old friend Prince Ang of Wei, whom he captured, to make the Qin state secure and [to] benefit its people." Cited in Li 1977, xxv.

[35] One *li* is roughly equivalent to 0.3 mile or 0.49 kilometer. It is not clear whether 600 *li* in the historical materials referred to a total area of 600 square *li* or 600 *li* on one side. WSWG exchanges, June 12–15, 2003.

great powers with formidable fighting capabilities. Although Qin had separately defeated them, the three states together could easily overpower
Qin. Qin thus pursued a strategy of allying with Chu when it attacked
Han and Wei, and allying with Han and Wei when it attacked Chu. To
make peace with Chu, King Zhao married a princess to Chu's King Huai
in 305 BC and returned a piece of territory in 304 BC. Chu and Qin then
invaded Han. Han sought help from Wei and Qi to punish Chu in 303 and
302 BC. When the Qin-Chu alliance broke down and Qin invaded Chu
in 301–298 BC, Wei and Han were only too happy to watch Chu suffer.
But Qin soon turned around to make peace with Chu again in 295 BC.
Qin then invaded Han and Wei in 294–286 BC and even annihilated their
240,000 core troops in a major battle in 293 BC. To preempt the severely
embattled Han and Wei from mobilizing another *hezong* alliance, Qin
married another princess to Chu's king in 292 BC and offered the title
dongdi or Eastern Emperor to Qi in 288 BC. After Qin turned around one
more time to make a crushing attack on Chu in 280–276 BC, Han and Wei
planned to join Qin to deal a further blow to Chu in 273 BC. To prevent
imminent annihilation, Chu sent an emissary to convince Qin to attack
Han and Wei instead.

   To deal with Qi, the strongest power from 341 BC on, Qin manipulated
the interplay of the *hezong* and *lianheng* strategies. Qin first broke up the
Qi-Chu alliance and scored a series of major victories over other great
powers. After catching up with Qi, Qin placated Qi by offering King Min
the title Eastern Emperor in 288 BC. After Qi conquered the prosperous
Song in 286 BC, Qin seized on Yan's desire to take revenge on Qi and the
widespread jealousy among other great powers. As a result of the anti-Qi
alliance in 284 BC, Qi lost both hegemonic and great-power status in one
stroke. After such a precipitous decline, Qi switched to an isolationist
policy and largely remained outside great-power competition for the rest
of the century.[36] Qin further bribed Qi officials so that Qi would not
engage in military buildup and would not lend any assistance to Qin's
targets.

   After Qin emerged as the unipolar hegemon, "the age of diplomatic maneuver" based on the manipulation of the *hezong* and *lianheng* strategies
gave way to "the time of 'total war'" marked by military prowess.[37] By
then, Zhao was the only great power still capable of resisting Qin. Zhao's

---

[36] Qi's withdrawal into isolationism after a precipitous decline is not unique. Britain in the
    interwar period is another example.
[37] Lewis 1999, 638.

King Wuling (325–298 BC) had earlier concluded that approaching Qin from its east would be too difficult because the only two passes which allowed easy passage across the Yellow River (Hangu and Wu Passes) had fallen into Qin's control. King Wuling thus secretly planned an operation from the northern frontiers. To attain that strategic position, Zhao first had to seize the region from northern nomadic tribes. For that purpose, King Wuling developed a highly mobile light cavalry on the model of northern nomads in 307 BC.[38]

Unfortunately, this plan died with King Wuling in a succession struggle. His successors even missed a prime opportunity to weaken Qin. When Qin poured massive armies to capture Chu in 280–276 BC, Qin's home territory was vulnerable to an attack by Zhao. Although Zhao was at war with Qin in 282–280 BC, King Hui (298–266 BC) agreed to a cease-fire agreement in 279 BC and remained neutral throughout the conflict. After Chu was decimated, Zhao, not surprisingly, became Qin's prime target. Qin attacked Zhao in 270–269 BC but was defeated. Qin tried again with larger forces in 262 BC. With a strong army developed by King Wuling, Zhao could hold its defense lines for over two years. Failing to defeat Zhao by force alone, Qin tried the tactic of *lijian* or estrangement (for the first time on its rise to domination). Qin bribed Zhao's high officials to spread the rumor that the commander in chief, Lian Po, who had defeated Qin earlier, could have easily fended off Qin's invasion but was avoiding combat. Zhao's King Xiaocheng (265–245 BC) became suspicious of Lian Po and dismissed him. The new commander, Zhao Kuo, changed the defensive strategy and launched an offensive against Qin's siege forces. In the famous battle of Changping in 260 BC, Qin's commander, Bo Qi, "allowed Zhao's forces to advance in the center, encircled them on the flanks, cut their supply lines, and seized the fortifications they had left behind."[39] Later in the war of unification in 236–228 BC, Zhao remained capable of resisting Qin for four years, from 236 to 232 BC. Zhao's forces even won two major battles in 233 and 232 BC. Qin thus resorted to the same *lijian* tactic to remove the able commander Li Mu in 229 BC. Qin conquered Zhao the following year.

---

[38] The light cavalry soon became a prime means for launching "unorthodox" battlefield tactics. For instance, the *Sun Bin* lists ten benefits: "reaching strategic points before the enemy, attacking undefended spots, pursuing fleeing soldiers, cutting supply lines, destroying bridges or ferries, ambushing unprepared troops, taking the enemy by surprise, burning stores and pillaging markets, and disturbing agriculture or kidnapping peasants. In short, cavalry were employed in skirmish, reconnaissance, ambush, and pillage." Lewis 1999, 624.

[39] Lewis 1999, 640.

Why Did the Balance-of-Power Strategy Fail – and Why Did the Divide-and-Conquer Strategy Work?

Why did the balance of power fail in the ancient Chinese system? As suggested in Chapter One, we should not make the a priori assumption that the European experience is the norm and treat the ancient Chinese experience as a deviant case. If international politics is supposed to be a game of fleeting alliances without permanent friends and enemies, then it is not obvious why we should expect Qin's targets to be united against Qin. Nevertheless, if we want to reflect on Eurocentric theories, it may still be useful to address this "Why not?" question in a factual manner. Kenneth Waltz argues that the balance of power should prevail wherever the international order is anarchic and constituent units wish to survive.[40] The anarchical nature of the *zhongguo* system is amply demonstrated by the prevalence of war and diplomacy. Is it then possible that the Chinese *zhongguo* did not seek survival? Some scholars of Chinese history who believe that unification was preordained indeed argue that there was an "urgent demand" for unification.[41] It is true that there was growing war weariness in the late Warring States period (as in many periods of intense warfare in Europe). But the vanquished states in fact mobilized their whole – adult and teenage, male and female – populations and fought to the bloody end in the final wars of unification. Could it be that the *zhongguo* did not understand that balancing would give them a better chance at maintaining survival? In light of various military alliances and other diplomatic efforts throughout the multistate era, it would be incredible to claim that ancient Chinese statesmen somehow did not understand the logic of the balance of power. As Han Fei characterized it, *hezong* strategists typically offered this advice to rulers: "If we do not rescue the smaller states and attack the powerful one, the whole world will be lost and, when the rest of the world is lost, our own state will be in peril!"[42] Xunzi, another scholar of the late third century BC, also observed that the victorious Qin "lived in constant terror and apprehension lest the rest of the world would someday unite and trample it down."[43] Most of all,

---

[40] Waltz 1979, 121.   [41] Yang 1986, 466.

[42] *Han Feizi*, ch. 45, trans. Watson 1964, 112.

[43] *Xunzi*, in Watson 1963, 70–71. The *Zhanguo ce* even includes a tale of what IR scholars call "security alliance." Su Qin, a fictitious persuader, fosters an alliance among the six states, which pledge that if Qin attacks any one of them, all other five states should send in elite troops to rescue it. This particular story is known to be sheer fabrication. Nevertheless, such imagined dialogues, which are analogous to political analyses in the modern times, can be of interest to students of international politics because they illustrate

previous domination-seeking states had been successfully checked – Qi in 284 BC, Wei in the midfourth century BC, and Chu, Jin, and Wu in the Spring and Autumn period.

If Chinese *guo* sought survival and were experienced balancers, then why were they "indifferent to mutual cooperation" during Qin's ascendance to hegemony?[44] Worse, why did they repeatedly follow the opposite strategy of allying with Qin? Although ancient Chinese strategists did not know about Mancur Olson's "logic of collective action,"[45] they understood that conflicts of interests would severely hinder the *hezong* strategy. As Zhang Yi, the mastermind of the *lianheng* strategy, observed, if even blood brothers would kill each other for money, then the impracticability of *hezong* was obvious.[46] Indeed, the vanquished states fought bitterly to seize territory from one another and from weaker states. The six states themselves devoured a number of medium-sized states: Wei conquered a non-Sinitic state, Zhongshan, in 406 BC (but Zhongshan managed to regain independence in 380 BC); Han conquered Zheng in 375 BC; Zhao conquered Zhongshan in 296 BC; Qi conquered Song in 286 BC; Wei conquered Wey in 254 BC; and Chu conquered Lu in 249 BC. Moreover, Yue set the precedent of conquering another great power, Wu, in 473 BC. Yue, in turn, was conquered by Chu in 306 BC. Although great powers generally did not have sufficient capabilities to launch full-scale conquest of other great powers, they would not hesitate to seize cities and counties from one another. Of the ninety-six "wars involving great powers" in the period 356–221 BC, as many as twenty-seven (or 28 percent) involved mutual attacks among the six states.[47] This systemic phenomenon of mutual aggression offered Qin many opportunities to seize territories with minimal efforts. As states could rarely do well in two-front wars, Qin would invade its targets when they were engaged elsewhere. For example, Qin recovered lost territory from Wei when Wei was preoccupied with Zhao

---

that ancient thinkers already understood the relationship between balancing and survival. See Mu and Wu 1992, vol. 1, 310–312.

[44] Sawyer 1994, 58–59.   [45] Olson 1965.

[46] Sanjun daxue 1976, vol. 2, 142. It is not clear whether Zhang Yi really said this. But the *Han Feizi* similarly argues that all human relations, including those between husbands and wives, fathers and sons, and elder and younger brothers, are characterized by calculation of material interests. Chang 1996, 159; Gao 1998, 524–526; Hsu 1965a, 151–153; Tian and Zang 1996, 192–194.

[47] Fifty-two of the remaining wars were initiated by Qin. Note that I underestimate the degree of mutual aggression by following Levy's rule of counting only wars involving great powers. Many wars that occurred after both (or all) belligerents lost their great-power status are not counted.

and Qi in 354 BC and then Han and Qi in 341 BC. Qin also started the war of unification against Zhao when Zhao attacked Yan in 236 BC.

The six states not only fought among themselves, but also solicited Qin's help in doing so. All of them wavered between the *hezong* and *lianheng* strategies. Indeed, the *lianheng* strategy could be understood in two senses: In addition to Qin's divide-and-conquer strategy, the term refers to efforts by Qin's targets to seize territorial gains from one another in order to compensate for their losses to Qin. Most notably, Qin's immediate neighbors, Chu, Han, and Wei, would bandwagon with Qin to make territorial gains from each other and from other states. Moreover, on a few occasions, the six states would even take advantage of their neighbors' recent defeats by Qin. For example, Qi attacked Wei and Zhao in 317 BC after the first *hezong* alliance was defeated by Qin in 318 BC. And Yan attacked Zhao in 251–250 BC after Qin killed a significant portion of Zhao's adult male population in 262–257 BC.

The fact that all great powers pursued opportunistic expansion also created the systemic scenario of multiple threats, which further complicated the balance-of-power mechanism. During the critical decades from 356 BC (when Qin began to launch self-strengthening reforms) to 284 BC (when Qi suffered near annihilation), it was not obvious to statesmen of the time that Qin was the main threat to their survival. Qin was originally a victim of Wei's aggression and had legitimate claims to recovering lost territory and securing defensible borders. When Wei first advocated the *hezong* strategy, other states were suspicious of Wei's hidden agenda. After Wei's downfall, Qi's aggression made it the most conspicuous threat. The situation of multiple threats thus allowed Qin to manipulate the interplay of the *hezong* and *lianheng* strategies to bring down its hegemonic rival with the help of other states.

In addition, the long-drawn-out process toward unification probably further weakened the balance-of-power mechanism. As Eric Labs argues, balancing "would be less likely or late" for states that made incremental, repeated, and localized expansion compared to states that made a conscious bid for hegemony.[48] Unlike Revolutionary France, which experienced a sudden jump in offensive capability and so became an unmistakable threat, Qin seized territory in bits and pieces over the course of 135 years. Even though piecemeal territorial gains and losses could

---

[48] Labs 1997, 12, fn. 38. Labs's argument is analogous to the frog analogy – that a frog would immediately jump out of a pot of boiling water but could be slowly cooked in a pot of cold water set on a low fire.

accumulate over time, it was not obvious to Qin's targets that their survival would ultimately be at stake. It was only when Qi's dramatic demise presented a "perceptual shock" that statesmen were first alerted to Qin's rise to domination.[49] By then, however, the dominoes had already fallen.[50] The peripheral Yan achieved the great-power status only during the anti-Qi war and lost this short-lived status when it was driven out of Qi in 279 BC. The once-hegemonic Wei had been pushed out of the great-power status earlier in 293 BC. A similar fate had fallen on Han, which began as the weakest among the three successor states of Jin. The once-largest Chu had been alternately weakened by Qi and Qin after it was deceived into breaking up with Qi in 312 BC. Chu further lost the western half of its core territory in 279 BC. At the end of the Yan-Qin war in 279 BC, therefore, Zhao was the only great power left. Unfortunately, Zhao's experience testified to the prevalence of opportunistic expansion and the weakness of the balance of power. When Chu, Han, and Wei were suffering repeated defeats, Zhao was preoccupied with conquering Zhongshan from 307 to 296 BC. Zhao even acquiesced to Qin's invasion of Chu in 279 BC. Zhao fought Qin only when Qin attacked it.

It may be argued that when survival became increasingly at stake, Qin's targets should be able to overcome the collective-action problem and engage in more effective balancing.[51] This view overlooks that there may be a disjuncture between the motivation to survive and the capability to resist domination. In general, weak states are more likely to pursue bandwagoning rather than balancing. Very weak states, in particular, do not balance against an overwhelming threat because such a policy is "futile and counterproductive."[52] After Qin conquered more than half of the system, even the combined capabilities of all six states would not match that of Qin. It is thus not surprising that Han Fei, who witnessed the last

---

[49] A perceptual shock is a single event which suddenly makes decision makers aware of the cumulative effects of gradual long-term power trends. Rose 1998, 160–61; see also Christensen 1996; Zakaria 1998. The growing awareness of the Qin threat generated two competing currents in strategic thinking. On the one hand, "the statecraft documents . . . increasingly take it as a given that unification will happen." At the same time, there was a "counter-unification movement," which included the *Zhuangzi*'s anti-statecraft doctrine, the Mohist school of defensive warfare, and the *Zuo zhuan*'s reconstruction of the Spring and Autumn hegemon as the paragon of virtue who defended the Zhou court and rescued weak states. Brooks, personal communication, July 14–17, 2002.

[50] For the domino dynamics, see Jervis 1997, 165–173.

[51] Snyder 1997, 51; Rosecrance 2001, 134–135.

[52] Schroeder 2003, 121. Schroeder notes that Denmark and Norway did not balance against Hitler in 1939–1940. See also Schweller 1998, 197.

decades of the Warring States period, had little faith in the balance-of-power strategy. As Paul Goldin summarizes Han Fei's view, "Joining the *lianheng* alliance means prostrating oneself before the might of Qin, and states that routinely prostrate themselves find their territory pared down until nothing is left. On the other hand, joining the *hezong* alliance means rescuing impotent states that are about to be annexed by Qin, and states that routinely rescue their impotent neighbors find their own strength weakened until their armies are defeated."[53]

Are the *zhongguo* unique in their failure at balancing? Balancing failures are in fact common in world history.[54] When the Roman Empire expanded, Macedonia, the Seleucid Empire, and Ptolemic Egypt "preferred to fight among themselves rather than form an alliance against the ascendant power."[55] As Niccolò Machiavelli observed,

The other powers who are not immediate neighbors and who do not have dealings with the victim will regard the whole business as taking place a long way off and think it no concern of theirs. They will keep making this mistake until they are next in line. By which time they have no defense available except to rely on their own troops. But by then their own troops will be inadequate, for the dominant power will have become overwhelmingly strong.[56]

A similar phenomenon occurred among Italian city-states at the end of the fifteenth century. Not only did they fail to join their forces against foreign encroachments, Milan even invited France to help subjugate fellow Italians in 1494. As a result, Italy became "overrun by Charles, plundered by Louis, raped by Ferdinand, and humiliated by the Swiss."[57] As Barry Buzan, Charles Jones, and Richard Little remark, in both the Roman and Italian cases, "Waltz's theory provides no obvious explanation as to why the necessary collaboration among the weaker powers failed to occur."[58]

In all, balance-of-power theorists are correct to argue that balancing against domination is a transhistorical phenomenon, but they are wrong to believe that balancing is normally effective. In ancient China, balancing alliances were formed as balance-of-power theorists would expect. But balancing efforts were not effective because targets of domination

---

[53] Goldin 2001, 152. See *Han Feizi*, ch. 45. Han Fei died in 233 BC.

[54] See Wohlforth et al. 2005.   [55] Buzan, Jones and Little 1993, 98.

[56] *Discourses* bk. 2, ch. 1, in Wootton 1994, 164. Machiavelli's account of the rise of Rome – and Polybius's, on which Machiavelli's is based – are probably less historical than *Zhanguo ce*'s and *Shi ji*'s accounts of the rise of Qin. Polybius 1979. But even retrospective accounts are useful if they illustrate understandings of international politics in earlier times.

[57] *The Prince*, ch. 12, in Wootton 1994, 42.   [58] Buzan, Jones, and Little 1993, 98.

shared the self-interest motivation, pursued their own opportunistic expansion, and thus had conflicts of interests among themselves. Qin further
weakened the balance-of-power mechanism by the divide-and-conquer
strategy and the use of unorthodox tactics. As a result, anti-Qin alliances
formed very slowly and infrequently, they did not have enough members
to overpower Qin, they rarely had unified command, and they readily
disintegrated. In the end, the balance of power merely slowed but did not
check Qin's rise to universal domination.

2.4   Overcoming the Rising Costs of Expansion

While many domination-seekers in world history were able to overcome
the inherently weak balance-of-power mechanism, some were ultimately
ruined by the rising costs of expansion. Qin was exceptional in that it
managed to overcome a second supposedly insurmountable obstacle by
self-strengthening reforms. Self-strengthening reforms are efforts to increase military and economic capabilities by enhancing the state's administrative capability. Self-strengthened states are much better at mobilizing war-making resources, solving logistical problems, developing clever
strategies, consolidating conquered territories, and extracting additional
resources from subjugated populations.

Improving National Strength

Scholars of international politics tend to place overwhelming emphasis on
the balance of power and overlook the importance of national strength as
the foundation for long-term success in international competition. However, statesmen in ancient China generally believed that self-strengthening
reforms, which involved reliance on one's own strength, were superior to
balancing alliances, which involved reliance on others' capabilities. When
Han Fei denounced both the *hezong* and *lianheng* strategies, he also advised state rulers "to strengthen the order within their domains, to make
their laws clear and their rewards and punishments certain, to utilize
the full resources of the land in building up stores of provisions, and
to train their people to defend the cities to the point of death."[59] This
view had a long tradition in the ancient Chinese world. The early hegemonic rivals Chu and Jin first established a tight relationship between
self-strengthening reforms and ascendance in relative capabilities.[60] As

[59] *Han Feizi*, ch. 45, trans. Watson 1964, 114–115.
[60] Qi under Duke Huan may be added if one believes that *Zuo zhuan* is credible about Qi's
nascent self-strengthening measures.

this relationship was proved again by the next generation of hegemonic rivals Wu and Yue, it became a well-accepted regularity in ensuing centuries. As Chen Enlin states, "The reality showed that any state that had successfully implemented *fuguo qiangbing* reforms also became militarily strong."[61]

As Qin was "relatively backward economically and politically,"[62] it was "relatively weak and passive in wars" in the early centuries[63] But late development could also produce the "advantage of backwardness."[64] Qin's reformers drew from the large repertoire of coercive tools that had been accumulated through previous centuries. Shang Yang, who masterminded Qin's self-strengthening reforms from 356 BC on, borrowed heavily from Wei (where he had lived some years). If Wei started the new round of self-strengthening reforms in the second half of the fifth century BC, then Qin pushed them to the climax in the second half of the fourth century BC. Scholars of international politics often presume that excellence in international competition rests on revolutionary innovations such as those introduced by Revolutionary and Napoleonic France. But excellence may also rest on "the ability to appropriate aspects of the rival solution and to make them subordinate parts of one's own approach."[65] While various elements of Qin's policies, strategies, and tactics were not new, Shang Yang adapted old models to changing circumstances and "put them into practice more systematically than had any of his precursors."[66]

In his efforts to build up *qianging* or a strong army, Shang Yang borrowed from Wei the mass infantry formed of peasant-soldiers and a professional standing army formed of elite soldiers. To encourage valor among all ranks, Shang Yang introduced a system of rewards and punishments that was designed – to borrow from Douglass North and Robert Thomas – to "bring social and private rates of return into closer parity."[67] According to the *Sunzi bingfa*, one of the critical estimates for victory and defeat is "whose rewards and punishments are clearer."[68] As the *Shang jun shu* (Book of Lord Shang) elaborates, "War is a thing that people hate,"[69]

---

[61] Chen 1991, 18.   [62] Yang 1977, 10.   [63] Gao 1995, 389.

[64] This concept is borrowed from Gerschenkron 1966.   [65] Unger 1987, 206, 176.

[66] Lewis 1999, 611; also Yang 1986, 194.   [67] North and Thomas 1973, 2.

[68] Other estimates are "Which ruler has the Way," "Which general has the greater ability," "Who has gained the advantage of Heaven and Earth," "Whose laws and orders are more thoroughly implemented," "Whose forces are stronger," and "Whose officers and troops are better trained." *Sunzi bingfa*, ch. 1, trans. Sawyer 1994, 167.

[69] *Shang jun shu*, ch. 4.18, trans. Duyvendak 1963, 286. This text was most likely written by Shang Yang's followers rather than Shang Yan himself, but it "contains much material about the reforms" and "very well may reflect [his] actual policies." Lewis 1990, 272,

but "a fearful people, stimulated by penalties, will become brave, and a brave people, encouraged by rewards, will fight to the death. If fearful people become brave and brave people fight to the death," then the country should have no match.[70] Compared with other reform programs, Qin's rewards were far more substantial (honors, lands, houses, servants, and other material reward) and its punishments far more severe (torture, death, and collective punishment).[71] Moreover, unlike other systems of rewards and punishments, which were introduced only in the course of certain battles and abandoned as soon as fighting subsided, Qin's system was fully institutionalized with the *Qin Law* and a twenty-rank honor system.[72] Qin's ranks and associated rewards were strictly meritocratic and not hereditary. But if a soldier died heroically in battle, his descendants would receive the number of ranks he earned. Given the incentive structure that "the gate to riches and honor should lie in war and in nothing else,"[73] Qin's populations were bent on exerting themselves in war.

To strengthen the material basis of *qiangbing* (military power), Shang Yang implemented a *gengzhan* or agriculture-for-war policy to establish *fuguo* (economic wealth). Building on Wei's model of small-scale household farming, Shang Yang granted small grids of lands to registered households and maximized extractions.[74] The Qin state further promoted economic growth by building large-scale irrigation projects and providing assistance with farm tools and technical advice. Although Qin more or

---

fn. 33; Watson 1964, 4. Moreover, some of the policies discussed in the text are corroborated by other texts such as the *Xunzi* and *Han Feizi*.

[70] *Shang jun shu*, ch. 1.3, trans. Duyvendak 1963, 201.

[71] Lewis 1990, 62–63. In Shang Yang's reforms, "[a]nyone who gained merit in battle by slaying enemies or commanding victorious units was rewarded with promotion in a twenty-rank hierarchy. Depending on their standing, they would receive stipulated amounts of land, numbers of dwellings, and quotas of slaves. Moreover, these ranks could be used to remit penalties for violations of the law or to redeem relatives from penal bondage." Lewis 1990, 62–63. As for punishment, any soldier who surrendered to an enemy would be subject to execution and confiscation of all property. Moreover, under the collective responsibility system, the other four members of his unit would be severely punished unless they redeemed themselves by killing enemy soldiers. Lewis 1999, 612–613; Yang 1986, 277–278.

[72] Wei also had *Fajing* (*Canon of Law*) but impersonal laws did not form the backbone of Wei's self-strengthening reforms. Laws in other states were even less systematic than those in Wei. Tian and Zang 1996, 280–288.

[73] *Shang jun shu*, ch. 4.17, trans. Duyvendak 1963, 282–283.

[74] Qin's peasants were subject to land tax, head tax, military service, and all kinds of corvée. One account estimates that nearly two-thirds of a household's productivity were taxed. Lin 1992, 328. But there is no systematic analysis of the total tax burdens of free peasants in the historical literature.

less followed Wei's blueprint, Shang Yang's package – economic as well as military – surpassed Wei's with an institutionalized system of handsome rewards and harsh punishments. Peasants who surpassed farming quotas would be rewarded with tax exemptions, but those who failed to fulfill quotas would have themselves and their dependents taken as government slaves. As Han Fei observed, with a population who became "diligent in production and courageous in war," it was hardly surprising that "the country became rich and strong."[75]

Did Qin's *gengzhan* policy face the so-called classical trade-off between guns and butter?[76] How did Shang Yang solve "the difficulty…of combining both intensive agriculture and frequent warfare"?[77] After all, in the age of the national army, the *gengzhan zhi shi* or men of agriculture and warfare were one and the same. The trade-off should be particularly acute for Qin, which had a relatively sparse population compared with that of central states. Shang Yang's solution was to encourage immigration from neighboring Han, Wei, and Zhao by giving immigrants lands and houses with tax exemption for three generations. As the *Shang jun shu* elaborates, "If the old population of Qin are engaged in warfare, and if the newcomers are caused to occupy themselves with agriculture, then, even though the army may stay a hundred days outside the frontier, within the borders not a moment will be lost for agriculture. Thus, you may be successful both in enriching and in becoming strong."[78] Even more notably, this policy allowed Qin to "hit two birds with one stone,"[79] in the sense of achieving *relative* as well as *absolute* gains.[80] As Qin's immigration policy drained peasant-soldiers from Han, Zhao, and Wei, "this way of inflicting damage on the enemy [was] just as real as a victory in war."[81] Shang Yang also promoted natural population growth by mandating marriage before age twenty and by providing increased subsidies to families who had more children. To open up wastelands in peripheral areas further, the Qin state sent convicts to build settlements and granted them amnesty in return. With these *gengzhan* measures, Qin's

---

[75] *Han Feizi*, cited in Yang 1977, 42. The uniform blocks of land also provided standardized rewards for military distinctions. Lewis 1999, 613.

[76] Powell 1993; 1999, 205–206.   [77] Duyvendak 1963, 50.

[78] *Shang jun shu*, ch. 4.15, trans. Duyvendak 1963, 270. Machiavelli also discussed how ambitious states should increase their population by attracting and compelling immigrants. *Discourses*, bk. 2, ch. 3, in Wootton 1994, 171.

[79] Ibid., trans. Duyvendak 1963, 272.

[80] For the IR concepts of relative and absolute gains, see Grieco 1988; Powell 1991.

[81] *Shang jun shu*, ch. 4.15, trans. Duyvendak 1963, 272.

food stores as well as weapon stores were well stocked to support war efforts.

After establishing basic military and economic reforms in 356 BC, Shang Yang introduced a second round of administrative reforms in 350 BC. Unlike balance-of-power theorists who pay little attention to state capacity, ancient Chinese reformers generally viewed administrative capacity as the basis of power and wealth. Indeed, the implementation of *fuguo qiangbing* reforms necessitated a whole range of administrative techniques, including accounting methods to record available resources and levy taxes, standardized measures and coinage to facilitate centralized accounting and prevent tax evasion, seals and tallies to bestow and withdraw military authority, regular procedures to appoint generals and administrators, and objective criteria to evaluate performance and reward meritorious service.[82] To ensure further that the central court was in full control of all human and material resources, Shang Yang required officials at all levels to submit annual reports on the actual circumstances of the previous year and on forecasts for the following year. Such reports should include "thirteen figures": "the number of granaries within its borders, the number of able-bodied men and of women, the number of old and of weak people, the number of officials and of officers, the number of those making a livelihood by talking, the number of useful people, the number of horses and of oxen, the quantity of fodder and of straw."[83]

More notably, Shang Yang built on Wei's two-layered administrative system of *jun* (prefectures) and *xian* (counties) and added two lower layers, *xiang* (townships) and *li* (villages). This measure represented the final step toward direct rule, giving the Qin court the capacity to penetrate the society down to the village level. Shang Yang then proceeded to systematize universal military conscription by grouping village

---

[82] Seals were used by civil officials to validate official commands. Tallies were used to validate military command. Tallies were usually made into two halves; the commander retained one-half and the ruler the other half. An army could be sent out only if the ruler's matching half was presented. Lewis 1999, 609; Sawyer 1998, 116.

[83] The *Shang jun shu* states, "If he, who wishes to make his country strong, does not know these thirteen figures, though his geographical position may be favourable and the population numerous, his state will become weaker and weaker, until it is dismembered." *Shang jun shu*, ch. 1.4, trans. Duyvendak 1963, 205. In a similar manner, Marquis de Vauban proposed an annual census to Louis XIV in 1686: "Would it not be a great satisfaction to the king to know at a designated moment every year the number of his subjects, in total and by region, with all the resources, wealth and poverty of each place; [the number] of his nobility and ecclesiastics of all kinds, of men of the robe, of Catholics and of those of the other religion, all separated according to the place of their residence?" Cited in Scott 1998, 11.

households into units of five on the model of five-man squads in military organizations. As eligible villagers could be mobilized easily as squads and platoons, "virtually an entire country could go to war."[84] Shang Yang also tightened the policy of household registration, which formed the basis of military service, land tax, and corvée. Although Duke Xian had borrowed Wei's household registration system in 375 BC, there were many loopholes in the implementation of this policy in Qin as in Wei.[85] Under Shang Yang, members of the Qin population were registered when they reached the height of four feet eleven inches (about sixteen to seventeen years of age); from then on, they were obliged to fulfill military and corvée obligations and to pay full taxes to the state until they retired at age sixty.[86] Later, in 348 BC, Shang Yang further broke up clan-based families into nuclear families by imposing double head taxes on households that had more than one adult male. As the system of extraction was household-based, a greatly increased number of households could provide the state with greatly increased power and wealth. With the ability to engage in *total* mobilization of national resources, Qin's power and wealth reached a new height.

Minimizing Emulation by Other States

Scholars of international relations may think that efforts at self-strengthening are elusive, because "states tend to emulate the successful policies of others" and to engage in what we call an "arms race."[87] In analyzing Qin's self-strengthening reforms, it is necessary to examine the strategic interaction between Qin and the six vanquished states. Before Qin's rise to domination, domination-seeking states would always be surpassed by new ones which borrowed from and improved upon successful models of previous powers. So why was there no other domination-seeking state which pursued even more comprehensive self-strengthening reforms and cleverer strategies and stratagems to overtake Qin? At the minimum, why did Qin's victims not imitate Qin's self-strengthening reforms and clever strategies in order to resist Qin?

In understanding the emulation problem, it is important to realize that the pursuit of self-strengthening reforms was a systemic phenomenon not unique to Qin. Qin's ascendance from relative weakness to hegemony in the period 356 to 284 BC was eclipsed by the growth of Qi – just as

---

[84] Sawyer 1994, 76.   [85] *Shang jun shu*, ch. 4.15, trans. Duyvendak 1963, 267.
[86] Commoners were required to begin lesser service at age fifteen. Yates 1987, 231.
[87] Waltz 1979, 124; also Jervis 1997, 75–76.

balancing against Qin was eclipsed by balancing against Qi. At the same time that Qin's Duke Xiao introduced Shang Yang's comprehensive reforms in 356 BC, Qi's King Wei launched reforms to build up Qi's strength. Although Qi's reforms might not be as comprehensive as Qin's, Qi enjoyed the initial upper hand because it had historically been a stronger power.[88] Qi was the first leader of Zhou states at the onset of the multistate period and remained a major player during the century-long Jin-Chu rivalry and the subsequent Warring States period. In 353 BC, Qi defeated Wei, the then-hegemonic power. In 341 BC, Qi further annihilated Wei's core forces and seized the hegemonic status. In ensuing decades, Qin gradually reversed its relative power vis-à-vis Wei, Han, and Chu. But not until at least 316 BC, when Qin doubled its size by conquering Ba and Shu, did Qin catch up with Qi. Qi recognized Qin's equal status when rulers of both states jointly proclaimed themselves emperors in 288 BC. Qi soon surpassed Qin after conquering the prosperous Song in 286 BC. At that stage, however, jealousy of Qi tilted the Qi-Qin competition in Qin's favor. An anti-Qi alliance almost annihilated Qi in 284 BC.

After Qin emerged as the unipolar hegemon, why did other states not emulate Qin's self-strengthening reforms? The answer is, timing matters. By the turn of the third century BC, all other Warring States had pursued some variants of self-strengthening reforms. As Ralph Sawyer indicates, "The period's insecurity compelled the surviving states to implement every possible measure to strengthen themselves economically, politically, and militarily."[89] During the bloody civil war which carved up Jin, Wei, Zhao, and Han had already begun to deepen Spring and Autumn practices. Around 445 BC, Wei started the new wave of self-strengthening reforms by systematizing preexisting practices and introducing innovative institutions. In the 380s BC, Chu introduced some of Wei's reform measures.[90] In 355 BC, Han formalized bureaucratic procedures for appointing and appraising officials at all levels of government. After Qi's invasion of 314 BC, Yan secretly carried out self-strengthening reforms while feigning

---

[88] Qi was also the state of high culture in the Warring States period. The language used in diplomatic exchanges was that of Qi.

[89] Sawyer 1998, 85.

[90] In conventional accounts, Wu Qi, a military general who arrived from Wei in 390 BC, introduced a self-strengthening program to eradicate the entrenched nobility and establish meritocracy. The reforms were so comprehensive that Wu Qi was much hated by the aristocrats. When the king died in 381 BC, Wu Qi was killed and the reforms were abandoned. *Shi ji*, ch. 65, cited in Lewis 1999, 601–602; Hsu 1965a, 97–98; Yang 1986, 457. Some historians doubt the historicity of Wu Qi. See Blakeley 1999b, 64; Lewis 1999, 601.

allegiance to Qi. Later in 307 BC, Zhao created the light cavalry on the model of northern nomadic tribes. In short, during Qin's early ascendance, all other great powers introduced various elements of self-strengthening reforms such as the mass army, national taxation, household registration, and hierarchical administration. Although no other reform programs matched Qin's in terms of comprehensiveness and institutionalization, other states were able to use their increased national strengths to pursue their own opportunistic expansion in the shadow of the Qin-Qi struggle for supremacy. Such a background is important. States which had recently pursued self-strengthening reforms and had already experienced rise and decline would find it more difficult to pick up renewed strength to play the game of catching up. As argued earlier, when Qin emerged as the sole hegemon at the end of the anti-Qi war in 279 BC, the dominoes had already fallen. Zhao was the only great power that had pursued self-strengthening reforms but had not started on the road to decline.

In deciphering the emulation problem, it is also important to keep in mind that there may be a disjuncture between motivation and capability. As in the balance of power, the pursuit of self-strengthening reforms is not simply a matter of will, or the desire to survive. As Jon Elster points out, "When people are badly off their motivation to innovate . . . is high. Their capacity or opportunity to do so, however, is the lowest when they are in tight circumstances."[91] Roberto Unger similarly argues that "[a] military threat, like any challenge, has double meaning. It can galvanize into reform as well as frighten into inaction."[92] Poland, for instance, failed to emulate its powerful neighbors. In ancient China, similarly, many weaker states were devoured by self-strengthened great powers. Qin's rulers and strategists seemed to understand this rationale. To weaken further targets' motivation and capability for renewed resistance, Qin engaged in massive brutality and massive bribery. In 268 BC, a strategist, Fan Sui, proposed to Qin's King Zhao the policy of "attacking not only territory but also people."[93] He argued that Qin should aim at the destruction of armies on such a scale that rival states would lose the capacity to fight. Before Fan Sui articulated this policy, however, Qin's commanders had already begun mass slaughters of defeated armies. According to classical texts, one talented commander, Bo Qi, alone killed 240,000 Han-Wei allied troops

---

[91] Elster 1989b, 18; also Homer-Dixon 2000, 288.   [92] Unger 1987, 54.

[93] *Shi ji*, ch. 79, cited in Lewis 1999, 639. Apparently, the *Sunzi*'s advice that "preserving their army is best, destroying their army second-best" had become outdated by then. *Sunzi bingfa*, ch. 3, trans. Sawyer 1994, 177.

in 293 BC, drowned several hundreds of thousands of Chu soldiers and civilians in 279 BC, killed 150,000 Zhao-Wei allied troops in 273 BC, and buried 400,000 Zhao forces in 260 BC.[94] On the whole, Qin is recorded to have killed more than 1.5 million soldiers of other states between 356 and 236 BC.[95] While these numbers are likely to be exaggerated and should be treated as reflecting the magnitude of battle deaths rather than absolute figures, they nevertheless reflect Qin's ruthless brutality in its pursuit of domination.[96]

As Qin's relative capability snowballed while its targets' relative capabilities dwindled, the defeated states found it increasingly difficult to engage in meaningful buildups. Han and Wei, in particular, became so frightened that they increasingly followed a policy of appeasement – ceding territory without fighting. Although appeasement is always a self-defeating policy in the long term,[97] it can be rational in the short term. As Stephen van Evera points out, "War is a trial of strength. If its results were foretold, the weaker could yield to the stronger and achieve the same result without suffering the pain of war."[98] In Han's and Wei's calculation, if they fought Qin, they would most likely lose and suffer further devastating losses of territory and troops; even if they happened to win, they would still suffer from exhaustion.[99] After the last hope for *hezong* vanished in the 240s BC, resistance was no less suicidal than appeasement. To weaken the motivation for both internal and external balancing further, Qin also bribed high officials in the courts of other states so that these corrupt officials would help convince their king that he would be better off to appease than to fight Qin.

Reducing the Costs of War
Superiority in relative capability is not sufficient to overcome the mechanism of rising costs of expansion. Even victorious wars impose undue burdens on national resources. As the *Sunzi bingfa* estimates, "When you send forth an army of a hundred thousand on a campaign, marching

---

[94] Yang 1986, 444.   [95] Lin 1992, 324; Yang 1986, 189.

[96] Lewis 1999, 626. For a more detailed discussion of battle death figures and their validity, see Chapter Three.

[97] An analyst in the Song dynasty, Su Xun, particularly highlighted this problem: "Of course the territory of the [six states] was limited while the avarice of Qin was not. The more diligently they served Qin the more importunate became her encroachments until primacy and submission, victory and defeat were decided without a battle." *Liu guo lun* (The Six States), cited in Crump 1996, 35.

[98] van Evera 1999, 14–15; also Gilpin 1981, 32.   [99] Zhang and Liu 1988, 94.

them out a thousand *li*, the expenditures...will be one thousand pieces of gold per day. Those inconvenienced and troubled both within and without the border, who are exhausted on the road or are unable to pursue their agricultural work, will be seven hundred thousand families."[100] Given the high costs of war, the *Sunzi* argues that "attaining one hundred victories in one hundred battles is not the pinnacle of excellence."[101] In the same manner, the *Wuzi* (named after Wu Qi, Wei's famous general who seized Qin's strategic territory between 413 and 385 BC) advises that "any state that constantly engaged in warfare would simply exhaust itself and, irrespective of its victorious record, ultimately be vanquished."[102] Indeed, the expansionist Wei lost hegemony in 341 BC and then great-power status in 293 BC. Qi similarly experienced exhaustion from the conquest of Song in 286 BC and then a dramatic defeat by a Yan-led alliance in 284 BC.

While Wei and Qi engaged in costly direct confrontations with enemies, Qin largely avoided such encounters during its ascendance to domination. It is most remarkable that although Qin's ascendance was successively blocked by Wei, Qi, and Zhao, Qin did not have to defeat the first two with its own troops. Wei was brought down by Qi; Qi, in turn, was toppled by a Yan-led alliance. It was only in its confrontation with Zhao that Qin had to fight a formidable foe in battle. Qin essentially lived up to the *Sunzi* ideal that "subjugating the enemy's army without fighting is the true pinnacle of excellence."[103] The military treatise suggests that "the highest realization of warfare is to attack the enemy's plans; next is to attack their alliances; next to attack their army."[104] Qin's divide-and-conquer strategy discussed earlier helped to overcome not only the mechanism of balance of power, but also the mechanism of rising costs of expansion. Qin's costs of war were much reduced by avoiding overwhelming alliances and multifront wars, making friends with targets' enemies and making tactical peace with secondary targets to isolate prime targets, launching

---

[100] *Sunzi bingfa*, ch. 13, trans. Sawyer 1998, 127. Ancient Chinese states would resort to a number of ways to alleviate logistical problems: First, they would forage for food supplies on the spot. Second, Chu pioneered the establishment of military bases in allied countries as early as in 597 BC. Third, Jin constructed through roads and Wu constructed a canal system before their attacks on Qi in 555 BC and 485 BC, respectively. Fourth, Wei built a fortified town on the Qin-Wei border before launching campaigns against Qin. Fifth, Qin, Han, Zhao, and Wei moved their capital closer to their targets to facilitate expansionist campaigns.

[101] *Sunzi bingfa*, ch. 3, trans. Sawyer 1994, 177.

[102] *Wuzi*, "Planning for the State," cited in Sawyer 1994, 308.

[103] *Sunzi bingfa*, ch. 3, trans. Sawyer 1994, 177.   [104] Ibid.

surprise attacks when targets were unprepared, seizing moments of opportunity when targeted states were preoccupied with other states, and threatening weakened states to make them cede territory without fighting at all.

When Qin could not avoid combat, it used unorthodox tactics to minimize war costs on the battle front. As Ralph Sawyer points out, the Chinese approach to battle generally followed "the theory of maneuver warfare, the key elements of which are indirection, manipulating the enemy into disadvantageous circumstances, surprise, the recognition and exploitation of topography."[105] Unorthodox tactics also included "using bribes, gifts, and other methods to induce disloyalty and cause chaos."[106] The use of bribes was particularly cost effective. In an age when victory hinged on forging the multitude of five-man squads into an integrated entity to strike at the decisive moment, "forcing a change in commander could reverse previous defeats, even result in complete victory."[107] Qin deployed this tactic against Wei in 340 BC, Zhao in 260 and 229 BC, and an anti-Qin alliance in 247 BC.

Moreover, Qin's commanders understood another *Sunzi* dictum, that army strength is "a question of dividing up the numbers."[108] Qin rarely relied on overwhelming army strength to secure victories. Qin's conquering armies, such as those commanded by Bo Qi, who "won all the wars he fought,"[109] were from time to time outnumbered by their enemies. For example, in a battle with Han and Wei in 293 BC, Bo Qi's troops were outnumbered by 240,000 allied troops.[110] But as Han's and Wei's armies fought separately without unified command, Bo Qi could defeat them one by one. Even in the direct confrontation with Zhao in 262–257 BC, Qin mobilized only its standing army plus male populations aged fifteen and older from the nearby Henei commandery. Classical texts report that Zhao lost more than 400,000 troops in this war. While this figure is likely to be inflated, Zhao apparently engaged in massive – if not total – mobilization to fend off Qin's aggression. For Qin, mobilization on a comparable scale

---

[105] Sawyer, see http://www.unc.edu/depts/diplomat/AD_Issues/amdipl_13/china_sawyer. html.

[106] Sawyer 1998, 19. [107] Ibid., 99.

[108] *Sunzi bingfa*, ch. 5. Ch. 6 continues, "If we are concentrated into a single force while [the enemy] is fragmented into ten, then . . . we are many and the enemy is few." Trans. Sawyer 1994, 187, 192.

[109] Lao 1985, 655.

[110] Classical texts record that Qin's army was outnumbered but do not report Qin's army strength.

occurred only in the final wars of unification. In the war against Chu in 226–223 BC, Qin is recorded to have mobilized 600,000 troops after the initial campaign with 200,000 troops went badly.[111]

Overcoming Offensive Disadvantages and Seizing Offensive Advantages

Some scholars of international politics concede that domination is possible if the domination-seeker enjoys offensive advantages. Robert Gilpin argues that "the imperial unification of China by Qin was due to advances in the offense over the defense."[112] More specifically, Stephen van Evera argues that conquest is easier if there are no major "oceans, lakes, mountains, wide rivers, dense jungles, trackless deserts, or other natural barriers that impede offensive movement or give defenders natural strong points."[113] Is geography responsible for Qin's ability to achieve the impossible? Graeme Lang believes so:

> Why was political power centralized in China, while a much more decentralized and fragmented system of political entities developed in Europe? Ultimately, the answer lies in the realm of geography. Europe is comprised of a number of sub-regions, each of which is relatively protected by substantial geographical barriers such as mountain ranges, major rivers, bodies of water, or dense forests. These regions ... were relatively difficult to conquer and hold within a unified empire. ... The geography of China, unlike that of Europe, ... facilitated conquest and unification over a vast area.[114]

However, any topographical map of the Chinese continent can show that the area of the *zhongguo* system is marked by significant geographical barriers, including the Qin Ranges, Taihang Mountains, Yellow River, Yangtze River, Dan River, Huai River, and other secondary rivers and mountains. John Fairbank observed that "the North China plain and its extension toward the Yangtze delta are no easier to traverse ... than the North European plain."[115] Indeed, China's geographical barriers were so important that the *Sunzi bingfa* systematically analyzes some twenty different configurations of terrain and associated operational

---

[111] For both army strengths and battle deaths, numbers in classical texts should be seen as representing the order of magnitude rather than actual figures. The figure of 600,000 is probably nominal rather than actual. The *Hou Han Shu*, written in the Han Dynasty, discounts the figure to 420,000. Sawyer, personal communication, February 12, 2004. Nevertheless, it is important to keep in mind that Qin had both the motivation and the capability to engage in near-total mobilization, "for in the previous campaign Qin, with 200,000 soldiers, had suffered a severe defeat." Sawyer 1994, 54.

[112] Gilpin 1981, 61.   [113] van Evera 1998, 19; 1999, 154.

[114] Lang 1997, 89–90.   [115] Fairbank 1974, 3.

principles.[116] It is no wonder that Hong Junpei remarks that "from the perspective of geography, it was a necessary development for China to have independent states" in the Spring and Autumn and Warring States periods.[117]

If there were no *systemic* geographical advantages in the ancient Chinese system, did Qin nevertheless enjoy some *dyadic* geographical advantages vis-à-vis its targets? Historians of ancient China indeed observe such offensive advantages. Mark Lewis believes that "Qin enjoyed a splendid geographic situation that combined productivity and security. It was accessible from the East only through the Hangu Pass and from the southeast through the Wu Pass."[118] Ralph Sawyer similarly thinks that Qin occupied a "virtually unassailable mountainous bastion."[119] However, as Zhao's King Wuling saw it, such a splendid location would still be assailable from the poorly guarded northern frontiers. Even more notably, various historians also highlight that Qin was originally blocked from the central plain by both the mighty Yellow River and by the powerful Jin and its successor states, Wei, Han, and Zhao. Qin even lost strategic territory on the west bank of the Yellow River to Wei from 413 to 385 BC, "thereby losing the natural protection of the Yellow River."[120]

Qin's ultimate success at universal domination calls for a rethinking of theories of offense-defense balance. Whereas most IR theorists of offense-defense balance treat geography as a "hard constraint" "which states cannot change or evade,"[121] strategists in ancient China believed that geographical disadvantages could be overcome and geographical advantages could be seized. Although mountains and rivers are technically insurmountable in the sense that they cannot be removed by human wishes, they present opportunities as well as constraints. It is true that "terrain that slows or channelizes movement" normally "strains logistics" and so may "strengthen the defense."[122] But, as Ralph Sawyer points out, difficult terrain may also be exploited to create "a force multiplier, possibly even a killing ground."[123] Qin's rulers took this malleable view of geography and were determined to recover lost territory on the west

---

[116] Sawyer 1998, 469–470.   [117] Hong 1975, 16; see also Ge 1989, 50; Sun 1999, 90.

[118] Lewis 1999, 596.   [119] Sawyer 1998, 405.   [120] Yang 1977, 43.

[121] Glaser and Kaufman 1998/99, 200. On the other hand, van Evera is correct to recognize that the offense-defense balance "can be shaped by national foreign and military policy." van Evera 1999, 179.

[122] Glaser and Kaufman 1998, 65.

[123] Sawyer 1998, 86. This was how Qi devastated Wei in the famous battle of Maling in 341 BC.

bank of the Yellow River. It was not until 328 BC that Qin achieved this daunting task and secured the splendid geographical advantages noted.[124]

The experiences of Wei and Han illustrate the perils of treating geography as a hard constraint. Before the rise of Qin, Wei was the most blessed with various natural barriers provided by the Yellow River. Although the *Wuzi* warns that "hegemony does not start from geographical advantages" and that "good policies are more important," such advice went unheeded.[125] Over the course of the fourth century BC, Wei gradually lost to Qin its strategic strongholds on both banks of the Yellow River. Han's fortified city Yiyang was another example. Siege warfare was inherently difficult in ancient China as elsewhere.[126] Yiyang, in particular, was like a natural fortress located on steep cliffs overlooking a section of the Yellow River. When Qin laid siege to Yiyang in 308 BC, the Han court did not believe that Qin could possibly capture this strategic city and did not send in reinforcements. However, Qin poured massive reinforcements to the siege and offered handsome rewards to soldiers who would risk death to break into the fortified city.[127] Although Qin suffered high casualties in this conflict,[128] it also gained a critical foothold in the center of the ancient Chinese system.

Chu's experience was no less remarkable. Chu was for centuries protected from Qin by the very steep and rough Qin Ranges. Before encroaching on Chu, Qin first conquered Ba and Shu in 316 BC. Located in the south of Qin and west of Chu (in modern Sichuan), these non-Sinitic states provided "a crucial base for launching expeditions against

[124] Lin 1992, 367. According to the *Shiji*, Shang Yang advised Qin's Duke Xiao, "Wei ... and Qin are separated by the Yellow River but only Wei enjoyed its natural barriers. Wei can attack Qin in the West when the circumstances are advantageous, and command the East even when circumstances are not so advantageous. Now Qin is becoming stronger and stronger, but Wei's national strength was hard hit in the war against Qi. Qin should take this opportunity to attack Wei to send it eastward. If Qin can occupy the natural barriers at the bend of the Yellow River, then we will be able to command various states in the East to establish hegemony." Cited in Zhang and Liu 1988, 92.

[125] Cited in Lao 1985, 505. According to the *Wuzi*, this advice was offered to Marquis Wu by Wu Qi, who seized strategic territory from Qin.

[126] For siege warfare in the Warring States period, see Needham and Yates 1994; Yates 1980; 1982.

[127] Gao 1995, 412–413. It is not clear how many troops Qin sent to capture Yiyang. But the reinforcements were apparently numerous enough that Qin became worried about its home defense. To prevent a surprise attack from Chu, Qin returned a piece of territory to Chu to keep it neutral. Lao 1985, 528.

[128] According to the *Sunzi* estimate, a siege army can easily lose one-third of its officers and troops. *Sunzi bingfa*, ch. 3, Sawyer 1994, 177. Lin estimates that Qin's casualty rate in this battle might be as high as 50 percent. Lin 1992, 406.

Chu."[129] In 312–311 BC, Qin seized Chu's Hanzhong area, which "linked the Qin heartland to Ba and Shu as a single territorial block."[130] When Qin planned to strike a fatal blow at Chu in 280 BC, Qin contemplated the alternative routes of (1) the easily accessible but heavily garrisoned central plain, (2) the similarly guarded Yangtze River valley, or (3) the rough but practically unguarded mountain ranges. Given such alternatives, the *Sunzi* would advise the conquering army to "traverse unoccupied terrain" and "strike positions that are undefended."[131] Qin's planners indeed decided to send expeditionary forces to climb the unguarded mountains to catch Chu off-guard and then send reinforcements and supplies downstream on the Yangtze River. In 278 BC, Qin successfully seized the western half of Chu's territory, including its capital. Zhao's experience was similar. Zhao was originally separated from Qin by the Yellow River and the steep Taihang Mountains. With such formidable geographical barriers, Zhao was relatively free of Qin's encroachment well into the early third century BC. However, Qin managed slowly to encircle Zhao after seizing territory from Han, Wei, and Chu on the central plain. By 270 BC, Qin was ready to launch full-scale campaigns against Zhao.

It may be said that Qin enjoyed a peripheral location which facilitated domination. Robert Gilpin, for instance, argues that "the ultimate beneficiaries of efforts to change international systems have more frequently than not been third parties on the periphery of the international system."[132] William McNeill even proclaims that the rise of peripheral states to dominance is "one of the oldest and best-attested patterns of civilized history."[133] Such states often have more room for expansion, fewer fronts to defend, and a lower number of conflicts with other states.[134] In the Warring States system, Qin was probably more advantaged than Wei, which was locked in, and Qi, which had no peripheral frontiers for easy expansion. However, Qin was not nearly as blessed as Chu, which enjoyed ready access to the central plain, plenty of room for easy expansion in the south, and the largest territory and the richest resources for most of the multistate period. (See Map 3.)

As Qin was situated on the west bank of the Yellow River, the peripheral location was a two-edged sword – while it provided some level of protection when Qin was on the defensive, it also hindered Qin's advance when

---

[129] Lewis 1999, 616.   [130] Ibid., 635.
[131] *Sunzi bingfa*, ch. 6, trans. Sawyer 1994, 191; also Sawyer 1998, 86.
[132] Gilpin 1981, 52; also Parker 1988.
[133] McNeill 1982, 148.   [134] Gilpin 1981, 181.

it switched to an offensive posture.[135] Most of all, the peripheral location lengthened the distance of expansion and aggravated the loss-of-strength gradient. As Charles Glaser and Chaim Kaufman argue, "Distance favors defense. If the attacker must travel a considerable distance just to reach the defender's territory, the amount of force it can project is reduced by the costs of transporting and supplying the projected force, as well as the costs of defending long lines of communication."[136] A strategist, Fan Sui, apparently understood this rationale. In 268 BC, he pointed out to Qin's King Zhao that long-distance campaigns that crossed over the territories of third parties entailed high costs and low benefits: Qin had to send large forces in order to win, but doing so would hurt Qin's self-defense; even if Qin won such wars, consolidating distant conquests would still be difficult. Fan Sui was referring to some territorial enclaves which Qin had seized from Qi in 284 BC; although they were prosperous cities of the former Song, occupation of such distant conquests diverted Qin's military strength from more immediate campaigns. To solve the problem, Fan Sui recommended the strategy of *yuanjiao jingong* or "befriending far-away [states] and attacking nearby [states]." This meant that Qin should make peace with Qi and attack more immediate neighbors which shared borders with Qin and which offered footholds in the center of the ancient Chinese world. Qin would then be able to expand as an integrated territorial unit. Probably out of cautious calculation of its relative capability, Qin had already been practicing piecemeal encroachment into neighboring Chu, Han, and Wei. This gradual approach helped minimize the costs of war further by allowing Qin to use pieces of territory taken earlier as forward bases to facilitate logistics and supplies, to safeguard its rear and sides, and to encircle its targets in future expansionist wars. In addition, piecemeal encroachment might have the added advantage of undermining the balance-of-power mechanism. As *hezong* is a geographical as well as a strategic concept, Qin could weaken the *hezong* strategy in geographical terms by taking bits and pieces of territory from Han, Wei, and Chu which occupied the intersection between the north-south and east-west axes.

---

[135] It is often argued that states that enjoy the natural protection of geography are more likely to be status quo powers. See Jervis 1978; van Evera 1998, 1999. But this view may have the causal direction reversed. That is to say, it may be that such states are more likely to support the status quo because the costs of pursuing an offensive policy are much higher. Sweden, which enjoyed defensive geographical advantages, faced the same problem as Qin when it took the offensive posture in the seventeenth century.

[136] Glaser and Kaufman 1998, 65; also Walt 1987, 23.

If Qin did not enjoy any geographical advantages, did it enjoy any military advantages? Stephen van Evera argues that the ancient Chinese system was characterized by offensive advantages because "[t]echnologies that favored mass infantry warfare (e.g. cheap iron, which allowed mass production of infantry weapons) strengthened the offense."[137] However, it severely strains credulity to argue that cold weapons in the ancient period would favor universal domination while hot weapons in the early modern period would favor system maintenance. Moreover, although iron was introduced to ancient China from Central Asia after 500 BC, this metal was generally used in agricultural implements rather than military weapons.[138] In addition, Qin did not enjoy superiority in the use of *any* weapons.[139] Rather, it was Chu that innovated advanced weapons such as crossbows and steel swords,[140] and Han that was skilled at making a wide range of weapons, including crossbows, swords, and halberds.[141]

There is no doubt that innovations in heavy crossbows, linked crossbows, and siege weapons such as catapults, rolling towers, mobile shields, scaling ladders, and battering rams facilitated the offense in the Warring States period. However, in ancient China as elsewhere, "[t]echniques for assault and defense advanced simultaneously."[142] Whereas military classics advocate the offensive doctrine, the less well-known Mohist school

---

[137] van Evera 1999, 152.   [138] Wagner 1996.

[139] For weapons in Warring States China, see Needham and Yates, 1994; "Zhongguo junshishi" editorial board, vol. 1, 1983–91. It is possible that Qin's production of weapons was more systematized. States in the Warring States period generally ran government bronze and iron foundries to produce weapons, agricultural implements, coins, and other items. Qin also forced large number of convicts to work at penal labor at such government workshops. "[B]y controlling the quantity and quality of the articles in their workshops and forcing large numbers of skilled workers to provide virtually free labor, the Qin may have been able to provide their armies with better quality equipment and have been able to resupply them even after defeats and loss of materiel and thus have been able to sustain their war efforts at a much higher level of intensity than their opponents." Yates 1982, 412.

[140] Crossbows first appeared in Chu in the early fifth century BC and were in general use in the fourth century BC. Brooks and Brooks 1998, 195; Yang 1986, 337. Their strength and effective killing range generally increased over the centuries as their mechanisms were perfected. Sawyer 1993, 387; fn. 52.

[141] Lin 1992, 346.

[142] Sawyer 1994, 55. Military historians have observed a marked difference between the earlier *Sunzi bingfa* and the later *Sunbin bingfa*. The *Sunzi bingfa* says that "the worst [strategy] is to attack . . . cities," though it does not dogmatically assert that one should never try to take cities. The *Sun Bin bingfa*, on the other hand, analyzes what types of cities could be attacked and what types should not be attacked. Sawyer 1998, 511–512; Yates 1982, 413.

emerged as "the defensive counterpart," so that various texts together "document a mutual escalation in the art of offense and defense."[143] As offensive weapons and techniques developed, various states also "undertook the expanded defense of borders, constructing great walls, ramparts, forts, and guard towers throughout the countryside to defend the entire territory against incursion."[144] The prevalence of conquests discussed earlier should not be interpreted as evidence that conquest was easy in the ancient Chinese system. Most major cities had such strong fortifications that they could not be taken except with resort to stratagems or at high cost. For instance, Qin's siege of Han's Yiyang produced high casualties. Qin's conquest of Ba and Shu, which were ringed by mountains, required most of a century. Similarly, Han's conquest of Zheng involved multiple wars fought intermittently over the course of five decades from 423 to 375 BC, and Zhao's conquest of Zhongshan lasted from 307 to 286 BC. At the same time, Qi failed to conquer Yan in 314 BC. Yan, in turn, was not able to take two well-fortified Qi cities, Ju and Jimo, after five years of siege.[145]

In short, Qin's success at domination was not facilitated by offensive advantages. On the contrary, Qin faced the barriers of geography in addition to the balance of power and the rising costs of expansion. Stephen van Evera believes that "the outcomes of battles and wars reveal the shift toward the offense" in the ancient Chinese system.[146] Such a view mistakenly imputes causes from the final outcome and overlooks the difficult struggles and maneuvers which had begun more than a century earlier. Overall, Qin's success involved the hard work of seven generations of rulers through fifty-seven wars involving great powers (fifty-two initiated by Qin and five initiated by other states) over the course of 135 years (356–221 BC). When Qin first emerged from relative weakness in the midfourth century BC, the obstacles it faced were considered insurmountable by statesmen of the time – and similar obstacles continue to be regarded as insurmountable by current theorists of international politics. Nevertheless, Qin managed to overcome various hurdles by employing

---

[143] Brooks, personal communication, May 8, 2000.

[144] Sawyer 1994, 55. After unification, the defense walls built by Qi, Yan, Zhao, and Qin against Xiongnu were connected to form the Great Wall, while those built by various states against one another were demolished.

[145] In comparison, while siege warfare was generally difficult in early modern Europe, even the great Dutch city of Antwerp was taken in thirteen months. Anderson 1998, 10.

[146] van Evera 1999, 181. He also emphasizes that "[t]he number of independent Chinese states declined from two hundred in the eighth century BCE to seven in the late fifth century, to one in the late third century – a clear measure of the growing power of the offense." Ibid., 181.

divide-and-conquer strategies and clever and cunning stratagems. At the same time, Qin also maximized its national strength so that it would enjoy higher chances of victory when it did have to engage in direct confrontation. In the end, what allowed Qin to roll up the *zhongguo* system was superiority in statecraft. As Xunzi remarked in the late Warring States period, "Qin's repeated victories... are no accident, but the result of policy."[147]

Consolidating Conquered Territories and Maximizing Extraction

Dissolving balancing alliances, avoiding direct confrontations, overcoming geographical obstacles, and scoring victories on the battlefields were significant markers of excellence in international competition. Nevertheless, to achieve universal domination, Qin still faced the additional challenges of consolidating conquests and making them pay. Stuart Kaufman argues that administrative capability was a critical "limiting factor" for system consolidation in world history.[148] In this regard, it is significant that China developed the centralized, bureaucratic state with "the ability to appoint officials, dispatch them to remote cities, maintain control over them at a distance, and remove them when necessary."[149] As Richard Walker remarked, "without this background of development," "the unification of China ... could never have taken place."[150]

As early as 686 BC (before the onset of the multistate era in 656 BC), Chu had already turned a newly conquered *guo*, Shen, into a *xian* or "an administrative district governed by an official appointed by and responsible to the central government."[151] In the ensuing "four centuries of almost uninterrupted expansion,"[152] Chu absorbed more and more *guo* as *xian*. Seeing Chu's success, Jin and Qin later copied Chu's practice.[153] With rudimentary centralized administration, the emergent great powers could not only consolidate conquests, but also extract handsome revenues – in

---

[147] *Xunzi*, in Watson 1963, 62.

[148] Kaufman 1997, 174; also Gilpin 1981, 150. This insight has a long pedigree. Niccolò Machiavelli had already observed that "conquests [were] dangerous in a thousand ways" – unless the conqueror had "good institutions and a Roman efficiency." *Discourses*, bk. 2, ch. 19, in Wootton 1994, 178, 181. Thomas Hobbes similarly argued that "ununited conquests... are many times a burthen." *The Leviathan*, pt. 2, ch. 29, in Morgan 1992, 711.

[149] Lewis 1999, 603.   [150] Walker 1953, 35.

[151] Creel 1970b, 132.   [152] Blakeley 1999a, 17.

[153] Some historians argue that the institution of *xian* was first established by Qin after conquering Gui and Ji in 688 BC. Lin 1992, 66, 84. Creel argues that Qin was unlikely to be the first such innovator, since Qin was generally "slow in developing governmental institutions." Creel 1970b, 153, 144.

terms of military service, land tax, and corvée – from subjugated populations. Indeed, the *xian* gradually became "the primary locus of military
recruitment."[154] For example, at the height of the Jin-Chu rivalry, Chu's
xian of Shen and Xi each provided one thousand chariots (including charioteers and foot soldiers). Jin's forces were likewise identified in terms of
the *xian* from which the troops were mobilized. In the late Spring and
Autumn period, Jin established another form of directly administered district, the *jun*, in "newly conquered, relatively under-populated, frontier
regions."[155] At the onset of the Warring States period, Wei reorganized
the whole *guo* – core as well as conquered territories – into a two-tier
structure of *jun* (commanderies) and *xian* (which evolved from dependent
districts to counties). As the *jun* and *xian* became standard administrative
units in the Warring States period, strategists could evaluate the relative
capabilities of various states in terms of their numbers of *jun* and *xian*.

By the time Qin rose to domination, therefore, ancient China had had
lengthy experience with consolidating conquests and making them pay.
Ba and Shu were particularly profitable. They not only provided a forward base for invading Chu, but also served as the granary for Qin's
conquering armies.[156] At the same time, all targeted states had developed
relatively coherent administrative and coercive apparatuses which facilitated wholesale takeovers.[157] As Max Weber pointed out: "The objective

---

[154] Lewis 1990, 63.

[155] In the beginning, the *jun* were "physically larger than the *xian* but lower in rank because
they were in areas of low population and little strategic value. As these *jun* were gradually filled in through resettlement and the opening of new lands during the Warring
States period, they were often subdivided into *xian*, thus creating a two-tiered system
of administration. This first appeared in the successor states of Jin [that is, Wei, Han,
and Zhao] during the fourth century, but it was imitated in Qin, Chu, and Yan and then
inherited by the Han dynasty." Lewis 1999, 614.

[156] Ba and Shu, located in modern Sichuan, were richly endowed with agricultural and
mineral resources. When Qin invaded Chu in 280–276 BC, Shu and Ba provided 100,000
troops and 10,000 ships of grains. Lin 1992, 393. The region's potential was further
realized after Li Bing built a massive irrigation project in the early third century BC. In
subsequent eras, this irrigation system at modern Dujiangyan made it "possible for an
area of 40 by 50 miles to support a population of about five million people. . . . That,
combined with a balmy climate and rich soil where farmers can grow up to four crops a
year from the same plot, helped earn Sichuan its reputation as China's granary." Murphy
2002.

[157] It is noteworthy that Qin could not immediately impose direct rule on the non-Sinitic
states of Ba and Shu after conquering them in 316 BC. Ba and Shu were chiefdoms and had
no prior experience with formal government. Qin appointed heirs of the original rulers
in the hope that they could better command compliance. However, three generations of
Shu rulers were killed for actual and suspected rebellions. Qin only imposed direct rule
in both Ba and Shu afterward. See Ge 1989, 95.

indispensability of the once-existing apparatus, with its peculiar, 'impersonal' character, means that the mechanism – in contrast to feudal orders based upon personal piety – is easily made to work for anybody who knows how to gain control over it . . . he merely needs to change the top officials."[158] When Qin advanced eastward in the ancient Chinese system, it could readily incorporate preexisting *jun* and *xian* into its own administrative hierarchy.

Qin's ability to roll up a whole, international system was also aided by the policy of gradual, piecemeal encroachment. Piecemeal encroachment not just weakened the awareness of Qin as a threat and alleviated the loss-of-strength gradient, but also allowed Qin to adjust territorial expansion with its gradual growth in relative capability. As Niccolò Machiavelli warned, a small country "cannot take control of cities or kingdoms stronger or larger than itself. Even if it conquers them, . . . [it] will carry its burden only with great effort."[159] Qin did not face this problem. By the time Qin launched the final wars of unification in 236 BC, it had already pushed its eastern borders to the central plain and consolidated more than half of the territory in the system. Moreover, the sovereign territorial states in the last decades were no longer the same entities they had been as hegemons and great powers: Han and Wei had been reduced to the size of single commanderies, and Chu and Zhao had been reduced by about half their size at the turn of the third century BC.

2.5 Launching the Final Wars of Unification

After overcoming of multiple layers of seemingly insurmountable obstacles – including the balance of power, the rising costs of expansion, the barriers of geography, and the consolidation of conquered territories – unification became increasingly feasible in the third century BC. By 257 BC, Qin had knocked down all other great powers and controlled half of the system. Qin further extinguished the Zhou court in 256 BC. However, Chinese history remained open-ended in the 250s and 240s BC.

---

[158] Weber 1958, 229. Machiavelli made the same observation long before Weber. He argued that while it would be difficult to conquer a kingdom with centralized authority, "it would be very easy to hold on to it" because there was "no reason to fear opposition." On the other hand, it would be easy to invade a kingdom ruled by a monarch in conjunction with nobles because there were always "malcontents." But "it simply is not sufficient to kill the ruler and his close relatives, for the rest of the nobility will survive to provide leadership for new insurrections." *The Prince*, ch. 4, in Wootton 1994, 16.

[159] *Discourses*, bk. 2, ch. 3, in Wootton 1994, 172.

International competition is not a simple function of the mathematical calculation of relative capabilities. The anti-Qin alliance of 247 BC still had a respectable chance of checking Qin's seemingly unstoppable rise to domination – that is, before it was dissolved by Qin's *lijian* tactic. Moreover, Qin fell into succession struggles and could be more vulnerable to estrangement tactics itself. Even more remarkably, Qin had no grand plan for universal domination despite its stunning victories for a century. Fan Sui, who propounded the strategy of both seizing territory and decimating enemy troops in 268 BC, was "the first politician to articulate a goal of irrevocable expansion for Qin."[160] But even Fan Sui did not advocate universal domination. Rather, Fan most systematically articulated the strategy of piecemeal encroachment – that of first attacking nearby states, so that "each inch or foot gained became the king's inch or foot."[161]

Universal domination finally appeared on the agenda when King Zheng reached adulthood and took over state affairs. In 237 BC, another strategist, Li Si, advised King Zheng to "*mie zhuhou* (vanquish various states), *cheng diye* (accomplish the enterprise of building an empire), and *wei tianxia yitong* (bring about unification to the world)."[162] He argued that "the states now listen to Qin as if they were our prefectures and counties. Qin's strength and your honor's competence are enough to annihilate the states to build an empire. This is a rare opportunity in history. If Qin still proceeds slowly, then the states may recover and form another *hezong* alliance. When that happens, even your competence will not suffice for unification."[163] It is worth noting that although "the condition for unification was ripe,"[164] King Zheng and his strategists apparently did not believe in the retrospective view that the task would be "as easy as dipping into one's pocket."[165] They seemed to understand that the targeted states, which should clearly know that death was imminent this time, would be highly motivated to engage in military buildups and form *hezong* alliances despite all odds. Wei Liao, for example, commented, "[M]y only fear is that [various states] will form an alliance, will unite to do something unexpected. This is how [previous hegemony-seekers] perished."[166] Thus, in launching the final wars of unification in 236 BC, Qin abandoned gradualism and sought to sweep through the system as fast as possible.

---

[160] Lewis 1999, 639.   [161] *Shi ji*, ch. 79, cited in Lewis 1999, 639.
[162] Cited in Gao 1995, 443.   [163] Cited in Mu and Wu 1992, vol. 2, 10.
[164] Yang 1986, 444–445.   [165] Guofangbu 1989, 43.
[166] *Wei Liaozi*, cited in Sawyer 1998, 99.

To achieve speedy victories and minimize last-minute resistance, Qin mobilized not just massive armies, but also handsome bribes. When Zhao sought help from Qi, for example, Qin preempted Zhao by sending in a team of envoys to bribe Qi officials and to dissuade Qi's king from helping Zhao. When faced with upright officials who refused lavish bribes, Qin sent assassins to get rid of them. In the face of imminent death, therefore, Qin's targets could only rely on "self-help" – in the literal sense of self-reliance. Fighting alone, the six states were defeated one after another. Qin conquered Han in 230 BC, Zhao in 228 BC,[167] Wei in 225 BC, Chu in 223 BC, Yan in 222 BC, and Qi in 221 BC. King Zheng became the First Emperor of the Qin Dynasty in 221 BC.

2.6   Why Did Qin Develop Cleverer Strategies?

Chapter One underscores that a theory of change requires more attention to agential strategies. In ancient China, Qin overcame the supposedly insurmountable countervailing mechanisms of the balance of power, the rising costs of expansion, and the barriers of geography by an aggressive grand strategy that combined the divide-and-conquer policy, self-strengthening reforms, and cunning stratagems and brutish tactics. To understand how Qin achieved the supposedly impossible, it is necessary to examine the role of leadership competence. Although leadership competence is widely regarded as one of the components of national strength,[168] its importance is rarely taken seriously in a field that is overwhelmed with structural constraints.

Leadership competence is particularly critical in the successful and persistent pursuit of self-strengthening reforms. As such reforms involve the establishment of meritocratic administration and the erosion of entrenched privileges, only competent rulers can take on such a daunting task and fend off inevitable resistance from powerful noble houses. As Thomas Ertman observes about early modern Europe, "Only when a ruler himself took an active role in the reform process . . . was it possible to replace proprietary officeholding with something closer to a proto-modern

---

[167] Zhao's crown prince fled to Dai, a very small area neighboring Yan, in 228 BC. Dai fought along with Yan in the final years and was vanquished at the same time as Yan in 222 BC.

[168] For example, Waltz's components of national capability include political stability and competence. Waltz 1979, 131. Morgenthau similarly discusses leadership competence under "the quality of government" and "the quality of diplomacy." Morgenthau 1973, 140–149.

bureaucracy."[169] Competent leadership in autocratic regimes, however, is subject to "a high degree of contingency."[170] Niccolò Machiavelli pointed out that "those states that depend entirely on the strength of a single individual do not last long, for his strength cannot outlive him. It is rare for his successor to be able to take over where he leaves off."[171] Throughout the multistate era in ancient China, the rise of great powers was often tied to the ascendance of competent rulers who pursued self-strengthening reforms, while the decline of these powers was generally linked to the death of such rulers, the dismissal of talented reformers, and the discontinuation of reforms. Thus, Qi lost the leadership of the northern states after Duke Huan died, Wei passed the zenith of its power after Marquis Wen died (and Wu Qi, who commanded Wei's victorious wars, left Wei), and Yan lost Qi after King Zhao died (and Yue Yi, who led the victorious anti-Qi war, was dismissed).

Qin's rise from weakness to strength followed this general pattern. Qin suffered from a series of power struggles and failed to respond to Wei's territorial encroachment at the turn of the fourth century BC. Only after Duke Xian seized the throne in 385 BC did Qin regain coherent leadership. The succeeding Duke Xiao was committed to rebuilding Qin's national strength and his reign was largely characterized by Shang Yang's reforms. Because Shang Yang ruthlessly stripped the nobility of all entrenched privileges, even the crown prince hated him. After Duke Xiao died in 338 BC, the new ruler, King Huiwen, accused Shang Yang of plotting a rebellion and sentenced him to torture and death. However, the institutionalization of Shang Yang's reforms allowed Qin to escape the fate of other states. Shang Yang had made his reforms far less vulnerable to reversal by, first, completely eradicating the hereditary nobility from government administration;[172] second, replacing the

---

[169] Ertman 1997, 125.

[170] In early modern Europe, Prussia's "swift rise" from weakness to strength was also attributable to the emergence of competent rulers, specifically, "the organizing and military genius of three leaders, the Great Elector (1640–1688), Frederick William I (1713–1740), and Frederick the Great (1740–1786)." Kennedy 1987, 91–92. However, "under monocratic rule a lasting defense against patrimonialist tendencies depends almost entirely on the degree of vigilance and the quality of supervision exercised by the executive, a condition subject to high degree of contingency in such a system. Thus following the death of Frederick the Great, his successors were far less interested in the day-to-day business of administration, and as a result the quality of the Prussian bureaucracy suffered noticeably." Ertman 1997, 323.

[171] *Discourses,* bk. 1, ch. 11, in Wootton 1994, 115–116.

[172] In order to establish a centralized bureaucracy from a clean slate, Shang Yang even moved Qin's capital in 350 BC.

traditional nobility with a new twenty-rank social hierarchy which was strictly based on military merits; and, third, anchoring all reform measures with a systematic body of impersonal laws, the *Qin Law*. Qin was also fortunate that Duke Xiao (361–338 BC) enjoyed a relatively long reign so that Shang Yang had sufficient time to prove the effectiveness of his reforms. Therefore, although King Huiwen killed Shang Yang, he did not kill Shang Yang's reforms. At the death of King Huiwen, Qin fell into another succession struggle between 310 and 307 BC. By then, Shang Yang's program had become so thoroughly institutionalized that its continuation was no longer dependent on the king's personal support.[173]

The establishment of meritocracy contributed to competent leadership in another crucial way. The quality of Qin's kingship was not free from the problem of high variability.[174] However, Qin benefited from the collective wisdom of various talented strategists, generals, and administrators. The list of such talents in Qin was extraordinary.[175] Shang Yang introduced self-strengthening reforms, employed cunning stratagems, and reversed the Qin-Wei balance of relative capabilities. Zhang Yi formulated the *lianheng* strategy, broke up the formidable Qi-Chu alliance, and divided and conquered Chu, Han, and Wei. Bo Qi commanded various decisive battles, knocked down once-great powers (Han and Wei in 293 BC, Chu in 279 BC, and Zhao in 260 BC), seized large tracts of territory from them, and slaughtered their armed forces. Fan Sui expounded the strategies of irrevocable expansion, "befriending far-away [states] and attacking nearby [states]" and "attacking not only territory but also people." Li Si later put universal domination on the agenda and masterminded Qin's final wars of unification. As these top talents were recruited from all over the ancient Chinese world and were astute at transnational learning, Qin enjoyed a higher capacity to learn from past experiences and to adapt to changing

---

[173] Sir George Downing's reform program in England also experienced some zigzags under Charles II and William. It was not until Anne's reign that "the survival of this system no longer depended on the skills or enlightened views of any one man." Ertman 1997, 218–219. See Chapter Three.

[174] Among the seven rulers who reigned from 356 to 221 BC, four were competent and enjoyed long reigns. They were Duke Xiao (361–338 BC), King Huiwen (337–311 BC), King Zhao (306–251 BC), and King Zheng (246–210 BC). But Qin suffered from weak leadership under King Wu (310–307 BC), King Xiaowen (250 BC), and King Zhuangxiang (249–247 BC).

[175] The ability to recognize talents and to keep them faithful is itself a mark of competence. As Machiavelli argued, "Rulers get the advisers they deserve, for good rulers choose good ones, bad rulers choose bad." *The Prince*, ch. 22, in Wootton 1994, 70.

times.[176] It was with the collective wisdom of these meritocratic officials that Qin could develop cleverer reforms, strategies, and tactics.

The superiority of Qin's strategies and tactics should not be overstated, however. Qin was generally "a borrower rather than an innovator."[177] In discussing both *fuguo qiangbing* reforms and Sunzian stratagems, it is important to keep in mind that they were systemic phenomena. Various military classics – none of which was written in Qin – uniformly speak of "the Way of deceit." Qin's grand strategy of shrewdly combining different policies, strategies, and tactics to dominate originally stronger enemies had precedents in the ancient Chinese system. In the Spring and Autumn period, Wu nearly conquered Chu at the turn of the sixth century BC, and Yue successfully annihilated Wu in the fifth century BC. "The unimaginable reversal of fortunes" between Wu and Yue, in particular, "left an indelible impression upon subsequent generations that subversive programs systematically implemented could achieve remarkable results."[178] It is striking how Qin's invasion of Chu in 280–278 BC was an almost exact replica of Wu's attempted conquest of Chu in 511–506 BC: Just as Wu made peace with its eastern neighbor, Yue, before sending massive forces into Chu's heartland in 506 BC, Qin made peace with Zhao before setting off for Chu in 279 BC; and just as Wu invaded Chu through mountainous and circuitous but poorly guarded terrain, Qin did the same except from the opposite direction (Qin was located in Chu's northwest, Wu in Chu's southeast). Similarly, Qin's *lijian* tactic closely resembled Qi's plot against Yan in 279 BC: Yan's commander in chief, Yue Yi, conquered most of Qi in 284 BC but could not take two heavily fortified and well-stocked cities, Ju and Jimo. Five years later, King Zhao, who appointed Yue Yi, died. Qi's surviving forces then bribed Yan's officials to spread the rumor that Yue Yi had ambitions to crown himself as Qi's ruler. The new Yan king then dismissed Yue Yi. Soon after, Qi drove away Yan's forces and restored independence. Qin successfully applied this tactic on Zhao in 260 BC and 229 BC, and the once-promising *hezong* alliance of 247 BC.

Was Qin the only state that learned lessons from history? Chu seemed to be unable to learn from history at all – it was conquered through mountainous ranges twice and it fell prey to Zhang Yi's deception twice.

---

[176] Zhang Yi and Fan Sui were originally Wei nationals. Li Si was a Wey national. Shang Yang was born in Wey but had lived many of his pre-Qin years in Wei. Some of the most reform-minded rulers had foreign experiences themselves. For example, Jin's Duke Wen and Qin's Duke Xian were in exile before they acceded to the throne. It is thus not surprising that these rulers were noted for their innovative reforms.

[177] Creel 1970b, 144.   [178] Sawyer 1998, 243.

However, Yan apparently learned a remarkably good lesson. Its revenge policy against Qi was very similar to Yue's against Wu: As did Yue, Yan feigned submission to Qi to preserve quasi independence but secretly carried out self-strengthening reforms. Yan also befriended Qi's actual and potential enemies to isolate Qi. Moreover, just as Yue encouraged Wu to fight Qi and to compete with Jin so that Wu would suffer from the problem of rising costs of expansion, Yan encouraged Qi to conquer the medium-sized Song so as to exhaust Qi and to stir up anti-Qi sentiment. Yan's plot materialized as Yue Yi commanded a five-state alliance to devastate Qi in 284 BC. However, Yan's initial success against Qi inadvertently helped Qin achieve unipolar hegemony, which in turn fundamentally altered the nature of international competition in ensuing decades.

If Qin's tactics were common knowledge of the time, then why were they so effective?[179] It is easier to understand ancient Chinese realpolitik if we realize that states are rarely unitary actors, as realist scholars assume. Moreover, there are often disjunctures between long-term rationality and short-term rationality, and between national interests and individual interests. Although the stratagems of bribery and deception are very simple and obvious, they can work on any individuals who desire power, profit, and pleasures. In dealing with self-indulgent individuals – whether rulers or officials – it would not be difficult to entice them with "the allure of beauty, and debauch them with scents, music, and sexual delights."[180] As Han Fei observed, "If the ruler is insatiably greedy and always wants to grab whatever profits are about, he can be destroyed."[181] Han Fei also believed that the ruler-minister relationship was one of mutual calculation, in which the ruler's interest and the minister's interest were diametrically opposed.[182] If the minister was someone who sold knowledge and wisdom in exchange for rewards and honors, it would not be very difficult to bribe him to sell his service to a higher bidder. The relationship between the ruler

---

[179] It may be conjectured that rulers of vanquished states were exceptionally stupid. As Sawyer puts it, it is an open question whether the effectiveness of *lijian* "illustrates the skillful employment of estrangement methods in creating disaffection through slander and calumny or simply the stupidity of rulers." Sawyer 1998, 115.

[180] Sawyer 1998, 231. See *Liu tao*, ch. 4. As various spy cases illustrate, this obvious and simple tactic was widely employed by both the United States and the Soviet Union during the cold war.

[181] *Han Feizi*, cited in Sawyer 1998, 416.

[182] *Han Feizi*, ch. 49. Han Fei was not alone in arguing that rulers should treat all ministers as potential traitors. The Prussian bureaucracy also worked with the assumption that "no official could be trusted any further than the keen eyes of his superiors could reach." Skocpol 1979, 107.

and the commander was even more problematic, because the commander's claim for autonomous authority on the battlefields inevitably clashed
with the ruler's claim for ultimate authority throughout the realm.[183] As
the commander could potentially use the army to take over the throne
(even though military command was strictly confined to specific campaigns in Warring States China), the ruler's personal interest in staying in
power in the short term could diverge from the national interest of survival in the long term.[184] Hence, the tactic of *lijian* could be astoundingly
effective wherever insecure kings were suspicious of competent generals
and high officials were at odds with their rulers and with one another.[185]

Why did Qin's targets fail to learn from Qin's stratagems? Interestingly, Zhao did. After inflicting a fatal blow on Zhao in 260 BC, Qin's
commander, Bo Qi, intended to ride the wave of victory and immediately
conquer Zhao. Zhao averted this attempted conquest by sowing discord
between Bo Qi and Qin's chief minister, Fan Sui. Zhao's envoy convinced
Fan Sui that if Bo Qi, who already had splendid military distinctions,
could conquer Zhao, Bo Qi would be ranked higher than Fan Sui in Qin's
hierarchy of honors. Fan Sui thus called off Bo Qi's follow-up campaign
in 260 BC. When Fan Sui renewed the war against Zhao in the following
year, Zhao had enjoyed a breathing space to regroup and to secure allied
assistance. Nevertheless, the human weaknesses of greed, jealousy, and
insecurity could not be easily corrected by historical learning. Zhao fell

---

[183] Lewis 1990, 122, 132. Various military texts such as the *Sunzi bingfa*, the *Sunbin bingfa*,
the *Six Secret Teachings*, and the *Wei liaozi* argue that the commander in the field should
not be controlled by the ruler. Lewis 1990, 126; Sawyer 1998, 113, 129.

[184] Machiavelli similarly observed, "A general who has brilliantly conquered an empire
for his employer, overcoming his enemies, covering himself with glory, and loading his
soldiers down with riches, inevitably acquires such a reputation – with his soldiers, with
his enemies, and with his ruler's own subjects – that his victory cannot taste good to the
ruler who sent him out.... This suspicion on the part of rulers is so natural that they
cannot help but give in to it." *Discourses* bk. 1, ch. 29, in Wootton 1994, 133–134.

[185] Consider the several classic cases. In Qi's plot against Yan in 279 BC, Yue Yi's remarkably
speedy success in the first six months of the anti-Qi war and his subsequent reluctance
to dissipate the army's strength in a horrendous urban assault naturally provided fertile
ground for the *lijian* tactic. Sawyer 1998, 103. In Qin's plot against Zhao in 260 BC,
similarly, Lian Po was a national hero who had defeated Qin ten years earlier. Thus,
his decision to wait out Qin's siege armies for more than two years this time provided
fuel for suspicion. Lewis 1999, 640. In Qin's plot against Wei's commander in 247 BC,
Qin bribed officials in Wei to spread the rumor that "the feudal lords have all heard of
the prince of Wei but not the King of Wei. The prince also wants to take advantage of
the moment to become king while the lords, fearing his might, jointly want to establish
him." Qin further sent agents ostensibly to offer congratulations that the prince would
soon become king. Sawyer 1998, 115.

into exactly the same trap again in 229 BC in the midst of Qin's large-scale wars of unification.

The fact that Qin could be a victim of the *lijian* tactic illustrates that even the Qin state was not unitary. However, Shang Yang's stringent system of rewards and punishments was much more effective in channeling individual self-interests to serve the national interest. The *Shang jun shu* understands that "the relation between public and private interests is what determines existence or ruin."[186] Hence, it advises rulers to give liberal rewards and impose severe penalties to ensure that "ministers will not hide things from their ruler, nor will inferiors deceive their superiors."[187] The effectiveness of Shang Yang's system of government was testified to by Xunzi, who visited Qin around 264 BC:

When I entered its frontiers . . . I saw that its people . . . stand in deep awe of their officials. . . . When I reached the yamens of the cities and towns, I saw that their officials are dignified. . . . When I entered the capital and observed its great prefects . . . I noticed that none of them engage in private business, have partialities, or form cliques. They are high-minded, and there are none who do not have understanding of the common welfare. They are worthy great prefects. When I observed its court, I noticed that in the hearing of affairs everything was attended to. . . . It is a worthy court.[188]

Thus, Shang Yang's administrative reforms not only facilitated total mobilization for war and consolidation of conquests, but also provided a more effective bulwark against the deployment of estrangement by other states. As *Shang jun shu* sums this up, "The strong are inevitably the well-regulated, and the well-regulated are inevitably the strong."[189]

2.7   Conclusion

To conclude briefly, both Sinocentric and Eurocentric perspectives are inadequate for understanding the triumph of domination in the ancient Chinese system. The Sinocentric view is wrong to presume that unification of the ancient Chinese system was inevitable. In fact, for more than three

---

[186] *Shang jun shu*, trans. Duyvendak 1963, 264; see also *Han Feizi*, ch. 45.
[187] *Shang jun shu*, trans. Duyvendak 1963, 261. This insight is similar to the argument in *The Prince* that men are "deceptive and deceiving [and] eager to gain. As long as you serve their interests, they are devoted to you." *The Prince*, ch. 17, in Wootton 1994, 52.
[188] *Xunzi*, cited in Li 1977, xviii.
[189] *Shang jun shu*, ch. 11, trans. Lewis 1990, 131. Remarkably, Machiavelli also argued that "where there are good armies, there must be good laws." *The Prince*, ch. 12, in Wootton 1994, 38.

centuries, that system was relatively stable. Various attempts at domination were invariably checked by the balance of power and the rising costs
of expansion. At the same time, the Eurocentric view is also wrong to
believe that universal domination is impossible. Although Qin faced the
balance of power, the rising costs of expansion, the barriers of geography,
and the challenge of consolidating conquests, Qin managed to overcome
them with the shrewd combination of self-strengthening reforms, divide-
and-conquer strategies, and ruthless stratagems. In examining Qin's phenomenal success, we should refrain from presuming that Qin's targets
must be uniquely incapable of balancing or that conquest must be inherently easy in the ancient Chinese system. Instead, we should reconsider the
Eurocentric perspective that countervailing mechanisms are immutable.

3

Rethinking the Dynamics of International Politics in Early Modern Europe

The outcome of international competition in early modern Europe was the exact opposite of that in ancient China: "No state has come to dominate the international system; few wars are total; losers rarely are divided up at the end of the war and indeed are reintegrated into the international system; small states, which do not have the resources to protect themselves, usually survive."[1] In light of the ancient Chinese trajectory, how did the logic of balancing and the logic of domination play out to bring about relative checks and balances in the early modern European system? Chapter Two illustrates that the countervailing mechanisms of balance of power and rising costs of administration were overcome by the coercive mechanisms of self-strengthening reforms, divide-and-conquer strategies, and ruthless stratagems in the ancient Chinese system. Did the checking mechanisms somehow present hard constraints in the European context?

Domination-seekers in early modern Europe failed because they did not follow the logic of domination fully. If the balance of power and the rising costs of expansion seemed insurmountable, it was because European states did not develop the strength of the lion and the wit of the fox, as urged by Machiavelli. While European rulers widely practiced counterbalancing strategies, they only belatedly pursued self-strengthening reforms and rarely employed ancient-Chinese-style ruthless stratagems against one another. As highlighted in Chapter Two, Sunzian stratagems were critical to Qin's ability to divide and conquer, minimize war costs, overcome relative weakness early on, and prevent other states from catching up after

[1] Jervis 1997, 131.

it achieved hegemony. Moreover, the earliest hegemonic rivals in Europe, Valois France and the United Habsburgs, adopted self-weakening expedients rather than self-strengthening reforms. Although these European competitors undertook internal balancing moves in the sense of building larger armies and raising higher revenues, they did so by relying on intermediate power holders instead of establishing administrative-extractive capacity. In their military measures, European rulers usually purchased foreign mercenaries rather than drafting their own populations. Although European states could build *numerically* stronger armies this way, mercenaries were immensely expensive to support and yet unreliable on the battlefields. In their financial measures, European rulers generally relied on tax farmers rather than appointed salaried officials. Although European states introduced various taxes to mobilize more revenues, middlemen at multiple layers could divert significant portions of tax receipts to their own pockets. With extremely high war costs and insufficient revenues, European states faced constant fiscal crises. Desperate for ready cash, early modern European rulers turned to hand-to-mouth measures, such as sale of offices and contraction of loans, which led to ever-escalating fiscal crises in the long term. As European states adopted self-weakening rather than self-strengthening measures, international competition for most of the early modern period is better characterized as competition of relative weaknesses rather than competition of relative capabilities.

It was not until the Revolutionary era that Europe caught up with ancient China. As in Qin's experience, the introduction of comprehensive self-strengthening reforms and the shrew manipulation of diplomatic and battlefield strategies allowed Napoleonic France to sweep through the European continent. Nevertheless, the adoption of self-defeating measures at the onset of system formation continued to shape the European trajectory. Most importantly, although France overthrew various centuries-old expedients, it inherited the crippling national debts which had led to the revolution. Despite dramatically increased revenues from reformed national taxation, France could not finance the empire-building project solely through its own national resources. France was heavily reliant on allies for human and material resources and was therefore vulnerable to their defection. Moreover, Napoleonic France faced a far more challenging environment than Qin: While Qin managed to defeat its cohegemon, Qi, with the help of an anti-Qi alliance, France had to confront its cohegemon, Britain, directly. It did not help that Britain had earlier developed a public credit system to address the problem of runaway war expenses. In a system where the balance of relative capabilities effectively meant the balance of relative wealth, the more resourceful Britain thus enjoyed the upper hand.

The first three sections of this chapter examine the successive competition between the self-weakened Habsburg empire and the equally self-weakened France, between the continually self-weakened France and the self-strengthened England/Britain,[2] and between the fiscally self-strengthened Britain and the militarily self-strengthened Revolutionary and Napoleonic France. As European attempts at domination were repeatedly thwarted by the early adoption of self-weakening expedients, the fourth section analyzes initial and environmental conditions that led the earliest hegemony-seeking states to follow self-weakening expedients rather than self-strengthening reforms. The fifth section argues that the legacy of self-weakening expedients brought about three different models of self-strengthening reforms in early modern Europe, rather than one single model, as in ancient China. The sixth section supplements historical analysis with rough quantitative indicators, including the frequency of war, deaths of soldiers, and elimination of political units. As both historical and quantitative accounts show that the ancient Chinese system was paradoxically more Hobbesian and more Machiavellian than the early modern European system, the following section examines why norms about the conduct of war and diplomacy failed to mitigate international competition. The chapter ends by addressing two most prominent "alternative" explanations for the divergent outcomes in the two systems: the offense-defense balance and the level of cultural homogeneity. Overall, this chapter presents an interlocking analysis of within-case comparison in early modern Europe and cross-case comparison with ancient China.

3.1 The Balance of Relative Weaknesses Between Self-Weakened France and the Self-Weakened Habsburg Empire (1495–1659)

Valois France and the United Habsburgs formed the first pair of hegemonic rivals in the early modern period. France emerged as the strongest state in Europe at the end of the Hundred Years' War. Similarly to powerful states in ancient China, the powerful France soon sought opportunistic expansion in surrounding areas. In 1463, Louis XI annexed the Catalan counties of Roussillon and Cerdagne. In 1494, Charles VIII took advantage of power struggles in the Italian peninsula and invaded Italy. In

---

[2] Britain was formed by the Union of England and Scotland in 1707.

response, other European countries formed the League of Venice in 1495, thus marking the onset of the early modern European system. France's neighbors also maneuvered a series of diplomatic marriages to merge their strengths. These marriages culminated in the Habsburg house's simultaneous ascendance to the crowns of Castile, Aragon, Burgundy, Austria, and the Holy Roman Empire in 1519, and also to the thrones of Hungary and Bohemia in 1526. As the resulting United Habsburgs encircled France, it became France's turn to feel threatened.

To mobilize for the Italian Wars and then to compete with the United Habsburgs, France needed larger armies and higher revenues. France had established the first standing army of Europe, the Compagnies d'Ordonnance or twenty companies of heavy cavalry formed by French knights, in 1445. But that was a relatively small force. Eager to expand military strength rapidly, France turned to military entrepreneurs to recruit mercenary troops. To raise more revenues, the French court increased various direct (e.g., *taille*) and indirect (e.g., *gabelle, aide,* customs) taxes. The court more than doubled its annual direct taxes from 2.1 million livres in 1497 to about 5.8 million livres in the 1550s, and more than tripled its total annual tax receipts from about 3.5 million livres to about 12 million livres in the same period.[3] Unfortunately, the costs of mercenaries increased at significantly faster rates, so much so that France's annual deficits reached an average of 1.5 million livres under Francis I (1515–1547) and more than 4 million livres under Henry II (1547–1559).[4] Mercenaries were not just expensive, they also caused a cash flow problem – while they had to be paid on a monthly basis during the six- to eight-month campaigning season, tax receipts "dribbled in small amounts throughout the year."[5] To keep expensive mercenaries in the fields, the French court began to sell public offices during the Italian Wars. After direct confrontation with the Habsburg empire began in 1521, Francis created ever more public offices in all spheres of government. In 1554, Henry even introduced the *alternatif,* that is, the sharing of an office by two holders.[6] From the 1520s onward, successive kings also contracted ever larger amounts of loans. By 1555, the court had accumulated a total debt of 4.9 million livres at 12–16 percent floating interest rates.[7] When investors became increasingly skeptical of the French court's ability to

---

[3] Ertman 1997, 96.   [4] Ibid., 97.   [5] Kaiser 1990, 20.

[6] Henri IV also granted full property right to officeholders in exchange for a special tax and "thereby sealed the transition from bureaucratic office to property." Moore 1966, 59.

[7] Ertman 1997, 97; Kennedy 1987, 57–58.

repay, Francis turned to the sale of *rentes*, whereby the court signed over sources of future revenues as security for repayment. Through this means, Francis raised 750,000 livres and Henry nearly 7 million livres.[8]

With these measures, France could command large armies but at the price of escalating fiscal crises. Over time, interest payments absorbed increasingly larger proportions of ordinary revenues. The sale of *rentes* and public offices further eroded the resource bases for future ordinary revenues. After four decades of struggle with the United Habsburgs, therefore, France declared bankruptcy in 1557. Such a bankrupt state would probably lose the great-power status, if not independence, in the ancient Chinese system. Nevertheless, France remained a first-rate power in the early modern European system. This was possible because its chief rival, the United Habsburgs, also adopted similar self-weakening expedients.

Compared with Valois France, the United Habsburgs seemed blessed at first sight. Charles V (1519–1555) had the fortune not only to obtain so many possessions by sheer inheritance, but also to enjoy the influx of silver from the discovery of the New World. It is sometimes argued that the Habsburg empire was doomed to fail because "[t]he disjointed Habsburg possessions, with their radically dissimilar political and social structures, were not of the material from which an imposing power, poised for action, could be formed."[9] This view fails to see that such "congeries of territories"[10] presented not just constraints, but also the opportunity to encircle France. If the Habsburgs had taken this opportunity to isolate Valois France by diplomacy and weaken it by overwhelming strength, "the mastery of Europe would virtually have been theirs."[11]

To be fair, the United Habsburgs did develop a strong army. To defend the far-flung empire, the Habsburg house developed a professional army formed of Spanish recruits, the *tercio*. New recruits received formal training for one or two years before leaving for active service. In combat, *tercio* troops would form into small companies of between 120 and 150 men

---

[8] Ertman 1997, 98–99.   [9] Dehio 1963, 33; also Kaiser 1990, 27; Kennedy 1987, 33.
[10] Kennedy 1987, 52.
[11] It may be argued that Charles V sought only the preservation of his legitimate possessions and not illegitimate conquest. From the perspective of opportunistic expansion and in light of Qin's experience, this point is rather irrelevant. As Kennedy points out, although Charles had "no conscious plan to dominate Europe in the manner of Napoléon or Hitler," "had the Habsburg rulers achieved all of their limited, regional aims – even their defensive aims – the mastery of Europe would virtually have been theirs." Kennedy 1987, 35.

each, which were then grouped into integrated regiments of up to three thousand pikemen, swordsmen, and arquebusiers who were trained to provide mutual support.[12] This professional, national force soon "swept aside innumerable foes and greatly reduced the reputation of French cavalry."[13] Unable to bear the full brunt of the *tercio* on the battlefront, France tried to outcompete the Habsburg empire on the diplomatic front. Although the Ottoman Empire was considered an outsider to European Christendom, France dragged this fearsome power into the hegemonic rivalry. Without a commensurate divide-and-conquer strategy, Charles had to fight the Turks and the French simultaneously in several major wars.[14] It was this strategic inadequacy that turned Charles's vast possessions from potential assets into sure liabilities, making him vulnerable to the mechanism of rising costs of expansion. To protect distant possessions from attacks, the Habsburg empire had to patrol the coastline from the Iberian peninsula to the Low Countries, the "Spanish road" from Lombardy to Luxembourg, and another road from Vienna to the lower Rhine. All such efforts required immense forces, but the number of Spanish recruits in the professional *tercio* could not be rapidly increased on short notice. Charles thus resorted to mercenary forces, thereby pushing up the costs of war even further.

To pay for various protection costs, Charles V turned to the cash cow of Castile. During his reign, Charles tripled tax receipts from *alcabala* (a 10 percent sales tax), *millones* (a tax on foodstuffs), *servicios* (extraordinary grants by estates), and customs.[15] The United Habsburgs also enjoyed handsome contributions from Italian and Dutch possessions and silver shipments from the New World. However, Charles' multifront wars were so expensive that they could not be paid for by an apparently wealthy court. As Paul Kennedy observes, "No state in this period, however prosperous, could pay immediately for the costs of a prolonged conflict; no matter what fresh taxes were raised, there was always a gap between government income and expenditure."[16] After the Habsburg-Valois rivalry began in 1521, the United Habsburgs quickly ran into fiscal crises. Charles thus sold numerous offices, privileges, monopolies, and

---

[12] Kennedy 1987, 44; Parker 1995, 39–40.   [13] Kennedy 1987, 44.

[14] During his reign, Charles was involved in the First War of Charles V (1521–1526), the Ottoman War (1521–1531), the Second War of Charles V (1526–1529), the Ottoman War (1532–1535), the Third War of Charles V (1536–1538), the Ottoman War (1537–47), the Fourth War of Charles V (1542–1544), the Ottoman War (1551–1556), and the Fifth War of Charles V (1552–1556).

[15] Ertman 1997, 112–116; Kennedy 1987, 47.   [16] Kennedy 1987, 72.

honors which carried exemptions from taxes. He further contracted *juros* (government bonds at high interest rates) and *asientos* (loans that used incoming silver shipments as security) to obtain more ready cash. Interest payments on *juros* quickly leaped from 36.6 percent of ordinary revenues in 1522, to 65 percent in 1543, to 103.9 percent by 1560.[17] The amounts of *asientos* contracted also quickly exceeded the value of the Treasure Fleet. While receipts from silver shipments reached between 200,000 and 300,000 ducats per year in the 1530s and 1540s and then 871,000 in the early 1550s, the amounts that had to be repaid annually on *asientos* averaged 1.2 million ducats and 2.5 million ducats in the respective periods.[18] Therefore, the Habsburg empire – along with Valois France – had to declare bankruptcy in 1557. The two bankrupt belligerents soon agreed to the Peace of Cateau-Cambresis in 1559.

When the exhausted Charles V abdicated his throne in 1555, his eldest son, Philip II, inherited the Spanish possessions (Castile, Aragon, the Netherlands, Italian possessions, and American colonies), and his brother, Ferdinand I, took over the Austrian possessions, thus splitting the United Habsburgs into Spain and Austria. Of the two Habsburg lines, Philip II (1556–1598) was better poised to revive the glory of the United Habsburgs. Philip restored royal control over the entire military establishment, which had fallen into private control during Charles's reign.[19] A special military treasury was established. The manufacture of gunpowder became a royal monopoly. The arms industries and the saltpeter makers were subsumed under strict royal supervision. The Mediterranean fleets and the garrisons of North Africa were controlled and provisioned by the royal commissariat in Seville. With formidable military strength, Philip thwarted the Ottoman Empire's ambitions on his possessions.

To the extent that Philip centralized the court's control over military forces and eliminated intermediate power brokers, he was engaged in self-strengthening reforms. But how did Philip mobilize his troops and pay for his wars? Philip doubled ordinary revenues from 1556 to 1573, and further redoubled them by the end of his reign.[20] However, Philip's army and navy also doubled and redoubled in the same period – and increasingly by hiring mercenaries. Moreover, Philip inherited not just Charles's Spanish possessions, but also his huge debts. When Philip assumed the Spanish throne, most of government revenues had been pledged to *juro*

---

[17] Ertman 1997, 116–117; Kennedy 1987, 54.   [18] Ertman 1997, 117.
[19] Parker 1995, 39; Thompson 1976, 6–7.   [20] Kennedy 1987, 47.

holders for years in advance. The court thus became more reliant on *asientos*, contracting far more loans that it could afford. When the value of silver shipments reached about 2.2 million ducats per year in the 1580s and 1590s, the value of *asientos* skyrocketed to between 4 and 6 million ducats a year.[21] At the same time, the huge influx of silver contributed to high inflation, thus making it increasingly expensive to put even the same number of men in arms.[22] To cover enlarging deficits, the Habsburg house sold not just public offices, but also revenues from whole villages and towns. In the late sixteenth century, the Spanish Crown retained control of only about 30 percent of the territory of Castile.[23]

Desperate for cash, Philip decided to increase extractions from the prosperous Italian and Dutch possessions. Philip met with little resistance in Italy, where Turkish vessels plied the waters and interdicted trade. However, the Netherlands had enjoyed a high degree of autonomy under Charles, as under the preceding Burgundian house. When the duke of Alva set out to "Castilianize" the territory, the Dutch revolted. As a result, the Habsburg house not only could not obtain new revenues, but even had to spend more traditional resources to suppress the rebellion. The Army of Flanders cost more than the combined revenues extracted from Castile and the West Indies.[24] At the same time, Dutch privateers captured Spanish fleets carrying treasures from the New World. To make matters worse, the Dutch seemed even more skillful than the French at soliciting foreign assistance in order to compensate for relative weakness in military strength. They raised troops from French, German, and English Protestants on the one hand, and encouraged the Ottoman Empire to launch a new offensive in the Mediterranean on the other. As Daniel Nexon remarks, "Under Philip's reign almost all of the factors leading to overextension were the result of war in the Netherlands."[25] Philip, on the other hand, did not seem to understand that even the most powerful state could ill afford multifront wars. He opened even more fronts by invading Portugal in 1579–1581[26] and intervening in the French civil

---

[21] Ertman 1997, 117.

[22] General prices climbed 200 to 300 percent over the course of the sixteenth century. North and Thomas 1973, 106.

[23] Ertman 1997, 119.   [24] Downing 1992, 228–229.   [25] Nexon 2003, 488.

[26] Philip claimed the Portugese throne through his mother. Portugal is sometimes treated as a hegemonic power because it established a global trading empire. See Rasler and Thompson 1994, 4. However, Portugal was marginal to international competition in early modern Europe and was even conquered by Spain for nearly nine decades. I follow Levy and do not treat Portugal as a great power. See Levy 1983.

wars in 1589–1598.[27] With dramatic increases in war expenditures and decreases in revenues, the inevitable result was bankruptcy in 1575 and 1596.

In such circumstances, even the *tercio* – the once strongest army of Europe – became severely weakened from within. The *tercio*'s strength in the early years lay in the centralization of command and use of Spanish recruits. From the late sixteenth century on, however, the Spanish court increasingly turned over the recruitment, administration, and provisioning of its troops to military entrepreneurs and Genoese financiers. The Habsburg house thus gradually lost control over its armed forces. To compound the problem, military entrepreneurs who were not paid surrendered to the enemy, and foreign mercenaries who were not paid deserted, mutinied, and pillaged the countryside.[28] For instance, unpaid troops in the Army of Flanders mutinied more than forty times between 1567 and 1609, thus weakening Spanish offense and strengthening Dutch defense.[29] The fiscal and military condition of Habsburg Spain continued to spiral downward during the reigns of Philip III (1599–1620) and Philip IV (1621–1665), resulting in three more bankruptcies in 1607, 1627, and 1647. Spain's kin, the Austrian house, did not fare any better.

Fortunately, Spain's foes were even weaker. Its primary rival, France, descended into decades of religious wars in the late sixteenth century and remained exhausted in the early seventeenth century. When the Thirty Years' War broke out, the joint forces of Habsburg Spain, Habsburg Austria, and Bavaria appeared triumphant everywhere. But Sweden unexpectedly entered the war (with French and Dutch subsidies) in 1630 and rolled back Catholic forces. When Sweden was dealt a severe blow at Nordlingen in 1634, France decided to pick up the fight. France and its allies engaged Habsburg forces on many fronts and attempted to block Habsburg supply lines on sea and land. Such an unexpected turn of events seriously deepened Spain's financial crisis. Philip IV thus turned to Catalonia, Portugal, and Spanish Italy for additional human and material resources. Similarly to the Netherlands, Catalonia and Portugal had been promised relative autonomy and fiercely resisted heightened coercion. Even Italy would not quietly swallow additional extractions this time.

---

[27] The Valois line ended with the death of Henry III in 1590. Philip intervened to prevent Henry of Navarre from taking the throne. Philip poured such tremendous resources into France that the intervention essentially "ensur[ed] the survival of the [Dutch] revolt." Nexon 2003, 480.

[28] The desertion rate could reach 50 to 70 percent. Parrott 1995, 243.

[29] Anderson 1998, 8; Downing 1992, 228–229.

The result was "[t]wo, three, many Hollands."[30] To complicate further the Habsburgs' troubles, France provided troops and subsidies to the rebellions. The Peace of Westphalia in 1648 and the settlement with France in 1659 finally sounded the death knell of Habsburg supremacy. While Spain could suppress the Catalonian revolt in 1652, the Dutch Republic became an independent state in 1648 and Portugal restored independence in 1668.

Although France appeared victorious over the Habsburg empire, this ascendancy was due not to French strength but to Spanish weakness. In the first round of hegemonic competition in early modern Europe, the adoption of self-weakening expedients by both sides essentially turned the balance of power into a balance of relative weaknesses. As Matthew Anderson observes, "the weaknesses of both economic structures and state machines" meant that international competition in this period was "a story of inflated ambitions, disappointed hopes and grudgingly accepted compromises."[31] Paul Kennedy even likens the two rivals to "punch-drunk boxers, clinging to each other in a state of near-exhaustion and unable to finish the other off. Each was suffering from domestic rebellion, widespread impoverishment, and dislike of the war, and was on the brink of financial collapse."[32]

Neither French nor Habsburg rulers were blind to the challenge of intensified geopolitical competition. Both states formed standing armies from their own nationals. The Habsburgs' *tercio* was particularly innovative and well deserved the reputation as Europe's most effective army. However, the success of the infantry (especially disciplined phalanxes of pikemen) over the heavy cavalry also meant that victory became a function of army size. To expand their army strength rapidly, both the French court and the Habsburg house increasingly turned to military entrepreneurs. Use of mercenary troops entailed not just high wages, but also increasing marginal costs. As Margaret Levi explains, once the initial pool of professional soldiers and unemployed young men had been tapped, it became increasingly costly to locate additional healthy men.[33] It was because the early hegemonic rivals relied on such an expensive means of war that they were easily crippled by the mechanism of rising costs of expansion.

The French and Spanish courts did not fail to raise more revenues to support their military ambitions. In fact, they managed to double and triple their tax receipts. What they failed to do was to improve their

---

[30] Downing 1992, 230.   [31] Anderson 1998, 203–204.
[32] Kennedy 1987, 58–59.   [33] Levi 1998, 112.

extractive capacity, that is, the ability to assess liability on the basis of productivity or wealth, to collect payments, and to remit tax receipts from the points of collection to the state treasury. Instead of appointing salaried tax collectors, French and Habsburg rulers were dependent on tax farmers over whom they exercised little control. At the same time, mercenary armies were so expensive that even significantly increased ordinary revenues could not cover war costs. When budget deficits escalated to fiscal crises, both France and the Habsburg empire deepened their reliance on intermediate resource holders by contracting loans and selling offices. Such measures could relieve burning fiscal crises in the short term but effectively incarcerated French and Spanish monarchs in "fiscal prisons" in the long term:[34] The more loans were contracted and the more exemptions were auctioned off, the more future sources of ordinary revenues were alienated; and the more ordinary revenues were signed away, the more desperate the court became in searching for additional extraordinary revenues. French and Spanish courts essentially "shifted revenue to earlier periods, to fight earlier wars, while restricting [their] ability to raise more money later."[35] Even worse, because capital holders were worried that kings and princes – who were above the law – would repudiate debts, they typically demanded that rulers sign away not just the yield but also the administration of future ordinary revenues. Fiscal expedients thus made it ever more difficult to construct a rational taxation system that would sustain military power over time. The consequences of fiscal troubles were military setbacks. Both French kings and Habsburg emperors had to subordinate strategic calculations to fiscal constraints. Worse, bankruptcies led to mutinies, thereby crippling the best armies with little fighting.

Fiscal expedients further distorted economic incentives and brought about economic stagnation and structural corruption. On the one hand, frequent debasement of coinage and high inflation made capital holders wary of long-term investments in the productive sectors of commerce and industry.[36] On the other hand, the reliance on military entrepreneurs, use of tax farmers, contraction of loans, and sale of public offices diverted capital to unproductive rent-seeking activities. Moreover, the conversion of state functions into profit-making ventures created a fundamental conflict between public interests and private interests, rendering the presumption of states as unitary actors in the pursuit of the national interest completely

---

[34] Brewer 1989, 16.   [35] Schultz and Weingast 2003, 26.
[36] Hoffman and Rosenthal 1997, 53; Kennedy 1987, 53; North and Thomas 1973, 130.

false. As argued previously, the divergence between national interests and individual interests allowed Qin to employ the stratagems of bribery and estrangement with stunning success. If even ancient Chinese states that had effective despots sitting on top of highly centralized bureaucracies were not unitary actors, then early modern European states were far less so. Bankers and creditors would of course charge handsome interest rates for their own personal profits. Tax farmers and venal officials would take their "cuts" before passing tax receipts to higher levels, leaving huge "wastes" between the taxes imposed on the subjects and the revenues collected by the Crown.[37] Military captains would maximize the margin between the payments provided by rulers and the actual costs of recruitment and provisioning, often by listing "phantom soldiers" on their payrolls and undercutting supplies and equipments.[38]

Spanish and French statesmen were not unaware of the acute financial problems venality caused – just as ancient Chinese rulers were not ignorant of the disastrous consequences of bribery and estrangement tactics. As Jan de Vries observes of Spain, "A whole school of economic reformers... wrote mountains of tracts pleading for new measures."[39] In France, Jean Bodin was one of the many enlightened thinkers who relentlessly attacked the use of mercenary troops and the sale of public offices.[40] However, even reform-minded rulers and ministers found it increasingly difficult – if not impossible – to redeem sold offices and contracted loans. At the same time, the increasingly large corps of farmers general, receivers general, treasures general, payers of the *rentes*, holders of *juros*, and other venal officials who enjoyed tax exemptions and reaped handsome profits from fiscal expedients would fiercely resist any efforts to end them. As a result, both hegemonic rivals sank deeper and deeper into the self-weakening vicious cycle. The Habsburg empire eventually "declined from the most powerful nation in the western world since the Roman empire to a second-rate power" over the course of a century and a half.[41] As France had equally rotten administration, it was to follow Spain's footsteps.

3.2 Competition Between Self-Weakened France and Self-Strengthened Britain (1661–1715)

If we set aside France's internal weaknesses for the moment, then Louis XIV's (1661–1715) position would seem "enviable" when he acceded to

---

[37] Kennedy 1987, 82; Tilly 1975, 57.   [38] Kaiser 1990, 146.   [39] de Vries 1976, 28.
[40] Franklin 1992, xxii.   [41] North 1990, 115.

the throne.[42] As Paul Kennedy observes,

To the South, Spain was still exhausting itself in the futile attempt to recover Portugal. Across the Channel, a restored monarchy under Charles II was trying to find its feet, and in English commercial circles great jealousy of the Dutch existed. In the North, a recent war had left both Denmark and Sweden weakened. In Germany, the Protestant princes watched suspiciously for any fresh Habsburg [Austrian] attempt to improve its position, but the imperial government in Vienna had problems enough in Hungary and Transylvania, and slightly later with a revival of Ottoman power.[43]

For Louis, such a window of opportunity was not to be missed. While the mutual animosity among his potential opponents already provided fertile ground for the divide-and-conquer strategy, Louis further used subsidies to buy bandwagons and to break up opposing alliances. With superb strategic maneuvering, Louis was remarkably successful at playing off his enemies against one another. In the Devolutionary War with Spain in 1667–1668, France secured the neutrality of the Dutch Republic and England, the alliance of Portugal, and the cooperation of Neubrug, Mainz, Cologne, and Munster.[44] In the Dutch War of 1672–1678, Louis similarly seduced England and Sweden to abandon the Dutch Republic and won the acquiescence of Austria and German states. In each of these wars, Louis managed to "gain the support of virtually all the powers that had previously opposed him."[45] According to the Great Elector of Prussia, the Sun King had become "the arbiter of Europe."[46]

Louis and his ministers apparently understood that the divide-and-conquer strategy must be backed by military strength. They also learned from the hegemonic struggle with the Habsburgs that they should centralize military command with a war ministry. French nationals were conscripted for both the army and the navy. Royal intendants were appointed to check on the recruitment, financing, and supply of troops. New standards of training and discipline were imposed by the inspector general. The ranking structure was revised and meritocracy was introduced to fill vacancies. The Academie Royale des Sciences was founded to engage the disciplines of cartography, chemistry, and engineering to the ends of naval warfare. Louis's ministers further enhanced a network of magazines near France's borders and a network of depots along marching routes that were initially built during the Thirty Years' War.

In addition, just as ancient Chinese strategists argued that the basis of *qiangbing* (strong army) was *fuguo* (rich country), European

---

[42] Sonnino 1987, 116.　　[43] Kennedy 1987, 100.　　[44] Kaiser 1990, 152.
[45] Schweller 1994, 11.　　[46] Cited in Schweller 1994, 90.

mercantilists believed that the pursuit of power must be based on the pursuit of wealth.[47] As Louis's finance minister, Jean-Baptiste Colbert, argued, "Trade is the source of finance and finance is the nerve of war."[48] The Finance Ministry under Colbert fostered economic growth by regulating the movement of bullion, reducing internal tolls and building infrastructures (bridges, roads, and canals), and encouraging immigration of skilled Dutch and Swedish mineralogical engineers. Colbert also took steps to improve the French court's financial situation. In the period 1661–1671, he was able to increase revenues from about 37 million livres to 65 million and reduce annual debt service from 30 million livres to 8 million.[49] It is notable that the increase in revenues was partly achieved by sidelining hereditary local magnates and appointing thirty-some removable royal intendants to assume direct responsibilities for tax collections, royal justice, economic regulation, and maintenance of law and order.

Despite these self-strengthening initiatives, Louis was eventually unable to track a different trajectory than his predecessors'. Although Louis raised native French forces, he did not develop a national conscription system but relied mostly on mercenary troops to expand his army strength.[50] Although Colbert made some efforts to improve state finance and promote economic activities, he did not reform the self-destructive fiscal arrangements inherited from the Italian Wars. Indeed, the French court had found it difficult to increase ordinary revenues since the last massive increases during the Thirty Years' War. When France was merely subsidizing the Habsburgs' enemies, it had increased direct taxes from 20.7 to 34.2 million livres between 1627 and 1634.[51] After France entered the war in 1635, the *taille* was doubled from about 36.3 million livres in 1635 to 72.6 million in 1643.[52] Moreover, a new sales tax was imposed throughout France in 1641. Heightened extractions resulted in widespread rebellions, often with local magnates siding with peasants. It was in such circumstances that royal intendants were dispatched to collect taxes in the provinces directly. Although the French court drastically increased tax receipts, it was still unable to cover all the bills. In 1643, for example, government expenditures were almost twice as great as revenues.[53] In fiscal crises, the court again sold public offices on a massive scale and even forced existing

---

[47] Viner 1948.   [48] Cited in Earle 1986, 217.   [49] Kaiser 1990, 144.

[50] According to Kaiser, the French army grew "from a few thousand men in 1661 to 72,000 in 1667 and 120,000 in 1672, and reached more than 150,000 even in the peacetime years of the early 1680s." Kaiser 1990, 145.

[51] Ertman 1997, 109; Sonnino 1987, 120.

[52] Kaiser 1990, 74.   [53] Kennedy 1987, 58.

officeholders to provide loans. By the time Louis ascended to the throne, therefore, management of state finance had fallen completely into the hands of venal officers, with the concomitant problems of exemption, deduction, and corruption at all levels of government. When the Sun King's wars rolled on, there was little left of the state that had not been sold into private hands. The view that Louis pioneered the *étatisation* of war – or "the mobilization of the total resources of the state, of the economy, as well as of manpower"[54] – is simply false. In reality, he "had lost direct control over much of the administrative, judicial, and financial infrastructure of [his] realm to proprietary officeholders, officeholder-financiers, and tax farmers."[55] Louis managed to prevail in the first half of his reign merely "by virtue of the weakness, decline, and undeveloped state of almost all the other powers."[56] When a self-strengthened foe eventually emerged, France was condemned to the road of decline.

Just as Sweden's and France's entry into the Thirty Years' War disrupted Spain's plan to reconquer the affluent United Provinces, England's intervention thwarted Louis's ambition on the same "jewel" of Europe. England was originally an unlikely candidate to challenge French supremacy, because it suffered from civil war and power struggles for most of the seventeenth century. England was also an unlikely ally for the Dutch Republic: England fought three Anglo-Dutch wars in the century and further sided with Louis during the Dutch War of 1672–1678. However, William of Orange, the commander in chief of the Dutch Republic and the husband of England's Mary, ascended to the English throne during the Glorious Revolution of 1688. This Anglo-Dutch union was analogous to a reincarnation of the United Habsburgs on a smaller scale. Overtaken by surprise, Louis declared war on England with little of his usual diplomatic preparation. He also had little idea that the nature of international politics was to undergo fundamental transformation. During the ensuing Nine Years' War (1688–1697), Louis deepened various centuries-old fiscal expedients such as sale of offices, sale of *rentes*, sale of lifetime exemption from *taille*, extraction of forced loans from existing officeholders, debasement of the currency, and default of loans, with the predictable consequences of bankruptcies and mutinies.[57] England, on the other hand, embarked on self-strengthening fiscal reforms.

---

[54] Treasure 1966, 257–258.   [55] Ertman 1997, 35.   [56] Schroeder 1994b, 132.

[57] When the court ran out of real offices for sale, it created "a host of entirely absurd offices . . . , including official burial announcer, barrel roller, and wall and room inspector." Ertman 1997, 136.

England's self-strengthening reforms did not develop naturally or easily. Similarly to other great powers, England had relied on self-defeating expedients to generate the wherewithal of war. When England fought France and Scotland in the 1540s, Henry VIII contracted loans with foreign bankers, imposed forced loans on officeholders, debased the coinage, sold religious properties at low rates, and seized noble properties on trumped-up charges.[58] When England entered wars with Spain and France in the late sixteenth and early seventeenth centuries, the court intensified various expedients. In 1604, even the customs, the Crown's largest source of ordinary revenues, was put to farm. Thus, the English state was not much different from the French state or the Spanish state: It was "a kind of parasite, extracting resources from the productive sectors of the nation and redistributing them among a small political class with access to power, offices, and contracts."[59] As elsewhere in Europe, fiscal weakness led to military weakness. During the Second Anglo-Dutch War, English defenses had deteriorated so much that the Dutch were able to sail up to the Thames and destroy the naval dockyard at Chatham in 1667. Nevertheless, English reformers seized on this humiliation to make reform a matter of national survival.

Sir George Downing was the chief architect of the reform package. The distinguishing mark of the reform was direct borrowing of ready cash from the general public rather than narrow groups of financiers. Hence, it was called the public credit system. Although the public credit system involved contraction of loans, it should count as a self-strengthening reform rather than a self-weakening expedient because it required concomitant administrative and fiscal reforms to generate public confidence in state finance. To enhance administrative efficiency and to reduce structural corruption, venality was replaced by meritocracy in all branches of government. Officials were appointed on the basis of objective criteria and remunerated with progressively higher salaries on a graded scale. To establish a centralized system of government revenues based on customs, excise, and land tax, tax farming was abolished and government agencies were created to collect taxes.[60] To rationalize government expenditures, the Treasury was established as the

---

[58] Kennedy 1987, 60. [59] Ertman 1997, 184.

[60] The customs was levied on international trade. The excise involved duties on domestically produced commodities, especially alcoholic drinks. The hearth tax was a graduated property tax based on the number of household hearths. Brewer 1989, 92. Together, these taxes provided about 90 percent of state revenues in the century after the Glorious Revolution. Brewer 1989, 95.

"master department" to exercise central budgetary control over all other departments, especially the main spending departments, the army and the navy.[61] With these measures, England became the first major European state to keep full accounts of total government revenues and expenditures. To improve administrative probity further, parliamentary oversight and market forces were also introduced. After the Glorious Revolution, parliamentary approval was required to wage war and to levy taxes. Parliament would vote on the war budget on an annual basis; the general public would then advance to the government the full amount of supply voted in cash in exchange for Treasury Orders secured on the tax funds.

Such a comprehensive restructuring of state institutions inevitably met resistance. Fortunately, the shocking defeat by a newborn, smaller power discredited conservative forces which blocked similar reforms in Habsburg Spain and Bourbon France. Moreover, Cromwell's Commonwealth had already experimented with fundamental administrative, military, and fiscal reforms. His victories over the Scots, Irish, and Dutch "served to establish a link in the minds of government officials and the general public alike between the administrative methods of the Interregnum and military prowess."[62] Equally important, England was only tangentially involved in the Habsburg-French rivalry and so the extent of venality was quite limited by Habsburg and French standards. As it turned out, the most formidable obstacles to reforms arose not from entrenched aristocrats, but from English kings themselves. Charles II appointed a Treasury Commission headed by Sir George Downing in 1667–1671 only after widespread pressure. He soon subverted the reform program when a new, less influential treasury minister rose to power. Nevertheless, Charles changed his mind again in 1679 and appointed another Treasury Commission, which reinstalled Downing's reform measures. After William of Orange plunged England into direct confrontation with Louis XIV in the Nine Years' War, the foreign king flirted with financiers for ready cash. Fortunately, William also restored fiscal authority to the Treasury. After some zigzags, the public credit system was finally institutionalized during the War of the Spanish Succession.

As the public credit system generated significant increases in ordinary revenues and higher credits at lower interest rates, it fundamentally altered the relative capabilities of England and France. Prior to the Glorious Revolution, England had only one-third of France's population, half of

[61] On Downing's reform package, see Brewer 1989, 129.   [62] Ertman 1997, 186.

France's economy, and one-fifth of France's revenues. After the reforms, England quickly doubled its average annual tax revenues to 3.64 million pounds during the Nine Years' War, and further to between 4 and 6 million pounds during the War of the Spanish Succession.[63] In the first quarter of the eighteenth century, Englishmen paid the equivalent of about 17.6 livres per capita in annual taxes while Frenchmen paid 8.1 livres.[64] The lower tax rates in France were further subject to huge wastes between the taxes collected from taxpayers and the revenues received by the Crown.[65] But England minimized this problem by eliminating tax farming and venality. In addition, Britain's superior access to credits allowed it to sustain protracted wars well in excess of normal receipts without exhausting its economy. In the average war year, Britain's military spending amounted to 1–1.5 years' worth of revenues, while France's comparable figure was 0.5–0.8.[66] It certainly helped that Britain's public credits took the form of perpetual redeemable securities at the low interest rates of 3–4 percent, but France had to rely on amortizing loans at two percentage points higher.[67] As before, France was constantly on the brink of bankruptcy. Britain, on the other hand, was able to translate economic wealth into military strength. During the Nine Years' War, England increased its army strength from 35,000 in 1688 to 87,440 in 1696, and expanded its navy from 173 ships in 1688 to 323 ships in 1697.[68] With an abundant supply of cash, moreover, England could afford to spend more than 20 percent of its war expenditures on subsidies to buy allies.[69] Consequently, the internally rotten France could not match the reformed Britain. Britain held off French might in the Nine Years' War (1688–1697), secured favorable terms in the War of Spanish Succession (1701–1713), and defeated France in the Seven Years' War (1755–1763). France was not able to renew its bid for hegemony until it embarked on even more comprehensive self-strengthening reforms than England's.

[63] Brewer 1989, 89; Ertman 1997, 218. A century later in the 1780s, English tax receipts experienced a sixfold increase.

[64] By the 1780s, the average Englishman paid the equivalent of about forty-six livres while the Frenchman paid seventeen livres in annual taxes. Brewer 1989, 89.

[65] In 1695–1715, the French court raised 505.7 million livres from sale of titles, offices, and lifetime exemption from future *taille*, but only 380 million livres actually reached the state. Ertman 1997, 137.

[66] Schultz and Weingast 2003, 21.

[67] Brewer 1989, 133; Ertman 1997, 141; Schultz and Weingast 2003, 20.

[68] Ertman 1997, 209.

[69] During the War of Spanish Succession, the British and the Dutch together spent about 8 million pounds on subsidies. Brewer 1989, 32; Kaiser 1990, 163.

3.3 Near Domination by the Self-Strengthened Revolutionary and Napoleonic France

Just as military defeat by the newborn Dutch Republic stimulated Dutch-style reforms in England, repeated defeats by the peripheral England generated mounting pressures for British-style reforms in France. Compelled by the exigencies of international competition, Louis XV and Louis XVI introduced reforms in 1770 and 1776, respectively. Unfortunately, the Bourbon court had become so thoroughly appropriated that every attempt to eliminate privileges and introduce an equitable tax system was undermined by vested interests.[70] The thorough subversion of state functions into private properties even allowed venal officials to resist reforms in the name of "the natural rights of man . . . [and] the social contract."[71] Louis XV's reforms were rolled back as soon as he died in 1774. Louis XVI's reforms were discontinued by the king himself in 1781. Eventually, it took a revolution from below to achieve what Prussian, English, and Chinese reformers could achieve from above.

The French Revolution was "a bureaucratic, mass-incorporating and state-strengthening revolution."[72] The national assembly quickly established a hierarchy of meritocratic and salaried officials under the central direction of an executive cabinet composed of six ministries. The assembly also founded a new treasury to exercise central control over state revenues and expenditures, the Bank of France to manage the money supply, an equitable system of direct and indirect taxation, and a nationalized system of short-term government credits. In addition to following the British model, French revolutionaries further installed direct rule for the first time in European history: The revolutionaries rationally divided France into eighty-three uniform *départements*, which were further subdivided into districts and communes.

With the capacity for direct rule, Revolutionary France was prepared to take another measure that was common in the late Warring States period

---

[70] Even Louis XIV had tried a more equitable capitation tax in 1695. The population was divided into twenty-two categories according to rank, with the highest group asked to pay two thousand livres and the lowest one livre. However, the court allowed the usual reductions and evasion for the privileged. Ertman 1997, 137. Moreover, regional estates had already provided guarantees to government bonds in a manner quite similar to that of British public credits. Unlike the debts issued directly by the French court, estates bonds were generally repaid on schedule. But as the estates had only limited leverage over state revenues, estates bonds composed only 15 percent of the total debts of the ancien regime. Rosenthal 1998, 83.

[71] Moore 1966, 61.   [72] Skocpol 1979, 179.

but unprecedented in early modern Europe: the introduction of universal military conscription in 1793.[73] The *levée en masse* soon revolutionized the character of international competition by facilitating significant reduction of war costs, drastic expansion of army strength, and dramatic improvement of fighting capability. Compared with employment of mercenaries, the use of national armies allowed the state to draw upon virtually the whole adult male population at little – and relatively constant – cost.[74] When the whole nation could be in arms, relative population size became a critical sinew of war. Revolutionary France was fortunate to be endowed with 25 million population, the largest in Europe. During the Revolutionary War, the French army quickly swelled from about 200,000 before the Revolution to 650,000 in 1793 and 730,000 in 1794.[75] When France embarked on the Napoleonic Wars, 2.4 million men were drafted in the period 1804–1813.[76] In the age of mercenaries, it had been impossible for armies to grow at such rates. This was not just because mercenaries were prohibitively expensive, but also because states that ruled indirectly through regional and local magnates simply did not have the administrative capacity to register young men on the national scale.

National conscripts were also better soldiers than mercenary troops. As Niccolò Machiavelli observed, a national army that "fights for its own glory" will display "sufficient firmness of purpose... to withstand an enemy who is at all determined."[77] In contrast, mercenaries "have no motive or principle for joining beyond the desire to collect their pay. And what you pay them is not enough to make them want to die for you."[78] Worse, unpaid mercenary armies would desert en masse, pillage the countryside, and mistreat the peasants. And unpaid military entrepreneurs would mutiny or surrender to the enemy side. Of course, national conscripts would also engage in evasion and desertion when they were not paid and when they faced the prospect of defeat. Nevertheless, a fiscally sound state was better able to pay monthly wages and reward outstanding contributions. The Revolutionary regime further instilled the nationalist sentiment that

---

[73] Strictly speaking, universal conscription did not become a reality in France until 1875, because commutation (payment to the government to draft someone else), substitution (payment to someone else to take one's place), and exemptions were legally allowed. Levi 1998, 109–111. This inadequacy might be another legacy of the feudal practice of *scutage*, whereby those obliged to provide military service had the option of paying a fee instead.

[74] Levi 1998, 112.   [75] Black 1994, 168; Kennedy 1987, 122; Skocpol 1979, 198.

[76] Skocpol 1979, 198.   [77] *Discourses*, bk. 1, ch. 43, in Wootton 1994, 139–140.

[78] *The Prince*, ch. 12, in Wootton 1994, 38.

each Frenchman "owe[d] himself to the defense of the Fatherland."[79] The overall result was phenomenal: Although the initially demoralized French armies suffered defeats in 1792, the *levée en masse* "mastered every major internal and external military threat to the Republic" by early 1794.[80]

France's fighting capability was further enhanced by the emergence of a military genius, Napoléon Bonaparte, who rose to the prominent position of commander in chief under the revolutionary principle of meritocracy. Napoléon put into effective use various organizational and battlefield tactics that had been developed earlier but could not be fully exploited without the centralized command structure and the disciplined national armies of the Revolutionary era. In the age of mercenaries, quasi-independent military entrepreneurs would not support one another to carry out any grand strategic plans, and mercenary troops could not be trusted to engage in any tactical maneuvering. As Jeremy Black puts it, wars were "'limited' in a very real sense – namely in the restricted ability of armed forces to carry out the grand strategic or political aims ordered by their rulers."[81] In sharp contrast, Napoléon could forge the multitude of national conscripts into "an articulated organism" composed of a hierarchy of units and divisions.[82] He could also order different divisions to take different routes and employ different tactics and yet make sure that the separate divisions would support one another. Napoléon further perfected various battlefield tactics, such as attack in independent columns, maneuver of the central position (dividing more numerous opposing forces and then defeating them separately), envelopment of weaker forces (pinning them down with part of the forces, and then cleaving past them and cutting their lines of supply with the rest), and surprise attacks by night.[83] As French troops could be trusted to forage for themselves without the support of cumbersome supply trains, Napoléon could move his armies so quickly as to strike "lightning war" against his enemies. Moreover, with a highly motivated army that would not disintegrate to search for booty the moment an advantage was seized, French commanders could pursue their enemies to achieve decisive victories. All these practices were common in Warring States China and are widely discussed in Chinese

---

[79] Cited in Skocpol 1979, 198.   [80] Ibid., 190.

[81] Black 1994, 67; also Parrott 1995, 243.

[82] Roberts 1995, 15. A division was composed of elements of all arms and could serve effectively both as a detached force and as part of a coordinated army. This method was developed shortly before the revolution and then put into effective use under Napoléon. Black 1994, 154.

[83] Black 1994, 173–174, 183.

military classics.[84] But they were revolutionary in the modern European world, which had followed self-weakening expedients for centuries. With overwhelming strength and innovative strategies and tactics, the French *levée en masse* easily outnumbered and outmaneuvered its targets.

Similarly to his French predecessors and ancient Chinese counterparts, Napoléon understood that military strength should be accompanied by the divide-and-conquer strategy. He was extraordinarily successful at turning enemies into allies and fighting enemies one at a time. Indeed, all continental great powers switched sides in the course of the Revolutionary and Napoleonic Wars.[85] Having seen Napoléon's spectacular victories, many of France's targets – as did Qin's targets – preferred to submit rather than waste their resources fighting futile wars. As Richard Rosecrance and Chih-Cheng Lo nicely put it:

> Napoleon, until 1813, always managed to recruit a major Continental ally to his side. Prussia was the initial favorite, and her ties with the French prevented the formation of an effective coalition against Napoleon up until 1806. After the French usurper was able to defeat both Austria and Russia at Austerlitz in 1805, however, he turned on his Prussian accomplice, and humiliated Berlin. He then occupied three fourths of Prussia and issued the 'Berlin Decrees' (1806) proclaiming French economic dominance over the European Continent. Not content with these gains, Napoleon pressed into Poland, encroaching upon Russia's sphere of influence. He defeated the tsar at the battle of Friedland, and then Russia sued for peace.... In all these proceedings, the essential feature is Napoleon's ability to isolate and divide his opponents.[86]

In several instances, Napoléon was even able to organize most of Europe for war against a single isolated foe – Britain in 1803 and 1807, Prussia in

---

[84] See Chapter Two. In particular, Warring States armies were regularly divided into several divisions. For example, "the campaign that culminated in Qi's defeat of Wei at Guiling in 353 BC entailed maneuvers by four distinct armies moving across much of modern Shanxi. The general war of 312 between the coalition of Qin, Wei, and Han against the forces of Chu and Qi involved simultaneous offensives on four separate fronts stretching across the loess highlands and the flood plain of the Yellow River. The great battle of Changping, though more geographically concentrated than the preceding campaigns, involved two armies deadlocked across a front that stretched for hundreds of *li*." Lewis 1999, 628–629.

[85] As Gulick vividly described it, "Austria, at war with France off and on between 1792 and 1809, became the ally of Napoleon and assisted his Russian campaign in 1812 – against her former Russian ally. Prussia, an enemy of France between 1792 and 1795 and again in 1806, began the same Russian campaign in 1812 as an ally of Napoleon, later to change sides again and fight the French as Austria did. Russia herself, an enemy of France in the second and third coalitions, became a French ally by the Treaty of Tilsit in 1807, later reversing herself again." Gulick 1955, 79.

[86] Rosecrance and Lo 1996, 492–493.

1806, Spain in 1808, Austria in 1809, Russia in 1812. Moreover, as with the situation in ancient China, France's divide-and-conquer strategy was much facilitated by the fact that its targets shared the same motivation for opportunistic expansion. Austria, Prussia, and Russia, in particular, were as worried about each other's intentions in Poland as they were about French ambitions. As Paul Kennedy states, "When the third and final partition did occur in 1795, it was all too evident that Poland had been a more effective ally to France in its death throes than as a living, functioning state."[87] Against this background of systemic aggression, "France could be said merely to have compensated herself for the earlier partitioning of Poland by the eastern monarchies."[88]

Combining overwhelming military strength and superior divide-and-conquer strategy, France was able to subdue large parts of Europe. At the height of its strength in 1810, the French empire under direct rule included all the areas on the left bank of the Rhine, central Italy, Corsica, the Illyrian Provinces, and most of the Low Countries. The "Greater Empire" subject to French control included the Confederation of the Rhine, the Kingdom of Italy, Switzerland, the Grand Duchy of Warsaw, and Spain. In addition, Napoleonic France had the alliance of the Austrian Empire, Prussia, Russia, Denmark, and Norway. Only Britain, Portugal, and Sweden opposed France. Even more notably, Napoléon succeeded where Charles V and Louis XIV had failed: at making conquests pay. The *levée en masse* overran neighboring countries so easily and so early that the burdens of maintaining this enormous force largely fell upon non-French populations. From losers, France would extract territorial concessions and crushing indemnities, confiscate their Crown properties and treasures, and take spoils from their armies and garrisons. From satellites and allies, France would extract contributions in money and troops. Italy, for example, had to remit to France about half of the taxes raised between 1805 and 1812. French regiments would also quarter on satellite states and require them to supply contingents.

With the capability to win decisive victories and to make war pay for war, France thus appeared to be leaping toward the coercive trajectory at long last. Nevertheless, the Napoleonic empire was heir to not only the French Revolution, but also the ancien regime. During the Anglo-French competition, Britain continued to raise tax revenues and cheap credits with relative ease and further introduced the unprecedented income tax in 1799. France, however, was unable to balance the budget except during

[87] Kennedy 1987, 123.   [88] Gulick 1955, 96.

the year of peace in 1802–1803. This was less because war making was draining France's ordinary revenues as in the old regime than because Revolutionary France inherited the crushing national debts which had ignited the revolution. The revolutionaries had tried to solve the debt crisis by nationalizing and selling church lands but failed. When France suspended its debt service in 1793 and annulled two-thirds of its debts in 1797, it ruined its creditworthiness and the fragile public credit system. When the empire-building project accelerated after 1803, Napoleon even subverted the independence of the treasury and resorted to financiers and contractors. Without fiscal health to support military strength, the Napoleonic empire was highly vulnerable to countervailing mechanisms that blocked attempts at domination.

"The beginning of the end was the campaign in Spain."[89] The Spanish rebelled after the French invasion in 1808. Rebellion in newly conquered territories was not at all unusual, whether in early modern Europe or in ancient China. With overwhelming military strength, rebellions could normally be crushed.[90] However, the Spanish hit upon a strategy tailored for fighting a superior power – guerrilla warfare.[91] Napoléon had overcome the loss-of-strength gradient largely by using local supplies to feed, clothe, and shelter his mass armies. But Spanish guerrillas were able to deny French regiments access to local supplies. For the first time in its empire-building project, France was forced to rely on supplies from home and to defend supply lines against raids. The guerrilla resistance managed to tie down about 300,000 French troops at times and more than a billion francs in various kinds of material supplies.[92] If the problem of

[89] Kaiser 1990, 249.

[90] In fact, guerrilla resistance alone was not sufficient to defeat the mighty Napoleonic empire. Spanish guerrillas fought along with British conventional forces. In Tyrol and Calabria, where guerrillas did not receive such outside support, the resistance movements failed. Beckett 2001, 9.

[91] The word "guerrilla," which literally means "little war," originates from the resistance of Spanish irregulars or *partidas* against France between 1808 and 1814. In general, "guerrilla groups operated in difficult terrain such as mountains or deserts. They possessed local knowledge denied to their opponents and, conceivably, had a degree of support among the populations who inhabited such remote and inaccessible regions. They were generally more mobile than their opponents and would undertake the kind of hit-and-run raids that would enable them to evade larger forces and so prolong their struggle." Beckett 2001, 2. Such tactics are evident in ancient China. As I discuss in Chapter Two, Wu practiced hit-and-run tactics to wear out the much stronger Chu in the late seventh century BC. Although Qin did not face guerrilla warfare in its wars of unification, the Qin empire faced guerrilla-type resistance as the imperial court attempted to conquer tribal groups in present-day Guangdong and Guangxi. Yang 1986, 455.

[92] Handel 1990, 100; Kennedy 1987, 134–135.

rising costs of expansion was not responsible for France's fiscal troubles earlier, it certainly began to aggravate the situation now.

As the Napoleonic empire was at the height of its strength, it would probably have been able to suppress the Spanish rebellion had it not opened another front. Although Napoléon had been exceptionally skillful at dividing and conquering his targets, he now put himself in the fatal situation of fighting two-front wars – and at two extreme ends of the stretched-out European continent. After Russia turned against France and readmitted British trade in December 1811, Napoléon launched a long-distance campaign against Russia in 1812. He mobilized a huge army of 600,000 men so as to guarantee a short and decisive victory. However, the Russians adopted a "scorched earth" tactic that had an effect similar to the Spanish guerrilla warfare's. Napoléon's troops entered an undefended Moscow on September 14, 1812, only to find that the whole city and the surrounding countryside had been burned. Denied access to local supplies, Napoléon was forced to retreat on October 19. Heavy snowstorms from November 4 on then "turned the retreat into a nightmare."[93] More than 300,000 troops died of disease, battle wounds, or famine or were taken prisoner. Meanwhile, the Spanish resistance made significant headway as Paris stopped the flow of French reinforcements to Spain.

The Russian debacle turned out to be the tipping point for Napoléon's fortune: Before this point, piling-on actions had allowed French strength to snowball; after this point, the same actions caused the empire to unravel quickly. France's bandwagons, which provided half of the 600,000 troops in the Russian campaign, began to realize that Napoléon was not invincible after all and so turned against France one after another. Prussia was the first to leave the French camp in December 1812 and then concluded a defense pact with Russia in March 1813. Austria joined the coalition in June 1813. Britain, whose efforts at forming an anti-French alliance had repeatedly failed, was delighted to facilitate this promising alliance. When conflicts broke out again in August 1813, Napoléon had to fight four great powers simultaneously for the first time in his military career. As France's defeat appeared more likely, other states also switched sides and jumped on the allies' bandwagon. Moreover, allied countries copied the French model of *levée en masse* and rapidly built up their military strength. At the same time, the prospect of likely defeat resulted in massive desertion among French troops and massive evasion among new draftees. At the battle of the Nations at Leipzig on October 16–19, 1813, Napoléon was

93 Black 1994, 187.

heavily outnumbered (195,000 to 365,000 by the time both sides were fully engaged).[94] The Napoleonic empire crumbled.

If the Russian setback reversed Napoléon's fortune, does it mean that Napoléon failed because he made the mistake of "overexpansion," as in most conventional accounts?[95] David Kaiser argues that the policy of using war to finance war "condemned Napoleon indefinitely to seek new prizes abroad. Each campaign was like another turn of the roulette wheel, which, if it did not bring him more good fortune, would start him down the road to bankruptcy."[96] However, we should not overlook that the ability to use war to finance war also helped to alleviate the mechanism of rising costs of expansion and should be considered a strength as well as a weakness. In addition, Randall Schweller suggests that "the Allied coalition . . . would never have come together . . . had Napoleon not attacked his own allies and neutrals."[97] This second view is factually accurate but misses a simple but critical aspect: Aspirants for universal domination rather than mere hegemony – whether Napoleonic France or Qin or Rome – inevitably had to attack bandwagons and neutrals. The question is not whether they should do so, but when they should do so and how they should design the grand strategy.

In light of Qin's experience, the more interesting question is why Napoleonic France was so vulnerable to the Spanish and Russian debacles. Qin also met with some serious setbacks on the road to domination. Qin's attempted conquest of Zhao in 260 BC was thwarted by Zhao's plot to sow discord between Qin's chief minister and commander in chief. A renewed effort to conquer Zhao in 259–257 BC was met by a balancing alliance and resulted in defeat and heavy casualties. Qin's attempt to conquer Wei in 247 BC also faced a balancing alliance and defeat. Even in the final war of unification against Zhao in 236–228 BC, Qin was effectively blocked by Zhao's defense for years and lost 100,000 men in one major battle. In the war to unify Chu in 226–223 BC, Qin's original army of 200,000 was defeated; not until Qin more than doubled its army strength and placed it under the command of the most experienced general did it eventually conquer Chu.

These setbacks clearly slowed Qin's drive for domination but were not nearly as fatal as the Spanish rebellion and Russian retreat for Napoleonic France. Qin could tolerate so many setbacks because it mobilized its own national resources to finance expansionist wars and used strategies and

---

[94] Ibid., 187–188.   [95] Vasquez 2003, 92; see also Rosecrance and Lo 1996.
[96] Kaiser 1990, 249.   [97] Schweller 1994, 92; see also Schroeder 1994b, 121; 2003.

stratagems to minimize the costs of war. Napoleonic France, however, failed to heed Machiavelli's advice that "auxiliaries" or allied troops could be "much more dangerous than mercenaries."[98] While Qin mobilized its own national resources and used bandwagons only to divide and conquer, France was heavily reliant on allies and satellites to contribute human and material resources. It is remarkable that while Qin mobilized only its nationals in the final wars of unification, France turned to allies for half of the 600,000 troops in the Russian campaign. Hence, Napoleonic France was critically vulnerable to defection by allies, whereas Qin was not. France's heavy reliance on allies for the wherewithal of war also created significant disincentives for the use of ruthless brutality. As Robert Jervis points out, if "today's adversary may be tomorrow's ally, crippling it would be foolish."[99] But the result was that Prussia, Russia, Austria, and other states could engage in rapid buildups after they turned against France. Disbanded Spanish troops could also launch a guerrilla war against French occupation. In sharp contrast, Qin, which did not need allies, slaughtered defeated armies en masse to prevent losing states from recovering rapidly. Moreover, while Qin had perfected the capacity for direct rule and could stamp out evasion and desertion, France was still experimenting with various administrative techniques. In addition, while Qin avoided long-distance campaigns and pursued a strategy of attacking nearby states and befriending faraway states, France engaged in long-distance campaigns and was thus vulnerable to the "scorched earth" tactic. Further, while Qin avoided two-front wars and even direct confrontations with targets' core forces, France plunged itself into the fatal situation of fighting on two fronts.

In short, European attempts at domination failed because they fell far short of the shrewd combination of comprehensive self-strengthening reforms, divide-and-conquer strategy, and Machiavellian stratagems and brutality. The old regimes of Spain and France were crippled by the mechanism of rising costs of expansion because they followed self-weakening expedients – use of expensive mercenaries, contraction of unsustainable loans, and sale of public offices. When Revolutionary and Napoleonic France embarked on self-strengthening reforms, it almost succeeded in rolling up the European continent. Nevertheless, even the

---

[98] *The Prince*, ch. 13, in Wooton 1994, 43. Machiavelli also thought that "of all the types of soldier, auxiliaries are the greatest liability." *Discourses*, bk. 2, ch. 19, in Wootton 1994, 183.

[99] Jervis 1997, 134.

self-strengthened France lived in the shadow of its own self-weakened past – Napoleonic France inherited such crushing national debts from the old regime that it failed to build *fuguo* (wealthy country) to support *qiangbing* (strong army). Moreover, European states did not employ Machiavellian or Qin-style stratagems against one another – not even Napoléon, who "avidly read and greatly admired" *The Prince*.[100] Although European rulers engaged in widespread subversion and assassinations[101] – as did ancient Chinese – they never engaged in mass killing of defeated troops. Unable to pursue domination on their own, European domination-seekers were heavily dependent on the assistance of allies. Hence, they made themselves vulnerable to the mechanism of the balance of power as well.

Was the Balance-of-Power Mechanism Stronger in Early Modern Europe?

Chapter One argues that the framework of competing logics requires the simultaneous examination of the relative weakness and strength of both the logic of domination and the logic of balancing. Chapter Two illustrates that coercive mechanisms were very strong and the balance-of-power mechanism was very weak in the ancient Chinese system. This chapter demonstrates that coercive mechanisms were significantly weaker in early modern Europe than in ancient China. To provide a more complete picture, it is necessary to analyze whether the balance-of power mechanism was nevertheless stronger in early modern Europe.

As the balance-of-power theory is Eurocentric, one would expect it to operate better in its home territory.[102] However, in early modern Europe as in ancient China, balancing alliances did not come about automatically; nor did they hold together easily after they were formed. Similarly to their counterparts in ancient China, European great powers generally shared the expansionist motive. As Jack Levy points out, the vast majority of peacetime alliances were offensive in that "the initiation of military action was explicitly called for in the treaty and not conditional upon an external military attack."[103] Jack Levy and William Thompson also observe that the size of the typical balancing coalition was only 2.7 great powers: considerably smaller than the average of four or five great

---

[100] Gulick 1955, 44.
[101] For assassination in early modern Europe, see Thomas 2000.
[102] This is another way to say that early modern Europe should provide a "most likely" case for the balance of power theory. On "most likely" cases, see Eckstein 1975.
[103] Levy 1981, 590.

powers available for balancing.[104] In addition, lesser states typically had to be bribed by substantial subsidies to join alliances; nevertheless, they shamelessly switched sides in the course of a war or accepted subsidies from both sides of the rivalry.

The first antihegemonic alliance at the onset of system formation, the League of Venice, already "showed all the fragility that was to mark every future combination of this kind."[105] At the height of Habsburg power in the Thirty Years' War, Sweden's Gustavus Adolphus could not build an anti-Habsburg coalition because most rulers were "intimidated by the relentless onslaughts of Tilly and Wallenstein."[106] In the age of Louis XIV, "social war" also failed because "[a]lmost every individual state in Europe would find it advantageous to make its own terms with the enemy and to hope for the best."[107] During the Revolutionary and Napoleonic Wars, great powers such as Prussia, Russia, and Austria not only did not balance against the rise of France, but also pursued their own territorial ambitions in Poland. Lesser states bandwagoned with France when Napoléon seemed invincible and joined the allied side only when it was winning.

If French bids for the mastery of Europe were repeatedly thwarted by England/Britain, is it correct to say that the European system was maintained because Britain played "the textbook example of the balancer"?[108] If "the balancer" is a powerful state that consistently "holds the balance" by "throwing its weight as the occasion required to the weaker and more threatened side to redress the equilibrium,"[109] then there was no balancer in either early modern Europe or ancient China.[110] In the wars against Louis XIV, Britain "balanced" against France for more or less the same reason that Zhao "balanced" against Qin in the face of attack in 262–257 BC. England originally took French subsidies in the Sun King's war against the Dutch Republic. England changed course only after the Dutch commander in chief, William of Orange, ascended to the English throne, thereby effectively changing England from an onlooker into a target of domination along with the Dutch Republic. If balancing is understood in terms of resistance to domination, then the Dutch Republic, which fought a lengthy war of independence against Habsburg Spain and two wars of resistance against Bourbon France, should deserve more credit

[104] Levy and Thompson 2002, 15, 18.   [105] Anderson 1998, 79.
[106] Downing 1992, 195–196.   [107] Schroeder 1994b, 135.
[108] Gulick 1955, 65.   [109] Kissinger 1994, 70.
[110] Waltz is correct to say that the "balance of power theory cannot incorporate the role of balancer." Waltz 1979, 164.

than England. Indeed, while all other European states including England switched sides during Louis's reign, the Dutch Republic was a rare exception that always fought against France. Nevertheless, as John Vasquez argues, the balance-of-power mechanism must mean more than just that states fight back when physically attacked.[111] After all, Qin's targets did engage in total mobilization to resist domination.

What of Britain's balancing against France in the Revolutionary and Napoleonic Wars? The assertion that Britain "balanced" against France means nothing more than the simple fact that Britain was France's cohegemon. Britain's efforts to forge anti-French coalitions were not much different from Qin's manipulation of an anti-Qi alliance in 284 BC. It is always in the self-interest of the cohegemon to prevent its equal from surpassing it. During the two-decade-long rivalry with France, Britain "took advantage of the situation every bit as fully as Napoléon and showed the same willingness to violate the rights of neutrals."[112] Britain seized many overseas colonies from France and French bandwagons, including its own longtime ally the Dutch Republic. As Paul Schroeder sarcastically states, the real British definition of the balance of power meant "a weakened France restrained by other Continental powers and barriers, giving Britain a free hand to intervene or not in European affairs as its interests required and freeing it from serious rivalry on the seas or overseas."[113]

In the limited sense that Napoleonic France had to confront a cohegemon which had both the motivation and the capability to thwart French ambitions, it is accurate to say that the balance of power was stronger in the modern European system than the ancient Chinese system. Britain would offer subsidies, munitions, and troops to states that fought France and provide leadership to help overcome the collective-action problem. France was thus in a much more difficult situation than Qin, which defeated its cohegemon, Qi, with the help of an anti-Qi alliance. However, it is noteworthy that Britain's generous offers found few takers when Napoleonic France seemed infallible. It is doubtful that the last coalition would have formed had Napoléon not put himself in the difficult situation of fighting multifront wars. Even when Napoléon's enemies eventually joined after the Spanish and Russian debacles, "internal troubles nearly visited disaster upon the coalition."[114] Austria, Prussia, and Russia continued to be mutually suspicious. A new war almost broke out over the disposal of Poland and Saxony.

---

[111] Vasquez 1997, 908.   [112] Kaiser 1990, 255.
[113] Schroeder 1992, 690.   [114] Gulick 1955, 149.

In addition to the continued existence of a co-hegemon, the early adoption of self-weakening expedients rather than self-strengthening reforms significantly facilitated the balance-of-power mechanism in early modern Europe. As even the most powerful European states had difficulty mobilizing ready cash to pay for mercenary armies and scoring decisive victories, they could not pursue opportunistic expansion on their own but needed allies. Whereas wars involving great powers were generally bilateral in ancient China, they became increasingly multilateral in early modern Europe.[115] The prevalence of coalitional warfare was conducive to system maintenance – even when many of the alliances were offensive rather than defensive, even when states joined coalitions late rather than early, and even when they were bandwagons rather than balancers. First, while the issue of military victory tended to be straightforward in ancient China, it often meant different things to different allies and became "profoundly ambiguous and divisive" in early modern Europe.[116] Second, while victors in ancient China could easily dictate territorial concessions from losers, those in early modern Europe were more likely to be inhibited by other participants, who "did not necessarily wish to make their allies too powerful by weakening rival powers excessively."[117] Overall, then, the balance-of-power mechanism was indeed stronger in early modern Europe than in ancient China. But this was the case because European domination-seekers were relatively weak in their pursuit of the logic of domination.

3.4 Initial and Environmental Conditions

This comparative historical analysis leads to another question: If international competition should compel self-strengthening reforms and self-strengthening reforms should maximize relative capabilities and minimize war costs, then why did the earliest hegemony-seeking rulers in Europe adopt self-weakening expedients? As a matter of fact, international

---

[115] Prior to the Thirty Years' War, most wars involved two great powers. From the early seventeenth century to the early nineteenth century, the number of warring great powers varied from one to six, with a median of four. Levy 1983, 146. Peace treaties often involved far more participants. For example, the Peace of Buda (1503), which settled the Venetian-Turkish War of 1499–1503, already included Turkey, Moldavia, Ragusa, Venice, the papacy, Bohemia-Hungary, Poland-Lithuania, Rhodes, Spain, Portugal, and England. The Treaty of Westphalia (1648) drew together 145 representatives from most parts of the European state system.

[116] Schroeder 1987, 288.   [117] Black 1994, 85.

competition did compel self-strengthening reforms in Europe. While this development occurred *belatedly* in the early modern period, it also once occurred *before* the onset of the era. During the Hundred Years' War, France was so severely beaten by England that Charles VI agreed to accept the English king as his heir before he died in 1422. But the Dauphin Charles did not relinquish his claim to the throne. To fight England, Charles VII established the first standing army in Europe, the Compagnies d'Ordonnance. He also imposed drastic increases in direct and indirect taxes. Though rudimentary, these were self-strengthening measures because they required the French court to improve its extractive capacity.[118] If France had carried forward these practices, European history would have been more like Chinese history.

However, Charles's policy package included other elements that were to divert Europe from the trajectory of domination. France had earlier adopted mercenary forces from England when its own feudal levies were outnumbered.[119] Charles created the standing cavalry because he already observed that unruly mercenaries plundered as ruthlessly as English troops. However, mercenaries did not disappear from the French military but continued to serve in the infantry. Equally important, Charles followed an earlier Capetian practice of selling public offices. When Charles VII's successors set their ambitions on Italy, it was to the latter measures that they turned. Rather than taking the harder course of building up administrative and extractive capacity, they followed the easier course of relying on intermediate resource holders such as military entrepreneurs and financiers. It is remarkable that Niccolò Machiavelli had identified the problem in the early sixteenth century. Machiavelli praised Charles VII's understanding that "it was essential to have one's own weapons."[120] He believed that "if the foundations laid down by Charles VII had been built upon," "the Kingdom of France would [have been] able to overcome any enemy."[121] Unfortunately, "King Louis abolished the infantry and began to recruit Swiss troops. It was this mistake, imitated by his successors, that was...the cause of the dangers faced by that kingdom. For...he destroyed his own infantry and made his own cavalry dependent on the

---

[118] Ertman argues that early state builders such as France tended to inherit patrimonial ruling methods from the medieval period. Ertman 1997, 26–27. This view is not false but glosses over the fact that France also had protobureaucratic methods at its disposal.

[119] English kings used mercenaries partly because they could not use national peasant militias on foreign soils.

[120] *The Prince*, ch. 13, in Wootton 1994, 44.   [121] *Ibid.*, in Wootton 1994, 45.

support of foreign troops."[122] From the Italian Wars onward, the most problematic practices of the late medieval period – the contracting of mercenary troops, the patrimonialization of public offices, and the dominance of financiers within the state – were increasingly elaborated and codified. Through international competition, moreover, France's self-weakening expedients were spread to other states, in particular France's prime rival, the United Habsburgs. As the Habsburg empire enjoyed additional contributions from various possessions and handsome treasures from the New World, there was even less incentive to carry out the difficult task of improving administrative-extractive capacity. Heavily dependent on non-Spanish resources for as much as 90 percent of its revenues, the Habsburg empire "waxed and waned with them."[123]

If self-strengthening reforms occurred in both Europe and China, why did self-weakening expedients exist in Europe but not in China? It is noteworthy that the practices of mercenary armies, venal offices, and sovereign loans involved commercialization and monetization of public functions. In Europe, trade and interdependence were as important as war and peace. As early as the medieval era, knight service was gradually commuted into *scutage* or money payment, which allowed rulers to substitute mercenary armies for feudal levies. The use of mercenaries, in turn, pushed up the costs of war so much that heavy borrowing became a usual recourse and bankruptcy a recurring threat in the midthirteenth century. During the Renaissance period, Italian bankers further developed elaborate credit instruments, including bills of exchange, demand notes, and deposit certificates, thus facilitating the contraction of increasingly larger loans. At the same time, the possibility of taxing dense trade flows provided security for loans and reduced the incentive to rationalize other taxes.

In ancient China, the existence of a multistate system also stimulated the expansion of international trade and the monetization of the economy.[124] What was different was the *relative timing* when trade expansion occurred. In Europe, trade began to expand from the eleventh century on. This early timing allowed the earliest domination-seeking rulers to rely on financiers. In ancient China, trade began to expand only after the onset of system formation. With a low level of monetization, the earliest hegemonic rivals had no easy recourse. The only way they could build larger armies and raise higher revenues was to extend military service and land

---

[122] *Ibid.*, in Wootton 1994, 44.   [123] North and Thomas 1973, 128.
[124] For a more detailed discussion of trade in ancient China, see Chapter Four.

tax ever deeper to the lower orders and ever wider to the hinterlands. Ancient China thus witnessed smooth transitions from feudal levies to national armies and then to universal conscription.

Different initial conditions set the two systems on two different trajectories; different environmental conditions further exacerbated the divergence over time. The ancient Chinese system was relatively enclosed, whereas the European system began to expand its reach to the rest of the world from the onset of system formation. The discovery of the New World generated a huge influx of bullion, which deepened the process of monetization and weakened the incentive for reforms. Moreover, European conflicts became increasingly global in scope, thus aggravating the mechanism of rising costs of expansion. In addition, overseas colonies provided outlets for territorial competition, thereby allowing international competition on the European continent to be far less zero-sum.[125] Colonies also provided outlets for Machiavellian stratagems, thus allowing Europeans to be ruthless against "uncivilized" populations but not against fellow Europeans. In comparison, not only did ancient China not have colonial outlets; the relatively compact size of the system and high population-to-land ratio further increased the payoffs from territorial conquest.

Thus, although the pressure of international competition propelled self-strengthening measures in both ancient China and early modern Europe, monetization of the economy and relative openness of the system diverted Europe from the self-strengthening path toward the self-weakening path. As the adoption of self-strengthening reforms versus self-weakening expedients fundamentally shaped relative capabilities and relative costs of war, this difference was able to trump the ongoing pressure toward convergence. Over time, the initial differences became increasingly magnified through path dependence. Although the pressure of war brought about another moment of near convergence in the Revolutionary era, the late timing in the adoption of self-strengthening reforms and the legacy of self-weakening expedients continued to derail the logic of domination in Europe.

3.5 Divergent Models of Self-Strengthening Reforms in Early Modern Europe

The early adoption of self-weakening expedients left another legacy: When European great powers eventually embarked on self-strengthening

---

[125] Dehio 1962; Gulick 1955, ch. 1; Herz 1959, ch. 4; Morgenthau 1973, ch. 14.

reforms, they developed different reform models. To solve the problem of runaway costs of war, Britain developed a fiscally based self-strengthening reform, the public credit system. In an international system in which war-making was essentially "a financial question,"[126] *fuguo* or economic strength could be directly translated into *qiangbing* or military capability. In comparison, the self-strengthening program of Revolutionary and Napoleonic France focused on innovative military organization, grand strategies, and battlefield tactics. As in ancient China, *qiangbing* could spill over to *fuguo* because the *levée en masse* helped to reduce the cost of war, improve fighting capability, and make conquest pay. But unlike Qin, Napoléonic France faced constant financial problems. France tried to copy British *fuguo* measures but failed. Thus, the hegemonic rivalry between Britain and France was also a competition between the British *fuguo*-oriented model and the French *qiangbing*-oriented model, rather than competition over the relative comprehensiveness of the same *fuguo qiangbing* model as in ancient China. Because the public credit system merely addressed the symptom of high war costs while universal military conscription cured the disease by eliminating expensive mercenaries altogether, one may argue that the *qiangbing* model was relatively more comprehensive than the *fuguo* model. Indeed, in the years when Napoléon seemed invincible, British economic wealth did not match French military might; nor could handsome subsidies lure allies away from the French side.

If European great powers had traditionally followed self-weakening expedients, how did Britain and France hit upon self-strengthening reforms? As discussed earlier, the British *fuguo* model originated with the Dutch. Sir George Downing had been ambassador to the Hague and had firsthand experience with the public credit system. Where did the Dutch model originate? Of course, the Dutch borrowed banking instruments from the Italians. But it is remarkable that Charles V, who resorted to dubious fiscal expedients and impeded the economy in Castile, played a critical role in establishing the public credit system in the Dutch possessions. Charles acquired the Netherlands indirectly from Burgundy through dynastic marriages. As his authority was more tenuous there than in Castile, he engaged in more bargaining than coercion in his efforts to seek new revenues. In 1515, Charles delegated the responsibility for debt collection and repayment from the Habsburg regent in Belgium to the Estates General, the uniform Dutch representative assembly, and empowered it to issue state-backed annuities secured on new taxes.[127] To improve administrative

---

[126] Hintze 1975b, 192.   [127] Hart 1993; Tracy 1990, 114–146.

efficiency, Charles also reduced the size of the government and appointed university-educated jurists. With the most efficient institutions of the time, the Netherlands reaped huge profits from trade expansion in the sixteenth century and quickly emerged as the shipper, exchanger, banker, and commodity dealer of Europe, taking over the functions of Italian city-states on a much larger scale. When the revolt occurred, the tiny but wealthy United Provinces managed to hold off mighty but bankrupt Habsburg Spain for decades and eventually won independence in 1648.[128] In the seventeenth century, the Dutch Republic not only defeated England and thwarted France, but also established a global trading empire. Nevertheless, the Holland regents were extremely mindful of state coercion and did not develop the state's bureaucratic capacity. Moreover, the country's small size meant that it could hold sway only when the sinew of war rested more with national wealth than with national population. When the age of universal conscription dawned, the Dutch Republic lost its independence to Napoleonic France.

Where did the powerful French model originate? Political scientists and Europeans often point to Enlightenment thoughts and Revolutionary ideas.[129] While indigenous ideas certainly played some role, transnational learning from the Prussian example should not be overlooked. Brandenburg-Prussia was a late developer less burdened by the self-weakening expedients of more established great powers. It thus developed a self-strengthening program which most closely resembled the ancient Chinese *fuguo qiangbing* model.[130] Similarly to Qin, which climbed from relative weakness to domination, the "little Brandenburg" that was severely exploited by great powers in the Thirty Years' War later became the mighty Prussia that prevailed over Austria in 1740. The first steps were taken by the Great Elector (1640–1688), who established a centralized hierarchy of salaried officials and avoided the venality of offices of Habsburg Spain and Bourbon France. Unlike Charles V of the United Habsburg, the Great Elector was able to integrate disjointed

---

[128] Spain essentially granted de facto recognition of Dutch independence in the Twelve Years' Truce of 1609. Spain formally recognized Dutch sovereignty in the Treaty of Münster in January 1648. This was a bilateral treaty and was not part of the Peace of Westphalia later in the same year.

[129] See, in particular, Avant 2000.

[130] It is often argued that late developers required direct state intervention while early developers could afford to rely on private initiatives. See Gerschenkron 1966. A comparative historical perspective suggests that the Prussian model of state-led development is the norm. Even the British model in fact involves state-led reforms.

possessions (which were obtained through dynastic marriages and the Peace of Westphalia) by a centralized governing structure. Equally important, Frederick William I (1713–1740) introduced national conscription in 1733. In the Kantonsystem, each company was assigned a canton as a fixed recruiting district. All adult male peasants were registered on a muster roll and were successively called up for military service. Nobles would serve as officers, free peasants as sergeants, and serfs as ordinary soldiers. With this conscription method, Prussia could more than double its army size, from forty thousand in 1710 to eighty-three thousand in 1740.

Generations of Prussian rulers built up not only *qiangbing* (military strength), but also *fuguo* (economic capability). Unlike French and Habsburg rulers, who relied on tax farmers, Prussian rulers appointed salaried officials to collect taxes and established a system of annual budgetary control. Moreover, the Great Elector undertook a land reform that bore some resemblance to the ancient Chinese experience. In 1684, he removed the administration of royal lands from the hands of the bailiffs and leased the lands to private farmers at fixed money rents. Frederick William I also used budget surpluses to buy new domain lands and used profits from these capital acquisitions to create a war chest to provide ready cash in time of war. Frederick the Great (1740–1786) further pursued mercantilist policies, including construction of infrastructures such as roads, bridges, and canals; promotion of nascent industries critical to military power; attraction of immigrants with needed skills; and establishment of a state academy to marshal the expertise of scientists in central planning. With a wide range of *fuguo* efforts, total revenues increased dramatically from 600,000 thaler to more than 1.6 million thaler during the reign of the Great Elector, and from 4.8 million thaler to 6.9 million thaler during the reign of Frederick William I.[131] A war chest of 8.7 million thaler allowed Frederick the Great to conquer Austria's Silesia in 1740.[132] With the administrative capacity to extract resources, military success generated further revenues. Silesia provided 3.2 million thaler per year during the war with Austria from 1740 to 1745 and continued to make handsome contributions to the war chest afterward.[133] As a result, the Prussian army could be further expanded to 137,000 men in 1756 and 200,000 in 1786.[134] Prussia moved on to acquire West Prussia from Poland in 1772.

---

[131] Ertman 1997, 248, 255.   [132] Prussia also obtained subsidies from great powers.
[133] Ertman 1997, 256.   [134] Ibid., 256–260.

Nevertheless, Prussia was soon eclipsed by France. Although Frederick the Great left a war chest of more than 50 million thaler when he died in 1786, the money was quickly used up in 1794, only two years into the Revolutionary Wars.[135] Prussia had to cede to France all territory on the west bank of the Rhine in that year, and all territory to the west of the Elbe in 1806. Thomas Ertman argues that the "realities of war" favored the British strategy of public credit and condemned the Prussian strategy of war financing by cash hoards and conquests.[136] This view overlooks that the Prussian model was a precursor to the French model and that the French model was a respectable contestant with the British model. Prussia's defeat by France is better attributable to, again, the use of mercenaries – the most self-weakening expedient. Prussia's Kantonsystem was not universal and involved only 7 percent of the population.[137] Prussia relied on mercenaries to fill the rest of its increasingly larger army. It was because Prussia adopted this European-style military expedient that its ancient-Chinese-style economic measures became inadequate in sustaining prolonged geopolitical competition. Nonetheless, the Kantonsystem laid the foundation for the *levée en masse*. When Prussia turned against Napoléon in 1813, it adopted universal conscription and quickly expanded its army size. Together with Britain, Russia, and Austria, which had also undergone self-strengthening reforms,[138] Prussia eventually emerged as a victorious power at the end of the Napoleonic Wars.

While France's administrative and military reforms were traceable to Prussia, the Prussian model should in turn be traced to Sweden, which occupied Germany during the Thirty Years' War.[139] Similarly to France's Charles VII, Gustav Vasa (1523–1560) found mercenaries unreliable. Interestingly, his solution was exactly what Niccolò Machiavelli

[135] Ibid., 261.

[136] Ibid., 263. Although Prussia did not introduce the public credit system, its direct and indirect taxes were modeled on the Dutch system. Ibid., 247.

[137] Downing 1992, 95.

[138] After the humiliating defeat by Prussia in 1740, Austria's Maria Theresa introduced military reforms by abolishing the system of military entrepreneurship and establishing meritocracy and central command.

[139] Another possible source was Hungary. Under Matyas Hunyadi (1458–1490), the Hungarian court replaced the quasi-private troops of the barons with the Black Army of some twenty-eight thousand men. To support this new army, Matyas levied new direct taxes and established a meritocratic bureaucracy of university-educated officials. After his death in 1490, however, the Hungarian Diet dismantled the new army and handed over government functions to local magnates. Ertman 1997, 31, 288.

advocated – the Roman model of a citizen army. Sweden introduced a cantonal system of national conscription and formed "the first truly national European army."[140] Moreover, as did the ancient Chinese model, the Swedish model rested on a "semifeudal military system" which exchanged land for military service.[141] Although Sweden became an independent state (from Finland) only in 1521, Gustavus Adolphus (1611–1632) commanded "perhaps the best fighting force in the world" a century later, defeating Tilly at Breitenfeld and Wallenstein at Lutzen in the 1630s.[142] However, Swedish rulers heavily relied on foreign mercenaries to supplement national conscripts. Of the 175,000 troops Gustavus Adolphus fielded in 1632, only 18 percent were Swedes.[143] He paid for war expenses mainly with foreign (French and Dutch) subsidies, tolls collected in occupied Baltic ports, and appropriations from Germany. As Sweden was neither wealthy nor populous, it could prevail over larger enemies only when those armies remained self-weakened. Charles XII's crushing defeat of the Russians at Narva in 1700 would be the last major Swedish victory. After the humiliation, Peter the Great adopted the canton system in 1705 and quickly raised more than 150,000 men in 1705–1709. Moreover, Peter supplemented the Swedish model with the Prussian model. The Swedes did not develop a centralized system of tax collection; however, Peter imposed heavy direct and indirect taxes and created a hierarchical bureaucracy to collect them. He further modernized and centralized the production of artillery. This self-strengthening program produced immediate results. In 1709, Peter took full revenge on Charles at Poltava.[144] Russia emerged as a first-rate power at the end of the Great Northern War (1700–1721).

If Prussia's Kantonsystem had a clear lineage in Europe, its centralized bureaucracy could have originated somewhere else. European rulers

---

[140] Roberts 1995, 16.

[141] Downing 1992, 203. The *indelningsverk* was formalized under Charles XI (1672–1697). Each soldier and officer was granted either a piece of land or a percentage of the revenue from one. The product was a network of yeoman militias of up to 100,000 troops. Downing 1992, 203.

[142] Kennedy 1987, 64–65.   [143] Downing 1992, 198.

[144] Sweden faced the same fatal blow that was to befall Napoleonic France later. The Swedish army relied on plundering local supplies in its long-distance campaigns. Peter the Great used his cavalry to conduct a scorched-earth policy by interdicting Swedish foragers. He aggravated Charles's supply problem by delaying decisive engagement. In 1709 Charles launched an attack on the Russian supply center at Poltava, where well-prepared and superior Russian forces crushed the Swedish army. Downing 1992, 207.

surely benefited from the rise of universities and the increasingly larger
corps of jurists. But Prussia's administrative practices of civil service examination, uniform taxation, and periodic censuses were unusual in Europe
and familiar in China.[145] After Europeans sailed to Asia, Jesuits took great
pains to learn about Chinese civilization. They were immensely impressed
by Chinese administration and wrote many tracts on the subject. A work
by Matteo Ricci, a pioneer of the Jesuit mission in China, appeared in five
European languages by 1648.[146] The new knowledge of China reached
Europe at precisely the time when progressive reformers were searching
for ways to address the problems of corruption and venality. Enlightenment thinkers "discovered to their astonishment" that Chinese thinkers
"had thought the same thoughts... and fought the same battles" more
than two thousand years earlier.[147] Chinese influence was particularly
strong in Prussia. The Great Elector was personally interested in books
on China and sponsored studies of China. In 1672, Samuel Pufendorf
published *De Jure Naturae et Gentium*, in which he contrasted European
methods of selecting men for office with the Chinese institution of civil service examination.[148] When Europe's first written civil service examination
was introduced in Berlin in 1693, Herrlee Creel believed that "the inspi-
ration came from China."[149] If the Prussian model was at least partially
borrowed from China, it is little wonder that it most closely resembled
the ancient Chinese model.

Prussia, Sweden, Russia, Britain, and Revolutionary and Napoleonic
France are often cited as quintessential examples of the "rise and fall of
the great powers" in international politics.[150] Although this phenomenon

[145] Blue 1999, 60–70. For the eastern origins of other Western practices, see Hobson 2004.
[146] Creel 1970a, 24. The Norman King Roger II (1093–1154) of Sicily had also sponsored a description of the entire world which mentioned China at length and with admiration. It may not be a sheer coincidence that Roger had already attempted to establish a protobureaucracy. Soon after, Thomas Brown, who had served in Roger's court, became one of the central officials in the English Exchequer under Henry's reign (1154–1189). Ibid., 12–15.
[147] Reichwein 1925, 77. Passmore even remarks that "European thought became Confu-cianized" in the seventeenth and eighteenth centuries. Passmore 1970, 160.
[148] Creel 1970a, 25–26.
[149] Creel 1970a, 24; also Elegant 1999, 68; Teng 1943. Similarly, British parliamentarians debated in 1853–1854 whether they should adopt such a "Chinese" scheme. Creel 1970a, 27. In China, objective criteria for selecting officials were developed in the late fourth century BC, the written civil service examination was introduced in the Han Dynasty in 165 BC.
[150] Kennedy 1987; also Olson 1982.

is usually attributed to uneven rates of economic growth,[151] it is better understood in terms of self-strengthening reforms. Until the Thirty Years' War, the system was so dominated by self-weakened states that there were few instances of either rise or fall. The Dutch Republic, which pioneered the public credit, and Sweden, which introduced the national army, were the only states that rose from the peripheral to the great-power status. These cases left their marks in history but were too isolated to make a difference to the overall pattern of international competition in their own time. When a significant cluster of states pursued self-strengthening reforms at the turn of the eighteenth century, Europe eventually witnessed the rise and decline of great powers. In the ancient Chinese system, in which states long pursued not only self-strengthening reforms but also Sunzian stratagems, the rise and fall of hegemons and great powers were far more dramatic. While all rounds of hegemonic competition in early modern Europe were initiated by France, the identities of domination-seekers were far more fluid in ancient China, including Chu, Qi, Jin, Wu, Wei, Qi, and then Qin. As we have seen, high variability in power growth rates makes a system more unstable and more vulnerable to system collapse.[152]

3.6 Comparing the Intensity of War

Overall, because ancient Chinese states pursued self-strengthening reforms early on while European states followed self-weakening expedients in the early centuries, international competition was far more intense in the ancient Chinese system than in the early modern European system. To complement the preceding historical analysis, the discussion that follows illustrates the intensity of international competition through some crude quantitative indicators: frequency of war, battle deaths, and unit deaths.[153] According to Jack Levy's data set, there were eighty-eight "wars involving great powers" in a period of 321 years (1495–1815) in early modern

---

[151] Gilpin 1981; Kennedy 1987.

[152] Computer simulation produces the same result. Cusack and Stoll 1990, 49, 112.

[153] These indicators are adopted from Levy 1983. I do not compare Levy's other indicators: duration of war and number of great powers involved. Duration is a fair indicator for the growing scale of war in ancient China, but it may indicate indecisiveness rather than severity in early modern Europe. Similarly, the number of participating great powers may reflect the scale of war but may also reflect the strength of the balance-of-power mechanism.

Europe.[154] That is to say, wars characterized by the participation of at least one great power on either side broke out every 3.65 years on average. The sixteenth and seventeenth centuries were "the most warlike" – nearly one war every three years – but there was a tendency for the frequency of war to decline in subsequent centuries.[155] Following Levy's criteria, my data set shows 256 "wars involving great powers" in a time span of 436 years (656–221 BC) in ancient China.[156] That is, such wars occurred every 1.7 years on average, more than twice as frequently as in early modern Europe.[157] In the period 356–221 BC during which Qin ascended to domination, "wars involving great powers" occurred even more frequent, at a rate of once every 1.42 years. As Warring States in ancient China developed the capacity to engage in near-total mobilization for war, they were literally war machines. International relations scholars argue that "[w]ar would be much more frequent if they were less...costly."[158] It is then not surprising that a system of relatively affordable national armies was more warlike than a system of prohibitively expensive mercenary troops.[159] Moreover, if contiguous neighbors are generally more likely to

---

[154] Levy 1983, 135. Both beginning and ending years are counted. The frequency of wars involving great powers is sensitive to the number of great powers in a system, which, in turn, is endogenous to the decisiveness of wars. As argued previously, the decisiveness of war is critically shaped by the adoption of self-strengthening reforms and the use of strategies and stratagems. Great powers in early modern Europe include France (1495–1815), Austrian Habsburgs/Austria/Austria-Hungary (1495–1519; 1556–1815), Spain (1495–1519; 1556–1808), United Habsburgs (1519–1556), England/Great Britain (1495–1815), the Netherlands (1609–1713), Sweden (1617–1721), Russia (1721–1815), and Prussia/Germany (1740–1815). See Levy 1983, ch. 2.

[155] Levy 1983, 140, 135.

[156] The list of great powers in ancient China was originally compiled on the basis of Levy's operational criteria. Such great powers include Qi (659–284 BC), Chu (659–278 BC), Qin (632–221 BC), Jin (632–453 BC), Wu (584–475 BC), Yue (482–335 BC), Wei (408–293 BC), Han (404–293 BC), Zhao (404–260 BC), and Yan (284–279 BC). See Appendixes II and III.

[157] Kiser and Cai similarly argue that warfare in ancient China was more severe than in other historical systems, thus accounting for the higher level of bureaucratization in Qin China. Kiser and Cai 2003, 519–525. While their argument is plausible, their data set is not credible because they do not follow standard procedures in international relations.

[158] Jervis 1978, 176; see also Cusack and Stoll 1990, 49, 110, 166; van Evera 1999, 15, 30.

[159] The smooth transition from feudal levies to national armies probably allowed the feudal practice of soldiers' supplying their own food and clothing to persist in the Warring States period. The *Shang jun shu* suggests that each peasant household with a land grant could afford to participate in one war per year. See Yang 1986, 182, 185. An unearthed letter shows that a Qin soldier fighting a war of unification asked his mother to send money so that he could buy clothes. Yang 1986, 131. While there is no further concrete evidence for this practice in the Warring States period, subsequent dynasties did follow more or

fight than distant neighbors,[160] then the more centralized distribution of great powers in the ancient Chinese system probably facilitated a higher frequency of war. (See the maps in Chapter Two.)

It is far more difficult to compare battle deaths than war frequency across early modern Europe and ancient China. While data on the beginnings and ends of wars are generally available, data on casualties in both systems are quite scattered and typically involve rough estimates rather than actual figures. Mark Lewis cautions that ancient Chinese data reflect not absolute figures but "orders of magnitude."[161] The quality of European data is not much better. Pitirim Sorokin, one of Jack Levy's sources, emphasizes that "the data for most of the wars of the period before the seventeenth century are estimates and therefore inaccurate."[162] Moreover, while Jack Levy's data set on early modern Europe reports *total* battle deaths of *all* participating great powers in *aggregated* wars, Chinese materials generally contain only the battle deaths of Qin's targets and only in major battles. Hence, the best one can do is to establish trends over time.

According to Levy, battle deaths before the Thirty Years' War were limited to a few thousands or at the most a few tens of thousands. The figures climbed up to 1,151,000 in the Spanish-French portion of the Thirty Years' War (1635–1648), 1,251,000 in the War of the Spanish Succession (1701–1713), 992,000 in the Seven Years' War (1755–1763), 663,000 in the French Revolutionary Wars (1792–1802), and 1,869,000 in the

---

less the same policy. European states, on the other hand, had to supply mercenary troops as well as pay them wages. During the later seventeenth century, for example, "a typical army of 60,000 men, with its 40,000 horses, consumed almost a million pounds of food per day.... [That was] the equivalent of the daily wages of about 90,000 ordinary laborers." Tilly 1992 [1990], 81. Thus, if ancient Chinese states did not have to pay wages or provide food and clothing to national conscripts, then the difference in the relative costs of war between the two systems would be even more considerable.

[160] Bau 1986, 136–138; Jones, Bremer, and Singer 1996.

[161] Lewis 1999, 626. Even the availability of modern, scientific counting techniques does not always produce absolute figures. For instance, politicians in Hong Kong have bitter debates over the number of demonstrators on July 1, 2004. The estimates range from 200,000 to 530,000.

[162] Sorokin 1962, 274. Sorokin's estimates are in fact quite inflated. As he states, "For each war the total strength of the army means the typical size of the army multiplied by the number of years of a given war," and "the total number of the casualties in a given war means the typical per cent of the casualty in regard to the strength of the army multiplied by the number of years during which the war lasted." He acknowledges that this method "presume[s] that for every additional year of the war duration the total typical size of the army is renewed." Sorokin 1962, 184–285. Levy does not change this method of generating estimates. Levy 1983, 85.

Napoleonic Wars (1803–1815).[163] As the Thirty Years' War established a high baseline, Levy concludes that "in general there [was] no significant increase in the total losses of life from wars involving great powers" and that the average number of battle deaths in each war doubled only "every 110 years or so."[164] The opposite trend occurred in ancient China. In the Spring and Autumn period, the scale of war was quite confined and battle deaths were limited to several thousands. Early hegemonic rivals typically attacked the lesser states that were sandwiched between them and largely avoided direct confrontations. Qi and Chu never directly fought each other in their brief hegemonic competition in the midseventh century BC. Jin and Chu clashed only three times (in 632 BC, 597 BC, and 575 BC) in their prolonged competition from 632 to 546 BC. However, with the transition from elite-based chariot warfare in the Spring and Autumn period to peasant-based infantry warfare in the Warring States period, the scale of war surged and battle deaths climbed to the tens of thousands.[165] In the third century BC, the system further witnessed a "shift from wars seeking advantage in a balance of power to the campaigns of all-out conquest launched by Qin."[166] As Qin pursued the policy of annihilating the fighting capabilities of other states so as to prevent them from recovering, wars were increasingly marked by "unlimited carnage and brutality."[167] Overall, classical texts record more than 1.5 million deaths among Qin's targets in major battles between 356 and 236 BC.[168] During

---

[163] Levy 1983, 88–91.

[164] Ibid., 135, 292. Note that Levy's data refer to the whole span of the modern period rather than the early modern period.

[165] While "armies never exceeded 100,000 during the first centuries of the Warring States period and were generally much smaller," they witnessed significant expansion after 356 BC. Lewis 1999, 627.

[166] Lewis 1999, 627–628.   [167] Sawyer 1994, 286.

[168] Rough estimates of battle death figures include the following: 7,000 Wei soldiers in 354 BC; 45,000 Wei soldiers in 330 BC; 82,000 allied troops of Han, Wei, and Zhao in 317 BC; 10,000 Han soldiers in 314 BC; 80,000 Chu soldiers in 312 BC; 60,000 Han soldiers in 307 BC; 20,000 Chu soldiers in 300 BC; 20,000 Chu soldiers in 298 BC; 240,000 Han and Wei soldiers in 293 BC; several hundreds of thousands of Chu soldiers and civilians in 279 BC; 40,000 Han soldiers in 275 BC; 40,000 Wei soldiers in 274 BC; 150,000 Wei and Zhao soldiers in 273 BC; 50,000 Han soldiers in 264 BC; 450,000 Zhao soldiers in 260 BC; 20,000 Chu and Wei soldiers in 257 BC; 40,000 Han soldiers in 256 BC; 90,000 Zhao soldiers in 256 BC; 30,000 Han soldiers in 245 BC; and 30,000 Wei soldiers in 244 BC. These battle death figures, which served as the basis for military rewards, are likely to be "biased upward." Lewis 1999, 626. The most controversial figure is the burying alive of 400,000 Zhao soldiers in Changping in 260 BC. Archaeological evidence indicates that a great battle was fought on the site, but there is no evidence for a massive burial of 400,000 men. However, Hsu thinks that the number is "not necessarily

the final wars of unification from 236 BC to 221 BC, the only available figure is 100,000 Zhao deaths in 234 BC. But it is certain that Qin killed many
adult males of vanquished states so as to minimize the potential for rebellion.[169] As the total population in the Warring States period was roughly
20 million[170] while the French population alone at the time of the revolution was 25 million, ancient Chinese figures are very high in per capita
terms.

The sharpest contrast between the two systems lies in the deaths of
sovereign territorial states. Kenneth Waltz argues that international competition is like the market: States that fail at self-help should fall by the
wayside.[171] Many scholars of international relations point out that this
analogy is a poor match with the reality. Even Waltz qualifies his own
argument by saying that "[t]he death rate among states is remarkably
low. Few states die; many firms do."[172] However, the market metaphor is
a very accurate characterization of the ancient Chinese system. The very
first line in the *Sunzi bingfa* reads: "Warfare is the greatest affair of state,
the basis of life and death, the Way to survival or extinction."[173] As great
powers were able to win wars and make conquest pay, survival was precarious for the less fit. It was fair game for winners to win territory and
losers to lose territory. As Alexander Wendt acknowledges, the Hobbesian state of war is "a world in which states do not recognize rights to
territory or existence."[174] A dialogue in the *Zuo zhuan* nicely illustrates
this point: "Territory is defined by battle. It belongs to one state at one
time, to another state at another time.... Where is the constancy?"[175]
Not surprisingly, the number of political units was reduced from about
170 in 770 BC to about 20 in the midfifth century BC.[176] In the early
Spring and Autumn period, death was inflicted on only the smallest and
weakest entities. There was a lingering rule that while great powers could

---

incredible" and Gao finds "no basis to reject it." Gao 1995, 435; Hsu 1965a, 67. Sawyer
believes that Warring States battle death figures may be "less inaccurate than thought"
because "states of the period were certainly capable of mobilizing a very high percentage
of their male population, particularly when threatened with extinction." Sawyer 1998,
559, fn. 38. Lewis concurs that ancient Chinese figures "present a consistent picture of
an expanding scale of military actions that fits well with what we know of the evolving
institutions and practices of the period" and are "not wholly out of line with what we
know of the size of armies that primarily live off the land." Lewis 1999, 626, 628.
[169] Gao 1995, 437–438; Yang 1986, 189–190.   [170] Yang 1986, 112, 484; Yang 1996, 54.
[171] Waltz 1979, 89–91, 93–94, 98; also Gourevitch 1978, 896.   [172] Waltz 1979, 95.
[173] *Sunzi bingfa*, ch. 1.   [174] Wendt 1992, 410.
[175] *Zuo zhuan*, ch. Duke Zhao first year, trans. Hsu 1999, 569.
[176] Mu and Wu 1992, vol. 2, 23–31, 132–133; Sanjun daxue 1976, 106–108.

annihilate small and isolated states, they should demand only allegiance from medium states and exercise limited aims against other great powers. It certainly helped that ambitious rulers could also expand their territorial reach by cultivating wastelands in uncharted hinterlands. When easy prey and buffer zones gradually disappeared, various great powers began to encroach on medium-sized states. From the late fourth century BC on, great powers even engaged in mutual aggression.[177] During the wars of unification from 236 to 221 BC, of course, all other states except the unifier fell by the wayside.

Ancient Chinese history calls for a reconsideration of European history. Even in Europe, territorial sovereignty did not always have the present-day normative conception of mutual respect for territorial integrity.[178] It is true that many small and weak states survived. But this was because great powers lacked adequate capabilities, not because they exercised normative restraints. In the era of self-weakened states, even the most powerful domination-seekers had difficulty mobilizing resources for war and consolidating conquered territories. As a result, "the political frontiers of western Europe in the early seventeenth century were strikingly similar to those of a hundred years earlier."[179] Indeed, the system witnessed not just few deaths, but even the *birth* of the Dutch Republic, which immediately became the world's prime commercial and maritime power. This scenario changed from the late seventeenth century on, when Prussia, Russia, Austria, and even France successively embarked on self-strengthening reforms. In a system of self-strengthened states, survival was reserved only for the fittest. In the so-called age of reason, territorial sovereignty was understood in terms of the right of war, "as a doctrine granting state leaders the right to do whatever was necessary to ensure the territorial viability of their domains, including launching an attack on a neighboring state."[180] Such an anarchical conception of sovereignty legitimized any territorial acquisition. The formalization of boundaries further provided a "legal concept ... through which the expansion and contraction of power in the form of territory could be measured."[181] Although European statesmen frequently spoke of preserving the independence of states and

---

[177] As early as 506 BC, Wu had already made the first attempt at conquering another great power, Chu. Wu failed to conquer Chu and was itself conquered by Yue a few decades later, in 473 BC.

[178] The territorial sovereignty norm is "the proscription that force should not be used to alter interstate boundaries." Zacher 2001, 215. For sovereignty as a historical variable in modern Europe, see Hui 2003a.

[179] Anderson 1998, 203.   [180] Murphy 1996, 94.   [181] Coplin 1968, 21.

restoring the balance of power, they referred only to great powers.[182] In such circumstances, the Prussian invasion of Silesia in 1740 quickly set in motion a series of territorial wars which "fundamentally recast the political geography of the region."[183] Although "[m]ost of the literate Europe was appalled at the successive carvings up of Poland"[184] – just as Warring States in ancient China were outraged by Qi's conquest of Song in 287 BC[185] – great powers did not restore Poland's independence at the end of the Napoleonic Wars.

Given this phenomenon of *systemic* conquests from the mideighteenth century on, it is surprising that Europeanists argue that the survival of weaker states was rarely at stake in Europe.[186] Andreas Osiander, in particular, argues that before the French Revolution not one European entity was destroyed simply because it was unable to defend itself.[187] It is important to keep in mind that history is always written by winners about winners; losers have left so few traces in historical records that the very issue of their existence is buried. As Brian Downing wryly remarks, "The histories, or lack thereof, of Livonia, Novgorod, and Burgundy" attest to the existence of military conquests in Europe.[188] While the number of

---

[182] Levy 2003, 48, fn. 11; Zacher 2001, 236.   [183] Murphy 1996, 93.

[184] Holsti 1995, 48. Note that Poland tried self-strengthening reforms but failed. Kings Sigismund the Old (1506–1548) and his son, Sigismund Augustus (1548–1572), made repeated attempts at building a modern army. As in other countries, reformist rulers faced fierce resistance from the entrenched nobility. Unlike Brandenburg-Prussia, which began as a small principality and fell prey to territorial encroachment in the Thirty Years' War, Poland began as a much stronger and resourceful power and so the ruling class grew complacent. Moreover, the legendary relief of Vienna in 1683 fostered the illusion that its small feudal levies "could still more than hold their own against the modern armies of the region" and thus further delayed military reforms. Downing 1992, 151. In addition, unlike that in England, where the parliament was increasingly infiltrated by yeomen and the rising commercial class, the Polish estate was solely occupied by the traditional, landed nobility. Furthermore, unlike in France, there was no revolution to sweep away such feudal vestiges. The consequence was disastrous. Poland ceded East Prussia to Brandenburg in 1660. Poland proved unable to defend itself in the Great Northern War (1700–1721). After the Treaty of Warsaw, Poland became Russia's protectorate. Poland was successively carved up by Prussia, Russia, and Austria in 1772–1773, 1793, and 1795.

[185] According to Brooks and Brooks's interpretation, the *Analects* ch. 16 first records "an impending outrage" and then "an accomplished outrage" about the conquest. Brooks and Brooks 1997, 29.

[186] For a study of the deaths of modern states, see Fazal 2001.   [187] Osiander 2001, 278.

[188] Downing 1992, 82. Similarly, although there were supposed to be about 170 units in the early Spring and Autumn period, *Chunqiu* records only about 30 relatively active states. WSW email communication, July 17, 2002. For the rest, we know nothing more than their names – and they typically appear as targets of conquests.

consequential states did not fluctuate much over time, the total number of political units was reduced from five hundred in 1500 to twenty-five in 1900.[189] Moreover, survival is not just the flip side of death: If we take survival as "the long-term continuation of states as sovereign entities in more or less the same geographical location and shape,"[190] many lesser states which had their boundaries redrawn again and again can only be said to maintain partial survival.

On the whole, it is fair to say that survival for weaker states was far less problematic in early modern Europe than in ancient China. The early modern European system was populated by self-weakened states for so long that wars were indecisive and conquest was difficult. Even the puny but wealthy Italian city-states could survive for most of the early modern period. The ancient Chinese system, by contrast, was populated by domination-seeking states which relentlessly pursued self-strengthening reforms, divide-and-conquer strategies, and Sunzian stratagems. This system thus witnessed recurrent warfare, frequent territorial transfers, and even deaths of great powers. As such, the ancient Chinese system better resembled the Hobbesian state of war in that international-political life was genuinely nasty, brutish, and short.[191] As Qin faced an increasingly Hobbesian world while Napoleonic France faced a less-than-Hobbesian world, it is not surprising that the former had a much better chance at becoming the universal Leviathan.

3.7 Was the Ancient Chinese System More Hobbesian and Machiavellian Than the Early Modern European System?

Is it too counterintuitive to argue that the ancient Chinese system was more Hobbesian and more Machiavellian than the early modern European system? Constructivists, cultural relativists, and Chinese alike may find the current analysis puzzling. Chen Jian, for example, proclaims that "[t]erritorial expansionism or imperialism as known in the West was never an active part of Chinese civilization."[192] Roland Bleiker similarly argues that "a Confucian-oriented foreign policy is less likely to resort to violent

---

[189] Tilly 1975, 15.   [190] Jackson 1990, 179.
[191] It may be argued that a unified China "added substantially to the peace of mankind" or "contributed more to human welfare than a multiplicity of political units." Loewe 1999, 1031–1032. It is true that there were no more interstate wars and no more battle deaths properly defined. However, it should not be overlooked that generations of imperial rulers practiced torture and killing on massive scales in order to maintain universal rule.
[192] Chen 1993, 194.

means" because it seeks to establish influence "not through wars, but via nonviolent and persuasive methods such as education and indoctrination."[193] For those who believe that "the Chinese people are a uniquely peace-loving people," even *Sunzi bingfa*'s dictum of subduing the enemy without fighting – a coercive strategy tailored to overcome the logic of balancing – somehow becomes proof for the "pacifist bias" in China's military tradition.[194]

True, the Chinese tradition can claim the Confucian-Mencian norm, which "assumes essentially that conflict is aberrant.... When force is used, it should be applied defensively, minimally, only under unavoidable conditions, and then only in the name of the righteous tradition of a moral-political order."[195] Among Confucian thinkers, Mencius was "the most forthright pacifist."[196] The *Mencius* argues that *renzheng* or benevolent rule was the key to hegemony because a state with good government will simultaneously secure its own strength and enjoy the sympathy of populations in other states.[197] In addition to Confucians and Mencians, the Mohists treated war as an unnecessary evil; they developed the concept of justified war and engaged in the art of defensive warfare for cities under siege.[198] These norms most likely originated from the elaborate system of *li* or rites codified in Western Zhou. In Zhou feudalism, honor dictated that one should not attack another *guo* of the same ancestral lineage, launch a surprise campaign, attack another state whose ruler recently died, take advantage of another state's internal power struggle except to help install the legitimate heir, employ a former official from the enemy camp to seek unfair advantage, injure or insult the ruler of the enemy state in combat, harm convoys sent from the enemy camp, kill prisoners of war, or cause casualties to civilians of the enemy state.[199]

If such extensive norms about the proper conduct of war and diplomacy had been regularly followed, Chinese history would have been very different. China's classical texts produced in this era are testimonies against the

---

[193] Bleiker 2001, 183.   [194] Johnston 1998, 7–8; also Johnston 1995, ch. 1.

[195] Johnston 1995, 249.   [196] Lewis 1990, 129.

[197] *Mencius* 1A5–6; see Brooks and Brooks 2002, 250, 260. However, Brooks and Brooks also observe that subsequent passages in 1B13–14 argue that small states, no matter how virtuous, have little hope of military success or even survival. Brooks and Brooks, WSWG communication, February 10, 2004.

[198] *Mozi* 50–71, discussed in Brooks and Brooks 1997, 22. For the European concept of just war, see Waltzer 1977.

[199] *Zuo chuan*, cited in Chen 1941, 641–642; Creel 1970a, 322; Hong 1975, 58–63, 266–276; Hsu 1965a, 70–71; Kierman 1974, 30; Lewis 1990, 38–39; Sawyer 1993, 7–9; 1994, 52; Shaughnessy 1996, 179.

"verbiage about China's pacific heritage."[200] Various military classics take "a *parabellum* or hard *realpolitik* view of security" and "accept that warfare and conflict are relatively constant features of interstate affairs, that conflict with an enemy tends towards zero-sum stakes, and consequently that violence is a highly efficacious means for dealing with conflict."[201] In such a brutish world, international politics was "a match of fraud and deceit"[202] in which "only the foolish and soon-to-be-defeated were burdened by the old code of ethics."[203] The *Zhanguo ce* offers "a vivid portrait of the ruthless amorality...that characterized the...interstate relations of the period in general."[204] Qin, in particular, could not have achieved domination had it not blatantly violated shared expectations.

For scholars who are aware of Sunzian stratagems in the ancient Chinese era, there is the opposite tendency to think that the European system is exceptionally normative. Kalevi Holsti, for instance, argues that Europe was a "society of states" because "European sovereigns more or less adhered to fundamental norms that provided some semblance of order and even security."[205] In contrast, ancient China was a "system of states" in which "insecure polities warred incessantly against each other and made conquest (and thereby obliteration) of neighboring states their ultimate political goal."[206] Holsti adds that treaties were generally binding in modern Europe but were merely "temporary stratagems" in ancient China.[207] It is true that there were extensive international treaties that formally codified norms about the conduct of war and diplomacy in Europe. But in early modern Europe as in ancient China, rules that interfered with *raison d'état* were readily discarded. Machiavelli advocated fraud and deceit because he already witnessed "how treaties and promises have been rendered null and void by the dishonesty of rulers."[208] For instance, Francis I accepted an unfavorable treaty while under Charles V's captivity but quickly renounced it as soon as he was released. Louis XIV later ushered "an age of treachery" with little regard for tradition, religion,

---

[200] Sawyer 1998, 111.

[201] Johnston 1995, 61. Johnston also observes that the seven military classics contain "at least 70 verbal expressions that describe offensive, invasive, and destructive actions: these include terms such as 'attack,' 'invade,' 'campaign against,' 'punish,' 'penetrate,' 'execute,' 'control,' 'threaten,' 'destroy,' 'suppress,' and 'dismember,' among others. There are also at least 15 terms used to describe legitimate outcomes of these actions against the enemy including the 'extermination,' 'execution,' 'killing,' and 'destruction' of the adversary'." Johnston 1995, 144–145.

[202] Lewis 1990, 124.   [203] Sawyer 1994, 52.   [204] Lewis 1999, 591.

[205] Holsti 1999, 284.   [206] Ibid.   [207] Holsti 1995, 47.

[208] *The Prince*, ch. 18, in Wootton 1994, 54.

or loyalty.[209] The self-strengthened Prussia and Russia further pursued a predatory foreign policy that made "a mockery of the conventions and constrictions of European statecraft."[210] Frederick the Great, in particular, disregarded the formalities of war declaration by attacking Austria at the death of Emperor Charles VI in 1740. Even the seemingly supreme norm about legitimate dynastic rights was either hypocritically exploited as an excuse for various wars of succession or conveniently ignored by self-strengthened states.[211] Ultimately, it was the legacy of self-weakening expedients rather than respect for international norms that tempered both Hobbesian competition and Machiavellian stratagems in early modern Europe. Europeans were also saved by the availability of overseas colonies where no normative standards applied and enemies could be wiped out completely.

3.8 "Alternative" Explanations

This chapter has so far argued that the relative weakness or strength of the logic of domination is the key to understanding the failure of domination in early modern Europe and its success in ancient China. There is an alternative view that the divergent outcomes in the two systems can be easily explained by the relative ease of conquest. That is to say, conquest was simply harder in early modern Europe and easier in ancient China. There are two variants of this argument. The first one says that the offense-defense balance in geography and technology favored universal domination in China but system maintenance in Europe. Chapter two subsumes the offense-defense balance under the mechanism of rising costs of expansion and discusses its configuration in ancient China. To complete the comparison, this section considers the importance of geography and technology in Europe. It also addresses the second variant which presumes that Europe was culturally more heterogeneous than ancient China and was thus less conducive to domination.

Offense-Defense Balance and Ease of Conquest
Stephen van Evera argues that the theory of offense-defense balance offers "a master-key to the cause of international conflict" and is more

---

[209] Kaiser 1990, 170, 198.   [210] Ingrao 1994, 695.

[211] As Krasner expresses it, various international norms should be characterized as "organized hypocrisy." Krasner 1999.

"elegant" and "parsimonious" than other explanations.[212] He believes that universal domination succeeded in ancient China simply because the offense was dominant, whereas all attempts at domination failed in Europe because the defense was dominant.[213] Van Evera follows a long tradition of scholars who hold the view that "[o]ffenses produce war and/or empire; defenses support independence and peace."[214] Chapter Two argues that there were no offensive advantages in ancient China – whether at the systemic or dyadic level, whether in geography or technology. What of early modern Europe? Was Napoleonic France condemned to failure by defensive advantages?

According to van Evera, "The geography of Western Europe, with its mountain ranges and ocean moats, is less favorable to conquest."[215] Eric Jones lists "mountain chains like the Alps and the Pyrenées and the chain between Norway and Sweden, the riverine marshes protecting the northern Netherlands, and the sea around peninsular Denmark and around Britain and Sweden and Norway."[216] Paul Kennedy concurs that Europe's "fractured" landscape "made difficult the establishment of unified control, even by a powerful and determined warlord."[217] He adds that France's geographical location was particularly unfavorable to domination because "in each direction she was hemmed in."[218] This view, though factually accurate, overlooks Qin's experience that geographic disadvantages could be overcome and geographical advantages could be seized. Even in Europe, various natural barriers blocked only the self-weakened old regimes of Bourbon France and Habsburg Spain, not the self-strengthened Napoleonic France.

This does not mean that geography is completely irrelevant. It is consequential that the ancient Chinese system was smaller in size and more centralized in the distribution of states, while the European system was more expansive and dispersed.[219] Thus, Napoleonic France faced the tyranny of distance in the Russian campaign. While Napoléon could have alleviated the problem by Qin's strategy of piecemeal encroachment, the distance problem was more serious for France than for Qin. The distance between Paris and Moscow was almost three times that between Qin's Xianyang and Qi's Linzi. Further compounding the problem, the European system

---

[212] Van Evera 1998, 196–197; 1999, 178. [213] Van Evera 1998, 36–37; 1999, 179–182.
[214] Quester 1977, 208. [215] Van Evera 1998, 19. [216] Jones 1988, 106–107.
[217] Kennedy 1987, 17. [218] Ibid., 89.
[219] The ancient Chinese system was also smaller than other historical systems. Kiser and Cai 2003, 529.

was sea-bound while the ancient Chinese system was largely land-bound. Although the southern states of Wu, Chu, and Yue developed warships to fight on the Yangtze River, naval warfare did not reach the scale of land warfare in ancient China. Because a navy entailed heavier capital investments than an army and yet the higher costs could not be billeted on occupied populations, naval warfare significantly advantaged wealthy states such as the Dutch Republic and Britain. At the same time, the coexistence of sea and land warfare meant that domination of Europe required mastery on both fronts. The Revolutionary and Napoleonic Wars thus witnessed a novel kind of competition unseen in the ancient Chinese system: While Britain dominated naval warfare but could do little about the French *levée en masse*, France dominated land warfare on the continent but could not subdue Britain across the Channel.

The offense-defense balance also involves the military sphere. As argued in Chapter Two, there were no inherent offensive advantages in ancient China. Were there some inherent defensive advantages in early modern Europe? In a review of the literature on the military offense-defense balance in Europe, Jack Levy concludes that

the period from 1450 to 1525 was characterized by offensive superiority. The authorities are split on the 1525 to 1650 period. There is complete agreement that defense was superior from 1650 to 1740. Some argue that this defensive superiority continued until 1789, though Frederick's emphasis on the tactical offensive leads some to assert the opposite and others to make no specific evaluation. The period from 1789 to 1815 is generally regarded to favor the offense but because of innovations in tactics rather than armaments."[220]

It is quite obvious that the invention of the artillery brought about offensive superiority at the dawn of the modern era. However, whereas offensive military technology witnessed few changes until the midnineteenth century, defensive techniques such as the *trace italienne* and Vauban's star-shaped fortifications were developed as bulwarks against artillery attacks after 1650. On the whole, military technology thus seemed to favor the defense for most of the early modern period.

Nevertheless, "[w]eapons do not fight";[221] it is people who use weapons to fight wars. Many military historians argue that the "military revolution" is not just about military technology, but also about military organization.[222] Military organization should be understood broadly to include the development of universal conscription, administrative

---

[220] Levy 1984, 233–234.   [221] Unger 1987, 155.
[222] See contributions in Rogers 1995; also Downing 1992, 10.

districts, and population registration.[223] The artillery in fact "could be exploited by either defenders or attackers, depending on their ability to protect and deliver their weapons."[224] Ted Hopf adds that although artillery produced "tactical offensive advantage" in the period from 1450 to 1525, the use of mercenary armies turned the situation into one of "strategic defensive advantage."[225] By the same token, although defensive fortifications did make siege warfare more difficult after 1650, cities defended by the *trace italienne* could still be taken if large enough forces were mobilized to starve out defending troops.[226] Ultimately, then, it was really the use of mercenaries that created "war of maneuver rather than . . . war of decisive battles."[227] As Niccolò Machiavelli observed, mercenaries "were in no hurry to assault fortifications under cover of darkness, while the defending troops were far from eager to mount sorties against their assailants."[228] Such problems, however, were alleviated by Frederick the Great and completely overcome by Napoléon Bonaparte. Although Prussia and France introduced no substantive changes in military technology, they reversed the offense-defense balance by innovative military organization, strategy, and tactics.[229] It is no coincidence that scholars date the end of defensive superiority to either 1740, when Prussia conquered Silesia, or 1789, when France launched comprehensive self-strengthening reforms. In ancient China, similarly, any offensive advantages Qin is said to enjoy were created by the relentless pursuit of the logic of domination – the shrewd combination of self-strengthening reforms, divide-and-conquer strategies, and Sunzian stratagems. It is noteworthy that Qin did not even introduce revolutionary breakthroughs in military organization and tactics.

---

[223] Yates makes a similar observation about ancient China: "None of [the] changes in military technique and technology can be divorced from the social, political, and economic changes that were also taking place." Yates 1982, 410–411; also Sawyer 1993, 373.

[224] Adams 2003/04, 55.

[225] Hopf 1991, 482–483. According to Hopf, a "tactical offensive advantage" means that it is cheaper to seize a piece of territory than to defend it. A "strategic offensive advantage" is "the ability to seize and/or occupy as much of an enemy's territory as is necessary to destroy its military potential at less cost to oneself than is required for the defender to protect its territory or retake it." Hopf 1991, 476.

[226] Parker 1995, 45.   [227] Gulick 1955, 91.

[228] *The Prince*, ch. 12, in Wootton 1994, 42.

[229] As Adams observes, "Frederick the Great's offensive breakthroughs . . . occurred with the same muskets and rifles used by his opponents; the difference lay in Prussia's tactics of marching in step, firing in unison, and reloading quickly, as well as its use of horse-drawn artillery." Adams 2003/04, 55. Levy similarly emphasizes that "the offensive character of Napoleonic warfare derived from the generalship of Napoleon and his changes in military organization, strategy, and tactics." Levy 1984, 232.

Qin's offensive advantages vis-à-vis its targets were simply achieved by *more* comprehensive self-strengthening reforms and *more* ruthless strategies and stratagems.

In short, theories of offense-defense balance may be parsimonious and elegant, but they are unhistorical and wrong. There were simply no inherent advantages that preordained Qin's success or inherent disadvantages that preordained France's failure. Both Napoleonic France and Qin faced geographical barriers, but they were able to overcome some or all of them. Napoleonic France and Qin may be said to enjoy military offensive advantages, but such advantages were products of their own self-strengthening efforts and strategic maneuvering. While the sea-bound geography (and the use of artillery) made conquest more expensive in Europe, the relative costs of war can be accounted for by the mechanism of rising costs of expansion. It is true that conquest was indeed easier in ancient China, but that was largely because states had higher coercive capabilities and wars were cheaper.

Cultural Homogeneity and Ease of Conquest

In addition to the offense-defense balance, it is also argued that domination was intrinsically difficult in early modern Europe because European states were culturally heterogeneous while it was intrinsically easier in ancient China because Chinese states were more culturally homogeneous. Eric Jones argues that expansion "tended to be along the lines of least resistance, into similar areas with similar languages" because "[e]thnic and linguistic diversity . . . made the cost of assimilating territory high."[230] Bau Tzong-ho suggests that ancient China represented such a "homogeneous international society," where the resistance of victims to the aggressor was weak and the problem of governance less daunting.[231] However, scholars should not impute causes from outcomes. The fact that domination eventually succeeded and resistance eventually failed does not mean that conquered rulers and populations welcomed domination as a result of some shared cultural affinity with the conqueror.

The *zhongguo* or central states certainly exhibited many common cultural characteristics: members of major ruling classes shared some blood ties as a result of common lineage to Zhou and/or diplomatic marriages; they spoke the language of Zhou states (especially that of Qi) in international meetings; and they aspired to a common standard of civilization which distinguished them from surrounding "barbarians." However,

[230] Jones 1988, 106–107.   [231] Bau 1986, 149–152.

such cultural affinity was also evident among European states. In the medieval period, Europe became "an identifiable cultural entity" through a process of "Europeanization" or "the spread of one particular culture through conquest and influence" similar to that of cultural assimilation in Zhou China.[232] By the modern era, the areas of France, Germany west of the Elbe, and north Italy shared not just a common religious belief, but also a common heritage of the Roman Empire and Charlemagne's Frankish empire. The conception of European Christendom as a single society and a single hierarchy was deeply held. European ruling families were also inextricably interwoven through diplomatic marriages, so much so that it was easy to claim "legitimate" dynastic rights in various wars of succession. Moreover, members of the nobility typically spoke Latin and French and aspired to the haute couture set by Paris.

Such cultural homogeneity is not a matter of concern for Europeanists. Indeed, cultural affinity is generally regarded as the glue that allowed European states to form an interdependent system in the first place. As Edward Gulick pointed out, "The 'unity' within the framework is important to our argument because it shows how this group of states was crisscrossed with a network of interrelationships and ties which were not duplicated in the relations of those states with the [extra-system] world."[233] Even more importantly, cultural homogeneity is believed to be the very foundation that allowed the balance-of-power mechanism to function more effectively. Hedley Bull thinks that Europe shared "common interests, common values, and a common set of rules and common institutions" that provided the cement for an international society.[234] This view is equally held by classical realists. Hans Morgenthau argued that European states "saw Europe as 'one great republic' with common standards of politeness and cultivation and a common system of arts, and laws, and manners. The common awareness of these common standards restrained their ambitions by the mutual influence of fear and shame, imposed moderation upon their actions and instilled in all of them some sense of honor and justice. In consequence, the struggle for power on the international scene was in the nature of 'temperate and undecisive contests.'"[235] Gulick went even further, arguing that "the balance-of-power system...creaked badly enough as it was, without a lubricating homogeneity it might well have broken down."[236] If this European view is right,

[232] Bartlett 1993, 269, 291.   [233] Gulick 1955, 12–13.   [234] Bull 1977, 11.
[235] Morgenthau 1973, 219.   [236] Gulick 1955, 23–24.

then the supposedly more homogeneous states in ancient China should have been able to preserve the system.[237]

Given the brutality of Qin in ancient China, it may be argued that Qin succeeded not because it was culturally similar to other states, but because it was culturally distinctive from them. In this account, Qin was a "march state," which was "obliged by constant contact and struggle with alien neighbors to develop a great military capacity and a firmer administrative structure than the more civilized, gracious and tradition-conscious communities in the relatively shielded heartland, as well as a greater readiness to innovate and to learn from experience."[238] Qin was indeed a "semibarbarian" state, so much so that it adopted full sinization as part of its self-strengthening program.[239] However, the argument works much better for Chu, which was regarded as wholly barbarian and which created the foundation for centralized administration as early as the onset of the ancient Chinese system. In addition to Chu, Zhongshan, Wu, Yue, and chiefdoms on the peripheries were also of different races than Zhou states, with very different sets of languages and customs. Even Zhou *guo* which originally shared a common lineage and shared the language of Qi developed regional variations in dialects, bronze forms, orthography, and architecture.[240] As both nobles and commoners of various *guo* extensively intermarried, there existed different mixes of ethnicity and customs within and across *guo*. Such differences were significant enough that authors of *Xunzi* and *Wuzi* developed "national combat profiles" – summary evaluations of an enemy's national character and fighting potential – and suggested corresponding tactical principles to achieve victory.[241]

On the whole, ancient Chinese *guo* resembled early modern European states in having a shared civilization amid distinctive cultural practices. As John Fairbank pointed out, "It would be an error...to imagine ancient China as an embryonic nation-state. We would do better to apply the idea of culturalism and see ancient China as a complete civilization comparable to Western Christendom, within which nation-states like France and England became political subunits that shared their common European culture."[242] Charles Tilly observes about Europe that "the myth of the

---

[237] However, Greek city-states which shared a single Hellenistic culture were as ineffective as ancient Chinese states in their balancing efforts. Anthropological studies also show that wars among units of the same culture are more frequent than wars between societies with different cultures. Snyder 2002, 28.

[238] Watson 1992, 194; also Gilpin 1981, 181.   [239] Lin 1992, 15–54.

[240] Blakeley 1970, 32; Lin 1992, 471.   [241] Sawyer 1998, 95–98.

[242] Fairbank 1992, 45.

nation-state, the claim that a given state's citizenry constituted a homogeneous community of common origin," is the product of the very process of homogenization under a central government.[243] Similarly, the level of cultural homogeneity in present-day China is better understood as the product rather than the cause of Qin's success. It was with the use of coercive tools – military strength, administrative capacity, counterbalancing tactics, brutal killing of adult male populations, demolition of the six states' defense structures, mass migration, and so on – that Qin could overcome the balancing logic, defeat targeted states, and suppress subjugated populations. After unification, the Qin Dynasty standardized the written language, the penal code, the calendar, through roads, weights, coinage, and other measures. The First Emperor further sent Qin's convicts en masse to build settlements in peripheral regions and moved some subjugated minorities to the capital area. While these massive relocations were intended to improve centralized control, they also had the side effect of homogenizing – and even cleansing – ethnic minorities.[244]

3.9   Conclusion

Scholars of international relations commonly believe that attempts at domination are doomed to fail as a result of the checking mechanisms of balance of power and rising costs of expansion, or what I call the logic of balancing. Scholars typically point to the modern European system as proof for their theories. As it turns out, such Eurocentric mechanisms represent only half of the picture even with regard to the early modern European system. In light of the ancient Chinese system, European attempts at domination were blocked by countervailing mechanisms only because domination-seekers did not develop sufficient coercive capabilities to overcome them. Among the three sets of coercive tools in the logic of domination, European rulers generally played the game of balancing and counterbalancing. However, they rarely pursued Machiavellian or ancient-Chinese-style stratagems against fellow Europeans. More importantly, the earliest hegemony seekers adopted self-weakening expedients rather than self-strengthening reforms. With lower coercive capabilities and higher war costs, international competition was

---

[243] Tilly 1992, 710.
[244] According to Ge Jianxiong, this policy of forced migration of minorities away from their localities wiped out the races of Dongyue, Minyue, and Dongou. Moreover, peoples who were moved from the south and Korea to the Chinese heartland also disappeared from subsequent historical records. "Apparently, they were homogenized." Ge 1989, 66–67.

more limited in early modern Europe than in ancient China. This scenario changed after Prussia, Russia, Britain, and Austria successively pursued self-strengthening reforms. International competition became further intensified as Revolutionary and Napoleonic France eventually developed the capacity for direct rule and introduced universal military conscription. However, with the legacy of self-weakening expedients, Napoleonic France amassed much weaker coercive capabilities but faced much stronger balancing mechanisms. In short, while it is factually accurate to say that the European outcome is attributable to the logic of balancing, the logic of balancing could be effective only because the logic of domination was very weak.

4

The Dynamics of State Formation and Transformation

War has fundamentally shaped not just international politics, but also domestic politics. Although war has brought about immense hardships and sufferings, theorists of state formation observe that military exigencies have also been conducive to citizenship rights and constitutional democracy. In Europe, when kings and princes pursued dynastic ambitions in the international arena, they were compelled to bargain with resource holders in the domestic realm. State-society bargaining for the wherewithal of war then created a variety of rights in the modern period. It is often presumed that this foundation for liberal democracy is unique to Western civilization and alien to non-Western cultures. From the perspective of comparative history, it is of critical importance that China was once a system of sovereign, territorial states in the classical era. As with the European experience, intense international competition gave rise to citizenship rights understood as recognized enforceable claims on the state that are by-products of state-society bargaining over the means of war.[1] To motivate the people to fight and die in war, ambitious rulers made three major concessions: first, freedom of expression, as testified by the "Hundred (meaning many) Schools of Thought"; second, the right of access to justice and the right of redress before higher judges; and, third, economic rights in terms of land grants and welfare policies. Hence, citizenship rights in fact indigenously sprouted on Chinese soil long before they blossomed on European soil.

[1] Tilly 1992 [1990], 101–102.

Nevertheless, in state-society struggles as in interstate competition, the logic of balancing faces the challenge of the logic of domination – and the outcome of this competition is shaped by the now-familiar self-strengthening reforms versus self-weakening expedients. As self-strengthening reforms are mutually constituted with state formation processes, they strengthen the logic of domination and weaken the logic of balancing in both arenas. In essence, processes of state formation involve monopolization of the means of coercion, nationalization of taxation, and bureaucratization of administration. *Qiangbing* or military reforms should facilitate monopolization of the means of coercion. *Fuguo* or economic reforms should bring about nationalization of taxation. And various military and economic reforms should result in bureaucratization of administration and centralization of authority. Such processes should simultaneously enhance rulers' ability to extract resources and enforce compliance. In ancient China, the Qin state was able to erode citizenship rights and achieve total domination. In early modern Europe, by contrast, the adoption of self-weakening expedients brought about state *de*formation rather than state formation, thus weakening the logic of domination and empowering the logic of balancing in state-society as well as interstate politics. In light of the ancient Chinese experience, the consolidation of citizenship rights and the evolution to constitutional democracy in modern Europe were far more contingent than is commonly presumed.

The following two sections discuss the early development of the logic of balancing and the ultimate triumph of the logic of domination in ancient China. The next section analyzes the development of state *de*formation and the uneasy balance between the logic of domination and the logic of balancing in early modern Europe. Then two initial and environmental conditions that are usually believed to shape state-society struggles are considered: the relations between rulers and ruled in the prior feudal era and the prevalence of civil wars in the multistate era. On the basis of this comparative history, two recent currents in the state formation literature are examined: a reorientation from the uniformity to the diversity of state formation processes and a movement away from a unidimensional to a multidimensional concept of state strength. This chapter closes with a discussion of the transformation of state capacity and state-society relations in postunification China. The overall aim is to trace the early convergence, gradual divergence, near convergence, and eventual divergence of two trajectories of state formation and transformation.

4.1   The Logic of Balancing in State Formation

Similarly to the international relations literature, the state formation literature presumes checks and balances. Europeanists argue that citizenship and democracy historically emerged out of the war-makes-state processes.[2] When European rulers mobilized higher revenues and larger armies, they had to encroach on societal actors who held the needed resources. Resource holders typically resisted extraction. Faced with resistance, kings and princes were compelled to engage in negotiations and make concessions. Charles Tilly observes that "even forceful repression of rebellions against taxation and conscription ordinarily involved both a set of agreements with those who cooperated in the pacification and public affirmation of the peaceful means by which ordinary citizens could rightfully seek redress of the state's errors and injustices. Those means commonly included petition, suit, and representation through local assemblies."[3] Thus, societal actors who were crucial to war-making efforts in different periods were gradually granted citizenship rights and democratic representation. This trend began with the "estatization" of capital holders in the age of mercenary troops and culminated in the extension of the franchise to male adults in the age of national armies.

If a "free constitution emerged...where a number of states existed next to each other on equal terms,"[4] then it is instructive to examine the domestic consequences of international competition in the Spring and Autumn and Warring States periods. Europeanists and sinologists alike tend to see the liberal tradition as deeply rooted in European history and the authoritarian tradition as deeply engrained in Chinese culture. In fact, in ancient China as in early modern Europe, "rulers had no choice but to make various concessions to obtain the cooperation of their people."[5] As discussed in previous chapters, warfare was a matter of life and death in ancient China. Ambitious rulers understood that they needed to win hearts and minds whether they wished to maintain survival or achieve hegemony. As Ralph Sawyer observes,

[S]tates that were well governed by reasonably compassionate, dynamic rulers enjoyed much greater support and even enthusiastic commitment from both the populace and officials. Their people went forth into battle ungrudgingly, with determination and intensity, unified and disciplined in defense of their interests. In

---

[2] Downing 1992; Ertman 1997; Giddens 1987; Kant 1970 [1795]; Levi 1988, 1997; Tilly 1992 [1990], 1992; Unger 1987.
[3] Tilly 1992 [1990], 102.   [4] Hintze 1975a, 164.   [5] Xu 1995, 543.

contest, under corrupt and extravagant rulers the people began military campaigns already weary and exhausted, and could only grow more dispirited and filled with rancor, even if initially motivated by 'national antagonisms' to fight the enemy.[6]

Out of the need to motivate the people to fight and die in war then emerged three major state-society bargains in ancient China: material welfare, legal protection, and freedom of expression. Because ancient China witnessed a smooth transition from feudal levies to national armies (without a detour to the mercenary stage, as in Europe), the basic material bargain retained the feudal form of land grants in exchange for military service, land tax, and corvée. As the security of the state was dependent on the well-being of peasants who cultivated food, paid taxes, and fought wars, ambitious rulers took steps to guarantee subsistence and improve production. The states of Wei and then Qin, in particular, rationally divided lands into grids of small areas and granted them to registered households. To promote agricultural productivity, they built large-scale irrigation projects, opened up wastelands, introduced planting of multiple crops in one year, and developed hybrid seeds. To stabilize the livelihood of peasants amid inevitable annual fluctuations in yields, different states established grain stores and provided disaster relief.[7] Wei and Qin further introduced a countercyclical policy, the "ever-normal granary," to provide a cushion against fluctuations in yields and grain prices. In addition to survival needs, Confucian and Mencian scholars argued that the people were entitled to reasonable prosperity before they could be called on to provide military service.[8] Even more notably, they regarded the state's provision of material welfare as representing a conditional state-society relationship: If the basic economic needs of the people were met, loyalty would ensue, and the state would be strong; if not, resentment would ensue, and the state would be weakened.[9]

However, economic welfare alone was not enough to motivate the peasant populations to fight and die for their rulers. The feudal bargain of land for military service and land tax arose from an era when armies

---

[6] Sawyer 1994, 108.   [7] Sawyer 1998, 237; Weld 1999.

[8] *Analects*, ch. 13.9, cited in Brooks and Brooks 1998, 100. Also *Mencius*, ch. 1A3, cited in Brooks and Brooks 2002, 250. Similarly, Hobbes argued that the sovereign was responsible for "the procuration of the safety of the people," which referred to not merely "a bare preservation, but also all other contentments of life, which every man by lawful industry, without danger, or hurt to the commonwealth, shall acquire to himself." *Leviathan*, pt. 2, ch. 30, in Morgan 1992, 711.

[9] Brooks and Brooks 2002, 259; also Wong 1997, 195.

were formed of aristocratic charioteers, among whom the warrior ethos was instilled from birth. As discussed in Chapter Two, *yeren* or subject populations began to be drafted into military service in 645 BC. It is noteworthy that *yeren* received in return not only land grants, but also an upgrade in social status. This is because, in the feudal order of the time, only *guoren* or those who could claim common lineage with the ruling house were entitled to military service and land ownership. But as military service and land tax were extended to ever more subject populations, military service evolved from a prized privilege to an onerous burden over time. When the age of mass armies dawned in the Warring States period, peasant-soldiers were more motivated to evade military service and desert the troops than to show off their martial skills.

To nurture an originally elite motivation for military service in the mass peasantry, Bruce Brooks observes that rulers introduced a "new legal quid" for a "new military quo."[10] In the feudal era, the common people had no right to know the law or why they were punished. In order to win popular support, some rulers began to promulgate legal codes publicly. As the law "was meant to bind rulers and ruled alike," it gradually became "the contractual basis on which the people would accept a given rulership."[11] At the beginning of the Warring States period, Wei's minister Li Kui consolidated the then-current laws of various states to form the *Fajing* (Canon of Law).[12] In the midfourth century BC, Qin's reformer Shang Yang institutionalized the principle of equality before the law – that "punishment should know no degree or grade...from ministers of state and generals down to great officers and ordinary folks."[13] When the

---

[10] Brooks particularly refers to a passage in the *Zuo zhuan:* "The ruler is about to go to war, and a commoner asks him: Why should I fight? The ruler says, The comforts of food and clothing; I do not dare to monopolize them; I always share with others. The commoner says, That is a petty kindness, not a general one; the people will not follow you. The ruler says, The sacrificial animals and jade and silk offerings, I do not dare to augment them; I am always sincere. The villager says, That is a petty sincerity, and not truly submissive; the spirits will not send blessings on you. The ruler says, In penal cases great and small, even if I cannot investigate, I always judge by the evidence. The village responds, *This* is the basis for loyalty. On this basis, you can fight a battle. If you do fight, I ask to be included." *Zuo zhuan*, ch. Zhuang 10th year, cited in Brooks 1998, 6.

[11] Xu 1995, 543.

[12] *Zuo zhuan* records some earlier instances, including Jin's casting of a new system of laws on an iron vessel in 513 BC and Zheng's inscribing of a new legal code on a bronze vessel in 536 BC. But Brooks believes that it is "grossly anachronistic to think of publicly promulgated law codes in the sixth century BC." Brooks, personal communication, May 25, 2002.

[13] *Shang jun shu*, ch. 4.17, trans. Duyvendak 1963, 279.

crown prince committed an offense, Shang Yang could not punish the future king but applied due punishments to the prince's guardian and tutor in order to demonstrate the impartiality of the law.[14] To ensure that local officials would not abuse the people, the Qin state dispatched law officers to educate the people on the law.[15] According to the *Shang jun shu* (Book of Lord Shang), the people had the right to "inquire of the law officer" when they believed that officials did "not act according to the law."[16] Qin legal documents unearthed at Yunmeng contain detailed instructions on how officials should conduct investigations and write reports.[17] A tomb of a Chu law magistrate at Baoshan yields summaries of legal proceedings and reports of investigations and hearings that are characteristic of evidential trials.[18] The *Guanzi* (Book of Guanzi), which reflects developments in Qi, similarly advocates the universality of the law, the right of access to justice, and the right to protest injustice before higher magistrates.[19] In short, the law provided "a means of affording protection from official oppression,"[20] and the central court served as "a focus for the redress of wrongs."[21] Although justice did not mean democracy, we should not overlook that Western constitutionalism was originally "symbolized not by the mass plebiscite but the impartial judge."[22]

Warring States China witnessed not only legal protection, but also freedom of expression. In the face of escalating international competition, it was essential to attract the best administrators and generals to help "develop clever strategies." In the open environment of the time, intellectuals could freely pursue their interests and travel across borders to seek appointments. Marquis Wen of Wei, King Xian and King Xiao of Qin, King Wei of Qi, and other successful rulers were renowned for their ability to attract the best minds of the times. Qi's King Wei also began the practice of granting stipends to scholars, who were expected to produce writings on government but had no official duties. Chosen scholars carried out their intellectual activities outside the Ji gate of the capital Linzi and came to be called *Jixia boshi* or scholars beneath

---

[14] *Shi ji*, ch. 68, trans. Li 1977, xxiv.

[15] *Shang jun shu*, ch. 5.26, Duyvendak 1963, 331–335.

[16] *Shang jun shu*, ch. 5.26, Duyvendak 1963, 330–331. Hobbes similarly argued, "To rule by words, requires that such words be manifestly made known; for else they are no laws." *Leviathan*, pt. 2, ch. 31, in Morgan 1992, 721.

[17] McLeod and Yates 1981, 129.

[18] Weld 1999; also Brooks, WSWG exchanges, June 2002.

[19] Brooks 1994, 40; Brooks and Brooks 1997, 26.

[20] Loewe 1999, 1009.   [21] Brooks 1998, 5.   [22] Zakaria 1999 [1997], 246.

the Ji gate.[23] Qi scholarship, in turn, stimulated a new era of intellectual debates, with writers arguing with each other rather than merely addressing rulers. The resulting "Hundred Schools of Thought" in the late fourth and early third centuries BC were remarkably progressive in comparison with Enlightenment thoughts in modern Europe.

Contra the conventional view that Chinese classics advocate autocracy, various classical texts written in this era – whether Confucian classics, Legalist statecraft texts, or military treatises – advance the common theme that state-society relations should be reciprocal and conditional.[24] The Legalist text *Guanzi* admonishes that "the rise of a state depends on the support of the people" while "the decline of a state lies in desertion by the people."[25] The Confucian texts *Chunqiu* (Spring and Autumn Annals), *Zuo zhuan* (Zuo's Tradition), and *Mencius* associate benevolent rule with not just survival, but also establishment of great-power status and hegemony.[26] The *Chunqiu* and *Zuo chuan* even document how bad rulers in the Spring and Autumn period lost the hegemonic or great-power status established by predecessors.[27] While the military classic *Sunzi bingfa* (Sunzi's Art of War) advises rulers to use "the unorthodox" (deceptive and manipulative tactics) to conquer other states, it tells rulers to practice "the normative" in commanding their armies or governing their states.[28] The reason is that it is only when the ruler "has established a mutual relationship with the people" that "they will die with him, they

---

[23] *Shi ji*, ch. 74, cited in Lewis 1999, 643. Lu was another center of scholarship. Qi-Lu texts set the standards for literary works. Brooks, personal communication, May 25, 2002.

[24] Philosophers have generally noticed relatively reciprocal state-society relations in classical texts but failed to situate the classics in the context of international competition. Note that the *Shang jun shu* is a notable exception. See later discussion.

[25] Cited in "Guanzi xuekan" editorial board 1993, 99, 107.

[26] Duke Huan of Qi (685–643 BC), Duke Mu of Qin (659–621 BC), Duke Wen of Jin (636–628 BC), King Helu of Wu (514–496 BC), King Goujiang of Yue (496–464 BC), Marquis Wen of Wei (445–396 BC), King Wei of Qi (356–320 BC), Duke Xian (384–362 BC) and Duke Xiao (361–337 BC) of Qin, King Wuling of Zhao (325–298 BC), and King Zhao of Yan (311–279 BC) were benevolent rulers who propelled their state from a relatively weak position to the great-power or hegemonic status.

[27] Examples of arbitrary rulers who lost the hegemonic or great-power status include Wu's Fucha (495–473 BC), Wei's Marquis Wu (395–370 BC) and King Huiwen (369–335 BC), Qi's King Min (300–284 BC), Chu's King Huai (328–299 BC), and Yan's King Wei (279–272 BC).

[28] Lewis 1990, 123. Machiavelli similarly advocated two sets of moral values: In relations between states, he believed that only success mattered. Within one's state, however, the prince should try to "make one's soldiers loyal and respectful" and "make oneself both loved and feared by one's subjects." *The Prince*, ch. 7, in Wootton 1994, 27.

will live with him and not fear danger."[29] Classical texts further argue that rulers who command the support of their populations should not be attacked, while rulers who brutalize and exhaust their people should be subject to "punitive expeditions."[30]

In addition, classical Chinese thinkers preceded modern theorists of state-society relations in making a clear distinction between the state and the ruler. For modern scholars, the state "is an abstract structure of offices endowed with powers, warrants, and resources which are distinguished sharply from the contingent human occupants of these offices."[31] Bruce Brooks observes that the term *gong* originally meant the feudal rank "duke" or the ruler in the Spring and Autumn period; it gradually evolved to mean "public" and then "fair" in the Warring States period.[32] In a similar vein, the term *zhong* originally referred to loyalty to the ruler as a feudal code of honor in the former period; it evolved to mean loyalty to the state in the latter period.[33] As government officials were supposed to serve the higher interest of the state rather than the personal interest of the ruler, classical thinkers argued that officials should be able to criticize rulers freely. Most notably, the *Analects* warns that flattering a bad ruler is tantamount to destroying the state.[34] It thus advises, "Do not deceive [the ruler]; rather, oppose him."[35] This obligation to criticize rulers in the multistate era was not the same as the duty to remonstrate in the imperial era.[36] When the difference between good and bad strategies could mean hegemony versus death, rulers generally would not take offense at free criticisms. The *Zuo zhuan* further extends the right to criticize

---

[29] *Sunzi bingfa*, chs. 9, 1, trans. Saywer 1994, 210, 167.

[30] Sawyer 1994, 280–281.

[31] Geuss 2001, 45. Thus, Hobbes speaks of "the office of the sovereign." *Leviathan*, pt. 2, ch. 30.

[32] Brooks and Brooks 1998, 34, 192, 197.

[33] Bruce Brooks, personal communication, June 15, 2002. It may be said that itinerant scholars had no sense of loyalty or nationalism in the modern sense. Confucians and Mencians were indeed criticized as disloyal by their contemporaries. The *Analects* ch. 14.32 provides an almost "postmodern" response, pointing out that the object of loyalty should be fundamental principles rather than individual rulers. Brooks and Brooks 1998, 124.

[34] *Analects* ch. 13.15 says: "If he is good and no one disobeys, is that not good? But if he is not good and no one disobeys, would this not be one saying that could destroy a state?" Trans. Brooks and Brooks 1998, 101. Machiavellli also discussed how a wise ruler should protect himself against flattery. *The Prince*, ch. 22, in Wootton 1994, 71.

[35] *Analects* ch. 14.22, trans. Brooks and Brooks 1998, 123.

[36] In the imperial era, high officials who remonstrated the emperor risked their life. Still, many heroic scholar-officials continued to insist on the obligation to criticize mistaken policies, thus carrying forth the dissenting intellectual tradition to this day. See de Bary 1998b, 1998c.

rulers from high officials to those in all walks of life: historians, teachers, blind musicians, artisans, and others.[37] The *Guoyu* (Discourses of States) adds that "stopping up the mouths of the people is more dangerous than stopping up a river."[38]

During the Chinese "enlightenment," progressive thinkers also advocated the doctrine of *tianming* or Mandate of Heaven, which was strikingly liberal in its insistence on the ultimate sovereignty of the people.[39] The *Mencius* articulates the *minben* (people as roots) principle, stating that "the people are of supreme importance, next comes the state, the ruler comes last."[40] Shendao similarly argued that "the king is installed for the state, not the state for the king; officials are installed for the people, not the people for officials."[41] Although the Mandate of Heaven would later be reinterpreted to rest with the *tianzi* or Son of Heaven in the imperial era, this was not the case in the multistate era. The *Mencius* unequivocally places the Mandate of Heaven in the hands of the people because "Heaven does not speak; it sees and hears as the people see and hear."[42] Xunzi likewise pointed out, "Heaven...establishes the ruler for the sake of the people."[43] Accordingly, rulers would enjoy the Mandate of Heaven only if they served the people; rulers would lose the Mandate if they abused the people. Even more notably, classical Chinese thinkers preceded modern resistance theorists in pushing the doctrine of popular sovereignty to its logical conclusion. The *Xunzi* suggests that "the ruler is like a boat and the people are like the water. While the water can float the boat, it can also capsize it."[44] The *Mencius* unambiguously states that the people had the obligation to depose and execute tyrants because

---

[37] *Zuo zhuan*, ch. Duke Xiang 14th year, trans. Watson 1989, xvi.

[38] *Guoyu*, Zhou yu I, trans. Watson 1989, xvii.

[39] It is important to restore China's hidden liberal legacy. As Schell observes, "All too many discussions of democracy in China have foundered precisely because they were viewed as overly...Eurocentric...This sensitivity toward 'foreign borrowing' means that, to be successful, Chinese democrats are advised first to draw on indigenous wellsprings of democratic thought." Schell 2004, 117. It may be said that the term "liberal" is inappropriate for ancient China. However, as Plattner puts it, "Liberalism did not originally insist on democracy as a form of government, but it unequivocally insisted upon the ultimate sovereignty of the people." Plattner 1999 [1998], 262.

[40] *Mencius*, ch. 7B14. The *Analects* expresses a similar idea that government exists to secure the well-being of the people, not the reverse. *Analects*, chs. 12–13, Brooks and Brooks 2002, 259.

[41] Cited in "Guanzi xuekan" editorial board 1993, 117. Shendao could be a "Jixia scholar."

[42] *Mencius*, ch. 5A5; see Lewis 1990, 236–237.

[43] *Xunzi*, ch. 27, trans. Chang 1998, 127.

[44] *Xunzi*, ch. 9, trans. Chang 1998, 127; Nivison 1999, 799.

they ceased to be rulers, properly speaking.[45] The *Zuo chuan* similarly remarks that if a ruler "exhausts the people's livelihood . . . and betrays the hopes of the populace, then . . . what use is he? What can one do but expel him?"[46] To illustrate the point, the *Chunqiu* and *Zuo chuan* chronicle many Spring and Autumn instances in which bad rulers were expelled or executed.[47]

In addition to the state-society bargains of material welfare, legal protection, and freedom of expression, the very existence of a multistate system further provided "the right of exit," which could serve as an implicit rein on arbitrary power.[48] In the multistate era, those who voted with their feet were members of all social classes, including traders with movable assets, itinerant scholars and persuaders in search of better employment opportunities, and peasants in search of better land and tax policies. As enlightened rule (*renzheng*) would motivate popular support in one's own state and attract the oppressed and dispirited from neighboring states, it was seen as intrinsic to self-strengthening reforms. Conversely, as oppressive rule would alienate the people and cause them to emigrate, it was tantamount to self-weakening. International competition thus brought about citizenship rights in ancient China as in early modern Europe.

[45] *Mencius* ch. 1B8 discusses the bad last Shang ruler: "I have heard about the killing of the ordinary fellow Zhou, but I have not heard of the assassination of any ruler." Trans. Brooks and Brooks 2002, 254. Hobbes made a similar comment on resistance theorists: "They say not regicide, that is, killing of a king, but tyrannicide, that is, killing of a tyrant, is lawful." *Leviathan*, pt. 2, ch. 29, in Morgan 1992, 708. Angle and de Bary believe that *Mencius* does not provide for the people's right to revolution because the obligation to remonstrate a bad ruler and to choose a new one was limited to high officials who had royal blood. Angle 2002, 124–125; de Bary 1998a, 8; WSWG exchanges, February 2004. It is interesting to note that French Huguenots similarly restricted the right to resistance. François Hotman argued that only the Estates General had the right to armed resistance. Théodore de Bèze extended the obligation to inferior magistrates of the realm. Nexon 2003, 512.

[46] *Zuo zhuan*, ch. Duke Xiang 14th year, trans. Watson 1989, xv–xvi.

[47] For example, a Zheng ruler was expelled to Cai in 697 BC, a Wey ruler was expelled to Qi in 696 BC, another Wey ruler was expelled to Chu in 632 BC, a Yan ruler was expelled to Qi in 539 BC, a Cai ruler was expelled to Chu in 521 BC, and a Ju ruler was expelled in 520 BC. Moreover, a Song ruler was killed in 611 BC, a Qi ruler was killed in 609 BC, a Ju ruler was killed in 609 BC, a Jin ruler was killed in 573 BC, a Zheng ruler was killed in 555 BC, another Zheng ruler was killed in 544 BC, another Ju ruler was killed in 542 BC and a Xue ruler was killed in 497 BC. See Tian and Zang 1996, 47–49, 90. However, as we shall see, such instances disappeared in the Warring States period.

[48] Jones 1988, 118; North and Thomas 1973, 87; Scott 2003 [2001], 5. Moravcsik argues that exit options "may be thought of as substitutes for formal representation." Moravcsik 1997, 518.

4.2   Self-Strengthening Reforms, State Formation, and the Coercive State in Ancient China

Unfortunately, citizenship was "an abortive development" in ancient China.[49] After establishing a universal empire in 221 BC, the First Emperor no longer needed to win the subjects' hearts and minds. As a result, all elements of citizenship rights disappeared. The principle of justice was eroded – punishments became so harsh that there were about 1.4 million convicts to provide forced labor to build the emperor's luxurious palaces and tomb. Freedom of expression was similarly stifled – all books except Qin's court records and those on medicine and agriculture were seized and burned, and 460 scholars who expressed doubts about the emperor's policies were persecuted.[50] Peasant welfare was likewise abandoned – the imperial court increased already high tax burdens and further drafted more than 800,000 men to stabilize the northern frontier and to expand the southern frontier. The Qin Dynasty ruled in a reign of terror.[51]

To understand the emergence and demise of citizenship rights in ancient China, we need to examine the logic of domination as well as the logic of balancing. Eurocentric theories of the state generally presume that the development of universal conscription and direct rule necessitated the enfranchisement of male adults. While agreeing with the mainstream view that "direct rule and mass politics grew up together," Tilly observes that direct rule also facilitated the transition from "reactive to proactive repression" in modern Europe.[52] When agents of the state penetrated local communities, they could prepare "dossiers, listening posts, routine reports, and periodic surveys of any persons, organizations, or events that were likely to trouble 'public order.'"[53] European states did not develop

---

[49] Brooks, personal communication, July 15, 2002.

[50] Li Si, the prime minister of the First Emperor, called for a complete crackdown on free criticisms of government policies. According to the *Shi ji*, Li Si told the emperor: "At present Your Majesty . . . has firmly established for yourself a position of sole supremacy. And yet these independent schools, joining with each other, criticize the codes of laws and instructions. Hearing of the promulgation of a decree, they criticize it, each from the standpoint of his own school. At home they disapprove of it in their hearts; going out they criticize it in the thoroughfare. . . . If such license is not prohibited, the sovereign power will decline above and partisan factions will form below. It would be well to prohibit this." Cited in de Bary 1998c, 39. The *Shi ji* records that 460 scholars were buried alive as a result. But the *Shi ji* most likely exaggerates Qin's ruthlessness. Lewis, personal communication, October 23, 2001.

[51] On the First Emperor's policies, see Fu 1993, 111; Lin 1992, 548–601; Yang 1986, 484–485. Similarly to numbers of army size and battle deaths in previous chapters, the numbers here reflect the magnitude of mobilization rather than actual figures.

[52] Tilly 1992 [1990], 115.   [53] Ibid.

this capacity to master the society until the nineteenth century. But Chinese states achieved this high threshold of stateness as early as the Warring States era. As Mark Lewis argues, the introduction of military service and land grants "entailed the development of new administrative organs for effective local government throughout the territory of the state, practices for registering and policing large populations, and methods to measure and allocate land. These policies, originally designed for mass mobilization and the control of infantry armies, became the basis of control of the civil population."[54] Thus, although ancient Chinese rulers did have to make concessions to generate active support for their international ambitions, the tendency for checks and balances was matched by the state's increasing capacity to compel military service and to prevent evasion and desertion.

As indicated previously, ancient Chinese states began to build up their administrative capacity to mobilize the wherewithal of war at the onset of system formation. As early as 686 BC, Chu had already begun to use centrally appointed officials in newly conquered territories. In 645 BC, Jin extended land grants, land tax, military service, and corvée to subject populations. Later in 548 BC, Chu conducted a general survey of its national resources (including mountain forests, salt ponds, fish ponds, and marshes) and redistributed fields through the introduction of irrigation channels.[55] Between 543 and 539 BC, Zheng reordered the fields of the state into grids and levied a tax on land.[56] In 483 BC, Lu instituted a direct land tax on the populace, which irreversibly eliminated the aristocracy who stood between the ruler and the people and converted "the previously endowed military elite into a salaried civilian elite."[57] At the interval between the Spring and Autumn and Warring States periods, various states adopted the direct land tax and expanded military conscription.

The extension of military service from aristocratic warriors to subject populations may be understood as a process of "punctuated equilibrium." The transition from elite-based chariot warfare to peasant-based infantry warfare proceeded very slowly in the Spring and Autumn period, but the development experienced a "punctuation" during the internecine wars in the interval between the Spring and Autumn period and the Warring States period in the midfifth century BC. While military defeat in an interstate

---

[54] Lewis 1990, 9.   [55] Creel 1970b, 152; Lewis 1990, 59.
[56] Lewis 1990, 59; Tian and Zang 1996, 119–120; Yang 1986, 151–154.
[57] Brooks and Brooks 1998, 271; Brooks 1998, 4.

war would mean loss of territory and some lives, defeat in a civil war could lead to total annihilation.[58] The six warring lineages in Jin were thus motivated "to recruit as many men as possible" by "continuing the process of socially extending military service to the lower levels of the population and geographically extending it to wider ranges of the hinterland."[59] After Han, Wei, and Zhao eliminated three rival lineages and partitioned Jin, they consolidated their power by carrying forth various reform measures introduced during the civil war. Wei's reforms were the most progressive, including the introduction of household registration, nationalization of conscription and taxation, rationalization of the administrative hierarchy into prefectures and counties, reorganization of rural hinterlands into small-scale peasant households, development of large-scale irrigation projects, and consolidation of the laws of various states into the *Canon of Law*.[60] With these efforts, Wei's state building reached a new level in the second half of the fifth century BC. But Wei still fell short in the capacity for direct rule. As the *Shang jun shu* remarks, many people in Han, Wei, and Zhao did not have their name registered and did not have lands or houses. Such "hidden" populations were beyond the reach of state extractions.[61]

It was Qin under Shang Yang that made the final leap toward universal conscription and direct rule, thus generating another "punctuation" in the midfourth century BC. When Shang Yang introduced universal military service, he also perfected the linked institutions of hierarchical administration, small-scale farming, household registration, collective responsibility, standardized weights and measures, systematic ranking of the population, and rigorous rewards and punishments.[62] It is not an exaggeration to say that Qin developed "the fine-grained administrative grid" characteristic of the "high modernist state."[63] With state agents deployed throughout the realm, the Qin court commanded huge quantities of reports and statistics necessary for both social engineering and political control. The division of the entire countryside into equal-sized plots of land is confirmed by the archaeological finding that "roads and footpaths form a striking pattern of rectilinear layouts" orienting north-south and east-west in the northern region (both Qin and Wei).[64] The unearthed *Qin Law*

---

[58] Similarly, civil wars have been far more brutal than interstate wars in the modern world. Holsti 1999.

[59] Lewis 1990, 60, 61.   [60] See Chapter Two.

[61] *Shang jun shu*, ch. 4.15, trans. Duyvendak 1963, 267. In a similar way, "underground economies" exist in many weak states in the Third World.

[62] See Chapter Two.   [63] Scott 1998, 88.   [64] Lewis 1990, 63.

contains very detailed specifications for (1) the household registration system; (2) crimes and corresponding punishments; (3) qualities of lands, animals, handicrafts, and corresponding tax payments; (4) administrative levels and corresponding criteria for the appointment, evaluation, and supervision of officials; (5) commercial activities and their minute management; and so on.[65] Moreover, Qin issued internal "passports" to chain the originally mobile traders, scholars, and peasants to their households.[66] The Qin state's immense administrative capacity was reinforced by its monopoly of the means of coercion. In Qin as in other Warring States, the central court monopolized not just the production of weapons but also the use of metals.[67] Weapons were stored in government armories and distributed only for specific military campaigns. With such a high level of state capacity, the Qin court could enforce extractions, encourage military performance, and repress any sign of resistance.

Is it a paradox that Shang Yang simultaneously championed the state's capacity to dominate the society and the state's commitment to the law? Scholars often presume that a body of impersonal law provides a bulwark against arbitrary rule. However, in the absence of constitutional democracy, feudal customs were in fact better than positive laws at checking against domination in both early modern Europe and ancient China. Feudal customs carried the weight of tradition and could not be arbitrarily changed by kings and princes. Positive laws, in contrast, were based on the will of the sovereign.[68] When the king could rewrite the law according to his wishes, there could be only the rule *by* law (with rulers above the law), not the rule *of* law (with rulers subject to the law).[69] As Baron de Montesquieu observed, "Mr. Law...was one of the greatest promoters of absolute power in Europe."[70] In Warring States China, *fa* or the law also served as a potent tool for promoting state power both internally and externally. The Legalist school argued that "the sovereign is the creator of the law. The officials are the followers of the law, and the people are the

---

[65] Hulsewé 1985.   [66] Yates 1980, 26.   [67] Yang 1986, 100; Yates 1982, 412.

[68] Hobbes, *Leviathan*, pt. 2, ch. 26, in Morgan 1992, 681.

[69] According to Hayek, "the Rule of Law...means that government in all its actions is bound by rules fixed and announced beforehand – rules which make it possible to foresee with fair certainty how the authority will use its coercive powers in given circumstances and to plan one's individual affairs on the basis of this knowledge." Rule by law, by contrast, means that "the use of the government's coercive powers will no longer be limited and determined by pre-established rules. The law can...legalize what to all intents and purposes remains arbitrary action." Hayek 1944, 80, 91.

[70] Montesquieu 1873, 19.

subjects of the law."[71] The unearthed Qin and Chu legal documents provide evidence for not just how the people could seek justice and redress, but also how they were treated as "objects of registration, surveillance, and punishment."[72] For Shang Yang, the principle of equal punishment was meant to promote compliance. Although he advised the king to establish "good faith" with the people and warned against arbitrary changes to publicly promulgated laws,[73] the rationale was that the people would be law-abiding if they firmly believed that transgression would be duly punished without exception. Moreover, Shang Yang seemed to share Niccolò Machiavelli's view that only "fear restrains men" and so "it is more compassionate to impose harsh punishments...than...to allow disorder to spread."[74] He argued that "if light offences do not occur, serious ones have no chance of coming."[75] To achieve maximal deterrence, he stipulated the death penalty for minor crimes (such as theft of horses and oxen) and savage corporal punishments for crimes against the state.[76] This Legalist-Machiavellian view stands in sharp contrast to the Confucian-Mencian view that all human beings are born with the "heart to discern right and wrong" (*shifei zhi xin*)[77] and so good government should "lead [the people] with virtue and regulate them by ritual."[78] Shang Yang believed that the free expression of such "private opinions" which denigrated positive laws would weaken the state.[79] Accordingly, he banned

---

[71] *Guanzi*, ch. 45, trans. Fu 1993, 39.   [72] Lewis 1999, 646; Weld 1999.

[73] Duyvendak 1963, 89, 119.

[74] *The Prince*, ch. 17, in Wootton 1994, 51. Hobbes similarly pointed out that "of all passions, that which inclineth men least to break the laws, is fear." *Leviathan*, pt. 2, ch. 27, in Morgan 1992, 696.

[75] *Shang jun shu*, ch. 2.5, trans. Duyvendak 1963, 209; also ch. 1.4, trans. Duyvendak 1963, 231–232. The general form of the penal code was "if one did (or did not do) x then he should be punished by y." Fu 1993, 110.

[76] Paradoxically, Shang Yang would later fall victim to his own statecraft. Shang Yang once punished the crown prince's tutor and guardian for the prince's wrongdoing. When the crown prince ascended to the throne, he accused Shang Yang of plotting a rebellion. Shang Yang was put to death by the cruelest penalty of "dismemberment by chariots." His whole family was also executed. *Shi ji*, ch. 68, cited in Yang 1977, 78.

[77] *Mencius*, chs. 2A6, 6A6.

[78] *Analects*, ch. 2.3. Thus, whereas Legalists viewed *fa* as penal codes, Confucians and Mencians saw *fa* as model institutions. de Bary 1998b, 45. However, Confucianism is correctly criticized for placing too much faith in the sage ruler, who would voluntarily refrain from abusing power. de Bary 1991. It was not until Huang Zhongxi (1610–1695) that a prominent Confucian scholar unambiguously insisted on institutionalized limits to the exercise of political power. See de Bary 1998c, 104–105.

[79] The *Shang jun shu* ch. 4.18 states "If a state is in disorder, it is because the people often have private opinions of what is their duty." Trans. Duyvendak 1963, 290. See also *Han Feizi*, ch. 45; *Leviathan*, pt. 2, ch. 29.

scholarly debates at court, burned Confucian books, and sent government critics to the frontier.[80]

If the law facilitated rather than checked attempts at domination, then the bureaucracy did not fare any better. Hsu Cho-yun argues that political authority in ancient China made the transition from the "traditional" to the "rational-legal" mode.[81] The Warring States bureaucracy was undoubtedly "legal" in that it was based on the rule *by* law, and "rational" in that it was based on ambitious plans to engineer whole societies. Unfortunately, as did the triumph of positive laws over feudal rites, the triumph of the rational-legal bureaucracy over traditional authority provided "the basis for the domination of the imperial state over society."[82] Under traditional authority, even an arbitrary ruler could not easily discharge his ministers because hereditary aristocrats were not appointed by him but were born to help him rule. Moreover, landed aristocrats had independent economic bases and were not vulnerable to the whims of rulers. It was in such circumstances that the nobility enjoyed "corporate immunity" in both feudal Europe and feudal China. Under rational-legal authority, in contrast, meritocratic officials were dependent on salaries and could be dismissed at will. As Thomas Ertman observes, the Weberian ideal-type bureaucracy "can only become a full-fledged reality when the possibility of arbitrary intervention on the part of the ruler has been eliminated by the introduction of a set of standard operating procedures subject to the strictures of a formalized, impersonal administrative law."[83] Such an independent bureaucracy remained an ideal in the early modern period and became "perfected" only in the post-Napoleonic era.[84] In ancient China, the early development of hierarchical administration made such a transition even more difficult.[85] When landholding ministers of noble blood were gradually displaced by salaried officials of humble origins, the traditional pattern of collegial, kinship-based authority also yielded to the new pattern of unchallenged authority.[86] Although the typical senior minister could discuss state affairs with the king on equal terms, the junior

[80] Yang 1986, 216–219.   [81] Hsu 1965a, 1.   [82] Fu 1995, 86.   [83] Ertman 1997, 9.
[84] Ertman 1997, 9; also Silberman 1993.
[85] Kiser and Cai argue that the Qin empire was not fully bureaucratic. One of the signs was that the system used "severe negative sanctions" for noncompliance. Kiser and Cai 2003, 532–533. This interpretation implicitly presumes the European experience as the norm and fails to see that the coercive state could well be the more natural outcome. It is also noteworthy that even European states did not reach the Weberian standard until the nineteenth century.
[86] In the Warring States period, "the practice of rewarding officials with salaries graded in quantities of grain was universal." Lewis 1999, 606.

official was supposed to be merely "a conduit who transmit[ted] the facts of his locality to the court and the decision of the court to the countryside without interposing his own will or ideas."[87] The Qin court aimed to control not just the general populations, but also officials charged with overseeing the people. The discovered *Qin Law* gives strict instructions to officials on how to inspect inferiors, how to keep accounts, how to check records, how to conduct criminal investigations, how to maintain government stores, and so on.[88] Officials who made mistakes in preparing household registries or investigating legal cases were subject to dismissals and severe punishments.

While monopolized coercion, legal positivism, and bureaucratic administration facilitated absolute rule, there was still a long way to go before Qin could establish total domination.[89] Theorists of state-society relations argue that attempts at domination typically fail. To begin with, administrative and coercive apparatuses are not just expensive to establish and maintain, but also subject to the law of increasing marginal costs. No matter how coercive a state is, it is simply impossible to send state agents to watch every individual around the clock. It is also impractical to send enough watchdogs to ensure that all state agents pursue the state's interests instead of their own personal interests. At the same time, even the most ruthless states typically face resistance. Repressed populations may be driven by "a human desire for freedom and autonomy" that is not easily deterrable by overwhelming state power.[90] Even under circumstances of extreme domination in which active resistance is guaranteed to face suppression, disgruntled populations may engage in "disguised, undeclared resistance."[91] For example, peasants may resort to "weapons of the weak"[92] by delivering inferior crops in paying land tax, shirking labor in performing corvée, and fighting halfheartedly on the battlefield.[93] If enough peasants take part in such foot-dragging activities,

---

[87] Lewis 1999, 610.   [88] Hulsewé 1985; McLeod and Yates 1981.

[89] It is often presumed that totalitarianism is a strictly modern phenomenon. See, for example, Giddens 1987, 57. But if we follow Giddens to find the "origins of totalitarianism" in "the curtailing of citizenship rights, the concentration of certain types of surveillance activity, and the systematic use of force based on the state's monopoly of the means of violence," then the Qin state was clearly totalitarian. Giddens 1987, 341.

[90] Scott 1990, 109. See also Fukuyama 1989; Goldston and Tilly 2001; Goodwin 2001; Migdal 1994. Svensson argues that Confucianism contains the concept of human dignity but not human rights and that one should not confuse the two by saying that Confucianism is conducive to human rights. Svensson 2002, 34. This view overlooks that human dignity is the fountain for resistance, which, in turn, generates human rights.

[91] Scott 1990, 198.   [92] Scott 1985.   [93] Scott 1990, 188.

"the aggregation of thousands upon thousands of such 'petty' acts of resistance [has] dramatic economic and political effects."[94] Thus, no matter how weighty the Qin legal code was as written, one should expect serious limits to its implementation.

Shang Yang and other statecraft specialists in the Warring States era apparently understood these interrelated problems and found solutions for them. The most fundamental issue is that resistance – whether open or disguised, declared or undeclared – must rest with dense social networks. If peasants are bound by communal land use and are connected to local and regional magnates with some independent resource bases, then collective actions are more likely. When such conditions are not available, resistance is far less likely. As Karen Barkey observes of the Ottoman Empire, the answer to "the puzzle of the missing rebellions to Ottoman rule" lies with the "relative barrenness" of the social structure.[95] Similarly, Chinese society is often characterized as "a loose tray of sand." This was not originally the case in the Spring and Autumn period, when state power was weak and social structure was strong. Hence, the *Chunqiu* and *Zuo zhuan* record many rebellions. By the Warring States period, however, states developed the capacity to destroy intermediate power holders and penetrate the society. The system of household farming further broke down extended lineages into nuclear families. Shang Yang even prohibited fathers and adult sons from living under one roof. As peasants in the Warring States era had little protection from social structures, they were more amenable to control from above.[96] Probably reflecting this phenomenon, classical texts of the Warring States period are notably silent on peasant rebellions.

But Shang Yang was not content with the mere absence of active resistance. In the passage "Weakening the People," the *Shang jun shu* argues that "a country which has the right way is concerned with weakening

---

[94] Ibid., 192.

[95] Barkey 1994, 11, 232. In the Ottoman Empire, collective action was difficult because "peasants were not organized, elites were split within their ranks, and peasants and elites had no preexisting basis for alliance." Ibid., 11.

[96] Against Legalist efforts at breaking down the family and the village, Mencians advocated communal land in the imaginary "well-field" system. In this design, eight families with nine plots formed one community. While each family had its private plot, all families should work together in the public plot. In the imperial era, generations of Confucian scholars continued to insist on "the principles of voluntarism, local autonomy, consensual and cooperative arrangement for the improvement of village life." de Bary 1998c, 88. However, the tradition of Confucian communitarianism remained politically ineffective.

the people" because "a weak people means a strong state and a strong state means a weak people."[97] Shang Yang wanted to create "a condition of complete good government" in which "husband and wife and friends cannot abandon each other's evil, cover up wrongdoing and not cause harm to relatives, nor can . . . the people mutually conceal each other from their superiors and government servants."[98] To achieve this goal, the Qin state introduced mutual surveillance so that "those whose businesses were connected should have different interests."[99] Based on the household registration system, the Qin state held households of five collectively responsible for any member's transgressions; at the same time, the state offered handsome rewards for family members and neighbors to report on one another. Shang Yang applied the same technique to state officials who were in charge of overseeing the people.[100] While the stated goal of linked liability was to create a condition in which "deserters from the ranks [had] no resort and stragglers [had] nowhere to go,"[101] the actual consequence was far more penetrating. By instilling mutual mistrust in the most basic social ties – between husband and wife in the family, between neighbors in the local community, and between colleagues in the workplace – even the mildest dissent could be nipped in the bud. By fashioning "a people who would of their own accord enforce the legal dictates of their masters,"[102] the Qin court could simultaneously maximize surveillance, minimize resistance, and lower the costs of domination. In short, Shang Yang achieved "the ultimate dream of domination: to have the dominated exploit each other."[103]

This does not mean that the Qin state eliminated all forms of concessions to society. As discussed previously, Qin's kings wanted to establish hegemony in the Warring States world. Given that Qin was originally weaker than other great powers, success in international competition would demand "a closer partnership between the working masses and central government and an ability somehow to translate this association into a structure of collaborative effort in warfare."[104] It is often presumed that only constitutional states can establish such "state-society

---

[97] *Shang jun shu*, ch. 5.20, trans. Duyvendak 1963, 303.

[98] Ibid., ch. 5.24, trans. Duyvendak 1963, 321. Item 4.151 of the *Qin Law* states, "A husband commits a crime, and his wife denounces him first (i.e., before the authorities are aware that he has committed the crime), she is not subject to seizure [of her maidservants, male and female slaves, clothes and utensils]." Cited in Yates, 1987, 203.

[99] *Shang jun shu*, ch. 5.24, trans. Duyvendak 1963, 322.

[100] Ibid., ch. 5.24, trans. Duyvendak 1963, 319–322.

[101] Ibid., ch. 4: 18, trans. Duyvendak 1963, 286–287.

[102] Lewis 1990, 93.   [103] Scott 1986, 30.   [104] Unger 1987, 170.

synergy."[105] But Qin's experience illustrates that economic rights can serve as substitutes for political rights, and that justice can be served in autocracy as in democracy.

Although the Qin state eroded the bargain of freedom of expression, it enhanced that of material welfare. Similarly to other states in the ancient Chinese system, the Qin state made land grants to peasants in exchange for military service, land tax, and corvée. Although state extractions were heavy, they were tied to peasants' ability to pay.[106] Moreover, the state actively promoted agricultural productivity by sponsoring irrigation projects and providing farm tools and other forms of technical assistance. Such welfare measures generated not only *fuguo* (economic wealth), but also compliance. As Joel Migdal points out, societal actors are likely to grant obedience and conformity to the state if they "see the state as a large piece of their personal life puzzles."[107] Because Qin's peasants owed their lands and livelihood ultimately to the state, they had little ground to resist state extraction. Because peasants could treat land grants as de facto private properties and pass them on to descendants, they were more content with being tied to the soil. Because peasants could generally maintain subsistence, they had little reason to stage food riots, which were common in early modern Europe. Thus, contrary to the liberal view that property provides the foundation for liberty, small-scale land ownership in fact served the authoritarian order in ancient China. Moreover, although the Qin state wielded the stick of harsh punishments for transgressions, it also offered the carrot of lucrative rewards for contributions. To motivate popular support for war further, the court systematically ranked the whole adult male population on the basis of military distinctions and assigned social status and allocated lands accordingly. Qin's stunning military victories, in turn, helped to justify heavy extraction and loss of personal freedom.

Qin's form of domination was successful also because it did not offend peasants' standards of justice.[108] Scholars who focus on France and

---

[105] Evans 1997, 81; also Ertman 1997; Levi 1997; Migdal 2001; Putnam 1993; Xu 1999.

[106] As Machiavelli observed, most subjects would "live contentedly" if the prince refrained from imposing crushing taxes on them. *The Prince*, ch. 19, in Wootton 1994, 56.

[107] Migdal 1997, 223.

[108] Injustice is often seen as inflammatory of popular protests. Moore believes that peasants have "folk conceptions of justice" that stress some rough parity between "the contributions of those who fight, rule and pray" and "peasants' return payments." Moore 1966, 471. Scott speaks of the "moral economy" of peasants. Scott 1976. See also Goodwin 2001, 45; Tilly 1992 [1990], 100–101.

England often believe that regressive tax structure was "a hallmark of absolutist regimes everywhere."[109] They point out that France had lower tax rates than England, but it was France that suffered from widespread tax rebellions. As the French tax system allowed innumerable privileges and exemptions, it was perceived as "exceptionally punitive and singularly unjust."[110] In contrast, English tax rates were higher but were uniformly applied to peers, gentlemen, clerics, and peasants alike without legal exemptions. Margaret Levi suggests that only democratic representation could guarantee the universality of the law and generate "contingent consent."[111] However, it is noteworthy that Thomas Hobbes simultaneously advocated the Leviathan and the principle that "justice be equally administered to all degrees of people."[112] And it is no coincidence that a demand for justice on the eve of the French Revolution was directed at the king: "Now we call on the king to mete out justice, and we express our most sincere desire for but one king, one law, one weight, and one measure."[113] Such a wish was realized in Qin under Shang Yang, who was keenly aware of the importance of justice for effective government. As the *Zhanguo ce* remarks, "Lord Shang implemented the laws with justice and impartiality. The high and powerful were not spared punishment, and friends and relatives were not favored in granting rewards."[114] Moreover, by preventing local officials from abusing the people and providing the right to seek redress at the central court, Shang Yang also avoided the "rightful resistance" that would become widespread in later times.[115] Thus, the justice-based element of citizenship strengthened the state more than the society in Warring States China.

---

[109] Ertman 1997, 111.

[110] Brewer 1989, 130; also Hoffman and Rosenthal 1997, 33–34.

[111] Levi 1988, 97–98. "Contingent consent is a citizen's decision to comply or volunteer in response to demands from a government only if she perceives government as trustworthy and she is satisfied other citizens are also engaging in ethical reciprocity." Levi 1997, 19, 205.

[112] *Leviathan*, pt. 2, ch. 30, in Morgan 1992, 715.   [113] Cited in Scott 1998, 31.

[114] *Zhangguo ce*, ch. *Qin 1*, cited in Li 1977, xxiv.

[115] O'Brien argues that "rightful resistance" has emerged in the Chinese countryside as a result of a wide gap between rights promised and rights delivered. Chinese peasants are "prepared to hand over whatever grain and fees are lawfully owed, provided the local representatives of state power treat them equitably, respect their rights, and deliver on promises made by officials at higher levels. When, however, grassroots leaders neglect the letter of the law or refuse to respect limits on their discretion, eagle-eyed villagers are quick to step in and to accuse them of engaging in prohibited behavior." O'Brien 1996, 37; also 2002.

On the whole, Shang Yang's package provided both a substitute for political rights in state-society relations and an engine for territorial expansion in interstate competition. In light of Qin's success at establishing universal domination, the Qin model may be more effective than the English model in motivating the active support of the general populace. Margaret Levi observes that in quasi-republican regimes in modern Europe there were often "tax evasion, draft evasion, and various other forms of disobedience" because "the provision of collective goods would never justify a quasi-voluntary tax payment and the benefits of a war could not possibly exceed the cost of dying."[116] Shang Yang similarly realized that "of the external affairs of the people, there is nothing more difficult than warfare."[117] However, he understood that the ruler could "compel [the people] by means of punishments and stimulate them by means of rewards."[118] Material incentives could motivate the people because "the people's attitude towards profit is just like the tendency of water to flow downwards."[119] Moreover, if the state could make the people have as much faith in the system of rewards and punishments as "in the shining of Sun and Moon," then the army would face no equals.[120] It is thus not surprising that Han Fei, a scholar of the late Warring States period, observed that Qin's people "were willing to die in war."[121] Similarly, Polybius remarked that the Romans enjoyed "brilliant success" in war because they had an "almost obsessive concern with military rewards and punishments."[122] In modern language, such material incentives effectively channeled individual interests to serve the state's interest in expansionism. As Robert Gilpin puts it, "If the growth and expansion of the state and the interests of powerful groups are complementary, then there exists a strong impetus for the state to expand and to try to change the international system."[123]

The use of economic instead of political bargains had significant implications for the further transformation of state-society relations. Cooperative state-society relations could survive in such an extremely dominant regime only because there were still checks and balances in the international system. The transformation of King Zheng (246–221 BC) of the state of Qin into the First Emperor (221–210 BC) of the Qin

---

[116] Levi 1997, 1–2.   [117] *Shang jun shu*, ch. 5.22, trans. Duyvendak 1963, 311.
[118] Ibid., ch. 5.26, trans. Duyvendak 1963, 326.
[119] Ibid., ch. 5.23, trans. Duyvendak 1963, 316.
[120] Ibid., ch. 3.9, trans. Duyvendak 1963, 242.
[121] *Han feizi*, cited in Tian and Zang 1996, 149.   [122] Polybius 1979, 335.
[123] Gilpin 1981, 97; also North and Thomas 1973, 1–2.

Dynasty was dramatic. On the eve of unification, the Qin court collected the best administrators, strategists, and generals of the time. To realize his formidable ambitions, King Zheng would humbly heed advice and even make apologies to his senior officials. The king also maintained the traditional policies of providing material welfare to peasant-soldiers and granting handsome rewards for military distinctions. After unification in 221 BC, the First Emperor no longer needed the subjects' active support. As a result, he abandoned Shang Yang's bargains of social welfare and legal justice and heightened extractions and punishments. In place of the tight state-society partnership that preceded unification, the imperial court entered into a state of war with the society.

4.3   Self-Weakening Expedients, State *De*formation, and the Constitutional State in Early Modern Europe

If processes of state formation favored the logic of domination and helped it rescind the logic of balancing in ancient China, then why did checks and balances become institutionalized in early modern Europe? The answer for state-society relations is the same as that for inter-state relations: Compared with the ancient Chinese trajectory, there was something deficient in the European trajectory. When international competition stepped up at the onset of the early modern period, Valois France and the United Habsburgs – as were their counterparts Chu, Qi, and Jin in ancient China – were motivated to build larger armies and raise more revenues. However, states across systems differed in the way they achieved the same objectives. In ancient China, the earliest domination-seeking rulers expanded army strengths by mobilizing their own populations, increased economic wealth by promoting agriculture, and consolidated conquered territories by appointing nonhereditary officials. As such efforts required enhancement of administrative capacity, the result was progress toward state formation. In early modern Europe, however, rulers turned to military entrepreneurs for mercenary armies and to capital holders for loans and credits. By relying on intermediate resource holders, these measures did not require the building up of administrative capacity. By converting public offices into private properties, European courts even weakened their already fragile administrative capacity. Thus, while war had the effect of making the state through self-strengthening reforms in ancient China, it had the opposite effect of *de*forming the state through self-weakening expedients in early modern Europe.

The heavy reliance on military entrepreneurs and mercenary troops was the root cause for state *de*formation. First, as the use of military entrepreneurs involved the delegation of the "power to recruit and to fight,"[124] monopolization of the means of coercion became impossible. Military entrepreneurs were also "dangerous" because the less competent among them could ruin their employers while the excellent would "always be looking for ways of increasing their own power."[125] During the Thirty Years' War, for instance, Wallenstein was an independent power more than equal to Holy Roman Emperor Ferdinand II and even conducted secret diplomacy on his own. Second, the dependence on mercenaries derailed efforts at rationalizing taxation. Both French and Habsburg rulers managed to double and redouble tax revenues during their prolonged hegemonic competition – even at the risk of inciting rebellions. But this European means of war was so expensive that ordinary revenues were simply inadequate. On the verge of bankruptcy, "the fiscal prudence of rulers was thrown to the winds."[126] Rather than rationalizing national taxation, most European rulers resorted to contraction of loans and sale of offices. Although such fiscal expedients helped to generate substantial cash for the moment, they worsened state finance and made reform ever more difficult in the long run. Third, the use of mercenaries and concomitant fiscal expedients further negated efforts at centralizing authority. With the creation of numerous offices that were for sale, war did make states in the sense that state apparatuses became increasingly bulky. But war in effect *de*formed European states by dispersing rather than concentrating state power. If the modern state is one where private officeholders should not have control over public resources and state institutions, then this conception is simply "a false characterization of early modern states."[127] When European rulers contracted out military command, tax collection, and public administration, they in effect signed away their control over state apparatuses and their populations. As Thomas Ertman pointedly remarks, "What was in fact 'rationalized' and 'reformed'... was a patrimonial state form wholly different in its logic and organizing principle from the rational-legal bureaucratic state."[128] With hollowed state structures, European rulers could not enhance their coercive capabilities as could their ancient Chinese counterparts.

---

[124] Unger 1987, 130.   [125] *The Prince*, ch. 12, in Wootton 1994, 39.
[126] Brewer 1989, 20.   [127] Goldstone 1991, 5, fn. 2.
[128] Ertman 1997, 154. Ertman also calls this process the "rationalization of irrationalization." Ertman 1997, 322.

The fateful reliance on military entrepreneurs not only weakened the logic of domination, but also empowered the logic of balancing. Compared with national armies, mercenary troops were prohibitively expensive. As Tilly argues, "[T]he more expensive and demanding war became, the more [rulers] had to bargain for its wherewithal."[129] The means of war also shaped the identity of the core groups of resource holders – whether they were massive groups of peasants or narrow groups of capital holders – which had important implications for state-society struggles. In ancient China, the basis of national strength was the peasantry. As peasants lived at subsistence, they were susceptible to state control through material incentives. Moreover, peasants had relatively low capacity for collective actions unless they had allies from other classes.[130] In early modern Europe, in contrast, the most critical resource holders were financiers. As wealthy individuals were few in number and concentrated in geographical location, they faced a much less daunting collective-action problem when they desired to rebel. Moreover, because many capital holders bought positions as military commanders, tax collectors, and the court's bankers, they effectively entered the state's decision-making process long before the dawn of representative democracy. Although state rulers were rarely threatened by disgruntled peasants, they were typically vulnerable to the noncooperation and defection of politically powerful and strategically positioned elites – not to mention that independent power lords could exploit peasant grievances to serve their own ambitions. If state-society bargains were more extensive in Europe, it was because state *de*formation made negotiations and concessions more compelling.

It was in a puny state that rulers began to pursue sustained self-strengthening reforms and alter the trajectory of state *de*formation. In the midseventeenth century, rulers of Brandenburg-Prussia established a centralized bureaucracy for military administration and revenue collection. Although the Prussian state still relied on mercenary troops, it could use the bureaucracy to establish central command. Building on this foundation, moreover, Prussia later introduced a canton-based national conscription system in 1733. The court also rooted out patrimonial tendencies by thorough militarization of the whole administration. Given

---

[129] Tilly 1992 [1990], 188.

[130] Barrington Moore argues, "By themselves, the peasants have never been able to accomplish a revolution. The peasants have to have leaders from other classes." Moore 1966, 479. Lin Jianming, who specializes on the history of Qin, likewise argues, "Peasants could not achieve the ultimate victory in a revolution, nor could they establish a new society." Lin 1992, 669. See also Barkey 1994; Goodwin 2001; Skocpol 1979.

the closer resemblance of this self-strengthening program to the ancient-Chinese model, it is hardly surprising that Prussia developed the most coercive state in early modern Europe. Criticisms of the state were not tolerated. Officials must be strictly subservient to the state or risked dismissal, imprisonment, and even execution if the king developed suspicion of their loyalty. As in Qin, a "consequentialist logic entered the judicial process: punishments served not only to punish offenders, but also to demonstrate overwhelming power, to intimidate and regiment the country."[131] Moreover, just as Qin's peasants were chained to the soil, Prussian peasants were tied to the canton and must seek approval for marriage and travel. In the early eighteenth century, the Prussian state introduced welfare measures such as maintaining grain stores, regulating food prices, and providing basic economic and medical care. Similarly to comparable provisions in ancient China, these welfare policies were meant to produce a population amenable to maximal extraction and to preempt popular demand for political reforms.

Just when Prussia was catching up with ancient Chinese developments, England embarked on a different self-strengthening model that was to divert early modern Europe from the logic of domination. As discussed previously, England borrowed from and improved on the Dutch system of public credit after a humiliating defeat by the Dutch Republic in 1667. The English model resembled the ancient Chinese or Prussian model in that it necessitated thorough administrative reforms to enhance state capacity, but it was unique in that it required "guarantees to investors that only a representative assembly could provide."[132] Coincidentally, the Glorious Revolution occurred soon after the introduction of the public credit system. As a foreign king, William was in a relatively weak bargaining position vis-à-vis the Parliament. Determined to secure English support in Dutch efforts to repel France, he agreed to parliamentary approval for the pursuit of war and the imposition of taxation. This conjuncture of events meant that at the same time that the English state was strengthened through bureaucratized administration, monopolized coercion, and nationalized taxation, the Parliament was simultaneously empowered to exercise constitutional checks and balances. The British state that emerged thus embodied a rough balance between the logic of balancing and the logic of domination.

Revolutionary and Napoleonic France offered Europe another chance to rejoin the trajectory of domination. Direct rule was introduced for

---

[131] Downing 1992, 93.   [132] Ertman 1997, 225.

the first time in Europe. Henceforth, France could introduce universal conscription, which allowed the state to simultaneously establish central command and minimize war costs. France could also launch a rational and equitable system of taxation which allowed the state to collect far more revenues to finance the empire-building project and, at the same time, freed the state from dependence on narrow groups of financiers. Such revolutionary breakthroughs significantly tilted state-society relations. Theorists of the state often presume that universal military service requires popular government, but this view is not borne out by either Chinese or European history. It is true that the Swedish national army was associated with the fourth estate formed of peasants, but the Swedish phenomenon was the exception rather than the norm. It was not military conscription per se but the self-equipped citizen army which historically served as a bulwark against domination. As Max Weber observed, "Whether the military organization is based on the principle of self-equipment or that of equipment by a military warlord who furnishes horses, arms and provisions, is a distinction quite as fundamental for social history as is the question whether the means of economic production are the property of the worker or of a capitalist entrepreneur."[133] Thus, when Prussia and Russia adopted the Swedish model of cantonal conscription in the context of state monopoly of military forces, they established the most coercive states in Europe. Although these states granted emancipation to serfs in exchange for military service, juridical equality did not mean freedom and democracy.[134] Similarly, the French Revolutionary regime was more "democratic" only in the sense that the monarchy was overthrown and the state reached "more even-handedly into society . . . without formal regard for social background."[135] Despite the rhetoric of "liberty, equality, and fraternity," revolutionaries in fact "strengthened executive-administrative dominance . . . rather than parliamentary-representative arrangements."[136] After Napoléon seized power, of course, the empire was anything but democratic. In early

---

[133] Weber 1982, 320. One can say that Machiavelli was as much a liberal as a realist to the extent that he relentlessly advocated the Roman model of the self-equipped citizen army.

[134] Downing insists that universal conscription "could only exist in a land of free peasants." Downing 1992, 204. It is true that peasants who paid taxes and fought wars could not be serfs or even slaves. That was why both Russia and Prussia emancipated serfs. Similarly, peasant-soldiers in Qin were free peasants who had "a wide range of economic resources at their disposal." Yates 1987, 231.

[135] Skocpol 1979, 179.   [136] Ibid., 178.

modern Europe as in Warring States China, therefore, the prerequisite for universal conscription was not the universal franchise but the capacity for direct rule.

Just as Qin organized the universal empire in its image, the Napoleonic Empire attempted to build replicas of the French form of government in conquered countries. Even in Britain, the French threat "put an end to all hope of reform" as conservative voices suppressed liberal voices in the name of national security.[137] Barrington Moore believes that "if the menace of revolution and military dictatorship had not ended at the battle of Waterloo, it is highly unlikely that England would have resumed in the nineteenth century those slow and halting steps toward political and social reform that she had given up at the end of the eighteenth."[138] At the end of the Napoleonic Wars, Britain remained a "liberal autocracy,"[139] and there was "nothing inevitable about the victory of parliamentary democracy."[140] Nevertheless, in comparison with Warring States, European states had a fighting chance to consolidate citizenship rights in the ensuing Pax Britannica. It was this historical contingency that laid the foundation for the ultimate triumph of liberal democracy in the Western world.

4.4   Initial and Environmental Conditions

Relations Between Rulers and Ruled in the Prior Feudal Era

The preceding historical comparison leads to another question: If processes of state formation should enhance rulers' coercive capabilities and facilitate domination of society, then why did European rulers not engage in state formation earlier? As state formation processes and self-strengthening reforms are mutually constitutive, this question is essentially the same raised earlier: Why is it that the earliest hegemony seekers in ancient China pursued self-strengthening reforms whereas those in early modern Europe resorted to self-weakening expedients? As I argued previously, practices such as the use of mercenaries, sale of offices, and contraction of loans were already commonplace in medieval Europe. This chapter further examines the same question from the perspective of state-society relations: Could it be that societal checks and balances were

---

[137] Moore 1966, 31.   [138] Ibid., 31.

[139] Zakaria 1999 [1997], 246. Britain allowed only 2 percent of its population to vote for the lower house in 1830. Democracy with universal suffrage is a twentieth-century phenomenon.

[140] Moore 1966, 30.

already in place in feudal Europe but not in feudal China? After all, it is widely believed that the existence of medieval constitutionalism accounts for the eventual emergence of constitutional democracy in Europe. For instance, Brian Downing insists that European and non-European countries are not comparable because medieval Europe uniquely enjoyed "citizenship rights, representative institutions, the rule of law, and a decentralized institutional basis for what could later become checks and balances on central authority."[141]

If we follow Downing's definition of feudalism as "a decentralized form of government by which a relatively weak monarch rules in conjunction with an independent, beneficed aristocracy that controls local administration and constitutes the basis of the military,"[142] then there are "startling" resemblances between European feudalism and Zhou feudalism in the relations between rulers and ruled.[143] In Zhou feudalism, *li* or rites provided elaborate normative restraints on the exercise of power and served the "constitutional function" of checking arbitrary rule.[144] The tradition of lineage participation in state affairs further placed real limits on royal authority.[145] The ruler of a feudal *guo* was only "first among equals."[146] The ruler's blood relatives all shared the right to rule

---

[141] Downing 1992, 36, 239. Moore similarly argues that Western feudalism, which generated "a rough balance between the crown and the nobility in which the royal power predominated but left a substantial degree of independence to the nobility," uniquely distinguished Europe from the rest of the world. Moore 1966, 417. Such a view expresses the fallacy of retrospective history. Until the nineteenth century, the Western world in fact had a negative view of democracies along the thoughts of Plato and Aristotle. However, once that situation changed in the early twentieth century, "Historians begin trying to trace a purportedly single line from the Athenian Assembly, through perhaps certain Roman popular institutions (especially the *comitia tributa*), various medieval forms of communal self-government, the French Revolution, etc., and ending this march of glory in, say, the Constitution of the Fifth French Republic or the Federal Republic of Germany; this historical account, however, is grossly incorrect." Geuss 2001, 111; also Rosanvallon 1995.

[142] Downing 1992, 249.

[143] Creel 1970a, 3. Creel's definition of Zhou feudalism as "a system of government in which a ruler personally delegates limited sovereignty over portions of his territory to vassals" is remarkably similar to Downing's definition of European feudalism. Creel 1970a, 320.

[144] Brooks and Brooks 1998, 117. Similarly, de Bary argues that the ritual order constitutes "a moral constraint on the exercise of power" and "occupies much of the space that in the modern West would be identified with a constitutional order." de Bary 1998b, 47, 43; also de Bary 1998c, 30.

[145] Blakeley, 1999b, 57; Guo 1994, 149; Hsu 1965a, 79; Lewis 1990, 8, 50–51; Tian and Zang 1996, 85–87.

[146] Lewis 1990, 33.

by birth in accordance with the closeness of their blood ties. Higher-level aristocrats had the right to hold public offices and the obligation to reprimand the ruler for his mistakes. The lowest level of the nobility or *guoren* formed the majority of the population and enjoyed substantial rights and duties.[147] Along with the obligations to fight war and pay taxes, *guoren* had the rights to bear arms and own lands. When the ruling court was contemplating war and peace or when there were succession disputes, the entire *guoren* should be assembled as a *hui* to make collective decisions. For instance, when Wu pressed Chen to join its side against Chu in 494 BC, Chen's ruler convened a *hui* and asked the people who supported Chu to stand to his right-hand side and those who supported Wu to stand to his left-hand side.[148] In this feudal order, the ruler would be obeyed only if he acted in the public interest of the whole *guo*. If the ruler became arbitrary and extravagant, aristocrats had the warrant to correct him. If the ruler failed to heed advice, the whole population had the obligation to expel or execute him and set up a successor. Given that the Huguenot doctrine of resistance was based on constitutional restraints developed in the medieval era,[149] it is quite probable that the Warring States doctrine of popular sovereignty was derived from the legacy of feudal relations in the Zhou era.

The case of Chen illustrates that such a balance of weak rulers and strong society lasted well into the middle of the Spring and Autumn period. However, Chen was a small state. Among great powers, feudal relations had already disappeared. A crucial turning point occurred when military service and land tax were extended from *guoren* to *yeren* in Jin in 645 BC. This measure was so effective in uplifting Jin's relative capability that it became institutionalized in Jin and gradually copied by other great powers. As ambitious rulers expanded their territorial reach through such self-strengthening reforms, various *guo* slowly evolved to become increasingly larger territorial states. Success at territorial expansion, in turn, allowed rulers to extend military service and land tax to ever expanding populations, thereby blurring the distinction between *guoren* and *yeren*. Moreover, the same self-strengthening reforms that facilitated territorial expansion in international competition also allowed rulers' amassing of coercive capabilities in state-society relations. The homogenized

---

[147] Hsu 1999, 572; Lewis 1990, 48; Shaughnessy 1996, 162; Tian and Zang 1996, 47–51, 384–385; Yang 1986, 146.

[148] Chen's *guoren* decided not to submit to either side. Tian and Zang 1996, 49; Yang 1986, 152.

[149] Franklin 1992, xxiii–xxiv.

populations were thus further reduced to mere subjects of their increasingly absolute rulers. But when military success in international competition required active support from the general populace, even absolute rulers had to make concessions to societal actors. Despite erosion of *guoren*'s feudal privileges, therefore, homogenized subjects in the Warring States period acquired juridical equality, legal protection, freedom of expression, and material welfare, as discussed earlier. Although autocracy heightened in Qin, Mencian scholars could still openly advocate tyrannicide in eastern states in the early third century BC.

Europe experienced a similar reversal in state-society relations during the transition from the feudal era to the multistate era. To be sure, there were representative bodies in Europe which did not exist in ancient China. Such assemblies first appeared sporadically in the Iberian kingdoms and Sicily in the late 1100s and early 1200s and became institutionalized throughout the regions west of the Elbe River during the period 1250–1350. From then on, approval for taxation became an established medieval custom. Hence, it may be argued that French and Habsburg rulers had no choice but to resort to self-defeating fiscal expedients. However, the principle of no taxation without representation could be readily trumped by the principle of "evident necessity" – that taxes could be levied without consent when the safety of the country was at risk.[150] Although most rulers originally felt compelled to seek approval for noncustomary taxes, they would quickly turn temporary levies based on consent into permanent taxes for which consent was not required. As the king alone had the authority to convene estates, it was not difficult to bypass them altogether.

Brandenburg-Prussia is a prime example. Although Prussia is known as the most absolutist state,[151] the region initially resembled much of western Europe. By the midseventeenth century, the estates of Brandenburg and Pomerania "had developed into able representative bodies that shaped foreign policy, supervised and audited the crowns' undertakings, influenced the appointment of ministers and local administrators, and handled the collection of taxes and tolls they had approved."[152] In fact,

---

[150] Bodin, *Commonwealth*, bk. 1, ch. 8; Brewer 1989, 10; Downing 1992, 75, 93; Ertman 1997, 73.

[151] Skocpol, for example, observes that the modern Prussian state could implement reforms from above because it "was already so very strong within society" and the Junkers were "in no institutional position to block concerted policy initiatives by the state." Skocpol 1979, 108.

[152] Downing 1992, 85–86; also Moore 1966, 415.

these estates were so powerful that their approval for new taxes was not gained easily even on the eve of the Northern War (1654–1660). In the Recess of 1653, the Great Elector had to agree to confirmation of privileges and exemptions (recognition of serfdom, administrative control of peasants, and exemption from the excise for most imports and exports) in exchange for funding for a new army. However, the establishment of a standing army, which was loyal to the prince, fundamentally altered the terms of subsequent state-society struggles. When the estates refused further funding in 1657, the Great Elector proclaimed his right to levy taxes without approval and used the army to collect them.

In the art of subverting estates, Prussia actually lagged behind Spain and France. Charles V had already weakened the *cortes* in Castile in the early sixteenth century. Compared with representative assemblies elsewhere in Europe, Spanish *cortes* were relatively weaker. However, the Habsburg emperor was also deprived of the appeal to *raison d'état* because Charles was not considered a Castilian and deputies had little interest in defending his far-flung empire. To convert these skeptical deputies into loyal supporters, Charles resorted to the divide-and-rule strategy with material enticements.[153] He first invited as few deputies as possible to the *cortes* to increase manageability; he then provided handsome salaries and expenses to bribe them. Moreover, Charles granted deputies a special lump-sum payment each time they voted a *servicio* (direct tax) and allowed them to retain 1.5 percent of all revenues derived from *servicios* and *millones* (food taxes). Consequently, although the *cortes* were once rebellious against Charles, they became rubber stamps that approved ever more taxes for the emperor's wars and those of his successors.

Compared with Prussia and Spain, France is often believed to have a stronger tradition of medieval constitutionalism. Even Niccolò Machiavelli, who wrote in the early sixteenth century, praised France as a "well-ordered and well-ruled" state[154] because French kings "obliged themselves to innumerable laws."[155] However, France was in fact the pioneer in establishing royal monopoly of taxation and coercion as early as the fifteenth century. During the last decades of the Hundred Years' War, Charles VII had a hard time fighting the English king both as a foreign enemy and as a rival claimant to the French throne. A turning point occurred in 1428, when the English assaulted Orléans. This threat permitted Charles

---

[153] Ertman 1997, 113–116. [154] *The Prince*, ch. 19, in Wootton 1994, 58.
[155] *Discourses*, bk. 1, ch. 16, in Wootton 1994, 123.

to raise 500,000 livres from the assembly at Chenon. From then on, the king increasingly treated imposition of taxes as his prerogative, which did not require consent. The assembly at Orléans in 1439 was the last time the French king sought approval for the *taille* (a direct tax). That, together with the establishment of the Compagnies d'Ordonnance in 1445, permitted Charles's authority to become supreme. Subsequent kings even bypassed and disbanded estates altogether. As a result, "the older, mutual obligations of king and people underwent a distinct transformation, emerging as little more than duties on the part of the people and prerogative rights on the part of the prince."[156]

French kings easily found theoretical justification for their efforts at destroying the medieval tradition. Similarly to Legalists in Warring States China, absolutists in Europe advocated the view that the law was nothing but the command of the sovereign. Jean Bodin argued that "the prince is not subject to the law"[157] and that "the main point of sovereign majesty... consists of giving the law to subjects in general without their consent."[158] Thomas Hobbes concurred that the sovereign "is not subject to the civil laws" and "is bound to himself only."[159] In response to the Huguenot doctrine of resistance, Bodin argued that medieval customs did not provide binding restraints on the sovereign and so subjects had no right to resistance "even if he has committed all the misdeeds, impieties, and cruelties that one could mention."[160] Bodin would go so far to advocate that "a subject is guilty of treason in the first degree not only for having killed a sovereign prince, but also for attempting it, advising it, wishing it, or even thinking it."[161] Although absolutist thinkers still held the sovereign answerable to the laws of God, moral admonitions that were not backed by enforceable constitutional requirements were as ineffective as the Mencian concept of Heaven.[162] By medieval standards,

---

[156] Church 1969, 335.

[157] *Six Books of a Commonwealth*, bk. 1, ch. 8, in Franklin 1992, 11.

[158] *Commonwealth*, bk. 1, ch. 8, in Franklin 1992, 23.

[159] *Leviathan*, pt. 2, ch. 26, in Morgan 1992, 681–682; also pt. 2, ch. 29.

[160] *Commonwealth*, bk. 2, ch. 5, in Franklin 1992, 115.   [161] Ibid.

[162] Bodin also believed that the sovereign had no right to levy taxes without consent. As he suggested, "[T]he saying that princes are the lords of everything applies only to legitimate governance and supreme judicial power, leaving to each the possession and property of his goods." *Commonwealth*, ch. 8, trans. Franklin 1992, 41. However, he so thoroughly destroyed the tradition of consent that it was quite pointless for him to continue to advise the king to seek approval from estates for taxation. Hobbes resolved this dilemma by denying that subjects had exclusive rights to their lands and goods. *Leviathan*, pt. 2, ch. 29.

therefore, early modern European kings were quite absolute in the extensive prerogative powers they enjoyed. It is by ancient Chinese and modern standards that absolutist kings were not absolute because they had no capacity to enforce their will on reluctant populations.

Nevertheless, Hobbes's call for the Leviathan in England was far less effective than Bodin's call for absolutism in France. If modern England innovated a unique model of self-strengthening reforms that enhanced checks and balances, medieval England also developed a unique form of representative assembly that was more resistant to subversion. While estates across Latin Europe were formed of the separate orders of the clergy, the nobility, and the burgher class, the Parliament of England was formed by geographically based representatives. As Thomas Ertman points out, "Estate-based assemblies were by definition strictly divided along status-group lines, the overriding concern of each of the individual chambers which composed such assemblies was to protect and, if possible, extend group-specific privileges. This made it very difficult for the chambers to cooperate among themselves in defense of the rights of the assembly as a whole vis-à-vis its royal master."[163] By contrast, "the structure of the territorially based parliaments encouraged cooperation at the level of the entire assembly."[164] Equally important, English parliamentarians had direct links to taxpayers in the localities – indeed, they were taxpayers themselves. Although England's Charles II did attempt to divide and rule parliamentarians,[165] he was deprived of the tactic of bribing representatives to approve new taxes that could be passed on to others. The Glorious Revolution further helped to check creeping absolutism and strengthen parliamentary oversight.

It may be argued that even though estate-based assemblies were less effective, the existence of representative bodies in Europe and their complete absence in ancient China should be responsible for the difference in outcomes. There is no doubt that the existence of representative assemblies

---

[163] Ertman 1997, 21. The same contrast between functional representation and geographical representation is evident in Hong Kong. See Hui 2003b.

[164] Ertman 1997, 22.

[165] The financial secretary Danby "made detailed surveys of the Commons in order to identify potential government supporters, and then used his control of revenue liberally to dispense pensions drawn on the excise in order to shore up their loyalty. These grants were supplemented by direct payments from the Treasury's discretionary fund, the 'secret service' account." Ertman 1997, 201. However, this effort failed. The Treasury Commission of 1667–1771 had laid the groundwork for Sir George Downing's reform program. Charles soon found it expedient to agree to another Treasury Commission in 1679 to restore Downing's reforms.

per se meant that checks and balances were relatively more institutionalized in feudal Europe than in feudal China. However, why did not assemblies of entire *guoren* or *hui* in feudal China become institutionalized into formal bodies? It is important to remember that "constitutional
government was intimately tied to the efforts of state makers to solve
their fiscal problems," whether in the medieval period or in the early
modern period.[166] Medieval rulers "were *forced* to call representative assemblies into being largely in order to seek...financial assistance."[167]
Feudal rulers in Zhou China did not face fiscal crises and so were not
compelled to establish checking institutions. Moreover, ancient Chinese
guos began as relatively small city-states comparable to the Greek polis.
When the *hui* was convened, the whole citizenry could participate and
there was no need to introduce representation.[168] By the time *guo* evolved
to become territorial states encompassing multiple city-states, however,
the balance of power between rulers and ruled had been fundamentally
altered. Moreover, although European estates had deeper roots, William
Church believes that they were "quite worthless...as a means of defending popular legal rights."[169] Jean Bodin provided the best testimony
for their worthlessness: "What semblance of a democracy is there in the
assembly of the Three Estates, where each individually and all collectively bend the knee and present humble requests and petition, which the
king accepts or rejects just as he sees fit? And what democratic counterweight against the monarch's majesty can there be in the assembly of the
Three Estates – or indeed in the whole people if it could be assembled in
one place – which requests, petitions, and reveres its king?"[170] In fact,
the Estates General failed to meet after 1614 and became "nothing more
than a historical precedent."[171] It was severe fiscal crises that restored
its life in 1789.

   From the perspective of comparative history, what was more consequential to European state formation was not the mere existence of
medieval assemblies, but the existence of three – instead of one – social

---

[166] Bin Wong 1997, 130.

[167] Ertman 1997, 60 (emphasis added). See also Downing 1992, 30; North 1990, 113;
North and Weingast 1989; Ruggie 1993, 166.

[168] There is a debate among some historians whether the *hui* was as democratic as citizen
forums in Greek city-states. See Blakeley 1970, 48–49. The crucial issue is that only the
ruler could convene the *hui*. However, medieval assemblies also had no right to convene
on their own. In fact, many medieval assemblies would not meet for decades, if not
centuries.

[169] Church 1969, 167–168.   [170] *Commonwealth*, bk. 2, ch. 1, in Franklin 1992, 101.

[171] Skocpol 1979, 182.

orders that were highly autonomous from kings and princes. A major reason why most assemblies were estate-based in feudal Europe was that there were multiple privileged orders: In addition to the nobility, there were the clergy and the burgher class. In feudal China, there was only the nobility. As the nobility already enjoyed privileged access to social status and economic benefits without fear of competition from other orders of society, there was little incentive to organize into a formal body. However, when hereditary aristocrats became subjugated in processes of state formation, there were no other independent forces that could mediate between the sovereign above and the subjects below. In Europe, in contrast, religious leaders and capital holders had both the motivation and the resources to check rulers *outside* assemblies.

The burgher class, as the source for intermediate resource holders, plays a central role in this analysis. Burghers not only inadvertently undermined the logic of domination by facilitating self-weakening expedients, but also directly strengthened the logic of balancing by engaging in extensive bargaining with rulers. Barrington Moore's proclamation of "no bourgeoisie, no democracy" is not groundless, but we need to study the circumstances that allowed the bourgeoisie to shape history.[172] To a large extent, it was because the means of war were so costly that "no ruler who seriously pursued war avoided reliance on capitalists of some sort."[173] Although absolutist kings were autonomous of the larger society, they were beholden to the burgher class. Although capital holders sought exemptions and privileges which had undesirable consequences for economic development, they also demanded institutional guarantees against arbitrary seizure of private properties which helped to lay the foundation for the rule of law. Although some capital holders became feudalized through the purchase of public offices and titles, others maintained "a preference for the greatest amount of independence possible."[174] In addition, as argued by Adam Smith, Baron de Montesquieu, Friedrich Hayek, and other classical liberal economists, commercial activities, if not heavily regulated, could create an autonomous space in the civil society which formed the basis for individual liberty.[175]

The role of religion was no less important in European politics – both international and domestic. The clergy in general and the Roman Catholic

---

[172] Moore 1966, 418. We also need to examine why some members of the bourgeoisie support dictatorship and others favor democracy. See Hui 2005.

[173] Tilly 1994, 11.   [174] Spruyt 1994, 63.

[175] Hayek 1944; Montesquieu, 1873; Smith 1976.

Church in particular controlled not just peoples' souls, but also immense economic resources.[176] For centuries, the papacy was in keen competition with lay authority and was instrumental in ensuring that no political authority would rise to dominance. In the feudal era, the struggle between the church and lay rulers gave rise to new representative bodies and strengthened preexisting ones.[177] During the Reformation, resistance to political domination was inextricably intertwined with resistance to religious domination.[178] It mattered that the Huguenots, unlike the Mencians, did not just advocate the doctrine of resistance but also acted on it.[179] When French Huguenots and other Calvinists launched armed resistance against Catholic rulers, they exhausted such states' already limited coercive capabilities and extorted more concessions. During the Napoleonic Wars, Catholic churches organized guerrilla resistance against French occupation, especially in Spain, Tyrol, and Calabria.[180] Throughout the ages, moreover, Christian churches – whether Catholic or Protestant – nurtured solidarity and trust among fellow believers and provided sanctuary for resistance fighters.[181]

With the existence of two additional orders that were both resourceful and autonomous, the balancing logic was therefore much stronger in Europe. When this was combined with rulers' own pursuit of self-weakening measures, checks and balances became increasingly entrenched in the early modern period. However, when European kings embarked on

---

[176] The church also subverted the coercive logic in a more roundabout way. In the medieval era, many rulers built their expanding bureaucracy on the model of the church hierarchy and appointed clerics to fill many positions. However, the church's administrative model "granted quasi-proprietary rights to officeholders from the start." Ertman 1997, 27–28.

[177] For instance, Philip the Fair (1285–1314) convoked the first meeting of the Estates General in 1302 in order to obtain broad support for his struggle against Pope Boniface VIII.

[178] Religion also interacted with trade. Merchants and craftsmen were the most important converts in the Reformation probably because they were discriminated against under the established order.

[179] However, the opportunity for resistance is itself shaped by the degree of state strength. See the next section. Moreover, Luther and Calvin originally rejected challenges to political authority in the early stage of the Reformation. It was only in the midst of the Wars of Religion that the Huguenots (mostly Calvinists) advocated armed resistance to tyranny. Théodore de Bèze's *The Right of Magistrates* (1574), François Hotman's *Francogallia* (1573), and Phillipe Du Plessis-Mornay's *Vindiciae contra tyrannos* (1579) were the most notable among Huguenot political theory.

[180] Beckett 2001, 6.

[181] Various churches have also played an important role in the third wave of democracy.

ancient-Chinese-style self-strengthening reforms, the logic of domination so unleashed was able to counteract even the much stronger logic of balancing. Europe was ultimately saved by the conjuncture of several historical accidents centered around England/Britain – its preservation of medieval constitutionalism, its adoption of the public credit system that strengthened rather than weakened Parliament, and its difficult but ultimate victory over Napoleonic France. European politics in the nineteenth century thus began to resemble the British state, embodying an uneasy balance between the logic of balancing and the logic of domination.

Civil Wars and Power Struggles

In addition to societal resistance to state domination, there is an alternative route to checks and balances in state formation. Just as international relations scholars believe that ambitions can check ambitions, theorists of the state observe that contending warlords in power struggles and civil wars may be able to check one another. As Joel Migdal argues, "[A]ttempts at domination are invariably met with opposition by others also seeking to dominate."[182] Mancur Olson similarly believes that "autocracy is prevented and democracy permitted by the accidents of history that leave a balance of power or stalemate – a dispersion of force and resources that makes it impossible for any one leader or group to overpower all of the others.... If no one leader can subdue the others ... then the alternative is either to engage in fruitless fighting or to work out a truce with mutual toleration."[183] Moreover, it is also argued that rival rulers in civil wars are less likely to be absolute monarchs because they have to compete for support from the people.[184]

Nevertheless, in civil wars as in interstate wars, the balance of power is not the only possible outcome. Winner-take-all is another possibility.[185] It is important to keep in mind that the very occurrence of civil

---

[182] Migdal 1994, 21.

[183] Olson 1993, 573. South Africa provides a present-day example. According to McAdam, Tarrow, and Tilly, the "conjuncture of the balance of forces" between the African National Congress and the apartheid regime "provided a classic scenario which placed the possibility of negotiations on the agenda." As a result, "a semi-revolutionary situation yielded to a remarkable negotiated compromise." McAdam, Tarrow, and Tilly 2001, 153.

[184] North 1981, 24–27; North and Thomas 1973, 120. However, this argument is baffling to the millions of refugees who have been fleeing from brutish civil wars in the Third World.

[185] The worst possibility is state collapse, as in Somalia.

wars testifies to the inadequacy and even failure of efforts at monopolizing the means of coercion. In China in the Spring and Autumn period, armed forces were controlled by multiple noble houses rather than titular rulers. As a result, civil conflicts were endemic, not only between ruling courts and noble houses, but also among noble houses. Violent internecine struggles reached their climax in the partition of Jin at the interval between the Spring and Autumn and Warring States periods. Among his various *fuguo qiangbing* reforms, Wei's Marquis Wen took the important step of centralizing military command in his own hands. In the ensuing Warring States period, various kings exercised effective control over salaried generals and secured effective monopoly of armed forces within their boundaries.[186] Consequently, civil wars became more or less extinct. This trend eventually culminated in total domination in Qin.

In light of the ancient Chinese experience, civil wars often resulted in stalemates in Europe largely because rulers had weak coercive capabilities to achieve decisive victories. The widespread occurrence of violence should facilitate the rise of absolutism because nobles and commoners alike became convinced that "[r]ebellion seemed more dangerous...than royal tyranny."[187] For instance, Niccolò Machiavelli urged that a strong prince unify Italy because he was disturbed by power struggles within city-states, wars among Italian city-states, and the French invasion of Italy.[188] Jean Bodin was horrified by the Wars of Religion and changed his position from limited sovereignty (that the sovereign was bound by well-established customs which he could not change without consent) in *Method for the Easy Comprehension of History* to absolute sovereignty in *Six Books of the Commonwealth*.[189] And it was against the backdrop of the Thirty Years' War and the English Civil War that Thomas Hobbes argued that it was better to give the Leviathan unlimited power than to suffer from "perpetual war of every man against his neighbor."[190] With the pursuit of self-weakening expedients, however, "the 'new monarchies' were rather inefficient despotisms."[191] Although European kings managed to pacify many religious rebellions and peasant revolts, such successes were typically achieved at the cost of major concessions.

---

[186] Lewis 1990, 243; Sawyer 1994, 51.   [187] Strayer 1955, 222.

[188] *Discourses*, bk. 1, ch. 12, in Wootton 1994, 118.   [189] Franklin 1992, xxi –xxii.

[190] *Leviathan*, pt. 2, ch. 20, in Morgan 1992, 657.

[191] Strayer 1955, 222. In addition to Prussia, a notable exception was Denmark in 1660. After a crushing defeat by Sweden, King Frederick III routed the estates and established an absolute monarchy with the support of burghers and clergymen. Ertman 1997, 309–310.

4.5 Diversity in State Formation and State Strength

This historical comparison demands reconsideration of not just the European experience, but also two recent currents in the state formation literature. The first current is a critique of unilinear theories and a call for attention to the diversity of state formation processes. The second is a reorientation from a unidimensional to a multidimensional conception of state strength. Ancient China presents a puzzle to these trends: While the ancient Chinese trajectory is clearly different from the early modern European trajectory, it is also a uniform and unidimensional one. What does this comparative historical analysis mean for the literature?

Uniformity Versus Diversity

There has been a wave of criticisms and self-criticisms of unilinear theories of European developments. For instance, Hendrik Spruyt critiques unilinear evolutionary theories that "assume continuity in history" and "contract the causes of the demise of feudalism with the causes of the rise of the state system."[192] He advocates a research design that analyzes "why some governments took the form of sovereign, territorial rule whereas others did not."[193] Similarly, Charles Tilly criticizes his own work of 1975 for posing "a unilinear story – one running from war to extraction and repression to state formation."[194] In his 1990 book, he examines instead "[w]hat accounts for the great variation over time and space in the kinds of states that have prevailed in Europe since AD 990, and why . . . European states eventually converge[d] on different variants of the national states."[195] Of course, history should not be seen as a long march toward progress. The initial emergence and ultimate demise of citizenship rights in ancient China should caution against any presumption that liberal democracy represents the ineluctable "end of history."[196] Yet, the Chinese state formation experience was remarkably unilinear: All *guo* evolved from feudal city-states to sovereign territorial states, and all states denied political concessions to society. Any variation was merely a matter of degree. As pointed out previously, similar patterns occurred in self-strengthening reform models. Whereas there was

---

[192] Spruyt 1994, 18, 5.   [193] Ibid., 3.   [194] Tilly 1992 [1990], 12.   [195] Ibid., 32.
[196] As we shall see, the initial expansion and ultimate contraction of international trade should also caution us against any presumption that capitalism represents the end of history. A modern analogy is the reversal of the third wave of democracy in the post–cold war era. See Huntington 1996 [1991]. For the argument that democracy and capitalism represent "the end of history," see Fukuyama 1989.

only one *fuguo qiangbing* self-strengthening model in ancient China, there were three – *fuguo qiangbing, fuguo*-oriented, and *qiangbing*-oriented – models in early modern Europe. What explains this phenomenon of diversity in the European experience and uniformity in the ancient Chinese experience in both state formation processes and self-strengthening reforms?

According to Tilly and Spruyt, the diversity within Europe rests on differential patterns of trade. Tilly states, "[W]hen men began to concentrate coercion in various parts of Europe the relative presence or absence of concentrated capital *predicted* (and to some degree *caused*) different trajectories of change in state structure."[197] The result was the alternatives of "capital-intensive," "capitalized-coercive," and "coercion-intensive" state forms.[198] In light of the European experience, was trade absent in ancient China? Quite the contrary, the existence of a multistate system stimulated dramatic expansion of international trade in the Spring and Autumn and Warring States periods. Douglass North and Robert Thomas observe that "the development and expansion of a market economy during the Middle Ages was a direct response to the opportunity to gain from the specialization and trade made feasible by population growth."[199] In ancient China, population growth and the migration of populations into virgin areas similarly brought about growing differentiation between regions and opportunity to trade. Moreover, as did advanced states in Europe such as the Dutch Republic and England/Britain, great powers in ancient China developed intensive farming with irrigation, fertilization, crop rotation, multiple cropping, iron tools, ox-drawn plows, and other techniques.[200] The result was significant increase in productivity, which, in turn, provided an additional driving force for trade expansion. Moreover,

---

[197] Tilly 1992 [1990], 133 (emphasis added).

[198] Tilly 1992 [1990], 30. Note that the coercive state in this analysis is not the same as the "coercion-intensive state" in Tilly's account. Tilly's definition of the "coercion-intensive state" is trade-centered, in terms of scarcity of capital. Tilly categorizes relatively constitutional states such as Hungary, Poland, and those in Scandinavia as "coercion-intensive," along with absolutist regimes such as Prussia and Russia. On the other hand, he classifies the old regimes of Spain and France as capitalized-coercive states, but they are closer to coercive states in my account.

[199] North and Thomas 1973, 26. As they explain, "Settlers moving out over Northwest Europe encountered different soils and climates, and of necessity they set up varied patterns of agricultural activity. While adjacent manors might produce an almost identical mix of goods and services, the growing differentiation between regions increased the profitability in trading." Ibid., 22.

[200] Ding and Wu 1993, 96–97; Gao 1998, 522; Hsu 1965a, 130–133; Lin 1992, 432; Sawyer 1994, 53; Xiao 1990, 120; Yang 1986, 22–79.

peasants who received land grants in areas of hills and streams turned to animal husbandry, fishery, and mineral mining and processing, which produced not for subsistence but for the market.[201] In addition, improvement in means of transportation promoted commercial exchanges. And the development of credit as well as media of exchange – from sea shells to silk to metal coins – facilitated business transactions.[202] With burgeoning trade, capital cities grew in size, and new cities and towns emerged. In particular, Qi's Linzi was "the largest metropolis" and Song's Dingtao "the wealthiest commercial center" of the time.[203] Although many merchants operated on a relatively small scale and were often artisans themselves, there were long-distance traders who made profits out of regional price differentials. The more venturesome would trade beyond the ancient-Chinese world to east Central Asia in the west, the steppes in the north, and tribal regions in the south. The richest businessmen of the time possessed wealth that rivaled state treasuries.

Despite the phenomenal growth of trade and the phenomenal wealth of capital holders, state formation in ancient China followed the "coercion-intensive" trajectory. Why did "capital" fail to check "coercion" in state formation in ancient China? As argued earlier, the "Why not?" question presumes that the European experience is the norm and that the ancient-Chinese experience is an anomaly. It may be helpful to take an alternative perspective and see whether there was something unusual about the rise of the trading class in Europe. As Robert Gilpin points out, the prominent role of the burgher class is "a distinctive feature of Western civilization," and "[t]he seeming ease with which this aggressive class achieved ascendancy in both domestic and international society in the Western

---

[201] As Tian and Zang argue, "Why did private commerce and artisanship develop so quickly? The usual answer is increase in productivity which encouraged division of labor. This is correct, but leaves too much unexplained. One has to trace the answer in land structure. Many traders and artisans were originally peasants with government land grants. As the size of land grants generally varied with arability, peasants who received mountains, streams, swamps, steep slopes, and so on were granted larger pieces of lands. As these landscapes were not suitable for farming, peasants turned to such activities as animal husbandry and fishery which produced for the market. Over time, people also acquired techniques to extract and process iron and salt ores. They thus became rich." Tian and Zang 1996, 357–358.

[202] Yang 1986, 136. Contracts of transaction or loans were written on pieces of bamboo. The certificates would be split into two halves, creditors or buyers holding the right sides, and debtors or sellers holding the left sides. Creditors or buyers could then use their halves of the certificates to press debtors or sellers to fulfill their obligations. Yang 1986, 136.

[203] Lewis 1999, 595, 637.

world obscures how extraordinary a development this was."[204] Immanuel Wallerstein similarly argues that "all other known systems have 'contained' capitalist tendencies, in both senses of the word 'contain.' They have had these tendencies; they have effectively constrained them."[205] Indeed, it was not at all preordained that European traders could translate economic wealth into political power. The burgher class was originally shunned by the clergy and the nobility. Hereditary nobles despised traders for their inferior birth and their inability to bear arms. Clergymen looked down on burghers because the church condemned profit-making activities. Many political rulers also ruined originally prosperous city-states and trading towns by all kinds of arbitrary actions: debt repudiation, debasements, confiscations, expulsions, irregular levies, forced loans, judicial murders, and the like. Nevertheless, commerce was occasionally promoted when it suited the Crown's interest. Although Charles V destroyed the Castilian economy, he built up financial institutions in the Dutch possessions because he badly needed ready cash. The conjuncture of expensive means of war and weak extractive capacity meant that European rulers had to rely on "formally independent capitalists for loans, for management of revenue-producing enterprises, and for installation and collection of taxes."[206] It was in such unusual circumstances that European capital holders enjoyed an "elective affinity" with coercion wielders,[207] achieving equal status with the clergy and the nobility and becoming "indispensable equals" to kings and princes.[208]

In ancient China, where the costs of war were much lower and the extractive capacity of the state was much higher, however, the trading class was unable to translate economic wealth into political power. Although in isolated cases wealthy merchants attained high offices, the business class as a whole was politically ineffective. This was not because trade did not generate revenues. In fact, commercial revenues from customs on international trade, duties on artisan merchandises, taxes on market transactions and on use of natural resources were quite lucrative[209] – so much so that the most prosperous cities of the time were prime targets of conquest. However, ancient Chinese rulers did not face fiscal difficulties and were not desperate for cash. Even more fundamentally, ancient Chinese rulers considered agriculture as the essence (*ben*) of economic wealth and commerce as a nonessential (*mo*) element. Land taxes first were rationalized in the

[204] Gilpin 1977, 25.   [205] Wallerstein 1999a, 43.   [206] Tilly 1992 [1990], 29.
[207] Spruyt 1994, 27.   [208] Tilly 1992 [1990], 60.
[209] Tian and Zang 1996, 179–180; Xiao 1990, 130; Yang 1986, 121.

Spring and Autumn period and then flowed steadily into state treasuries in the Warring States period.[210] While land taxes were used to support state apparatuses, commercial revenues were typically assigned for the use of the ruling court and major noble houses.[211] Qin's kings would use commercial revenues from whole cities as reward (along with offices, social status, land grants, servants) for the highest military contributions, even though land taxes were strictly reserved for the state.[212] In early modern Europe, in contrast, rulers were heavily dependent on commercial revenues because they were unable to produce sufficient revenues from land taxes.[213]

In addition to the degree of state formation, the timing of trade expansion relative to system formation was also critically important. In Europe, as noted previously, trade expansion occurred centuries before the onset of system formation. The early timing in trade expansion facilitated the adoption of self-weakening expedients, which, in turn, weakened the logic of domination in both state formation and international competition. When European rulers eventually developed coercive capabilities in the second half of the millennium, capital holders had already established relative autonomy – even independence in the Dutch case. In ancient China, by contrast, trade expansion was originally a by-product of international meetings in the Spring and Autumn period. The conjuncture of late timing

---

[210] The *Analects* ch. 12.9 and a recently discovered chapter of the *Sunzi bingfa* mention a tax rate of 20 percent. Brooks 1994, 39; Sawyer 1998, 413–414.

[211] Yang 1986, 260.

[212] Commanders who received such "tax-paying cities" (*shiyi*) were enfeoffed as "lords" or "dukes." These lords enjoyed taxes but possessed no political or military authority over either the land or the inhabitants. Nor were the titles and privileges hereditary. A notable example was Shang Yang, who received "Shang" as his tax-paying city and was ennobled as "Lord Shang." Tian and Zang 1996, 303; Yang 1977, 91.

[213] Europeanists often presume that land taxes were more difficult to collect than commercial taxes. Tilly argues that "the institution of head taxes and land taxes created ponderous fiscal machines, and put extensive power into the hands of landlords, village heads, and others who exercised immediate control over essential resources." Tilly 1992 [1990], 99. However, "[w]hile states which derived substantial income from land taxes like France and Castile might well have possessed very large fiscal apparatuses, this had more to do with the proliferation of venal offices than with any difficulties involved in collecting such taxes." Ertman 1997, 16; also Brewer 1989, 101. It is noteworthy that trade was regarded as "less amenable to taxation" in ancient China. Lewis 1999, 613. Indeed, when Europe abandoned communal landholding, taxation on land became relatively easy. As Scott explains, the "heroic simplification" of "the thicket of common property and mixed forms tenure" into "individual freehold tenure" makes it "much easier... to assess such property and its owner on the basis of acreage, its soil class, the crops it normally bears, and its assumed yield." Scott 1998, 36.

in trade expansion and early timing in state formation meant that by the time traders accumulated wealth, rulers had developed coercive capabilities to control them.

Indeed, control was the characteristic form of ruler-trader relations in ancient China. If European rulers had an "uneasy" *"liaisons dangereuses,* love-hate" relationship with capital holders,[214] then it is not surprising that ancient Chinese rulers viewed wealthy traders with intense suspicion. Compared with other classes, itinerant traders who had movable assets particularly "lacked firm allegiance to any state or community."[215] Merchants also "seemed odd to the ruling groups because they held no offices and were of no political consequence, yet they could live as luxuriously, even spend as much money, as state rulers."[216] Worse, trade was seen to undercut the foundation of *fuguo qiangbing.* Traders would entice peasants away from the hard labor of farming and fighting by their ostentatious wealth and consumption.[217] Unscrupulous businessmen who charged high interest for loans and who engaged in opportunistic buying and selling of farm lands even drove many peasants into bankruptcy and slavery, thereby making them unavailable for state extractions.[218] Ancient Chinese states thus generally included the policy of "promoting agriculture and suppressing commerce" in their self-strengthening reforms. Rather than enjoying equal status with coercion wielders, traders in ancient China were "inferior people," who ranked below officials, peasants, and artisans, in descending order.[219]

Compared with other Warring States, Qin introduced the harshest measures to suppress traders and commerce. Shang Yang believed that the people should be made poor so that they would be entirely dependent on the state. As the *Shang jun shu* explains, "If the people live in humiliation they value rank; if they are weak, they honor office, and if they are poor, they prize rewards.... If the people have private honors, they hold rank cheap and disdain office, if they are rich, they think lightly of rewards."[220] The means to make the rich poor were to stifle commercial

---

[214] Tilly 1992 [1990], 58–59.

[215] Chang 1996, 147. Scholars often think that traders who have movable assets are in the best bargaining position to compel concessions from rulers. See Bates and Lien 1985; Levi 1988, 97–112. Ancient Chinese statesmen apparently understood the problem and found a way to handle it.

[216] Hsu 1965a, 128.

[217] *Han Feizi,* ch. 49; *Shang jun shu,* ch. 1.3. See Chang 1996, 147; Wong 1997, 146; Yang 1986, 110.

[218] Hsu 1965a, 113; Xiao 1990, 131; Yang 1986, 93, 110, 456–457.

[219] Lewis 1999, 613.   [220] *Shang jun shu,* ch. 5.20, trans. Duyvendak 1963, 306.

activities and to apply severe penalties.[221] The Qin state prohibited the private use of national resources in mountains, forests, and swamps so that merchants had no access to necessary raw materials; outlawed the private sale of grains so that merchants had to cultivate their own food; banned the hiring of waged workers so that merchants had no access to helping hands; provided farm tools to peasants so that they had no need to buy them on the market; and imposed sale taxes on wine and meat that were ten times as high as costs. Shang Yang also created a merchant registry (which paralleled the peasant registry) to regulate merchants' movements, to subject them to extended terms of garrison duty at the frontier, and to impose extra head tax and corvée on their slaves. Needless to say, such extreme measures destroyed the traders in Qin. Although merchants continued to flourish in eastern states, they faced ultimate suppression at the establishment of the Qin Dynasty. The First Emperor moved merchant households from conquered states to Qin's capital so as to uproot them from their normal environment and to keep them under surveillance.[222]

As "capital" was severely decapacitated by "coercion," state formation in ancient China had little chance of following the "capitalized-coercive" path and became an increasingly "coercion-intensive" process. This phenomenon of uniformity was further enhanced by the strength of the logic of domination in system formation. Kenneth Waltz argues that regime types do not matter in international politics. Interestingly, his argument is more applicable to the ancient Chinese system than to the early modern European system. Since "competition produces a tendency toward sameness of the competitors," it is not surprising that states in ancient China

---

[221] On Qin's policies to suppress commerce, see Lewis 1999, 613; Lin 1992, 283; Mu and Wu 1992, vol. 2, 45; Tian and Zang 1996, 359–366; Yang 1986, 179–187, 216–219. The *Shang jun shu* argues: "If the poor are encouraged by rewards, they will become rich and if penalties are applied to the rich, they will become poor. When in administering a country one succeeds in making the poor rich and the rich poor, then the country will have much strength." *Shang jun shu*, ch. 1.4, in Duyvendak 1963, 201. Machiavelli similarly argued that the prince "should make the rich poor and the poor rich" so that there was "no office, no rank, no authority, no wealth which [was] not acknowledged by its possessor as being his gift." *Discourses*, bk. 1, ch. 26, in Wootton 1994, 131.

[222] Creel 1970a, 89; Lin 1992, 587; Mu and Wu 1992, vol. 2, 29. Although all other states also promoted agriculture and suppressed commerce, they never did so to the same extent as Qin. For example, Qi and Chu nationalized only the most important mountains, rivers, forests, swamps, and other natural resources to guarantee supplies to the military and to the court; the rest were granted to peasants. Tian and Zang 1996, 144, 358–359. As a result, there was a sizable group of merchants in the other six states on the eve of universal domination. After Qin, subsequent dynasties continued to weaken merchants by heavy taxes, by state management of intraregional trade, and by salt and iron monopolies. Hsu 1965b, 363–364.

developed the same regime type. Although all Warring States made important concessions to society in order to generate active support for war, they uniformly excluded societal actors from decision-making processes. At the triumph of universal domination, even minor differences in terms of the degree of coerciveness were eliminated.

Whereas the early development of internal state strength intensified Darwinian selection and foreclosed domestic variation in the ancient Chinese system, the late development of internal state strength allowed domestic forces to attain vital importance to international politics in the early modern European system. State *de*formation meant that domination-seeking states had great difficulty in mobilizing resources for war, consolidating conquered territories, and making conquest pay. Because international competition was significantly tempered for most of the early modern period, states were not compelled to have the same coercive form. As Arnold Wolfers indicates, "[W]here less than national survival is at stake, there is far less compulsion and therefore a less uniform reaction."[223] The higher tendency to form alliances further reduced the extent of domestic resource mobilization which would have fostered domination.[224] At the same time, because monarchs could assemble the means of war only with the collaboration of capital holders, the latter managed to take over considerable political power with varying degrees of success. Moreover, as Habsburg Spain and Bourbon France were too self-weakened to overcome the geographical barriers of the Dutch waterways, the Dutch Republic could establish independence, maintain survival, and serve as a shining model for the public credit system and the republican form of government. Although Europe faced the prospect of ancient-Chinese-style uniformity when international competition intensified in the Revolutionary and Napoleonic era, Napoleon was eventually defeated. Modern states that emerged thus reflected the diversity among the winning allies – with Britain's constitutional state coexisting with Prussia's and Russia's coercive states.

"Strong" State Versus "Weak" State

The uniformity of authoritarian regimes in the Warring States period presents another puzzle to the literature on state-society relations. For decades, theorists of both international relations and state-society relations defined state strength as the degree of centralization of state

---

[223] Wolfers 1962, 15.   [224] Downing 1992, 78.

institutions.[225] As Ira Katznelson expresses it, many scholars took "a single conflated continuum of 'weak' and 'strong' states. The latter were portrayed as states that captured more and more functions from civil society, constructed clear lines of demarcation between the public and private domains, and developed the administrative capacity to manage state functions and secure the goals of the managers of the state."[226] Various theorists of the state have moved away from such a unidimensional conception of state strength to a multidimensional conception. It is now generally agreed that state capacity – the state's ability to mobilize resources and implement policies – should be differentiated from state autonomy – the state's ability to formulate policies independently of or against the will of divergent societal interests.[227] In this new framework, constitutional states may be weak in state autonomy but are in fact strong in state capacity because they can generate societal cooperation. By the same token, coercive states may appear strong in state autonomy but are in fact weak in state capacity. This "paradox of state power"[228] neatly captures historical development in early modern Europe. Although French and Spanish rulers were strong in terms of their subjugation of estates and establishment of royal monopoly over coercion and taxation, they were weak in terms of their ability to mobilize the wherewithal of war and to implement grand strategies. In contrast, English kings seemed weak after the Parliament took over the power of the purse and the gun. Yet, the Crown-in-Parliament could generate popular support and mobilized unprecedented amounts of ready cash for Britain's war involvement.

A comparison with ancient China shows that the real paradox may lie more with the European trajectory. In theory, processes of state formation should enhance both state capacity and state autonomy. Bureaucratization of administration – especially when it culminates in direct rule – should allow rulers to impose their will throughout the realm. Nationalization of taxation should provide rulers with higher and more steady flows of revenues and free them from dependence on narrow groups of resource holders. Monopolization of the means of coercion should further facilitate autonomy because the standing army can easily suppress resistance. Hence, it is not surprising that ancient Chinese rulers enjoyed both state capacity and state autonomy and established domination over society. In

---

[225] See, for example, Krasner 1978; Skocpol 1979; Watkins 1934.

[226] Katznelson 1992, 730; see also Nettl 1968.

[227] See Barkey and Parikh 1991, 525–526; Goodwin 2001, 11, 37–38; McAdam, Tarrow, and Tilly 2001, 78; Migdal 1994, 12.

[228] Brewer 1989, 137–161.

light of the ancient Chinese experience, the disjuncture in state strength in European development is probably another legacy of self-weakening expedients. As the French and Habsburg states resorted to sale of offices, contraction of loans, farming of tax revenues, and use of mercenaries, they became composites of contradictions: despotic but ineffective, autonomous but incapable, and bulky but rotten from within. When England entered the hegemonic competition with Louis XIV, it adopted a self-strengthening model which strengthened rather than weakened parliamentary constitutionalism. Britain thus created the converse hybrid of decentralized but strong state. However, as the cases of Prussia, Russia, and Revolutionary and Napoleonic France illustrate, European rulers did not really face a stark choice between the coercive-but-weak state and the constitutional-but-strong state. As could their counterparts in ancient China, European states could achieve both state capacity and state autonomy once they pursued self-strengthening reforms. Nevertheless, the triumph of the British model fundamentally redefined the modern conception of state strength. In the image of the Crown-in-Parliament, the modern "state-in-society" perspective regards a strong state as one that embeds itself in and cooperates with strong social power.[229]

4.6   Collapse of the Qin Dynasty and Transformation of State-Society Relations in the Han Dynasty

The Qin example demonstrates that domination can go very far in suppressing checks and balances. Yet, similarly to modern totalitarianism, Qin's coercive power was not without limits. Although the state of Qin beat all odds to establish a coercive universal empire in 221 BC, the Qin Dynasty collapsed in 206 BC. The rapid downfall of the Qin Dynasty calls for an extended analysis of the logic of domination and the logic of balancing. With regard to system formation, although the mechanism of balance of power ceased to exist in a universal empire, the mechanism of rising costs of expansion remained and eventually caught up with the Qin Dynasty. As for state formation, both countervailing mechanisms of resistance and costs remained operative in a universal empire as in a national state.

Although the Qin state was able to keep the costs of expansion under control, the Qin Dynasty began to face increasing costs. This was because the First Emperor was not content with ruling only the preexisting

---

[229] Evans 1997; Hobson 2000, 2002; Migdal 1994, 2001; Wang 1999.

areas of the conquered states but sought to rule *tianxia* or "all under Heaven." To consolidate the new empire, the court drafted hundreds of thousands of laborers to demolish previous defense walls between states and to construct standardized through roads linking the capital with major regions of the empire. While these projects were probably necessary and certainly affordable, the Qin Dynasty engaged in other expansionist campaigns which entailed immense costs.[230] In 221 BC, the imperial court sent some 500,000 troops to conquer what are now the Guangdong and Guangxi areas in the south. Lined with rivers and streams and occupied by numerous less developed chiefdoms, the southern region presented serious logistical problems to the northern troops. The emperor had to build a canal linking the Yangtze and Pearl Rivers before he finally conquered the area in 214 BC. In 215 BC, the imperial court also mobilized 300,000 troops to seize territories within the northern bend of the Yellow River from the Xiongnu. To consolidate the region, the court built new settlements and another new through road. In addition to initiating various public projects, the First Emperor further enslaved the populations for his own extravagance. He drafted more than 700,000 prisoners to build his private tomb and 700,000 castrated convicts to build more than 270 imperial palaces.[231] With onerous military service, corvée, land tax, and head tax, the subjects lived on the verge of starvation.

If the mechanism of costs had not been joined by the mechanism of resistance, the Qin Dynasty could well have lasted longer. Even under such extreme domination, effective resistance was not a likely scenario because the Qin court monopolized the means of coercion and atomized the society. Moreover, Qin had experience with suppressing rebellions in conquered states even before the wars of unification. For instance, the people of Shu rebelled (or plotted to rebel) three times. Han's people in the Shangdang commandery also resisted Qin's rule. As Qin swept through the ancient Chinese system in the final wars of unification, Qin resorted to a series of brutish measures to control conquered populations: mass

---

[230] As the southern region provided vast arable lands, its exploitation did pay off for subsequent dynasties in the long term. However, the same cannot be said of the deserts in the north. Cosmo also argues that the Xiongnu did not originally present any security threats to the Qin Dynasty. Cosmo 1999, 964. Instead, Qin's massive campaigns compelled the dispersed Xiongnu tribes to unify and centralize. It was this interactive process which led the Xiongnu to become a real threat to subsequent dynasties.

[231] For the First Emperor's measures, see Fu 1993, 111; Lin 1992, 548–601; Yang 1986, 484–485. Note again that the numbers reflect the magnitude of mobilization but not absolute figures.

killing of royal families and defeated armies, enforced mass migration of noble and wealthy families to the capital, demolition of the six states' defense structures, imposition of direct rule with collective responsibility and mutual surveillance, establishment of settlements in problem-prone areas by Qin's convicts, and so on.[232] Thus, no matter how disgruntled the subjects might be, the First Emperor was able to keep them in awe.

The situation changed after the competent First Emperor died in 210 BC. The Second Emperor usurped the throne by forging the First Emperor's will and forcing the crown prince to commit suicide.[233] He imposed even heavier extractions and harsher punishments than the First Emperor but was uninterested in the administration of the empire. When compliance meant not just hard labor but also harsh punishments and even death, the people were left with "no other way out" but to engage in resistance.[234] Rebellions began when Chen Sheng and Wu Guang were delayed by torrential rains on their way to report corvée. Under Qin laws, delay in reporting duty was punishable by death. Even if they were spared for this offense, they would still be worked to death by hard labor. Chen and Wu thus concluded that rebellion would involve little cost.[235] Not surprisingly, this rebellion was readily crushed by the imperial court's military might. However, the Second Emperor was so arbitrary and ruthless that he soon alienated his own military generals.[236] With this golden window of opportunity, multiple rebellions sprang up throughout the empire.

In the ensuing chaos, China had a second chance to restore a multistate system because surviving descendants of prior ruling houses sought to revive independence. However, Liu Bang, the first rebel leader to capture the capital, stepped into Qin's shoes and proclaimed the Han Dynasty

---

[232] Yang 1986, 455, 461–464. As Machiavelli advised, the prince of new acquisitions should "leave nothing as it was" by "mov[ing] populations from one place to another" and establishing colonies rather than relying on an occupying army. *Discourses*, bk. 1, ch. 26, in Wootton 1994, 131; also *The Prince*, ch. 3.

[233] The crown prince Meng Tian was a competent general in charge of seizing northern territories and guarding the northern frontiers. Soon after his death, the Xiongnu overtook the defense lines and recovered lost territories. Cosmo 1999, 966.

[234] Extreme repression that leaves the people with "no other way out" has always been the recipe for armed resistance. Goodwin 2001. When the "current threats" are extremely severe, actors may become insensitive to "repressive threats" and the absence of opportunities. Goldstone and Tilly 2001.

[235] Lin 1992, 640.

[236] As noted in Chapter One, the mechanism of "regime defection" is the key to understanding the collapse of dictatorships. See McAdam, Tarrow, and Tilly 2001, 196.

in 206 BC.[237] As Qin had established a set of unified bureaucratic and coercive apparatuses, Liu could attempt a wholesale takeover.[238] However, he also had to placate the ambitions of allies and relatives who had helped him seize the empire and who commanded their own armies. The result was a "modified form of the multi-state system of the Warring States period,"[239] something akin to the "one country, two systems" model today.[240] While Han Gaozu directly controlled the capital and surrounding area in the Guanzhong region, he grudgingly agreed to the establishment of feudatory principalities in the east. At the founding of the Han Dynasty, these principalities enjoyed independent political authority with large armed forces. The passes between the imperial regions and the eastern states were guarded, and "passports" were required of all travelers. However, over the course of several generations, Han emperors cited rebellions – actual or fabricated – as excuses for eroding the autonomy of the principalities and turning them into prefectures and counties.

In the art of domination, Han Gaozu apparently learned some lessons from the contrast between the well-ordered Qin state and the short-lived Qin Dynasty.[241] The Han court revived state interest in peasant welfare by restoring the Warring States practice of land grants and reducing land taxes and other extractions. But this policy was introduced "not from an altruistic sense of charity or benevolence but because an economically viable peasantry was understood to be the basis for a politically successful government."[242] More importantly, the Han court had no desire to revive legal rights and freedom of expression that were once prevalent in the Warring States era. When Liu Bang first seized the capital, he criticized the cruelty of Qin's penal code and lightened punishments. After the Gaozu had consolidated his power, however, he compiled the Han penal code on the basis of the Qin code, including its harshest elements, "the consorted five punishments and execution of the person charged along

---

[237] The characters for the state of Han in the multistate period and the Han Dynasty are different. There was no relationship between the two.

[238] Motyl argues that "the degree to which a polity possesses a coherent bureaucratic and coercive apparatus able to administer, police, and tax a certain territory and the amount of material resources at the disposal of state elites" is the necessary condition for successful reimperialization. Motyl 1999, 135–136.

[239] Lewis 2000, 42.   [240] Guan 1995.

[241] In the "Discourses on Salt and Iron" under Emperor Wu (140–87 BC), officials debated whether Shang Yang's reforms laid the foundation for Qin's unification of China or led to Qin's downfall. Yang, trans. Li 1977, 95.

[242] Wong 1997, 77.

with three branches of relatives."[243] Gaozu also followed Qin's policy of moving remnants of prior royal families – who were instrumental in overthrowing the Qin Dynasty – to the capital to facilitate surveillance. As subsequent dynasties further heightened the cruelty of punishments and the number of capital offenses,[244] the authoritarian tradition became firmly institutionalized in Chinese history.

Nevertheless, the Han court's statecraft surpassed Qin's in one crucial respect: it created the façade of legitimacy.[245] Confucianism was elevated and then formally established as the official state ideology in 136 BC. As John Fairbank pointed out, "Han emperors took great pains to claim that their rule was based on the Confucian teachings of social order, even while they used the methods of the Legalists as the basis for their institutions and policy decisions."[246] As all ensuing dynasties followed this policy of "Legalism with a Confucian façade,"[247] many Chinese and sinologists have been led to believe that China's imperial tradition was Confucian. However, as Hsiao Kung-chuan observed, the label "Confucian state" "would have puzzled Confucius himself, horrified Mencius, and failed even to please Xunzi."[248] If Confucian moral restraints had little impact in the Warring States era, then they had an even shakier foundation in the imperial era.[249] The Mandate of Heaven was reinterpreted to rest with the imperial emperor, who was now the Son of Heaven. As "all under Heaven" was the emperor's private property, there was simply no

---

[243] Fu 1993, 111.

[244] Although imperial emperors abandoned Shang Yang's bargain of justice, they seemed to understand his insight that clear procedures would help to generate compliance. Thus, the application of harsh punishments was not completely arbitrary in imperial China. For example, although the Qing Code was probably the harshest and allowed extraction of confession by torture, it also stipulated concrete procedures for various punishments and provided a system of review. Conner 1998.

[245] As Machiavelli advised, the wise ruler should know how to be a "clever counterfeit and hypocrite." *The Prince*, ch. 18, in Wootton 1994, 54.

[246] Fairbank 1974, 11.   [247] Hsiao 1977, 137.

[248] Ibid. It was only at the local level that Confucian ethos generally prevailed. de Bary 1998b, 94.

[249] The proper Confucian tradition was not completely lost in the imperial era. Generations of Neo-Confucians, from Wang Anshi (1021–1086) in the Song Dynasty to Liang Qichao (1873–1929) in the late Qing Dynasty, sought to revive classical doctrines "as a critique of imperial power's encroachment upon the locality and community." Duara 1995, 153; also de Bary 1998c, 98–99. But this does not mean that the Confucian ritual tradition continued to obtain "something of the status of a 'constitution,' . . . limiting the exercise of dynastic rule." Chu 1998, 174. Any limits to power were more or less confined to the need to create a façade of legitimacy. Confucian scholar-officials had to risk their life just to remonstrate the emperor.

effective sanction to prevent him from enslaving *his* subjects.[250] Although imperial emperors who openly upheld Confucianism could not burn Confucian classics as Qin's First Emperor did, Ming's Taizu and Qing's Kangxi extirpated offensive passages from the *Mencius* and *Chunqiu Zuozhuan* that were at odds with the Legalist authoritarian order.[251]

As for state institutions, although the Han court reorganized Qin's administrative structure and added the formal written examination in 165 BC, the imperial state gradually lost the capacity for direct rule. The burden of ruling "all under Heaven" meant that the central court became increasingly dependent on local leaders to maintain social order throughout the realm. This reliance on local notables recreated intermediate power holders, who could ignore court orders and subvert imperial power.[252] The danger of indirect rule was particularly acute when it was combined with the institution of universal military service. Without centrally appointed officials, the authority to command peasants and control weapons must be delegated to clan elders and other local elites who could turn national armies into semiprivate armies. As Mark Lewis observes, "[T]he problems that discouraged monarchs in early modern Europe from creating armies of national service also argued against mass mobilization of the peasantry in imperial China."[253] Indeed, although peasant rebellions were rare in the Warring States era, they became a constant possibility in the Han Dynasty because disgruntled peasants were ready allies for ambitious local magnates. Seeing this danger, the early Han court informally modified the institution of universal conscription by "the commutation of service into monetary payment, the recruitment of long-term volunteers or convicts, and the increased reliance on non-Han cavalry."[254] After Wang Mang seized the throne in AD 9–24 – thereby dividing the Han Dynasty into the Former Han (206 BC–AD 8) and the Eastern Han (AD 25–220) – Emperor Guangwu formally abolished universal military service in AD 30–31. To rebuild army strength, the Han court resorted to mercenary

---

[250] A Neo-Confucian scholar, Huang Zhongxi (1610–1695), explicitly criticized the imperial court for serving only its selfish interests in his 1663 treatise *Waiting for the Dawn*. Trans. de Bary 1993, 98.

[251] In the late fourteenth century, Emperor Ming Taizu ordered an abridged version of the *Mencius* without such passages as "The people are the most elevated, next comes the state, the sovereign comes last." In 1699, Qing's Emperor Kangxi ordered a team of scholar-officials to edit a new imperial edition of the *Chunqiu Zuozhuan*, purging passages that suggest the removal of tyrannical rulers. Chu 1998, 172–173; Fu 1993, 60–61.

[252] Hsu 1965b, 369.   [253] Lewis 2000, 42.   [254] Ibid., 74.

troops, both Han and non-Han, who were recruited through payments in grain and cash. To cover heavy expenses in times of war, Han emperors sold public offices in AD 109 and then AD 178. To prevent the repetition of usurpation, the Eastern Han court gradually filled top military positions with civilian officers who were chosen for their loyalty but had no military expertise. As the art of war perfected in the Warring States era was neglected, the seemingly mighty empire became vulnerable to encroachments by nomadic tribes in the peripheries.[255] Paradoxically, the Chinese imperial state began to resemble old-regime European states – it was coercive in terms of state autonomy but weak in terms of state capacity and international competitiveness.

The Han Dynasty managed to linger on until AD 220. The Middle Kingdom then disintegrated into the Three Kingdom period (AD 220–280). From then on, Chinese history was characterized by cycles of unification and division.[256] However, the dynamics of politics in subsequent eras of division was fundamentally different from that in the Spring and Autumn and Warring States periods. In terms of military competition, whereas rulers in the ancient multistate era took for granted that the system of *zhongguo* or central states was the normal existence, power contenders in subsequent periods of division understood that taking "all under Heaven" was possible. In terms of state-society relations, the balance of state power and social forces remained unfavorable to citizenship rights. Although ambitious rulers from time to time introduced welfare measures to buy political support, the reasonably high level of administrative and coercive capacity meant that the imperial court could continue to compel compliance with minimal concessions. At the village level, although the lineage structure reemerged, Qin's pattern of household production (without communal land use) remained, thus leaving peasant households in the same situation of competitive isolation.[257] Although rebellions occurred from time to time, they were typically too sporadic to challenge the imperial court because different regions were kept divided from one another. The court also sought to tie the upper class to the imperial order by an elaborate civil service system. Consequently, various unmistakably

---

[255] The Han Dynasty was menaced by the Xiongnu. The Chinese empire was later conquered by Mongolians, who formed the Yuan Dynasty (1271–1368), and Manchus, who formed the Qing Dynasty (1644–1911).

[256] See Appendix IV.

[257] Hsu 1965b, 365–366; Wong 1997, 45. The situation is similar to that of "amoral familism" in southern Italy. Both cases are products of state domination. Fukuyama 1995, 75.

"modern" institutions and practices developed in the classical era were buried deeper and deeper in the postunification era.

Even though China was once two thousand years ahead of Europe in the development of self-strengthening reforms and state formation, it fell into stagnation in the imperial era. At the other end of the Eurasian continent, Europe made great strides in the post-Napoleonic era. When the British navy knocked on China's door in the nineteenth century, the militarily weak and economically backward "sick man of Asia" was no match. When the Qing Dynasty launched the "self-strengthening movement" (*ziqiang yundong*) in the face of Western encroachment, it resembled Bourbon France in its inability to pursue fundamental administrative, fiscal, and military reforms.[258] It was only after the Communist Revolutionary regime implemented comprehensive self-strengthening reforms that the Middle Kingdom could restore its rightful place in a completely transformed world.

[258] On the *ziqiang yundong*, see Liu 1994. For a comparison of Bourbon France and Qing China and the subsequent revolutions, see Skocpol 1979.

5

Conclusion and Implications

5.1 Rejoining the Dynamics of International Politics and State Formation

This book has examined why ancient China and early modern Europe shared similar processes but reached diametrically opposite outcomes in international competition and state formation, why the ancient Chinese and early modern European trajectories experienced early convergence but eventual divergence, and why ancient China witnessed checks and balances for more than three centuries but eventually succumbed to a coercive universal empire. To answer these questions, this book has advanced a dynamic theory of world politics that can account for endogenous transformation and alternative trajectories. In essence, world politics should be seen as strategic interaction between domination-seekers and targets of domination who employ competing strategies and who are simultaneously facilitated and hindered by competing causal mechanisms. Scholars of international politics and state formation generally presume that attempts at domination are checked by the mechanism of balance of power or resistance and that of rising costs of expansion or administration. This view is not wrong but is flawed with unilinear thinking. First, effective balancing or resistance is inherently difficult because targets of domination (other states in interstate competition and societal actors in state-society struggles) face the daunting collective-action problem. Second, international competition unleashes not just countervailing mechanisms, but also coercive mechanisms. Domination-seekers can significantly enhance their coercive capabilities and lower the costs of domination by self-strengthening reforms, divide-and-conquer strategies, and Machiavellian stratagems. The term "logic of balancing" here refers to the set of countervailing mechanisms, and the "logic of domination" to the set of coercive mechanisms. When politics is seen as strategic interaction between the logic of domination and the logic of balancing, both the balance of power and the triumph of domination are possible outcomes.

The mechanism of self-strengthening reforms is of utmost importance: It shapes the competition between the logic of balancing and the logic of domination; it bridges the mutual constitution of international competition and state formation; and it drives the endogenous transformation of both processes. Kenneth Waltz argues that international competition compels states to take "internal balancing" moves "to increase economic capability, to increase military strength, to develop clever strategies."[1] He is correct to highlight the structural pressures of war. However, he misses the dynamism of international politics by presuming that states make such efforts only to counterbalance attempts at domination. States may use their higher economic capabilities, increased military strengths, and cleverer strategies to establish domination. In addition, if states seek to "increase economic capabilities" by rationalizing national taxation, "increase military strengths" by building national armies, and "develop clever strategies" by establishing meritocratic administration, then they are also building state capacity. State capacity is critical to the relative success or failure of attempts at domination in both interstate and state-society competition. First, military reforms simultaneously improve fighting capabilities in international politics and tilt state-society struggles in rulers' favor. When states establish standing armies and monopolize the means of coercion, unarmed resistance can be more readily crushed. Second, economic reforms provide more revenues for both international competition and internal repression. When states introduce national taxation, they can also enjoy much wider resource bases and, hence, relative autonomy from narrow groups of resource holders. Third, meritocratic administration facilitates not just central command and strategic planning in international competition, but also control and surveillance of societal actors in state-society relations. Overall, self-strengthened states with enhanced administrative capacity can mobilize more of the wherewithal of war, enjoy higher chances of victory, consolidate conquered territories, extract resources from conquered populations, and prevent and suppress likely resistance.

---

[1] Waltz 1979, 118.

Chapters Two to Four demonstrated the playing out of the dynamics of competing logics in ancient China and early modern Europe. Although the logic of balancing is Eurocentric in its origins, it operated in the ancient Chinese system for more than three centuries from 656 BC to the turn of the third century BC. In international competition, ambitious states made their bids for hegemony but were checked one after another, nonhegemonic states generally engaged in balancing in their foreign policy, and opposite camps repeatedly restored roughly equal distribution of relative capabilities. Checks and balances similarly occurred in state-society relations. Ancient Chinese rulers understood that they needed the active support of their population if they wanted to excel in international competition. The desire to motivate the people to fight and die in war gave rise to the bargains of material welfare, legal rights, and freedom of expression. As the use of peasant-soldiers to provide military service, taxes, and corvée formed the basis of national strength, the security of the state rested with the well-being of the peasantry. Various states made land grants to guarantee subsistence, launched state-led irrigation projects to promote productivity, and introduced countercyclical measures to stabilize grain prices. To encourage commitment to the state, enlightened rulers promulgated impersonal laws and universally applied them to aristocrats and officials as well as commoners. In an age when good strategies could make a state and bad strategies could break it, moreover, many rulers treated their ministers, generals, and administrators on equal terms. The atmosphere of free thinking and free discussion further nurtured the Hundred Schools of Thought, which was akin to the Enlightenment. Some thinkers advocated the unmistakably liberal view that the people form the basis of government and that rulers are mere servants of their people. Mencians even preceded Huguenots in propounding the doctrine of resistance and tyrannicide.

Nevertheless, ancient Chinese history shows that war could be destructive as well as constructive of checks and balances. Although the logic of balancing prevailed in both interstate and state-society relations for several centuries, the state of Qin, which began to emerge from relative weakness from 356 BC on, eventually established universal domination in 221 BC. This outcome occurred not because the logic of balancing somehow ceased to operate during Qin's rise to domination. In international politics, other states in the system did form balancing alliances. However, as the logic of collective action would predict, alliances came about slowly and disintegrated quickly. Qin's targets fought bitterly among themselves to seize territorial gains from weaker neighbors and from one another. Qin therefore could defeat them seriatim with the shrewd combination of self-strengthening reforms, divide-and-conquer strategies, cunning stratagems in diplomatic and military maneuvers, and mass killings of enemy soldiers on the battlefields. Moreover, Qin faced the problem of rising costs of expansion because it was located in the peripheral west and had to travel long distances when it conquered eastward. But Qin overcame this obstacle by proceeding with piecemeal encroachment and by using already conquered pieces of territory as forward bases for targets further away. Consequently, the logic of balancing managed to slow but did not block Qin's rise to domination.

In state-society relations, similarly, the Qin state exerted total control and eroded the bargains of legal rights and freedom of expression. The processes of bureaucratization of administration, monopolization of the means of coercion, and nationalization of taxation significantly enhanced state domination. The capacity for direct rule, in particular, facilitated mutual surveillance and collective responsibility at the household level. The Qin state sought to divide and rule the people by holding family members and neighbors collectively responsible for crimes committed by any one member, and by encouraging them to report on one another with handsome rewards. However, the desire to achieve hegemony and domination in the international realm meant that Qin's rulers could not enslave their own people in the domestic realm. The Qin state fulfilled the bargain of economic rights which served as substitutes for political rights. Qin's rulers also provided justice by consistently applying rewards and punishments to all social classes and preventing local officials from abusing the people. Qin used the same system of handsome rewards and severe punishments to motivate peasant-soldiers to work hard in agriculture and to fight hard in war. Material incentives proved to be extremely effective in pushing forward the logic of domination – they simultaneously dampened constitutional bargains in state formation and generated enthusiastic support for expansionism in international competition.

Qin's shrewd application of the logic of domination clearly illustrates what agency can achieve in macrohistorical processes. But this does not mean that structure was irrelevant. Qin's success was immensely facilitated by the conjuncture of the early development of self-strengthening reforms in the ancient Chinese system and the late development of Qin. At the onset of system formation in ancient China, the earliest hegemony-seeking states were already compelled to pursue nascent elements of self-strengthening reforms. As self-strengthened states could maximize coercive capabilities and minimize costs, weak states faced territorial losses and even conquest. With survival at stake, states were in turn compelled constantly to deepen their self-strengthening reforms and even to pursue dirty stratagems and barbaric tactics. The system thus witnessed increasingly intense international competition, with frequent warfare, recurrent territorial transfers, and dramatic rise and decline – even death – of great powers. It was in such an already brutish and nasty world that the latecomer Qin could pursue the most comprehensive self-strengthening reforms and the most ruthless stratagems and tactics. In the end, Qin pushed the mutually constitutive and mutually reinforcing processes of international competition and state formation to the logical conclusion. The state of Qin established a coercive universal empire, the Qin Dynasty, in 221 BC.

If international competition tends to favor the logic of domination – and Qin indeed achieved universal domination in ancient China – then why did the logic of balancing prevail in early modern Europe? In light of the ancient Chinese trajectory, I have argued that European attempts at domination were inadequate. Among various coercive tools, European states generally practiced the counterbalancing strategy. However, the ancient Chinese stratagems of deceit and bribery were much less practiced in European diplomacy, and brutal killing of whole defeated armies was almost never attempted against fellow Europeans. Most important of all, the earliest domination-seekers adopted self-weakening expedients rather than self-strengthening reforms. To state it briefly, self-strengthening reforms refer to internal balancing moves that mobilize the wherewithal of war by enhancing administrative capacity. Self-weakening expedients refer to internal balancing moves that mobilize additional resources by relying on intermediate resource holders.

In ancient China, the earliest domination-seeking rulers of Chu, Qi, and Jin gradually built up administrative capacity, expanded army strength from their own populations, promoted agricultural productivity as the basis of national wealth, and consolidated central control over conquered territories. The situation in early modern Europe was different: With a higher level of monetization at the onset of system formation, the earliest domination-seeking rulers, Valois France and the United Habsburgs, could follow the easier course of relying on intermediate resource holders. Instead of building up state capacity, French and Habsburg rulers turned to military entrepreneurs to raise mercenary armies and to bankers and capital holders to provide loans and credits. Although such measures could generate additional resources for immediate campaigns, they were self-defeating in the long term. The use of mercenaries was particularly problematic. Mercenary troops not only had serious discipline problems, but also were prohibitively expensive. To relieve burning fiscal crises, rulers then contracted more loans and sold more offices. As such fiscal expedients alienated ever more future ordinary revenues, European states were driven into ever-escalating fiscal crises. Because European domination-seekers adopted self-weakening rather than self-strengthening measures, they could not maximize coercive capabilities and minimize war costs as their counterparts in ancient China could. Consequently, warfare was less frequent, combats were often indecisive, conquest was very difficult, and survival of sovereign states was rarely at stake.

The heavy reliance on intermediate resource holders further undermined already weak state authority in the domestic realm, resulting in state *de*formation rather than state formation. When the recruitment and command of troops were contracted to military entrepreneurs, the collection of tax revenues and management of public finance were auctioned to private financiers, and the administration of the realm was sold to venal officers, early modern European states were seriously hollowed out from within. As the state's administrative, extractive, and coercive institutions were effectively controlled by quasi-independent power holders, European kings had little choice but to make major concessions in state-society struggles. In short, it was because the logic of domination was so weak that the logic of balancing could survive for most of the early modern period.

This changed when the Great Elector and his successors embarked on ancient-Chinese-style self-strengthening reforms. Brandenburg-Prussia was able to rise from a weak state to a great power and achieve domination over the society. But Prussia's further ascendance was thwarted by the sudden turnaround of France. Through a revolution, various centuries-old self-weakening elements were overthrown overnight. Revolutionary France then launched comprehensive self-strengthening reforms which were common in Warring States China but revolutionary in early modern Europe: universal conscription, national taxation, and direct rule. Under Napoléon, France could even outmaneuver its targets on both the diplomatic and battle fronts. Living up to Machiavelli's ideal of combining the strength of the lion with the wit of the fox,[2] the Napoleonic empire was able to sweep through the European continent. After the missed

---

[2] *The Prince*, ch. 18.

opportunity at the onset of system formation, Europe was on the verge of following the coercive trajectory tracked in ancient China two millennia earlier.

Nevertheless, the early pursuit of self-weakening expedients meant that even the self-strengthened Napoleonic France lived in the shadow of a self-weakened past. France inherited huge national debts from the old regime, so much so that it could not finance the empire-building project solely out of its own national resources. As France was heavily reliant on allies to provide human and material resources, it was vulnerable to their defection. At the same time, the early use of mercenaries had led Britain to develop the public credit system to generate ready cash in time of war. This development not only made the cash-tight France even more vulnerable to the balance of power in international competition, but also strengthened checks and balances in state-society relations. While the ancient-Chinese-style or Prussian-style comprehensive self-strengthening model facilitated the state's domination over the society, the public credit system required parliamentary oversight to generate public confidence in state finance. The modern state that emerged thus maintained an unusual balance between the logic of domination and the logic of balancing – it possessed bureaucratized administration, monopolized coercion and nationalized taxation, on the one hand, but was checked by democratic representation, on the other.

Overall, the theoretical framework of the dynamics of competing logics not only accounts for alternative trajectories and endogenous transformation in ancient China and early modern Europe, but also highlights the contingency of both historical trajectories. In light of the European experience, the triumph of domination in ancient China was not at all a foregone conclusion. Qin's success at unifying the system involved overcoming not just the balance of power and the rising costs of expansion, but also the barrier of geography and the difficulty of consolidating conquests. If the Warring States system had survived, then citizenship rights would also have been preserved. In light of the ancient Chinese experience, the ultimate institutionalization of the logic of balancing in modern Europe was not at all inevitable. The pressure of international competition was so powerful that it unleashed similar causal mechanisms in both ancient China and early modern Europe, but different initial conditions set the two systems onto divergent trajectories. As the adoption of self-strengthening reforms versus self-weakening expedients fundamentally shaped relative capabilities and relative costs of war, this difference was able to trump the pressure toward convergence for some time. When the pressure of war built up in Europe and eventually com-pelled European states to embark on self-strengthening reforms, the Chinese and European trajectories had a second chance of convergence. Nevertheless, the late pursuit of self-strengthening reforms and the early adoption of self-weakening expedients continued to deflect Europe from the coercive trajectory.

5.2 Transformation of World Politics in the Post-Napoleonic Era

Although this historical comparison ends in 1815, the decisive defeat of the Napoleonic empire did not mark the end of history. It is often argued that the long and bitter war against Napoleonic France had the laudable effect of transcending narrow self-interests to enlightened self-interests in the Concert of Europe. According to Robert Jervis, for example, European statesmen learned that "the fates of the major powers were linked" and so the definition of self-interest became "broader than usual" and "longer-run than usual."[3] However, if peace was a function of war-weariness, then it would last for only as long as all great powers were exhausted. Not surprisingly, the Concert of Europe began to decay as early as the 1820s.[4]

When history is seen in the *longue durée*, it is more accurate to say that Revolutionary and Napoleonic France ushered a new era of heightened international competition in the modern period. After other European powers emulated French self-strengthening reforms, European politics evolved from competition of relative weaknesses to competition of rel-ative strengths. As illustrated by the ancient Chinese system, a world of self-strengthened states could be very dangerous (unless great pow-ers do not pursue opportunistic expansion). Indeed, Hobbesian compe-tition and Machiavellian stratagems deepened in the post-Napoleonic period, eventually culminating in the Darwinian struggle of survival of the fittest in the early twentieth century. Industrialization became the new formula for *fuguo* (by increasing economic efficiency and gener-ating unprecedented economic growth) and *qiangbing* (by facilitating the development of increasingly lethal military technology). At the same time, developments in administrative and communication technologies significantly eased the mechanism of rising costs of expansion, thus facil-itating the extension of power struggles beyond the European continent.

---

[3] Jervis 1982, 364; also Jervis 1997; Schroeder 1992; 1994a; 1994b.
[4] Jervis 1982, 368.

Samuel Huntington observes that "Britain and France, Germany and Japan, the United States and the Soviet Union, all became expansionist and imperialist powers in the course of industrialization."[5] Britain exploited its industrial and naval power to build a global empire. Prussia accelerated its self-strengthening efforts and unified Germany. Japan in the Meiji era likewise embarked on an ambitious modernization program to pursue *fukoku kyohei* (rich nation and strong army). All these self-strengthened powers scrambled for colonial concessions around the world. As colonial outlets gradually disappeared at the turn of the twentieth century, international competition became intensely zero-sum. In such an increasingly competitive world, international-political life again became nasty, brutish, and short. Moreover, domination-seeking states in the twentieth century did not hesitate to resort to ruthless tactics – not just against "uncivilized" populations, but also against fellow Europeans. Despite elaborate laws of war, they followed the principle that "all is fair in war."[6] The Axis countries, in particular, not only practiced mass killings of soldiers and civilians, but also experimented with chemical and bacteriological weapons.

Fortunately, such stronger coercive forces were matched by stronger normative forces in ways that were not seen in the ancient Chinese system. Although Britain was hardly a textbook case of the selfless "balancer," it continued to "balance" against any rising powers which challenged its leading position in the world. Even more notably, Britain refrained from pursuing traditional territorial expansion against its European neighbors even though it faced no serious challengers in the post-Napoleonic era. This phenomenon is even more remarkable as British power rose from strength to strength by commanding the lead in industrialization. Alexander Wendt argues that anarchy is what states make of it and so states may unmake it, but he cautions that transformation of a competitive international system is "extremely difficult."[7] He suggests that the unmaking of a Hobbesian world order requires at least two preconditions: "First, there must be a reason to think of oneself in novel terms. . . . Second, the expected costs of intentional role change – the sanctions imposed by others with whom one interacted in previous roles – cannot be greater than its rewards."[8] In the Pax Britannica, Britain certainly had the capability to bring about changes without serious risks. But where was the motivation? Immanuel Kant argued that "if by good fortune one powerful

---

[5] Huntington 1999 [1989], 35.   [6] Sorokin 1962, 339.
[7] Wendt 1992, 423.   [8] Ibid., 419.

and enlightened nation can form a republic (which is by nature inclined to seek peace), this will provide a focal point for federal association among other states."[9] It is doubtful that Britain was inherently more altruistic and more peaceful than other states. But Kant also suggested that international commerce would provide material incentives for moral commitments. Indeed, Britain had undergone a radical transformation in the definition of the self- or national interest.

As a result of the development of industrialization and capitalism from the mideighteenth century on, Adam Smith and other classical liberals argued that Britain should build an empire of trade rather than one of territory. They completely reframed the relative costs and benefits of war by arguing that Britain's strength rested with its superior productivity, that the costs of war involved the loss of trade benefits (or opportunity costs) as well as the actual costs of war making, and that the costs of consolidating conquests and extracting resources from resistant populations far outweighed the benefits.[10] Moreover, liberals made innovations to the idea of comparative advantage, which offered a positive-sum view of international competition as a counterweight to the mercantilist zero-sum view. During the Revolutionary and Napoleonic Wars, therefore, the competition did not simply involve the hegemonic status, but also involved different world orders. Britain desired the creation of a laissez-faire liberal world order centered on its industrial and financial core, while the Napoleonic empire wanted to establish a territory-based, autarkic continental system. The victory of the British world order would fundamentally transform the character of international politics in the modern period. As Henry Kissinger indicates, "England was the one European country whose *raison d'état* did not require it to expand in Europe."[11] For the first time in world history, the national interest of the most powerful state converged with the common interest of *relatively* peaceful coexistence. Although Britain dominated international trade and profited enormously from it, it also provided public goods to maintain the stability of the modern international system. With British leadership, some great powers and lesser states found it easier to forgo opportunistic expansion and to engage in concerted balancing against heightening threats. As Jack Levy observes, offensive alliances were common before 1815 but became "an extremely rare phenomenon" in the post-1815 period, and various

[9] Kant 1970 [1795], 104.
[10] Cain 1979; Doyle 1997; Rosecrance 1986; Schumpeter 1951; Zacher 2001.
[11] Kissinger 1994, 70.

indicators of balancing exhibit "stronger patterns in the second half of the half-millennium than in the first half."[12] Some scholars believe that hegemony, rather than the balance of power, is conducive to peace and stability.[13] Although the theory of hegemonic stability was quite alien to both the ancient Chinese and early modern European worlds, it finally became the reality in the Pax Britannica.

When Britain declined from the top rank in the early twentieth century, the national interest of the latest comer, the United States, grew even closer to the public interest of peaceful coexistence. Under Wilsonian liberalism, the United States saw its national interest as in harmony with a liberal world order in which states were bound by multilateral institutions, trade interdependence, and liberal democracy.[14] To be sure, the United States pursued opportunistic expansion in its own sphere of influence.[15] Yet, as a former colony itself, the United States was far more restrained in territorial expansion. It even persuaded European powers to grant independence to the colonial world at the end of the Second World War. As a trading state, the United States adopted Britain's positive-sum view of international competition and promoted interdependence. As a liberal democracy, it imposed democratization on Germany and Japan, encouraged democratization among decolonized states, and promoted democratic norms in international relations. No wonder even Lee Kuan Yew, a strong critic of the United States, remarks that "America has been unusual in the history of the world.... Any old and established nation would have ensured its supremacy for as long as it could. But America set out to put her defeated enemies on their feet.... That's unprecedented in history."[16]

Liberal transformation in the postwar (post–World War II) era has significantly surpassed that in the Pax Britannica. The logic of balancing in system transformation came to be buttressed by not just mutual trade benefits, but also the logic of balancing in state transformation. While the evolution from monarchical sovereignty to popular sovereignty suffered major setbacks and reversals in the nineteenth and early twentieth centuries, the process was eventually consolidated in the Western world in the postwar era. If state capacity is the key to understanding coercive transformation in earlier times, then democratic transition is the key to peaceful transformation in the modern era. A world of self-strengthened

---

[12] Levy 1981, 590; Levy and Thompson 2002, abstract.
[13] Gilpin 1981.   [14] Smith 2000.   [15] Zakaria 1998.
[16] Zakaria 1994, 124–125. The London-based *The Economist* concurs in its Millennium Special Edition that "of all history's great powers," the United States is "surely the strangest." *The Economist* 1999, 18.

states can be relatively peaceful if great powers respect the territorial integrity of one another and of smaller and weaker states. States with internal checks and balances are far more likely to pursue external checks and balances than domination and coercion. Liberal democracies not only do not fight each other, they are also far less likely to use their superior capabilities to pursue opportunistic expansion. Liberal democracies are also far less likely to employ Machiavellian stratagems in their conduct of war and diplomacy because democratic norms proscribe cunning and brutal tactics and democratic decision-making processes make keeping such plots secret more difficult. With a significant cluster of great powers sharing the logic of balancing in both interstate and state-society relations, the area of European Christendom was completely transformed from a war zone into a peace zone. Thus, although Germany and Japan underwent a new round of self-strengthening reforms in the postwar era, neither has renewed traditional opportunistic expansion or Machiavellian stratagems. After abandoning the traditional model of unification by coercion, moreover, European states have embarked on the U.S. model of unification by consensus.[17] Although a "United States of Europe" is nowhere in sight, the European Union is an unusual achievement in world history.

The end of the cold war and the beginning of the third millennium have sparked new debates about the transformation of world politics. The lesson from world history is that politics is transformable, history is open-ended, and state policies can shape the direction and process of transformation. Although world politics has been transformed in the more peaceful and rule-based direction in the modern era, this development should not be taken for granted. World politics will continue to be vulnerable to the logic of domination because the coercive tools of self-strengthening reforms, divide-and-conquer strategies, and Machiavellian stratagems remain available to political actors who wish to upset the liberal world order. Liberal democracies cannot rely on some structural countervailing mechanisms automatically to correct any deviations from the current equilibrium. Although universal domination – as the path not taken – has become increasingly impossible, attempts at regional domination can still be highly disruptive.

It may be argued that liberal democracies enjoy such insurmountable leads in military strengths, economic capabilities, and advanced technologies that any attempts at disrupting the status quo would be doomed to

---

[17] On the Philadelphian model, see Deudney 1995.

fail.[18] However, we should not overlook that the worst troublemakers in world history were originally insignificant lesser states. In ancient China, the Qin Dynasty, which ruled the entire Chinese world in 221 BC, was once a relatively weak state among great powers and was blocked from the central plain by the Yellow River a century earlier. In modern Europe, the Germany that made a bid for world hegemony in the twentieth century was once the puny Brandenburg-Prussia that was ravaged by great powers during the Thirty Years' War. Similarly, the Japan that defeated Qing China in 1895–1896 and pushed European powers out of Asia during the Second World War was once a tributary state of imperial China. In each of these cases, their originally more powerful neighbors did not imagine that such apparently weak states would be able to subjugate them several decades later.[19] To achieve the seemingly impossible, ambitious rulers in Qin, Germany, and Japan did not just pursue self-strengthening reforms to catch up, they also resorted to asymmetrical warfare to bridge any seemingly unbridgeable gaps in relative capabilities.[20] Moreover, the long-term dynamics of the rise and decline of hegemons further favored these challengers over the preexisting hegemons. Thus, the current liberal peace will be sustainable only if liberal democracies work to sustain – and expand – it.

The liberal peace should be expanded to the non-Western world because many parts of the Second and Third Worlds have descended into "zones of turmoil," infected with atrocious religious violence, ethnic cleansing, genocide, and transnational terrorism.[21] There is a growing consensus that the root cause of most conflicts in the less developed world lies in widespread failures at state building.[22] Upon independence, all the new countries acquired juridical sovereignty or international recognition almost overnight. But few developed the necessary state capacity for effective governance. Newly independent states typically copied the shells of the modern state but left out the substance: They established bureaucratic offices without centralization and meritocracy; they formed treasury and

---

[18] See, for example, Wohlforth 1999.

[19] It is noteworthy that Germany and Japan caught up twice in the twentieth century – both before and after the Second World War. Moreover, the most dramatic catching up in history occurred in modern Europe. Europe lagged behind China in processes of state formation and system formation for more than two millennia, but it eventually caught up and surpassed China in the eighteenth century.

[20] On asymmetrical warfare, see Arreguín-Toft 2001; Paul 1994.

[21] Singer and Wildavsky 1993; also Kaplan 1994.

[22] Ayoob 1998; Fukuyama 2004; Herbst 2000; Holloway and Stedman 2002; Jackson 1990.

internal revenue departments without nationalization of taxation and centralization of finance; and they built up the army, the navy, the air force, and the police without centralization of command and monopolization of the means of coercion. Yet, at the same time, many nationalist rulers treated international sovereignty as "their license to exploit people."[23] The combination of repressive rule and weak state capacity is a recipe for widespread civil wars whether then or now, east or west, north or south. But the Third World situation is unique in history in that even weak and small states have not had to face life-and-death struggles in interstate relations. Paradoxically, then, the territorial integrity norm enshrined in the United Nations Charter deprived newly independent states of the most crucial mechanism which compelled successful state building and state-society bargains in earlier eras.

If the Weberian state with both capacity and legitimacy solved the problems of state *de*formation and Darwinian competition in Europe, then it may also be the solution to state failures in the non-Western world. It may be argued that the ideas of constitutionalism, democracy, rule of law, human rights, and so on, are unique to Western civilization and incompatible with non-Western cultures.[24] However, if state-society bargains and citizenship rights indigenously sprouted on Chinese soil two thousand years before they blossomed on European soil, then the roots of liberal democracy are far more universal than Western. The real problem with state building and democracy building is not the incompatibility of non-Western cultures, but the weakness of the emerging view that the fates of the Western and non-Western worlds are interlinked. The reconstruction of collapsed states requires such immense resources and long-term commitment that great powers are reluctant to provide them unless geopolitical or business interests are at stake. Only history can tell whether world politics can be so thoroughly transformed that great powers will ultimately agree with the United Nations secretary-general Kofi Annan that "the collective interest is the national interest."[25]

---

[23] Jackson 1990, 140.

[24] However, there is a significant difference between the promotion of liberal-democratic ideals and institutions, on the one hand, and the imposition of elections by force, on the other. See Patten 2003.

[25] Kofi Annan, "Secretary-General Presents His Annual Report to General Assembly," 1996, United Nations website www.un.org, UN NewsCentre, Press Releases, search for "SG/SM/7136 GA/9596." See also Evans and Sahnoun 2002; Hui 2003a.

Appendix I

List of Wars Involving Great Powers in
Early Modern Europe (1495–1815)

This list is reproduced with permission from Jack S. Levy, *War in the Modern Great Power System* (Lexington: University Press of Kentucky, 1983), pp. 88–91, © 1983 The University Press of Kentucky.

1. *War of the League of Venice	1495–1497
2. Polish-Turkish War	1497–1498
3. Venetian-Turkish War	1499–1503
4. First Milanese War	1499–1500
5. *Neapolitan War	1501–1504
6. War of the Cambrian League	1508–1509
7. *War of the Holy League	1511–1514
8. *Austro-Turkish War	1512–1519
9. Scottish War	1513–1515
10. *Second Milanese War	1515–1515
11. *First War of Charles V	1521–1526
12. *Ottoman War	1521–1531
13. Scottish War	1522–1523
14. *Second War of Charles V	1526–1529
15. *Ottoman War	1532–1535
16. Scottish War	1532–1534
17. *Third War of Charles V	1536–1538
18. *Ottoman War	1537–1547
19. Scottish War	1542–1550
20. *Fourth War of Charles V	1542–1544
21. *Siege of Boulogne	1544–1546
22. *Arundel's Rebellion	1549–1550
23. *Ottoman War	1551–1556
24. *Fifth War of Charles V	1552–1556

* Denotes great power wars, that is, wars involving great powers on both sides.

25.	*Austro-Turkish War	1556–1562
26.	*Franco-Spanish War	1556–1559
27.	*Scottish War	1559–1560
28.	*Spanish-Turkish War	1559–1564
29.	*First Huguenot War	1562–1564
30.	*Austro-Turkish War	1565–1568
31.	*Spanish-Turkish War	1569–1580
32.	*Austro-Turkish War	1576–1583
33.	Spanish-Portuguese War	1579–1581
34.	Polish-Turkish War	1583–1590
35.	*War of the Armada	1585–1604
36.	Austro-Polish War	1587–1588
37.	*War of The Three Henries	1589–1598
38.	*Austro-Turkish War	1593–1606
39.	Franco-Savoian War	1600–1601
40.	*Spanish-Turkish War	1610–1614
41.	Austro-Venetian War	1615–1618
42.	Spanish-Savoian War	1615–1617
43.	Spanish-Venetian War	1617–1621
44.	*Spanish-Turkish War	1618–1619
45.	Polish-Turkish War	1618–1621
46.	*Thirty-Years' War – Bohemian	1618–1625
47.	*Thirty-Years' War – Danish	1625–1630
48.	*Thirty-Years' War – Swedish	1630–1635
49.	*Thirty-Years' War – Swedish-French	1635–1648
50.	Spanish-Portuguese War	1642–1668
51.	Turkish-Venetian War	1645–1664
52.	*Franco-Spanish War	1648–1659
53.	Scottish War	1650–1651
54.	*Anglo-Dutch Naval War	1652–1655
55.	*Great Northern War	1654–1660
56.	*English-Spanish War	1656–1659
57.	Dutch-Portuguese War	1657–1661
58.	*Ottoman War	1657–1664
59.	Sweden-Bremen War	1665–1666
60.	*Anglo-Dutch Naval War	1665–1667
61.	*Devolutionary War	1667–1668
62.	*Dutch War of Louis XIV	1672–1678
63.	Turkish-Polish War	1672–1676
64.	Russo-Turkish War	1677–1681
65.	*Ottoman War	1682–1699
66.	*Franco-Spanish War	1683–1684
67.	*War of the League of Augsburg (Nine Years' War)	1688–1697
68.	*Second Northern War	1700–1721
69.	*War of the Spanish Succession	1701–1713
70.	Ottoman War	1716–1718
71.	*War of the Quadruple Alliance	1718–1720

72. *British-Spanish War   1726–1729
73. *War of the Polish Succession   1733–1738
74. Ottoman War   1736–1739
75. *War of the Austrian Succession   1739–1748
76. Russo-Swedish War   1741–1743
77. *Seven Years' War   1755–1763
78. Russo-Turkish War   1768–1774
79. Confederation of Bar   1768–1772
80. *War of the Bavarian Succession   1778–1779
81. *War of the American Revolution   1778–1784
82. Ottoman War   1787–1792
83. Russo-Swedish War   1788–1790
84. *French Revolutionary Wars   1792–1802
85. *Napoleonic Wars   1803–1815
86. Russo-Turkish War   1806–1812
87. Russo-Swedish War   1808–1809
88. War of 1812   1812–1814
89. Neapolitan War   1815–1815

Appendix II

List of Wars Involving Great Powers in Ancient China (656–221 BC)

Only major belligerents are listed; minor allies are omitted. Initiators are listed first. All years are in BC.

1. Chu, Cai, Xu vs. Qi, Lu, Song, Chen, Wey[1]		656–653
2. Qi, Lu vs. Chen		656–656
3. Chu vs. Qi		645–643
4. Song vs. Qi		642–642
5. Chu, Zheng vs. Song		639–638
6. Chu vs. Chen		637–637
7. Qi vs. Song		637–637
8. *Qi vs. Lu, Chu		634–634
9. Chu, Cao, Wey and other allies vs. Jin, Song and other allies		634–632
10. Jin and allies vs. Wey		632–632
11. Jin and allies vs. Chu and allies		627–627
12. *Qin vs. Jin and allies		627–623
13. Jin vs. Wey		626–626
14. Jin vs. Lu		625–625
15. *Jin vs. Qin		620–615
16. Jin vs. Lu		619–619
17. Chu vs. Zheng		618–618
18. Chu vs. Chen		618–618
19. Jin vs. Cai		613–613
20. Qi vs. Cao		612–612
21. Qi vs. Lu		612–610
22. Yong vs. Chu, Qin, Ba		611–611

* Denotes great power wars, or wars involving great powers on both sides.

[1] The proper romanization for this state should be "Wei." To distinguish this medium-sized state from the hegemonic power that emerged later in the Warring States period, the convention is to reserve "Wei" for the latter and use "Wey" for the former.

23. *Jin vs. Qin and allies	608–607
24. *Chu and allies vs. Jin and allies	608–597
25. *Jin vs. Qin	601–601
26. Qi, Lu vs. Ju	598–596
27. Chu vs. Xiao, Cai, Song	597–596
28. Song vs. Chu, Chen, Wey	597–594
29. *Qin vs. Jin	594–594
30. *Qi, Chu vs. Jin, Lu, Wey	589–589
31. Jin and allies vs. Zheng	588–588
32. Zheng vs. Xu, Jin	588–587
33. Jin and allies vs. Song	585–585
34. *Chu and allies vs. Jin and allies	585–581
35. Wu vs. Chu and allies	584–584
36. Chu vs. Ju	582–582
37. *Qin and allies vs. Jin and allies	582–578
38. Zheng vs. Xu, Chu	577–576
39. Chu vs. Wey	576–576
40. Jin vs. Cao	576–576
41. *Wu vs. Chu	575–574
42. *Chu, Zheng, Chen, Cai vs. Jin, Song, Wey and other allies	575–571
43. *Jin vs. Qi	572–572
44. Jin vs. Xu	570–570
45. *Chu vs. Wu	570–570
46. Chu vs. Chen	570–566
47. *Jin, Song, Wey, Lu and other allies vs. Chu, Qin, Cai and other allies	565–559
48. *Wu vs. Chu	560–559
49. *Jin vs. Chu	558–557
50. Qi, Zhu vs. Lu	558–556
51. *Jin, Zheng vs. Qi, Chu	555–555
52. *Qi, Chu and other allies vs. Jin, Lu, Zheng	550–547
53. Qi vs. Ju	550–550
54. *Chu vs. Wu	549–548
55. Wey vs. Jin and allies	547–547
56. *Chu and allies vs. Wu, Xu†	538–536
57. Qi vs. Yan	536–535
58. Chu vs. Chen	534–534
59. Chu vs. Cai	531–531
60. *Chu vs. Wu, Xu†	530–529
61. Jin vs. Zhongshan	530–529
62. Ye, Chen, Cai, Xu vs. Chu	529–529
63. *Wu vs. Chu	529–529
64. *Wu vs. Chu	525–525

† Two states had the same romanized spelling "Xu." I use this symbol to differentiate one from the other.

112. Qi vs. Lu   408–408
113. Wei vs. Song   408–408
114. Han vs. Zheng   408–407
115. Wei vs. Zhongshan   408–406
116. Qi vs. Wey   407–407
117. *Qi vs. Wei, Han, Zhao   405–404
118. *Qin vs. Wei   401–401
119. *Wei, Han, Zhao vs. Chu   400–400
120. Zheng vs. Han   400–400
121. Qi vs. Lu   394–394
122. *Chu vs. Han   393–393
123. Wei vs. Zheng   393–393
124. *Wei vs. Qin   393–385
125. *Han, Wei, Zhao vs. Chu, Qin   391–391
126. Wei vs. Song   391–391
127. *Qi vs. Wei   390–390
128. Lu vs. Qi   390–390
129. Qin vs. Shu   387–387
130. *Wei vs. Zhao   386–386
131. Han vs. Song   385–385
132. Han vs. Zheng   385–385
133. Qi vs. Lu   385–385
134. *Qi vs. Wei, Zhao   384–384
135. *Zhao, Chu vs. Wey, Wei, Qi   383–379
136. Zheng vs. Han   380–380
137. *Qi vs. Yan, Wei, Han, Zhao   380–378
138. Shu vs. Chu   378–378
139. Zhao vs. Zhongshan   377–376
140. Han vs. Zheng   375–375
141. Yan vs. Qi   373–373
142. *Wei vs. Qi   373–373
143. Lu vs. Qi   373–373
144. *Zhao vs. Wey, Wei   372–372
145. Wey vs. Qi   372–372
146. *Wei vs. Chu   371–371
147. *Qin vs. Zhao   371–371
148. *Zhao vs. Qi   370–368
149. *Wei vs. Zhao   370–370
150. *Han, Zhao vs. Wei   369–369
151. *Qi vs. Wei   368–368
152. *Qin vs. Wei   366–361
153. Wei vs. Song   365–365
154. *Wei vs. Han   365–365
155. Zhao vs. Wey   365–365
156. *Wei vs. Zhao, Han   362–362
157. *Han vs. Wei   358–357
158. *Qin vs. Han   358–358

206. Chu vs. Yue	306–306
207. *Chu, Qin vs. Han, Wei, Qi	303–302
208. *Qin vs. Han	301–301
209. *Qin vs. Chu	301–298
210. *Qi, Han, Wei vs. Qin	298–296
211. Qi vs. Yan	296–296
212. *Qin vs. Han, Wei	294–286
213.*Qin vs. Zhao	288–288
214. Zhao vs. Song	288–288
215. Qi, Wei, Chu vs. Song	286–286
216. *Qi vs. Chu	286–286
217. Qi vs. Wei	286–286
218. Qin vs. Qi	285–285
219. *Yan, Qin, Zhao, Wei, Han v. Qi	284–284
220. Yan vs. Qi	284–279
221. Qin vs. Wei	283–283
222. Zhao vs. Qi	283–283
223. *Qin vs. Zhao	282–280
224. Zhao vs. Qi	280–280
225. *Qin vs. Chu	280–276
226. Zhao vs. Wei	276–275
227. Qin vs. Wei, Han	276–274
228. Zhao vs. Qi	274–274
229. *Wei, Zhao vs. Han, Qin	273–273
230. Qin vs. Yiqu	272–272
231. Wei, Han vs. Yan	272–272
232. Qin vs. Qi	270–270
233. *Qin vs. Zhao	270–269
234. Qin vs. Wei	268–266
235. *Qin vs. Zhao	265–265
236. Qi, Zhao vs. Yan	265–265
237. Qin vs. Han	265–261
238. *Qin vs. Zhao	262–257
239. Qin vs. Han	256–256
240. Qin vs. Zhao	256–256
241. Wei vs. Qin	254–254
242. Qin vs. Wei	254–254
243. Qin vs. Han	249–249
244. Qin vs. Zhao	248–247
245. Qin vs. Wei, Zhao, Han, Chu, Yan	247–247
246. Qin vs. Han	246–244
247. Qin vs. Wei	244–238
248. Zhao, Wei, Han, Yan, Chu vs. Qin	241–241
249. Qin vs. Zhao	240–239
250. Qin vs. Zhao	236–228
251. Wei, Qin vs. Chu	235–235
252. Qin vs. Han	231–230

² *Zhanguo ce* records that Qi surrendered to Qin without a fight because the chief minister took a bribe. Brooks argues that relevant *Shi ji* passages, which record that Qin had to fight Qi in 221 BC, seem more credible. Brooks, WSWG communication, October 21, 2002.

Appendix III

Operational Criteria for the Lists of Wars Involving Great Powers

Inclusion and Exclusion of Wars Involving Great Powers

The list of wars involving great powers in early modern Europe is adopted from Jack Levy's *War in the Modern Great Power System*.[1] I compiled the list of wars involving great powers in ancient China using Levy's operational criteria and procedure. The first step is to generate a tentative list of wars based on the most comprehensive chronologies available.[2] These sources include Gao Rui's *Zhongguo Shanggu Junshishi* (Military History of Ancient China), Lin Jianming's *Qin Shi* (A History of Qin), Mu Zhongyue and Wu Guoqing's *Zhongguo Zhanzhengshi* (History of War in China), Yang Kuan's *Zhanguo Shi* (History of the Warring States), the Academy of Military Sciences' *Zhongguo lidai zhanzheng nianbiao* (Chronology of Wars in China Through Successive Dynasties), the Military Museum's *Zhongguo Zhandian* (A Military Dictionary of China), and the Armed Forces University's *Zhongguo lidai zhanzhengshi* (History of Wars in China Through Successive Dynasties).[3] The second step is systematically to exclude conflicts that are not interstate wars. Civil wars are taken out except those which began with or ended as separate political units, and those in which outside powers intervened militarily against the government.[4] Wars involving nomadic tribes such as *rong* and *di* are also excluded because such entities did not exert centralized authority

---

[1] Levy 1983, 88–91.   [2] Ibid., 58.

[3] Gao 1995; Junshi bowuguan 1994; Lin 1992; Mu and Wu 1992; Sanjun daxue 1976; Yang 1986; "Zhongguo lidai zhanzheng nianbiao" editorial board 2003. Levy includes only those wars identified by at least two authoritative sources. Levy 1983, 58, 63. This is not a problem for my data set because Chinese sources agree on most of the wars involving great powers. The listed chronologies have two major types of differences: First, some omit less important wars, thus making it imperative to compile a list of wars involving great powers rather than a list of general interstate wars. Second, different sources may report the same events one year earlier or later because there was no uniform calendar in the multistate era.

[4] Levy 1983, 63.

over relatively stable territorial bases.[5] But wars involving "barbarian" entities such as Ba, Shu, Yiqu, and Zhongshan, which formed states over relatively defined territories, are included. The third step is to exclude interstate wars that did not involve any great powers (see later discussion) so as to generate a list of "wars involving great powers," that is, wars that involved the participation of at least one great power on either side. This category subsumes great power wars, which involve great powers fighting on both sides, and general wars, which involve two-thirds of the great powers in the system.[6] It is necessary to focus on great powers not just because the most powerful states "determine the structure, major processes, and general evolution of the system,"[7] but also because we know so little about small entities that it is impossible to develop comprehensive lists of general interstate wars for either ancient China or early modern Europe.

Following a standard practice in international relations, Jack Levy also uses the threshold of 1,000 battle deaths as an additional criterion for the inclusion of a war. To make the two lists of wars as comparable as possible, I need to apply the same standard to ancient Chinese wars.[8] Unfortunately, battle-death figures in Chinese sources are very sporadic. The best one can do is to make estimates based on army strengths. In the early seventh century BC, the typical army size was about 10,000 on each side.[9] This means that a casualty rate of 5 percent would yield 1,000 *total* battle deaths. This is comparable to the average battle death rate of 5 percent in early modern Europe.[10] It is often pointed out that Chu and Qi did not engage in direct confrontation and so the very first war which marks the onset of system formation may fail the test. While Qi and Chu did not fight in 656 BC, the hegemonic rivals attacked each other's allies over several years between 656 and 653 BC. The total battle death figure should be very close to 1,000. In the ensuing rivalry between Chu and Jin in 634–632 BC, the 1,000 battle-death

---

[5] Sun 1999, 61.   [6] Levy 1983, 51, 75.

[7] Levy 1983, 8. Levy follows Waltz, who argues that "the units of greatest capability set the scene of action for others as well as for themselves." Waltz 1979, 72, 94.

[8] However, it is worth reflecting whether this threshold is applicable at all times. For instance, Cioffi-Revilla and Lai do not follow the one thousand battle-death threshold in their data set for the period 7200–722 BC Cioffi-Revilla and Lai 2001. Anthropological studies of war similarly do not observe any cutoff points. Snyder 2002, 13. This threshold is also problematic for the post–cold war era. Wang and Ray exclude the first Iraq War because it did not involve more than one thousand battle deaths. Wang and Ray 1994, 143. As the tolerance for casualty is dramatically lower in the present age than in historical times, and as advanced military technology allows the precise striking of military targets with minimal human casualties, quantitative analysts in international relations should reconsider this threshold in future research. Otherwise, the third millennium will be very peaceful just by definitional fiat.

[9] Lewis 1990, 61; Sawyer 1994, 52. For a general discussion of army size and battle deaths in ancient China, see Lewis 1999.

[10] The estimates for the French-Habsburg rivalry are 5 percent or higher. Sorokin 1962, 305, 313, 318. Those for subsequent centuries are 3 to 5 percent. Ibid., 543–577. Sorokin's average casualty rate is estimated on the basis of well-studied battles of a particular war or of similar wars during the general period. Sorokin 1962, 184–285; see also Levy 1983, 85.

threshold is no longer in doubt.[11] According to Ralph Sawyer, each camp mobilized 12,000 to 20,000 troops at the great battle of Chengpu in 632 BC.[12] Archaeological evidence shows that more than 600 lower-ranked soldiers from one side (most likely the losing side, Chu) were buried in the site.[13] If we add a small number of senior officers whose corpses were taken home and the casualties suffered by the other side (probably the winning side, Jin), then the total battle death figure should exceed 1,000.[14] From then on, army strengths steadily increased as Jin and other great powers extended military service to subjugated populations. Major battles between Chu and Jin, Chu and Wu, and Wu and Yue involved 20,000 to 50,000 on each side.[15] By the Warring States period, armies could reach 100,000 in the fifth and fourth centuries BC and then several hundred thousands from the late fourth century BC on.[16] In the ensuing wars of mutual aggression and annihilation, recorded battle deaths were in the tens – and hundreds – of thousands.

Nevertheless, great powers also fought weak and small states and probably could win victories with minimal casualties. To minimize this potential bias, I exclude about thirty-six wars in which great powers attacked very small entities and the very weak Zhou court.[17] This is in addition to the exclusion of thirty-five wars between medium-sized states, nine wars in which medium-sized states attacked small entities, and six wars of mutual aggression among Qin's targets after they had lost their great-power status. Surprise attacks that involved only minimal fighting may present a similar problem. But it is not always clear which particular wars involved surprise attacks and whether reinforcements were sent to front lines, so this category of easy victories cannot be systematically excluded. This is not to mention that surprise attacks frequently resulted in consequential territorial transfers, which would be an important consideration in the European context. Similarly, punitive campaigns in which Jin and Chu punished lesser states for not participating in international meetings or multistate alliances might merely involve a show of force with little fighting. But Jin and Chu also used the pretext of "punitive campaigns" to expand their spheres of influence and to engage in territorial expansion. This may explain why some punitive wars escalated to mutual retaliation and expanded to include allies on both sides. As it would be too arbitrary to exclude some punitive campaigns but include others, I include them

---

[11] I exclude two wars between Qin and Jin which occurred before these states became great powers in 632 BC. Jin became a great power after winning Chu. Qin participated on Jin's side.

[12] Sawyer, Warring States Workgroup (WSWG) communication, November 26, 2002. These are probably the most conservative estimates available.

[13] Brooks, WSWG communication, November 24, 2002.   [14] Ibid.

[15] Sawyer, WSWG communication, November 24, 2002; Sawyer 1994, 52, 122–125.

[16] Lewis 1999, 627; Sawyer 1993, 10–11; 1998, 463.

[17] Some of those very small entities could be nomadic units which should be excluded by a previous criterion. Note that Levy excludes wars between German principalities and the Holy Roman Emperor because he treats them as civil wars. Levy 1983, 59. While I regard wars between *guo* and the Zhou court as interstate wars, I exclude them because they are unlikely to pass the one thousand battle-death threshold.

so long as military actions were involved. To minimize any possible inflation, I exclude conflicts in which punitive forces withdrew without fighting.

Delineation of Wars Involving Great Powers

In compiling the list of wars involving great powers in ancient China, there is also the challenge of "how to draw a line around a single war, both temporally and spatially," that is, "[w]hen are a series of wars over time to be aggregated or compounded into one larger war?"[18] Chinese materials typically record *zhan*, which means both "battle" and "war." "For instance, *Zuo zhuan* lists some 540 interstate *zhan* in a time span of 259 years.[19] If all *zhan* are treated as wars, then the frequency of war in ancient China would be seriously inflated.[20] In the data set for the modern European system, Jack Levy follows the criteria of issue linkage, peace duration, and military coordination:

> [The] problem of temporal aggregation is particularly difficult for the wars... which were fought continuously but intermittently over long periods of time.... [N]ot all wars end with formal settlements.... For these cases, criteria for defining the end of war might include the existence of a significant period of peace (and not simply a temporary cease-fire or tactical withdrawal) separating intense military conflicts, or a reversal in the military alliances that generate a new conflict.... Not all simultaneous wars are interrelated. Conflicts with different participants or totally unrelated issues should not be compounded. Wars involving coordinated military planning should be aggregated. In this compilation, ambiguous cases are compounded into a single war unless there are compelling reasons to do otherwise.[21]

Levy's criteria provide useful guidelines for the aggregation and disaggregation of *zhan*, except for a few caveats. First, because most wars in ancient China involved opportunistic expansion and subsequent mutual revenge, it is very difficult to use the criterion of issue linkage except in wars of annihilation or unification. In cases in which there is evidence for overall strategic planning, discrete battles that are up to four years apart are aggregated as single wars. The two examples are Yue's battles with Wu in 482 BC, 478 BC, and 475–473 BC, and Qin's battles with Yan and Dai in 227–226 BC and then 222 BC. In all other cases, battles that should be unambiguously aggregated are less than three years apart. So a peace of more than three years is treated as significant and warrants disaggregation. Borderline cases with peace duration of exactly three years are generally aggregated. In analyzing the ancient Chinese system, this criterion of peace duration is far more

[18] Levy 1983, 65.

[19] Lewis 1990, 36. According to Brooks, the *Chunqiu* records 421 *zhan* for the Spring and Autumn period. Brooks, WSWG communication, November 18, 2002.

[20] This is the major problem with Bau's quantitative comparison of the modern international system with the Warring States system. By treating conflicts under a single name as a single war, Bau derives an extremely high frequency of war for the Warring States period. Bau 1986, 232. This problem is made even more acute as he treats the Thirty Years' War (1618–1648) and the Revolutionary and Napoleonic Wars (1803–1815) as one war each, while Levy disaggregates the former into four wars and the latter into two. Levy 1983, 68.

[21] Levy 1983, 65–67.

useful than the existence of peace agreements or the results of decisive battles. This is because peace agreements were rarely binding, and combat often resumed immediately after a settlement. For example, Qi and Chu agreed to a peace settlement in 656 BC but quickly resumed their rivalry. Similarly, the Jin-Qin war of 582–578 BC began after a peace agreement in 582 BC. In addition, wars in ancient China frequently continued after decisive battles because the winning side pursued the losing side to consolidate or enlarge gains. For instance, in Qin's war against Han and Wei in 294–286 BC, Qin annihilated 240,000 allied forces in 293 BC and continued to attack them. In Qin's war against Zhao in 262–257 BC, Qin killed up to 450,000 Zhao troops in 260 BC and then resumed attack the following year. As for military coordination, bilateral battles are aggregated into a multilateral war when one belligerent was a common enemy of others. Existence of a formal alliance or fighting on the same battleground is not required.[22] Qin's wars of unification against each state are disaggregated because there was no coordination among the targets. The only exception was the Yan-Dai alliance in 227–222 BC, and so the relevant battles are aggregated as one war. If there are still ambiguities after these procedures, the *zhan* in question are aggregated. To preclude inflating the frequency of war in ancient China, I prefer to err on the conservative side.

Identification of Great Powers

Another challenge in compiling a list of wars involving great powers is to identify the great powers. For the Spring and Autumn period, there is no agreement among historians on the great powers. For the Warring States period, there is some consensus that Chu, Han, Qi, Qin, Wei, Yan, and Zhao were the *zhanguo qixiong* (the big seven of the Warring States period). But Chinese historians do not have the practice of specifying the dates of entry and exit, thereby giving the impression that all seven states were comparable great powers for the whole Warring States period (453–221 BC). To improve precision, I again turn to Levy's criteria: First, "a state whose security rests on a broad territorial expanse or natural barriers to invasion but that is unable to threaten the security of other states is not a great power"; second, great powers "think of their interests as continental or global rather than local or regional" and so "account for a disproportionate number of alliances and wars in the international system, particularly those designed to maintain the balance of power and prevent the dominance of any single state"; third, great powers "defend their interests more aggressively and with a wider range of instrumentalities, including the frequent threat or use of military force"; and, fourth, great powers are "differentiated from others by formal criteria, including identification as a Great Power by an international conference, congress,

---

[22] Bau also too rigidly defines military coordination. For example, he disaggregates the war of Wei versus Zhao and Qi in 354–352 BC into two bilateral wars because Qi did not directly send troops to lift Wei's siege of Zhao. The same applies to the war of Wei versus Han and Qi in 344–340 BC. Bau 1986, 232. However, Qi would not have had an excuse to invade Wei had Zhao and Han not asked for assistance. And even though the battlefields were different, Qi's interference put Wei in the position of fighting two-front wars, a very important factor, which contributed to Wei's decisive defeats and decline.

organization, or treaty."[23] Most of all, Levy adds that "the end of a decisive war is the most obvious symbol marking the rise of a new power or decline of an old one and is used as a primary indicator of change in great power status."[24]

According to Jack Levy, the list of great powers in the early modern European system includes France (1495–1815), Austrian Habsburgs/Austria/Austria-Hungary (1495–1519; 1556–1815), Spain (1495–1519; 1556–1808), United Habsburgs (1519–1556), England/Great Britain (1495–1815), the Netherlands (1609–1713), Sweden (1617–1721), Russia (1721–1815), and Prussia/Germany (1740–1815).[25] The list of great powers in ancient China with their dates of entry and exit is as follows: Qi (656–284 BC), Chu (656–278 BC), Qin (632–221 BC), Jin (632–453 BC), Wu (584–475 BC), Yue (482–335 BC), Wei (408–293 BC), Han (404–293 BC), Zhao (404–260 BC), and Yan (284–279 BC). I discuss the rise and decline of these great powers in Chapter Two. Let me elaborate on the dating of their entry to and exit from the great-power status here.

In identifying great powers in ancient China, two of Levy's criteria generate different exit dates for Chu, Han, Wei and Zhao. The criterion of active involvement with international politics generates much later exit dates than the criterion of decisive defeat in war. As Chu, Han, Wei, and Zhao shared borders with Qin and suffered the immediate threat of domination, they were generally more active in balancing efforts. Wei was the initiator of the *hezong* strategy. It led the first balancing alliance in 318–317 BC, the fourth one in 247 BC, and the rescue of Zhao in 259–257 BC. Han participated in seven of the eight anti-Qin alliances. Zhao did not participate in the second balancing alliance in 298–295 BC but led the last one in 241 BC. Chu was also involved in the alliances of 259–257 BC, 247 BC, and 241 BC. Thus, the criterion of concern with the balance of power would generate exit dates as late as 241 BC. However, if I follow the criterion of decisive defeat in war and the resultant loss of core territories, then the exit dates should be set earlier, as listed previously. The ancient Chinese system shows that scholars should not take for granted the balance-of-power mechanism and underestimate the frequency of decisive defeats. Han and Wei, in particular, quickly became Qin's prime targets for territorial encroachment. After they lost 240,000 core forces in 293 BC, both were dramatically weakened, seriously demoralized, and put on the defensive in Qin's continued territorial onslaught. Chu's defeat in 278 BC was even more phenomenal. In one stroke, Chu lost not only several hundreds of thousands of soldiers and civilians, but also the western half of its territory, including its capital. Similarly, Zhao was unable to recover from the crushing defeat of 260 BC. At the end of this war, moreover, Qin managed to control about half of the territories in the system. By the time of the *hezong* alliance in 247 BC, Han and Wei were further reduced to the size of Qin's prefectures. When the last alliance failed in 241 BC, the capitals of Han and Wei were encircled by Qin's newly conquered territory. Because active involvement with the balance of power by Qin's targets was generally ineffective and became increasingly so over time, I use decisive defeat in war as the single most important criterion for the loss of the great-power status. To maintain consistency, decisive victory over

---

[23] Levy 1983, 16–18.   [24] Ibid., 24.   [25] Ibid., ch. 2.

an established great power is the marker for a state's entry to the great-power status.

Two other cases warrant some discussion: First, historians usually exclude Yue from the list of the "big seven of the Warring States period." After conquering Wu in 482 BC, Yue stayed out of great-power competition thereafter. However, Yue continued to encroach on small neighbors to expand its strength. Indeed, Yue's great-power capability was not challenged until it was decisively defeated by Chu in 335 BC. Therefore, Yue's exit date from the great-power status should be 335 BC, rather than the end of the Spring and Autumn period. Second, the case of Yan presents the converse problem. Yan is usually included as one of the "big seven" by historians. However, Yan was merely a medium-sized power for most the multistate period. It was not heavily involved in great-power competition and its security rested more on its peripheral northeastern location than on its relative capability. In fact, Yan was almost conquered by its strong neighbor, Qi, in 314 BC and could maintain a precarious existence only by feigning submission to Qi. Yan achieved the great-power status in 284 BC when it defeated Qi with the assistance of an anti-Qi alliance. But this status was short-lived and ended when Yan's forces were driven out of Qi in 279 BC.

The obvious omissions from this list of great powers are Zheng, Lu, and Song, which are usually regarded by historians as great powers in the Spring and Autumn period. In the eighth and the early seventh centuries BC (that is, before the onset of system formation), Zheng was originally quite strong among Zhou *guo*. Lu was an enduring rival with Qi and probably enjoyed the same ranking. Song was similarly an important state – it was even confident enough to face the mighty Chu in 639–638 BC. It is probable that Zheng, Lu, and Song maintained their absolute power. However, as Chu encroached on the Zhou world and the relative capabilities of Qi and Jin rose in the midseventh century BC, Zheng, Lu, and Song gradually sank to the status of medium-sized states.[26] Moreover, as Zheng and Song (Lu to a lesser extent) were sandwiched between Jin and Chu, they unfortunately became battlefields in the rest of the Spring and Autumn period. The competing hegemons would coerce them into diplomatic submission. When these states submitted to one hegemon, however, the other one would attack them to force them to switch sides. In the Warring States period, Zheng, Song, and Lu further fell prey to territorial expansion by neighboring great powers. Zheng was conquered by Han in 375 BC, Song by Qi in 286 BC, and Lu by Chu in 249 BC.

Participation

According to Jack Levy, participation of a state is determined by "a minimum of 100 battle fatalities or the involvement of 1,000 armed personnel actively engaged in combat."[27] As such figures are not available for ancient China, I follow Kevin Wang and James Lee Ray's criterion and code participation on the basis of a state's actual involvement in combat with its own military forces.[28]

---

[26] Rui 1995, 158; Guo 1994, 75–76, 93–94. [27] Levy 1983, 63.
[28] Wang and Ray 1994, 144.

Identification of Initiators, Winners, and Losers

Jack Levy does not identify initiators, winners, and losers in his data set. I follow Melvin Small and David Singer, who define the initiator of a war as the side whose troops "made the first attack in strength on their opponent's armies or territories" according to "historians' consensus."[29] Kevin Wang and James Lee Ray similarly consider "the side that perpetrated the first among the following actions as the initiator of the war: declaration of war, blockade (resulting in fatalities), and obvious instances of attack and invasion."[30] In a few cases in which military attacks were ostentatiously provoked, however, the provoker rather than the actual attacker is treated as the initiator. For instance, Chu attacked Qin in 312 BC, but Qin is coded as the initiator. This is because Qin cheated Chu, inducing it to break with Qi by falsely promising six hundred *li* of territory. If historical records do not show the initiator but specify the battlefield, then the state in which the war is fought is regarded as the target and its opponent as the initiator.[31] In general, the identification of winners and losers is often clearly stated in historical materials. If this is not the case, then I consider as the winner(s) the side which successfully occupied the territory of its opponent(s),[32] or the side whose political objectives for entering to the war were the closest to being achieved according to the result of the war.[33]

Despite these cautious steps to follow conventional practices strictly, this data set on ancient China should still be subject to high rates of error. But historical data inevitably are of much poorer quality than contemporary data. Jack Levy estimates that the error for fatality estimates in modern Europe reaches 25–30 percent.[34] Pitirim Sorokin, on whom Levy's data are based, cautioned that his error could be as high as 300 percent.[35] Nevertheless, as Sorokin also suggested, if the purpose of a study is to trace developments over centuries, then "even a very imperfect, grossly representative map may be of value, sometimes of great value."[36] Moreover, as I use hard data not for hypothesis testing but merely for complementing a historical-institutionalist account, I can tolerate a higher margin of error than strictly quantitative accounts.

[29] Small and Singer 1982, 194.   [30] Wang and Ray, 1994, 143.
[31] Bau 1986, 236–237.   [32] Ibid. 234–235.   [33] Wang and Ray 1994, 143–144.
[34] According to Levy, "The measurement error ranges from 5–10 percent for the frequency and extent of war to 10–15 percent for the duration and magnitude of war and 25–30 percent for the fatality-based indicators." Levy 1983, 138.
[35] Sorokin 1962, 274.   [36] Ibid., 270.

Appendix IV

Chronology of Periods of Unification and Division in Chinese History

This chronology is adopted, with some amendments, from Fu 1993, 359–60.

Xia	2070?–1600? BC[1]	
Shang	1600?–1045? BC	
Zhou	1045?–256 BC[2]	
Western Zhou[3]	1045?–771 BC	
Spring and Autumn period	770–453 BC	
Warring States period	453–221 BC	
Qin dynasty	221–206 BC	(214–206 BC[4])
Han dynasty	206 BC–AD 220	(108 BC–22 AD; 36–184)
Western Han	206 BC–AD 8	
Xin	9–24	
Eastern Han	25–220	
Three Kingdom period	220–280	
Wei	220–265	
Shu	221–263	
Wu	222–280	

[1] Dates of any events before 841 BC are rough estimates and subject to intense disputes. Even the very existence of Xia is hotly contested.

[2] The Zhou court continued to exist through the Spring and Autumn and Warring States periods until it was extinguished by Qin in 256 BC.

[3] For Zhou as for ensuing dynasties, the label "western" (or "northern") was added retrospectively after rulers were forced to move eastward (or southward) at the end of decisive defeats.

[4] Years in brackets denote periods of unification defined by the establishment or restoration of the Qin Dynasty's maximal territorial reach. That territorial reach is marked by the Great Wall in the north, the Yungui plateau in the southwest, the Pearl River valleys in the south, and the coastline in the east. Ge 1989, 29.

Jin dynasty	265–420	
Western Jin	265–316	(280–301)
Eastern Jin	317–420	
Sixteen Kingdoms	304–439	
Northern and Southern dynasties	386–589	
Southern dynasties	420–589	
Song	420–479	
Qi	479–502	
Liang	502–557	
Chen	557–589	
Northern dynasties	386–581	
Northern Wei	386–534	
Eastern Wei	534–550	
Northern Qi	550–577	
Western Wei	535–557	
Northern Zhou	557–581	
Sui dynasty	581–618	(589–616)
Tang dynasty	618–907	(630–755)
Five dynasties period	907–960	
Ten kingdoms	907–979	
Song dynasties	960–1279	
Northern Song	960–1127	
Southern Song	1127–1279	
Liao dynasty	960–1125	
Western Xia	1032–1227	
Jin dynasty	1115–1234	
Yuan dynasty	1271–1368	(1279–1351)
Ming dynasty	1368–1644	(1382–1644)
Qing dynasty	1644–1911	(1683–1850; 1865–1911)
Republic of China	1912–	
On mainland	1912–1949	
In Taiwan	1949–	
People's Republic of China	1949–	(1949–)

Bibliography

Romanization of Chinese names follows Beijing's *pinyin* system unless the authors in question have followed the Wade-Giles system or Cantonese system in English publications.

Adams, Karen Ruth. 2003/04. Attack and Conquer? International Anarchy and the Offense-Defense-Deterrence Balance. *International Security* 28 (3): 45–83.

Almond, Gabriel A., with Stephen Genco. 1990. Clouds, Clocks, and the Study of Politics. In *A Discipline Divided: Schools and Sects in Political Science*, 32–65. Newbury Park, California: Sage Publications.

Anderson, Matthew Smith. 1998. *The Origins of the Modern European State System, 1494–1618*. New York: Longman.

Andreski, Stanislav. 1971. *Military Organization and Society*. Berkeley: University of California Press.

Angle, Stephen C. 2002. *Human Rights and Chinese Thought: A Cross-Cultural Inquiry*. Cambridge: Cambridge University Press.

Archer, Margaret S. 1995. *Realist Social Theory: The Morphogenetic Approach*. Cambridge: Cambridge University Press.

Arthur, Brian. 1989. Competing Technologies, Increasing Returns, and Lock-in by Historical Events. *Economic Journal* 99 (394): 116–131.

Arthur, Brian. 1990. Positive Feedbacks in the Economy. *Scientific American* 262 (2): 92–99.

Arreguín-Toft, Ivan. 2001. How the Weak Win Wars: A Theory of Asymmetric Conflict. *International Security* 26 (1): 93–128.

Avant, Deborah. 2000. From Mercenary to Citizen Armies: Explaining Change in the Practice of War. *International Organization* 54 (1): 41–72.

Axelrod, Robert. 1984. *The Evolution of Cooperation*. New York: Basic Books.

Axelrod, Robert. 1997. *The Complexity of Cooperation: Agent-Based Models of Competition and Collaboration*, Princeton; New Jersey: Princeton University Press.

Ayoob, Mohammed. 1998. Subaltern Realism: International Relations Theory Meets the Third World. In *International Relations Theory and the Third World*, edited by Stephanie G. Neuman, 31–54. New York: St. Martins Press.

Barkey, Karen. 1994. *Bandits and Bureaucrats: The Ottoman Route to State Centralization*. Ithaca, New York: Cornell University Press.

Barkey, Karen, and Sunita Parikh. 1991. Comparative Perspectives on the State. *Annual Review of Sociology* 17: 523–549.

Bartlett, Robert. 1993. *The Making of Europe: Conquest, Colonization and Cultural Change, 950–1350*. Princeton, New Jersey: Princeton University Press.

Bates, Robert H., Avner Greif, Margaret Levi, Jean-Laurent Rosenthal, and Barry R. Weingast. 1998. Introduction. In *Analytic Narratives*, 3–22. Princeton, New Jersey: Princeton University Press.

Bates, Robert H., and Donald Lien. 1985. A Note on Taxation, Development, and Representative Government. *Politics and Society* 14 (1): 53–70.

Bau, Tzong-ho. 1986. The Stability of International Systems: A Study of the Warring States System of Ancient China. Ph.D. dissertation, University of Texas at Austin.

Bean, Richard. 1973. War and the Birth of the Nation State. *Journal of Economic History* 33 (1): 203–221.

Beckett, Ian F. W. 2001. *Modern Insurgencies and Counter-Insurgencies: Guerrillas and Their Opponents Since 1750*. New York: Routledge.

Black, Jeremy. 1987a. Introduction. In *The Origins of War in Early Modern Europe*, edited by Jeremy Black, 1–27. Edinburgh: John Donald.

Black, Jeremy. 1987b. Mid-Eighteenth Century Conflict with Particular Reference to the Wars of the Polish and Austrian Successions. In *The Origins of War in Early Modern Europe*, edited by Jeremy Black, 210–241. Edinburgh: John Donald.

Black, Jeremy. 1994. *European Warfare, 1660–1815*. New Haven, Connecticut: Yale University Press.

Blakeley, Barry B. 1970. Regional Aspects of Chinese Socio-Political Development in the Spring and Autumn Period (722–464 BC): Clan Power in a Segmentary State. Ph.D. dissertation, University of Michigan.

Blakeley, Barry B. 1999a. The Geography of Chu. In *Defining Chu: Image and Reality in Ancient China*, edited by Constance A. Cook and John S. Major, 9–20. Honolulu: University of Hawaii.

Blakeley, Barry B. 1999b. Chu Society and State. In *Defining Chu: Image and Reality in Ancient China*, edited by Constance A. Cook and John S. Major, 51–66. Honolulu: University of Hawaii.

Bleiker, Roland. 2001. East-West Stories of War and Peace: Neorealist Claims in the Light of Ancient Chinese Philosophy. In *The Zen of International Relations: IR Theory from East to West*, edited by Stephen Chan, Peter Mandaville, and Roland Bleiker, 177–201. New York: Palgrave.

Blockmans, Wim P. 1994. Voracious States and Obstructing Cities: An Aspect of State Formation in Preindustrial Europe. In *Cities and the Rise of States in Europe AD 1000 to 1800*, edited by Charles Tilly and Wim Blockmans, 218–250. Boulder, Colorado: Westview Press.

Blockmans, Wim P. 2002. *Emperor Charles V, 1500–1558*. London: Arnold.

Bloodworth, Dennis, and Ching Ping Bloodworth. 1976. *The Chinese Machiavelli: 3,000 Years of Chinese Statecraft*. New York: Farrar, Straus & Giroux.

Blue, Gregory. 1999. China and Western Social Thought in the Modern Period. In *China and Historical Capitalism: Genealogies of Sinological Knowledge*, edited by Gregory Blue and Timothy Brook, 57–109. Cambridge: Cambridge University Press.

Blue, Gregory, and Timothy Brook. 1999. Introduction. In *China and Historical Capitalism: Genealogies of Sinological Knowledge*, edited by Gregory Blue and Timothy Brook, 1–9. Cambridge: Cambridge University Press.

Bodin, Jean, edited and translated by Julian H. Franklin. 1992. *On Sovereignty: Four Chapters from the Six Books of the Commonwealth*. Cambridge: Cambridge University Press.

Bonney, Richard. 1978. *Political Change in France Under Richelieu and Mazarin*. Oxford: Oxford University Press.

Bonney, Richard. 1981. *The King's Debts: Finance and Politics in France, 1589–1661*. Oxford: Clarendon Press.

Boulding, Kenneth E. 1963. *Conflict and Defense*. New York: Harper & Row.

Brewer, John. 1989. *The Sinews of Power: War, Money and the English State, 1688–1783*. New York: Alfred A. Knopf.

Brook, Timothy. 1999. Capitalism and the Writing of Modern History in China. In *China and Historical Capitalism: Genealogies of Sinological Knowledge*, edited by Gregory Blue and Timothy Brook, 110–157. Cambridge: Cambridge University Press.

Brooks, E. Bruce. 1994. The Present and Future Prospects of Pre-Han Text Studies." *Sino-Platonic Papers*, No. 46.

Brooks, E. Bruce. 1998. Evolution Toward Citizenship in Warring States China. Paper presented at the European–North American Conference on "The West and East Asian Values," Victoria College, University of Toronto, July 31–August 2.

Brooks, Bruce E. 1999. Alexandrian Motifs in Chinese Texts. *Sino-Platonic Papers*, No. 96.

Brooks, E. Bruce, and A. Taeko Brooks. 1997. Intellectual Dynamics of the Warring States Period. University of Massachusetts at Amherst, *Studies in Chinese History*, No. 7.

Brooks, E. Bruce, and A. Taeko Brooks. 1998. *The Original Analects: Sayings of Confucius and His Successors*. New York: Columbia University Press.

Brooks, E. Bruce, and A. Taeko Brooks. 2002. The Nature and Historical Context of the *Mencius*. In *Mencius: Contexts and Interpretations*, edited by Alan K. L. Chan, 242–281. Honolulu: University of Hawaii Press.

Bull, Hedley. 1977. *The Anarchical Society: A Study of Order in World Politics*. New York: Columbia University Press.

Buzan, Barry, and Richard Little. 1996. Reconceptualizing Anarchy: Structural Realism Meets World History. *European Journal of International Relations* 2 (4): 403–438.

Buzan, Barry, and Richard Little. 2000. *International Systems in World History: Remaking the Study of International Relations*. New York: Oxford University Press.

Buzan, Barry, Charles Jones and Richard Little. 1993. *The Logic of Anarchy: Neorealism to Structural Realism*. New York: Columbia University Press.

Cain, Peter. 1979. Capitalism, War and Internationalism in the Thought of Richard Cobden. *British Journal of International Studies* 5 (3): 229–247.

Carr, Edward Hallett. 1964. *The Twenty Years' Crisis, 1919–1939: An Introduction to the Study of International Relations*. New York: Harper & Row.

Cassirer, Ernst. 1946. *The Myth of the State*. New Haven, Connecticut: Yale University Press.

Cederman, Lars-Erik. 1996. Rerunning History: Counterfactual Simulation in World Politics. In *Counterfactual Thought Experiments in World Politics: Logical, Methodological, and Psychological Perspectives*, edited by Philip Tetlock and Aaron Belkin, 247–267. Princeton, New Jersey: Princeton University Press.

Cederman, Lars-Erik. 1997. *Emergent Actors in World Politics: How States and Nations Develop and Dissolve*. Princeton, New Jersey: Princeton University Press.

Chan, Gerald. 1998. Toward an International Relations Theory with Chinese Characteristics? *Issues and Studies* 34 (6): 1–28.

Chan, Gerald. 1999. The Origin of the Interstate System: The Warring States in Ancient China. *Issues and Studies* 35 (1): 147–166.

Chan, Stephen, Peter Mandaville, and Roland Bleiker, eds. 2001. *The Zen of International Relations: IR Theory from East to West*. New York: Palgrave.

Chang, Kwang-chih. 1983. *Art, Myth and Ritual: The Path to Political Authority in Ancient China*. Cambridge, Massachusetts: Harvard University Press.

Chang, Wejen. 1996. Traditional Chinese Legal Thought. Unpublished lecture notes.

Chang, Wejen. 1998. Confucian Theories of Norms and Human Rights. In *Confucianism and Human Rights*, edited by William Theodore de Bary and Tu Weiming, 117–141. New York: Columbia University Press.

Checkel, Jeffrey T. 1998. The Constructivist Turn in International Relations Theory. *World Politics* 50 (2): 324–348.

Chen, Enlin. 1991. *Xianqin junshi zhidu yanjiu* (A Study of the military system in the pre-Qin period). Changchun: Jilin Wenshi chubanshe.

Chen, Jian. 1993. Will China's Development Threaten Asia-Pacific Security? *Security Dialogue* 24 (2): 193–196.

Chen, Shih-tsai. 1941. The Equality of States in Ancient China. *The American Journal of International Law* 35 (4): 641–650.

Chi, Hsi-sheng. 1968. The Chinese Warlord System as an International System. In *New Approaches to International Relations*, edited by Morton A. Kaplan, 405–425. New York: St. Martin's Press.

Cioffi-Revilla, Claudio, and David Lai. 2001. Chinese Warfare and Politics in the Ancient East Asian International System, 7200 B.C. to 722 B.C. *International Interactions* 26 (4): 1–23.

Christensen, Thomas J. 1996. *Useful Adversaries: Grand Strategy, Domestic Mobilization, and Sino-American Conflict, 1947–1958*. Princeton, New Jersey: Princeton University Press.

Christensen, Thomas J., and Jack Snyder. 1990. Chain Gangs and Passed Bucks: Predicting Alliance Patterns in Multipolarity. *International Organization* 44 (2): 137–168.

Chu, Ron Guey. 1998. Rites and Rights in Ming China. In *Confucianism and Human Rights*, edited by William Theodore de Bary and Tu Weiming, 169–178. New York: Columbia University Press.

Chu, Samuel C., and Kwang-Ching Liu. 1994. *Li Hung-chang and China's Early Modernization*. Armonk, New York: M. E. Sharpe.

Church, William F. 1969. *Constitutional Thought in Sixteenth Century France: A Study in the Evolution of Ideas*. New York: Octagon Books.

Clausewitz, Carl von, translated by J. J. Graham. 1968. *On War*. New York: Penguin.

Collier, Ruth Berins, and David Collier. 1991. *Shaping the Political Arena: Critical Junctures, The Labor Movement, and Regime Dynamics in Latin America*. Princeton, New Jersey: Princeton University Press.

Conner, Allison W. 1998. Confucianism and Due Process. In *Confucianism and Human Rights*, edited by William Theodore de Bary and Tu Weiming, 179–192. New York: Columbia University Press.

Coplin, William. 1968. International Law and Assumptions About the State System. In *International Law and Organization*, edited by Richard Falk and Wolfram Hanrieder, 15–34. New York: J. B. Lippincott.

Cosmo, Nicola Di. 1999. The Northern Frontier in Pre-Imperial China. In *The Cambridge History of Ancient China: From the Origins of Civilization to 221 B.C.*, edited by Michael Loewe and Edward L. Shaughnessy, 885–966. New York: Cambridge University Press.

Crawford, Neta C. 2000. The Passion of World Politics: Propositions on Emotion and Emotional Relationships. *International Security* 24 (4): 116–156.

Creel, Herrlee G. 1954. *The Birth of China: A Study of the Formative Period of Chinese Civilization*. New York: F. Ungar.

Creel, Herrlee G. 1970a. *The Origins of Statecraft in China*. Chicago: University of Chicago Press.

Creel, Herrlee G. 1970b. The Beginnings of Bureaucracy in China: The Origins of the Hsien. In *What Is Taoism? And Other Studies in Chinese Cultural History*, 121–159. Chicago: Chicago University Press.

Creel, Herrlee G. 1970c. The Fa Chia, Legalists or Bureaucrats? In *What Is Taoism? And Other Studies in Chinese Cultural History*, 92–120. Chicago: Chicago University Press.

Crump, J. I., Jr. 1964. *Intrigues: Studies of the Chan-kuo Ts'e*. Ann Arbor: The University of Michigan Press.

Crump, J. I., translation and annotation with an introduction. 1996 [1970]. *Chan-kuo Ts'e*, rev. ed. Ann Arbor: University of Michigan Press.

Cusack, Thomas R., and Richard J. Stoll. 1990. *Exploring Realpolitik: Probing International Relations Theory with Computer Simulation*. Boulder, Colorado: Lynne Rienner.

de Bary, William Theodore. 1991. *The Trouble with Confucianism*. Cambridge, Massachusetts: Harvard University Press.

de Bary, William Theodore. 1998a. Introduction. In *Confucianism and Human Rights*, edited by William Theodore de Bary and Tu Weiming, 1–26. New York: Columbia University Press.

de Bary, William Theodore. 1998b. Confucianism and Human Rights in China. In *Democracy in East Asia*, edited by Larry Diamond and Marc F. Plattner, 42–54. Baltimore: Johns Hopkins University Press.

de Bary, William Theodore. 1998c. *Asian Values and Human Rights: A Confucian Communitarian Perspective*. Cambridge, Massachusetts: Harvard University Press.

de Vries, Jan. 1976. *Economy of Europe in An Age of Crisis, 1600–1750*. Cambridge: Cambridge University Press.

Dehio, Ludwig. 1963. *The Precarious Balance: Four Centuries of the European Power Struggle*. New York: Random House.

Deudney, Daniel H. 1995. The Philadelphian System: Sovereignty, Arms Control, and Balance of Power in the American States-Union, Circa 1787–1861. *International Organization* 49 (2): 191–228.

Ding, Chenyan and Qingtong Wu. 1993. *Chunqiu zhanguo shiqi guannian yu siwei fangshi piange* (Changes in concepts and modes of thinking in the Spring and Autumn and Warring States periods). Hunan: Hunan Publisher.

Downing, Brian M. 1992. *The Military Revolution and Political Change: Origins of Democracy and Autocracy in Early Modern Europe*. Princeton, New Jersey: Princeton University Press.

Doyle, Michael W. 1986. Liberalism and World Politics. *American Political Science Review* 80 (4): 1151–1169.

Doyle, Michael W. 1997. Commercial Pacifism: Smith and Schumpeter. In *Ways of War and Peace: Realism, Liberalism, and Socialism*, 230–250. New York: W. W. Norton.

Duara, Prasenjit. 1995. *Rescuing History from the Nation: Questioning Narratives of Modern China*. Chicago: University of Chicago Press.

Duyvendak, J. J. L., translation with an introduction. 1963 [1928]. *The Book of Lord Shang: A Classic of the Chinese School of Law*. Chicago: University of Chicago Press.

Earle, Edward Meade. 1986. Adam Smith, Alexander Hamilton, and Frederick List. In *Makers of Modern Strategy: from Machiavelli to the Nuclear Age*, edited by Peter Paret, 217–261. Princeton, New Jersey: Princeton University Press.

Eckholm, Erik. 2000. In China, Ancient History Rekindles Modern Doubts. *New York Times*, November 10, A3.

Eckstein, Harry. 1975. Case Studies and Theory in Political Science. In *Handbook of Political Science*, vol. 7, edited by Fred Greenstein and Nelson Polsby, 79–138. New York: Addison Wesley.

Economist, The. 1999. The Millennium of the West. *The Economist* Millennium Special Edition, December 31.

Editorial Department of the "Complete Works of Confucian Culture," translated by Baihua He. 1992. *Zhongyong*. Jinan, China: Shandong youyi shushe.

Elegant, Robert. 1999. Asian Millennium – What Went Wrong. *Far Eastern Economic Review*, April 15, 37–70.

Elster, Jon. 1989a. *The Cement of Society: A Study of Social Order*. Cambridge: Cambridge University Press.

Elster, Jon. 1989b. *Nuts and Bolts for the Social Sciences*. Cambridge: Cambridge University Press.

Elster, Jon. 1993. *Political Psychology*. Cambridge: Cambridge University Press.

Elster, Jon. 1999. *Alchemies of the Mind: Rationality and the Emotions*. Cambridge: Cambridge University Press.

Elster, Jon. 2000. Rational Choice History: A Case of Excessive Ambition. *American Political Science Review* 94 (3): 685–695.

Ertman, Thomas. 1997. *Birth of the Leviathan: Building States and Regimes in Medieval and Early Modern Europe*. Cambridge: Cambridge University Press.

Evans, Gareth, and Mohamed Sahnoun. 2002. The Responsibility to Protect. *Foreign Affairs* 81 (6): 99–110.

Evans, Peter. 1997. The Eclipse of the State? Reflections on Stateness in an Era of Globalization. *World Politics* 50 (1): 62–87

Evans, Peter, Dietrich Rueschemeyer, and Theda Skocpol, eds. 1985. *Bringing the State Back In*. Cambridge: Cambridge University Press.

Fairbank, John K. 1974. Introduction. Varieties of the Chinese Military Experience. In *Chinese Ways in Warfare*, edited by Frank A. Kierman, Jr. and John K. Fairbank, 1–26. Cambridge, Massachusetts: Harvard University Press.

Fairbank, John K. 1992. *China: A New History*. Cambridge, Massachusetts: Harvard University Press.

Fazal, Tanisha. 2001. Born to Lose and Doomed to Survive: State Death and Survival in the International System. Ph.D. dissertation, Stanford University.

Fearon, James D. 1991. Counterfactuals and Hypothesis Testing in Political Science. *World Politics* 43 (2): 169–195.

Fearon, James D. 1995. Rationalist Explanations for War. *International Organization* 49 (3): 379–414.

Fearon, James D. 1996. Causes and Counterfactuals in Social Science: Exploring an Analogy Between Cellular Automata and Historical Processes. In *Counterfactual Thought Experiments in World Politics: Logical, Methodological, and Psychological Perspectives*, edited by Philip Tetlock and Aaron Belkin, 39–67. Princeton, New Jersey: Princeton University Press.

Fearon, James D. 1997. The Offense-Defense Balance and War Since 1648. Paper presented at a brownbag at Columbia University, April 23.

Franklin, Julian H. 1992. Introduction. In *On Sovereignty: Four Chapters from the Six Books of the Commonwealth* by Jean Bodin, ix–xxvi. Cambridge: Cambridge University Press.

Fu, Zhengyuan. 1993. *Autocratic Tradition and Chinese Politics*. Cambridge: Cambridge University Press.

Fukuyama, Francis. 1989. The End of History? *The National Interest* 16: 3–18.

Fukuyama, Francis. 1995. *Trust: The Social Virtues and the Creation of Prosperity*. New York: Free Press.

Fukuyama, Francis. 2004. *State-building: Governance and World Order in the 21st Century*. Ithaca, New York: Cornell University Press.

Gao, Guangjing. 1998. *Zhongguo guojia qiyuan ji xingcheng* (The origins and formation of the Chinese state). Changsha: Hunan renmin chubanshe.

Gao, Rui, ed. 1992. *Zhongguo Junshishilue* (A brief military history of China), vol. 1. Beijing: Junshi kexue chubanshe (Academy of Military Sciences).

Gao, Rui. 1995. *Zhongguo Shanggu Junshishi* (Military history of ancient China). Beijing: Junshi kexue chubanshe (Academy of Military Sciences).

Ge, Jianxiong. 1989. *Putian zhixia: tongyi fenlie yu zhongguo zhengzhi* (All under heaven: Unification, division, and Chinese politics). Changjun: Jilin Education Press.

Geortz, Gary, and Paul Diehl. 1992. *Territorial Changes and International Conflict.* London; New York: Routledge.

Gerschenkron, Alexander. 1966. *Economic Backwardness in Historical Perspective: A Book of Essays.* Cambridge, Massachusetts: Harvard University Press.

Geuss, Raymond. 2001. *History and Illusion in Politics.* Cambridge: Cambridge University Press.

Gibler, Douglas M., and John A. Vasquez. 1998. Uncovering the Dangerous Alliances, 1495–1980. *International Security Quarterly* 42 (4): 785–807.

Giddens, Anthony. 1987. *The Nation-State and Violence.* Berkeley: University of California Press.

Gilley, Bruce. 2000. Digging into the Future. *Far Eastern Economic Review*, July 20, 74.

Gilpin, Robert. 1977. Economic Interdependence and National Security in Historical Perspective. In *Economic Issues and National Security*, edited by Klaus E. Knorr and Frank N. Trager, 19–66. Lawrence: National Security Education Program, Regents Press of Kansas.

Gilpin, Robert. 1981. *War and Change in World Politics.* Cambridge: Cambridge University Press.

Glaser, Charles L., and Chaim Kaufman. 1998. What Is the Offense-Defense Balance and Can We Measure it? *International Security* 22 (4): 44–82.

Glaser, Charles L., and Chaim Kaufman. 1998/99. Correspondence: Taking Offense at Offense-Defense Theory. *International Security* 23 (3): 200–206.

Goldin, Paul R. 2001. Han Feizi's Doctrine of Self-Interest. *Asian Philosophy* 11 (3): 151–159.

Goldstone, Jack A. 1991. *Revolution and Rebellion in the Early Modern World.* Berkeley: University of California Press.

Goldstone, Jack A., and Charles Tilly. 2001. Threat (and Opportunity): Popular Action and State Response in the Dynamics of Contentious Action. In *Silence and Voice in the Study of Contentious Politics*, edited by Ronald R. Aminzade, Jack A.Goldstone, Doug McAdam, Elizabeth J. Perry, William H. Sewell, Sidney Tarrow and Charles Tilly, 179–194. Cambridge: Cambridge University Press.

Goodwin, Jeff. 2001. *No Other Way Out: States and Revolutionary Movements, 1945–1991.* Cambridge: Cambridge University Press.

Gourevitch, Peter. 1978. The Second Image Reversed: The International Sources of Domestic Politics. *International Organization* 32 (4): 881–911.

Graff, David A., and Robin Higham, eds. 2002. *A Military History of China.* Boulder, Colorado: Westview Press.

Green, Donald, and Ian Shapiro. 1994. *Pathologies of Rational Choice Theory: A Critique of Applications in Political Science.* New Haven, Connecticut: Yale University Press.

Grieco, Joseph. 1988. Anarchy and the Limits of Cooperation: A Realist Critique of the Newest Liberal Institutionalism. *International Organization* 42 (3): 485–507.

Griffith, Samuel B., translated with an introduction. 1963. *Sun Tzu: The Art of War*. New York: Oxford University Press.

Gross, Leo. 1968. The Peace of Westphalia, 1648–1948. In *International Law and Organization*, edited by Richard Falk and Wolfram Hanrieder, 45–67. New York: J. B. Lippincott.

Gu, Jiegang. 1982 [1926]. *Gushipian* (Ancient history disputes), vol. 2, 1–10. Shanghai: Shanghai Classics.

Guan, Donggui. 1995. One Country, Two Systems in the Qin-Han Periods – Contradiction and Integration of Political Structures. In *Zhongguo lishishang de fenyuhe xueshu yantaohui lunwenji* (Collection of essays from the Seminar on Unification and Division in Chinese History), edited by Zhongguo lishishang de fenyuhe xueshu yantaohui editorial board, 57–68. Taipei: Lianjing chubanshe.

Guanzi xuekan editorial board. 1993. *Qi wenhua zonglun* (A general discussion of Qi's culture). Beijing: Huaming chubanshe.

Gulick, Edward. 1955. *Europe's Classical Balance of Power*. New York: W. W. Norton.

Guo, Baojun. 1963. *Zhongguo qingtong zhi shidai* (China's Bronze Age). Beijing: Sanlian.

Guo, Keyu. 1994. *Luguoshi* (History of the state of Lu). Beijing: Renmin.

Guofangbu (Ministry of Defense). 1989. *Zhongguo zhanshi dacidian* (Great dictionary of Chinese military affairs). Taipei: Liming wenhua.

Gurr, Ted Robert. 1988. War, Revolution, and the Growth of the Coercive State. *Comparative Political Studies* 21 (1): 45–65.

Handel, Michael I. 1990. *Weak States in the International System*. London: Frank Cass.

Hart, Marjolein C't. 1993. *The Making of a Bourgeois State: War, Politics and Finance During the Dutch Revolt*. Manchester: Manchester University Press.

Havel, Václav, translated by Paul Wilson and others. 1997. *The Art of the Impossible: Politics as Morality in Practice: Speeches and Writings, 1990–1996*. New York: Knopf.

Hayek, Friederick. 1944. *The Road to Serfdom*. Chicago: University of Chicago Press.

Herbst, Jeffrey. 2000. *States and Power in Africa: Comparative Lessons in Authority and Control*. Princeton, New Jersey: Princeton University Press.

Herz, John, H. 1959. *International Politics in the Atomic Age*. New York: Columbia University Press.

Hintze, Otto. 1975a. The Formation of States and Constitutional Development: A Study in History and Politics. In *The Historical Essays of Otto Hintze*, edited by Felix Gilbert, 157–177. New York: Oxford University Press.

Hintze, Otto. 1975b. Military Organization and the Organization of the State. In *The Historical Essays of Otto Hintze*, edited by Felix Gilbert, 178–215. New York: Oxford University Press.

Hirschman, Albert O. 1945. *National Power and the Structure of Foreign Trade*. Berkeley: University of California Press.

Hirschman, Albert O. 1977. *The Passions and the Interests: Political Arguments for Capitalism Before Its Triumph*. Princeton, New Jersey: Princeton University Press.

Hirschman, Albert O. 1992. *Rival Views of Market Society and Other Recent Essays*. Cambridge, Massachusetts: Harvard University Press.

Hobbes, Thomas. 1992. *Leviathan*. In *Classics of Moral and Political Theory*, edited by Michael Morgan, 571–732. Indianapolis: Hackett.

Hobson, John M. 2000. *The State and International Relations*. Cambridge: Cambridge University Press.

Hobson, John M. 2002. The Two Waves of Weberian Historical Sociology in International Relations. In *Historical Sociology of International Relations*, edited by Stephen Hobden and John M. Hobson, 63–81. Cambridge: Cambridge University Press.

Hobson, John M. 2004. *The Eastern Origins of Western Civilisation*. Cambridge: Cambridge University Press.

Hoffman, Philip T., and Jean-Laurent Rosenthal. 1997. The Political Economy of Warfare and Taxation in Early Modern Europe: Historical Lessons for Economic Development. In *The Frontiers of the New Institutional Economics*, edited by John N. Drobak and John V. C. Nye, 31–56. New York: Academic Press.

Holloway, David, and Stephen John Stedman. 2002. Civil Wars and State-Building in Africa and Eurasia. In *Beyond State Crisis?* edited by Mark R. Beissinger and Crawford Young, 161–188. Washington, D.C.: Woodrow Wilson Center Press.

Holsti, Kalevi J. 1991. *Peace and War: Armed Conflicts and International Order, 1648–1989*. Cambridge: Cambridge University Press.

Holsti, Kalevi J. 1995. *International Politics: A Framework for Analysis*, 7th ed. Englewood Cliffs, New Jersey: Prentice Hall.

Holsti, Kalevi J. 1999. The Coming Chaos? Armed Conflict in the World's Periphery. In *International Order and the Future of World Politics*, edited by T. V. Paul and John A. Hall, 283–310. Cambridge: Cambridge University Press.

Homer-Dixon, Thomas F. 2000. Environment, Scarcity and Violence. In *Perspectives of American Foreign Policy*, edited by Bruce W. Jentleson, 278–290. New York: W. W. Norton.

Hong, Junpei. 1975. *Chunqiu guoji gongfa* (International law in the Spring and Autumn period). Taipei: Wenshizhe chubanshe.

Hook, Brian, ed. 1991. *The Cambridge Encyclopedia of China*, 2nd ed. Cambridge: Cambridge University Press.

Hopf, Ted. 1991. Polarity, the Offense-Defense Balance, and War. *American Political Science Review* 85 (2): 475–494.

Hsiao, Kung-chuan. 1977. Legalism and Autocracy in Traditional China. In *Shang Yang's Reforms and State Control in China*, edited by Yu-ning Li, 125–143. White Plains, New York: M.E. Sharpe.

Hsu, Cho-yun. 1965a. *Ancient China in Transition: An Analysis of Social Mobility*. Stanford, California: Stanford University Press.

Hsu, Cho-yun. 1965b. The Changing Relationship Between Local Society and the Central Political Power in Former Han: 206 B.C.–8 A.D. *Comparative Studies in Society and History* 7 (4): 358–370.

Hsu, Cho-yun. 1997. War and Peace in Ancient China: The History of Chinese Interstate/International Relations. The Woodrow Wilson Center Asia Program Occasional Paper Number 75, October 3.

Hsu, Cho-yun. 1999. The Spring and Autumn Period. In *The Cambridge History of Ancient China: From the Origins of Civilization to 221 B.C.*, edited by Michael Loewe and Edward L. Shaughnessy, 545–586. Cambridge: Cambridge University Press.

Huang, Zhongxi, translated by William Theodore de Bary. 1993. *Waiting for the Dawn*. New York: Columbia University Press.

Hui, Victoria Tin-bor. 2001. The Emergence and Demise of Nascent Constitutional Rights: Comparing Ancient China and Early Modern Europe. *Journal of Political Philosophy* 9 (4): 372–402.

Hui, Victoria Tin-bor. 2003a. Problematizing Sovereignty: Relative Sovereignty in the Historical Transformation of Inter-State and State-Society Relations. In *International Intervention in the Post-Cold-War World: Moral Responsibility and Power Politics*, edited by Michael C. Davis, Wolfgang Dietrich, Bettina Scholdan, and Dieter Sepp, 83–103. Armonk, New York: M. E. Sharpe.

Hui, Victoria Tin-bor. 2003b. Heaven's Mandate Lies with the People. *South China Morning Post* (Hong Kong), July 11, A15.

Hui, Victoria Tin-bor. 2004. Toward a Dynamic Theory of International Politics: Insights from Comparing the Ancient Chinese and Early Modern European Systems. *International Organization* 58 (1): 175–205.

Hui, Victoria Tin-bor. 2005. Globalization, Development, and Constitutionalism in Historical Perspective: Lessons from the West on the Rest. Unpublished manuscript, University of Notre Dame.

Hulsewé, A. F. P. 1985. *Remnants of Ch'in Law: An Annotated Translation of the Ch'in Legal and Administrative Rules of the 3rd Century BC Discovered in Yun-meng Prefecture, Hu-pei Province in 1975*. Leiden: Brill.

Huntington, Samuel P. 1996 [1991]. Democracy's Third Wave. Reprinted in *The Global Resurgence of Democracy*, 2nd ed., edited by Larry Diamond and Marc F. Plattner, 3–25. Baltimore: Johns Hopkins University Press.

Huntington, Samuel P. 1999 [1989]. No Exit: The Errors of Endism. Reprinted in *The New Shape of World Politics*, a Foreign Affairs reader, 26–38. New York: Foreign Affairs.

Ingrao, Charles W. 1994. Paul W. Schroeder's Balance of Power: Stability or Anarchy? *The International History Review* 16 (4): 681–700.

Jackson, Patrick Thaddeus, and Ronald R. Krebs. 2003. Twisting Tongues and Twisting Arms: The Power of Political Rhetoric. Paper presented at the 99th Annual Meeting of the American Political Science Association, Philadelphia, August 28–31.

Jackson, Robert H. 1990. *Quasi-States: Sovereignty, International Relations and the Third World*. Cambridge: Cambridge University Press.

Jervis, Robert. 1978. Cooperation Under the Security Dilemma. *World Politics* 30 (2): 167–214.

Jervis, Robert. 1982. Security Regimes. *International Organization* 36 (2): 357–378.

Jervis, Robert. 1997. *System Effects: Complexity in Political and Social Life.* Princeton, New Jersey: Princeton University Press.

Jervis, Robert. 1998. Realism in the Study of World Politics. *International Organization* 52 (4): 971–991.

Johnston, Alastaire Iain. 1995. *Cultural Realism: Strategic Culture and Grand Strategy in Chinese History.* Princeton, New Jersey: Princeton University Press.

Johnston, Alastaire Iain. 1998. China's Militarized Interstate Dispute Behaviour 1949–1992: A First Cut at the Data. *The China Quarterly* (153): 1–30.

Jones, Eric L. 1988. *Growth Recurring: Economic Change in World History.* New York: Oxford University Press.

Jones, Daniel M., Stuart A. Bremer, and J. David Singer. 1996. Militarized Interstate Disputes, 1816–1992: Rationale, Coding Rules, and Empirical Patterns. *Conflict Management and Peace Science* 15 (2): 163–213.

Junshi bowuguan (the Military Museum of China). 1994. *Zhongguo Zhandian* (A military dictionary of China), vol. 1. Beijing: Jiefangjun chubanshe.

Kahler, Miles. 1998. Rationality in International Relations. *International Organization* 52 (4): 919–941.

Kaiser, David. 1990. *Politics and War: European Conflict from Philip II to Hitler.* Cambridge, Massachusetts: Harvard University Press.

Kant, Immanuel. 1970 [1795]. Perpetual Peace: A Philosophical Sketch. In *Kant's Political Writings*, edited by Hans Reiss and translated by H. B. Nisbet, 93–130. Cambridge: Cambridge University Press.

Kaplan, Morton A. 1979. *Towards Professionalism in International Theory.* New York: Free Press.

Kaplan, Robert D. 1994. The Coming Anarchy. *The Atlantic Monthly* 273 (2): 44–76.

Kapstein, Ethan B. 1995. Is Realism Dead? The Domestic Sources of International Politics. *International Organization* 49 (4): 751–774.

Katznelson, Ira I. 1992. The State to the Rescue? Political Science and History Reconnect. *Social Research* 59 (4): 719–737.

Katznelson, Ira I. 1997. Structure and Configuration in Comparative Politics. In *Comparative Politics: Rationality, Culture, and Structure*, edited by Mark Irving Lichbach and Alan S. Zuckerman, 81–112. Cambridge: Cambridge University Press.

Katznelson, Ira I. 2003. Periodization and Preferences: Reflections on Purposive Action in Comparative Historical Social Sciences. In *Comparative Historical Analysis in the Social Sciences*, edited by James Mahoney and Dietrich Rueschemeyer, 270–304. Cambridge: Cambridge University Press.

Kaufman, Stuart J. 1997. The Fragmentation and Consolidation of International Systems. *International Organization* 51 (2): 173–208.

Kaysen, Carl. 1990. Is War Obsolete? A Review Essay. *International Security* 14 (4): 42–64.

Kennedy, Paul. 1983. *Strategy and Diplomacy 1870–1945.* London: George Allen and Unwin.

Kennedy, Paul. 1987. *The Rise and Fall of the Great Powers: Economic Change and Military Conflict from 1500 to 2000.* New York: Random House.

Keohane, Robert O. 1984. *After Hegemony: Cooperation and Discord in the World Political Economy*. Princeton, New Jersey: Princeton University Press.

Kierman, Frank A., Jr. 1974. Phases and Modes of Combat in Early China. In *Chinese Ways in Warfare*, edited by Frank A. Kierman, Jr. and John K. Fairbank, 27–66. Cambridge, Massachusetts: Harvard University Press.

Kiser, Edgar, and Yong Cai. 2003. War and Bureaucratization in Qin China: Exploring an Anomalous Case. *American Sociological Review* 68 (4): 511–539.

Kiser, Edgar, and Margaret Levi. 1996. Using Counterfactuals in Historical Analysis: Theories of Revolution. In *Counterfactual Thought Experiments in World Politics: Logical, Methodological, and Psychological Perspectives*, edited by Philip Tetlock and Aaron Belkin, 187–207. Princeton, New Jersey: Princeton University Press.

Kissinger, Henry. 1994. *Diplomacy*. New York: Simon & Schuster.

Kohli, Atul, and Vivienne Shue. 1994. State Power and Social Forces: On Political Contention and Accommodation in the Third World. In *State Power and Social Forces*, edited by Joel S. Migdal, Atul Kohli, and Vivien Shue, *State Power and Social Forces: Domination and Transformation in the Third World*, 293–326. New York: Cambridge University Press.

Krasner, Stephen D. 1978. *Defending the National Interest: Raw Materials and U.S. Foreign Policy*. Princeton, New Jersey: Princeton University Press.

Krasner, Stephen D. 1984. Approaches to the State: Alternative Conceptions and Historical Dynamics. *Comparative Politics* 16 (2): 223–246.

Krasner, Stephen D. 1999. *Sovereignty: Organized Hypocrisy*. Princeton, New Jersey: Princeton University Press.

Kydd, Andrew. 1997. Sheep in Sheep's Clothing: Why Security Seekers Do Not Fight Each Other. *Security Studies* 7 (1): 114–154.

Labs, Eric J. 1992. Do Weak States Bandwagon? *Securities Studies* 1 (3): 383–416.

Labs, Eric J. 1997. Beyond Victory: Offensive Realism and the Expansion of War Aims. *Security Studies* 6 (4): 1–49.

Lang, Graeme. 1997. Structural Factors in the Origins of Modern Science: A Comparison of China and Europe. In *East Asian Cultural and Historical Perspectives: Histories and Society – Culture and Literatures*, edited by Steven Totosy de Zepetnek and Jennifer W. Jay, 72–96. Edmonton: Research Institute for Comparative Literature and Cross-Cultural Studies, University of Alberta.

Lao, Gan. 1985. Zhanguo qixiong ji qita xiaoguo (The Big Seven and other smaller states in the Warring States period). In *Zhongguo Shanggushi*. vol. 3. *The Two Zhou*, 499–533. Taipei: Zhongyan Yanjiuyuan Lishiyuyan Yanjiushuo.

Lasswell, Harold. 1941. The Garrison State. *American Journal of Sociology* 46 (4): 455–468.

Layne, Christopher. 1993. The Unipolar Illusion: Why New Great Powers Will Rise. *International Security* 17 (4): 5–51.

Layne, Christopher. 1994. Kant or Cant: The Myth of the Democratic Peace. *International Security* 19 (2): 5–49.

Lebow, Richard Ned. 2000. What's So Different About a Counterfactual? *World Politics* 52 (4): 550–585.

Levi, Margaret. 1988. *Of Rule and Revenue*. Berkeley: University of California Press.

Levi, Margaret. 1997. *Consent, Dissent, and Patriotism*. Cambridge: Cambridge University Press.

Levi, Margaret. 1998. Conscription: The Price of Citizenship. In *Analytic Narratives*, edited by Robert H. Bates et al., 109–147. Princeton, New Jersey: Princeton University Press.

Levy, Jack S. 1981. Alliance Formation and War Behavior: An Analysis of the Great Powers 1495–1975. *Journal of Conflict Resolution* 25 (4): 581–613.

Levy, Jack S. 1983. *War in the Modern Great Power System, 1495–1975*. Lexington: University Press of Kentucky.

Levy, Jack S. 1984. The Offensive/Defensive Balance of Military Technology: A Theoretical and Historical Analysis. *International Studies Quarterly* 28 (2): 219–238.

Levy, Jack S. 2003. Balances and Balancing: Concepts, Propositions, and Research Design. In *Realism and the Balancing of Power: A New Debate*, edited by John A. Vasquez and Colin Elman, 128–153. Englewood Cliffs, New Jersey: Prentice-Hall.

Levy, Jack, and William R. Thompson. 2002. Hegemonic Threats and Great Power Balancing in Europe, 1494/5–2000. Paper prepared for delivery at the 2002 Annual Meeting of the American Political Science Association, Boston, August 29–September 1.

Lewis, Mark E. 1990. *Sanctioned Violence in Early China*. Albany: State University of New York Press.

Lewis, Mark E. 1999. Warring States Political History. In *The Cambridge History of Ancient China: From the Origins of Civilization to 221 B.C.*, edited by Michael Loewe and Edward L. Shaughnessy, 587–650. Cambridge: Cambridge University Press.

Lewis, Mark E. 2000. The Han Abolition of Universal Military Service. In *Warfare in Chinese History*, edited by Hans van de Ven, 33–75. Leiden: Brill.

Li, Yu-ning. 1977. Introduction. In *Shang Yang's Reforms and State Control in China*, by Kuan Yang, xiii–cxx. White Plains, New York: M. E. Sharpe.

Liberman, Peter. 1993. The Spoils of Conquest. *International Security* 18 (2): 125–153.

Lin, Jianming. 1992. *Qin Shi* (A history of Qin). Taipei: Wunan chubanshe.

Liu, Kwang-Ching. 1994. The Beginnings of China's Modernization. In *Li Hung-chang and China's Early Modernization*, edited by Samuel C. Chu and Kwang-Ching Liu, 1–16. Armonk, New York: M. E. Sharpe.

Locke, John. 1992. *Second Treatise of Civil Government*, edited by Michael Morgan, 736–817. Indianapolis: Hackett.

Loewe, Michael. 1999. The Heritage Left to the Empires. In *The Cambridge History of Ancient China: From the Origins of Civilization to 221 B.C.*, edited by Michael Loewe and Edward L. Shaughnessy, 967–1032. Cambridge: Cambridge University Press.

Lynn-Jones, Sean M. 1998. Realism and America's Rise. *International Security* 23 (2): 157–182.

Lynn-Jones, Sean M. 2000. Does Offense-Defense Theory Have a Future? Research Group in International Security Working Paper 12, McGill University.

Machiavelli, Niccolò, edited and translated by David Wootton. 1994. *Selected Political Writings: The Prince, Selections from the Discourses, Letter to Vettori.* Cambridge: Hackett.

Mahoney, James. 2000. Path Dependence and Historical Sociology. *Theory and Society* 29 (4): 507–548.

Mahoney, James, and Dietrich Rueschemeyer. 2003. Comparative Historical Analysis: Achievements and Agenda. In *Comparative Historical Analysis in the Social Sciences*, edited by James Mahoney and Dietrich Rueschemeyer, 3–40. Cambridge: Cambridge University Press.

Mann, Michael. 1986. *The Sources of Social Power.* vol. 1. *A History of Power from the Beginning to A.D. 1760.* Cambridge: Cambridge University Press.

Mann, Michael. 1988. *States, War and Capitalism.* Oxford: Blackwell.

McAdam, Doug, Sidney Tarrow, and Charles Tilly. 2001. *Dynamics of Contention.* Cambridge: Cambridge University Press.

McAdams, A. James. 2001. *Judging the Past in Unified Germany.* Cambridge: Cambridge University Press.

McLeod, Katrina C. D., and Robin D. S. Yates. 1981. Forms of Ch'in Law: An Annotated Translation of the *Feng-chen shih. Harvard Journal of Asiatic Studies* 41 (1): 111–163.

McNeill, William H. 1982. *The Pursuit of Power: Technology, Armed Force, and Society Since A.D. 1000.* Chicago: University of Chicago Press.

Mearsheimer, John J. 2001. *The Tragedy of Great Power Politics.* New York: Norton.

Migdal, Joel S. 1988. *Strong Societies and Weak States: State-Society Relations and State Capabilities in the Third World.* Princeton, New Jersey: Princeton University Press.

Migdal, Joel S. 1994. The State in Society: An Approach to Struggles for Domination. In *State Power and Social Forces: Domination and Transformation in the Third World*, edited by Joel S. Migdal, Atul Kohli, and Vivien Shue, 7–36. Cambridge: Cambridge University Press.

Migdal, Joel S. 1997. Studying the State. In *Comparative Politics: Rationality, Culture, and Structure*, edited by Mark Irving Lichbach and Alan S. Zuckerman, 208–235. Cambridge: Cambridge University Press.

Migdal, Joel S. 2001. *State in Society: Studying How States and Societies Transform and Constitute One Another.* Cambridge: Cambridge University Press.

Milner, Helen V. 1998. Rationalizing Politics: The Emerging Synthesis of International, American, and Comparative Politics. *International Organization* 52 (4): 759–786.

Montesquieu, Baron de. 1873. *The Spirit of the Laws.* Cincinnati: Robert Clarke.

Moore, Barrington. 1966. *Social Origins of Dictatorship and Democracy.* Boston: Beacon.

Moravcsik, Andrew. 1997. Taking Preferences Seriously: A Liberal Theory of International Politics. *International Organization* 51 (4): 513–553.

Morgan, Michael, ed. 1992. *Classics of Moral and Political Philosophy.* Indianapolis: Hackett.

Morgenthau, Hans J. 1973 [1948]. *Politics Among Nations: The Struggle for Power and Peace.* New York: Knopf.

Motyl, Alexander. 1999. Why Empires Reemerge: Imperial Collapse and Imperial Revival in Comparative Perspective. *Comparative Politics* 31 (2): 127–145.

Mu, Zhongyue, and Guoqing Wu. 1992. *Zhongguo Zhanzhengshi* (History of war in China). Beijing: Jincheng chubanshe.

Murphy, Alexander B. 1996. The Sovereign State System as Political-Territorial Ideal: Historical and Contemporary Considerations. In *State Sovereignty as Social Construct*, edited by Thomas J. Biersteker and Cynthia Weber, 81–120. Cambridge: Cambridge University Press.

Murphy, David. 2002. Dujiangyan Rules River for 2,000 Years: Irrigation System Secured Sichuan's Place as China's Granary. *Far Eastern Economic Review*, May 23, available at http://www.feer.com/articles/2002/0205_23/po3ochina.html.

Needham, Joseph, with Wang Ling. 1954. *Science and Civilisation in China*, vol. 1. Cambridge: Cambridge University Press.

Needham, Joseph, and Robin D. S. Yates, eds. 1994. *Science and Civilisation in China*. vol. 5. *Part VI: Military Technology: Missiles and Sieges*. Cambridge: Cambridge University Press.

Nettl, J. P., 1968. The State as a Conceptual Variable. *World Politics* 20 (4): 559–592.

Nexon, Daniel H. 2003. Sovereignty, Religion, and the Fate of Empires in Early Modern Europe. Ph.D. dissertation, Columbia University.

Nivison, David S. 1999. The Classical Philosophical Writings. In *The Cambridge History of Ancient China: From the Origins of Civilization to 221 B.C.*, edited by Michael Loewe and Edward L. Shaughnessy, 745–812. Cambridge: Cambridge University Press.

North, Douglass C. 1981. *Structure and Change in Economic History*. New York: W. W. Norton.

North, Douglass C. 1990. *Institutions, Institutional Change and Economic Performance*. Cambridge: Cambridge University Press.

North, Douglass, and Robert Paul Thomas. 1973. *The Rise of the Western World: A New Economic History*. Cambridge: Cambridge University Press.

North, Douglass C., and Barry Weingast. 1989. Constitutions and Commitment: The Evolution of Institutions Governing Public Choice in Seventeenth Century England. *Journal of Economic History* 49 (4): 803–832.

Nuyen, A. T. 2002. Confucianism and the Idea of Citizenship. *Asian Philosophy* 12 (2): 127–139.

O'Brien, Kevin J. 1996. Rightful Resistance. *World Politics* 49 (1): 31–55.

O'Brien, Kevin J. 2002. Villagers, Elections, and Citizenship. In *Changing Meanings of Citizenship in Modern China*, edited by Merle Goldman and Elizabeth J. Perry, 212–231. Cambridge, Massachusetts: Harvard University Press.

Olson, Mancur. 1965. *The Logic of Collective Action*. Cambridge, Massachusetts: Harvard University Press.

Olson, Mancur. 1982. *The Rise and Decline of Nations: Economic Growth, Stagflation, and Social Rigidities*. New Haven, Connecticut: Yale University Press.

Olson, Mancur. 1993. Dictatorship, Democracy, and Development. *American Political Science Review* 87 (3): 567–576.

Osiander, Andreas. 2001. Sovereignty, International Relations, and the Westphalian Myth. *International Organization* 55 (2): 251–287.

Owen, John M. 1994. How Liberalism Produces Democratic Peace. *International Security* 19 (2): 87–125.

Parker, Geoffrey. 1988. *The Geopolitics of Domination*. London: Routledge.

Parker, Geoffrey. 1995. The Military Revolution 1550–1660 – a Myth? In *The Military Revolution Debate: Readings on the Military Transformation of Early Modern Europe*, edited by Clifford J. Rogers, 37–54. Boulder, Colorado: Westview Press.

Parrott, David A. 1987. The Causes of the Franco-Spanish War of 1635–59. In *The Origins of War in Early Modern Europe*, edited by Jeremy Black, 72–111. Edinburgh: John Donald.

Parrott, David A. 1995. Strategy and Tactics in the Thirty Years' War: The "Military Revolution." In *The Origins of War in Early Modern Europe*, edited by Jeremy Black, 227–252. Edinburgh: John Donald.

Parrott, David A. 1995. Strategy and Tactics in the Thirty Years' War: The Military Revolution. In *The Military Revolution Debate: Readings on the Military Transformation of Early Modern Europe*, edited by Clifford J. Rogers, 227–251. Boulder, Colorado: Westview Press.

Passmore, John Arthur. 1970. *The Perfectibility of Man*. London: Gerald Duckworth, 1970.

Patten, Chris. 2003. Democracy Doesn't Flow from the Barrel of a Gun. *Foreign Policy* 138, 40–45.

Paul, T. V. 1994. *Asymmetric Conflicts: War Initiation by Weaker Powers*. Cambridge: Cambridge University Press.

Philpott, Daniel. 2001. *Revolutions in Sovereignty: How Ideas Shaped Modern International Relations*. Princeton, New Jersey: Princeton University Press.

Pierson, Paul. 2000. Not Just What, but When: Timing and Sequence in Political Process. *Studies in American Political Development* 14 (1): 72–92.

Pines, Yuri. 2002. *Foundations of Confucian Thought: Intellectual Life in the Chunqiu Period (722–453 B.C)*. Honolulu: University of Hawaii Press.

Plattner, Marc. F. 1999 [1998]. Liberalism and Democracy. *Foreign Affairs* 77 (2): 171–180; reprinted in *The New Shape of World Politics*, 259–270. New York: Foreign Affairs.

Poggi, Gianfranco. 1990. *The State: Its Nature, Development and Prospects*. Stanford, California: Stanford University Press.

Polanyi, Karl. 1944. *The Great Transformation*. New York: Rinehart.

Polybius, translated by Ian Scott-Kilvert, selected with an introduction by F. W. Walbank. 1979. *The Rise of the Roman Empire*. New York: Penguin Books.

Porter, Bruce. 1994. *War and the Rise of the State: The Military Foundations of Modern Politics*. New York: Free Press.

Powell, Robert. 1991. Absolute and Relative Gains in International Relations Theory. *American Political Science Review* 85 (4): 1303–1320.

Powell, Robert. 1993. Guns, Butter, and Anarchy. *American Political Science Review* 87 (1): 115–132.

Powell, Robert. 1994. Anarchy in International Relations Theory: The Neorealist-Neoliberal Debate. *International Organization* 48 (2): 313–344.

Powell, Robert. 1999. *In the Shadow of Power: States and Strategies in International Politics*. Princeton, New Jersey: Princeton University Press.

Putnam, Robert D. 1993. *Making Democracy Work: Civic Traditions in Modern Italy.* Princeton, New Jersey: Princeton University Press.

Quester, George. 1977. *Offense and Defense in the International System.* New York: John Wiley & Sons.

Rasler, Karen, and William Thompson. 1989. *War and State Making.* Boston: Unwin Hyman.

Rasler, Karen, and William Thompson. 1994. *The Great Powers and Global Struggle, 1490–1990.* Lexington: University Press of Kentucky.

Reichwein, Adolf. 1925. *China and Europe: Intellectual and Artistic Contacts in the Eighteenth Century.* New York: A. A. Knopf.

Risse, Thomas. 2000. Let's Argue! Persuasion and Deliberation in International Relations. *International Organization* 54 (1): 1–39.

Roberts, Michael. 1995. The Military Revolution, 1560–1660. In *The Military Revolution Debate: Readings on the Military Transformation of Early Modern Europe,* edited by Clifford J. Rogers, 13–36. Boulder, Colorado: Westview Press.

Rogers, Clifford J. 1995. The Military Revolution in History and Historiography. In *The Military Revolution Debate: Readings on the Military Transformation of Early Modern Europe,* edited by Clifford J. Rogers, 1–12. Boulder, Colorado: Westview Press.

Rogowski, Ronald. 1983. Structure, Growth, and Power: Three Rationalist Accounts. *International Organization* 37 (4): 713–738.

Rosanvallon, Pierre. 1995. The History of the Word "Democracy" in France. *Journal of Democracy* 6 (4): 140–154.

Rose, Gideon. 1998. Neoclassical Realism and Theories of Foreign Policy. *World Politics* 51 (1): 144–172.

Rosecrance, Richard. 1986. *The Rise of the Trading State: Commerce and Conquest in the Modern World.* New York: Basic Books.

Rosecrance, Richard. 2001. Has Realism Become Cost-Benefit Analysis? *International Security* 26 (2): 132–154.

Rosecrance, Richard. 2003. Is There a Balance of Power? In *Realism and the Balancing of Power: A New Debate,* edited by John A. Vasquez and Colin Elman, 154–165. Englewood Cliffs, New Jersey: Prentice-Hall.

Rosecrance, Richard, and Chih-Cheng Lo. 1996. Balancing, Stability, and War: The Mysterious Case of the Napoleonic International System. *International Studies Quarterly* 40 (4): 479–500.

Rosen, Sydney. 1976. In Search of the Historical Kuan Chung. *Journal of Asian Studies* 35 (3): 431–440.

Rosenthal, Jean-Laurent. 1998. The Political Economy of Absolutism Reconsidered. In *Analytic Narratives,* edited by Robert H. Bates et al., 64–108. Princeton, New Jersey: Princeton University Press.

Ruggie, G. John. 1986. Continuity and Transformation in the World Polity: Toward a Neorealist Synthesis. In *Neorealism and Its Critics,* edited by Robert O. Keohane, 131–157. New York: Columbia University Press.

Ruggie, G. John. 1993. Territoriality and Beyond: Problematizing Modernity in International Relations. *International Organization* 47 (1): 139–174.

Sanjun daxue (Armed Forces University). 1976. *Zhongguo lidai zhanzhengshi* (History of wars in China through successive dynasties), vols. 1 and 2. Taipei: Liming wenhua chubanshe.

Sawyer, Ralph D., with the collaboration of Mei-chun Sawyer, translation with a commentary. 1993. *The Seven Military Classics of Ancient China*. Boulder, Colorado: Westview Press.

Sawyer, Ralph D., with the collaboration of Mei-chun Sawyer. 1994. Introduction. In *Sun Tzu: The Art of War*, 29–162. Boulder, Colorado: Westview Press.

Sawyer, Ralph D., with the collaboration of Mei-chun Sawyer. 1998. *The Tao of Spycraft: Intelligence Theory and Practice in Traditional China*. Boulder, Colorado: Westview Press.

Schell, Orville. 2004. China's Hidden Democratic Legacy. *Foreign Affairs* 83 (4): 116–124.

Schelling, Thomas. 1960. *The Strategy of Conflict*. Cambridge, Massachusetts: Harvard University Press.

Schmitter, Philippe C., and Terry Lynn Karl. 1996 [1991]. What Democracy Is . . . and Is Not. Reprinted in *The Global Resurgence of Democracy*, edited by Larry Diamond and Marc F. Plattner, 2nd ed., 49–62. Baltimore: Johns Hopkins University Press.

Schroeder, Paul. 1987. The Collapse of the Second Coalition. *Journal of Modern History* 59 (2): 244–290.

Schroeder, Paul. 1992. Did the Vienna Settlement Rest on a Balance of Power? *American Historical Review* 97 (3): 683–706.

Schroeder, Paul. 1994a. *The Transformation of European Politics, 1763–1848*. New York: Oxford University Press.

Schroeder, Paul. 1994b. Historical Reality vs. Neo-realist Theory. *International Security* 19 (1): 108–148.

Schroeder, Paul. 2003. Why Realism Does Not Work Well for International History. In *Realism and the Balancing of Power: A New Debate*, edited by John A. Vasquez and Colin Elman, 114–127. Englewood Cliffs, New Jersey: Prentice-Hall.

Schultz, Kenneth A., and Barry R. Weingast. 2003. The Democratic Advantage: Institutional Foundations of Financial Power in International Competition. *International Organization* 57 (1): 3–42.

Schumpeter, Joseph, translated by Heinz Norden. 1951. *Imperialism and Social Classes*. New York: Augustus M. Kelley.

Schweller, Randall L. 1994. Bandwagoning for Profit: Bringing the Revisionist State Back In. *International Security* 19 (1): 72–107.

Schweller, Randall L. 1996. Neorealism's Status-Quo Bias: What Security Dilemma? *Security Studies* 5 (3): 90–121.

Schweller, Randall L. 1998. *Deadly Imbalances: Tripolarity and Hitler's Strategy of World Conquest*. New York: Columbia University Press.

Scott, Bruce R. 2003 [2001]. The Great Divide in the Global Village. Reprinted in *Developing World*, edited by Robert J. Griffiths, 13th ed., 2–8. New York: McGraw-Hill.

Scott, James C. 1976. *The Moral Economy of the Peasant: Rebellion and Subsistence in Southeast Asia*. New Heaven, Connecticut: Yale University Press.

Scott, James C. 1985. *Weapons of the Weak: Everyday Forms of Peasant Resistance*. New Haven, Connecticut: Yale University Press.

Scott, James C. 1990. *Domination and the Arts of Resistance: Hidden Transcripts.* New Haven, Connecticut: Yale University Press.

Scott, James C. 1998. *Seeing like a State: How Certain Schemes to Improve the Human Condition Have Failed.* New Haven, Connecticut: Yale University Press.

Scott, James C., and Benedict J. Tria Kerkvliet, eds. 1986. *Everyday Forms of Peasant Resistance in South-East Asia.* London: Frank Cass.

Shaughnessy, Edward. 1996. Military Histories of Early China: A Review Article. *Early China* 21: 159–182.

Silberman, Bernard. 1993. *Cages of Reason: The Rise of the Rational State in France, Japan, the United States, and Great Britain.* Chicago: Chicago University Press.

Singer, Max, and Aaron Wildavsky. 1993. *The Real World Order: Zones of Peace/Zones of Turmoil.* Chatham, New Jersey: Chatham House.

Sivin, N. 1982. Why the Scientific Revolution Did Not Take Place in China – or Didn't It? In *Explorations in the History of Science and Technology in China,* edited by Guohao Li, Mengwen Zhang, and Tianqin Cao, 89–106. Shanghai: Shanghai Chinese Classics.

Skinner, Quentin. 1978. *The Foundations of Modern Political Thought,* vol. 1. Cambridge: Cambridge University Press.

Skocpol, Theda. 1979. *States and Social Revolutions: Comparative Analysis of France, Russia and China.* Cambridge: Cambridge University Press.

Small, Melvin, and David Singer. 1982. *Resort to Arms: International and Civil Wars 1816–1980.* Beverly Hills, California: Sage.

Smith, Adam, edited and with an introduction by Edwin Cannan. 1976. *An Inquiry into the Nature and Causes of the Wealth of Nations.* Chicago: University of Chicago Press.

Smith, Tony. 2000. National Security Liberalism and American Foreign Policy. In *American Democracy Promotion: Impulses, Strategies, and Impacts,* edited by Michael Cox, G. John Ikenberry, and Takashi Inoguchi, 85–102. Oxford: Oxford University Press.

Snyder, Glenn H. 1997. *Alliance Politics.* Ithaca, New York: Cornell University Press.

Snyder, Jack L. 1991. *Myths of Empire: Domestic Politics and International Ambition.* Ithaca, New York: Cornell University Press.

Snyder, Jack L. 2002. Anarchy and Culture: Insights from the Anthropology of War. *International Organization* 56 (1): 7–45.

Sonnino, Paul. 1987. The Origins of Louis XIV's Wars. In *The Origins of War in Early Modern Europe,* edited by Jeremy Black, 112–131. Edinburgh: John Donald.

Sorokin, Pitirim. 1962. *Social and Cultural Dynamics.* vol. 3. *Fluctuation of Social Relationships, War and Revolution.* New York: American Book Company.

Spruyt, Hendrik. 1994. *The Sovereign State and Its Competitors.* Princeton, New Jersey: Princeton University Press.

Strayer, Joseph R. 1955. *Western Europe in the Middle Ages: A Short History.* New York: Appleton-Century-Crofts.

Sun, Yurong. 1999. *Gudai zhongguo guojifa yanjiu* (Studies of international law in ancient China). Beijing: Zhongguo Zhengfa daxue chubanshe.

Sunzi, translated by Ralph D. Sawyer with the collaboration of Mei-chun Sawyer. 1994. *Sun Tzu: The Art of War*. Boulder, Colorado: Westview Press.

Svensson, Marina. 2002. *Debating Human Rights in China: A Conceptual and Political History*. Totowa, New Jersey: Rowman & Littlefield.

Tarrow, Sidney. 1998. *Power in Movement: Social Movements and Contentious Politics*. Cambridge: Cambridge University Press.

Taylor, A. J. P. 1971. *The Struggle for the Mastery of Europe, 1848–1918*. Oxford: Oxford University Press.

Teng, Ssu-yu. 1943. Chinese Influence on the Western Examination System. *Harvard Journal of Asiatic Studies* 7 (2): 267–312.

Tetlock, Philip E., and Richard Ned Lebow. 2001. Poking Counterfactual Holes in Covering Laws: Cognitive Styles and Historical Reasoning. *American Political Science Review* 95 (4): 829–843.

Thelen, Kathleen. 1999. Historical Institutionalism and Comparative Politics. *Annual Review of Political Science* 2: 369–404.

Thelen, Kathleen. 2003. How Institutions Evolve: Insights from Comparative Historical Analysis. In *Comparative Historical Analysis in the Social Sciences*, edited by James Mahoney and Dietrich Rueschemeyer, 208–240. Cambridge: Cambridge University Press.

Thomas, Ward. 2000. Norms and Security: The Case of International Assassination. *International Security* 25 (1): 105–133.

Thompson, I. A. A. 1976. *War and Government in Habsburg Spain 1560–1620*. London: Athlone Press.

Thompson, I. A. A. 1995. "Money, Money, and Yet More Money!" Finance, the Fiscal-State and the Military Revolution: Spain 1500–1650. In *The Military Revolution Debate: Readings on the Military Transformation of Early Modern Europe*, edited by Clifford J. Rogers, 273–298. Boulder, Colorado: Westview Press.

Tian, Changwu, and Zhifei Zang. 1996. *Zhou Qin shehui jiegou yanjiu* (A study of the social structure in the Zhou and Qin periods). Xian: Xibei daxue chubanshe.

Tilly, Charles. 1975. Reflections on the History of European State-Making. In *The Formation of the National States in Western Europe*, edited by Charles Tilly, 3–83. Princeton, New Jersey: Princeton University Press.

Tilly, Charles. 1992 [1990]. *Coercion, Capital, and European States, AD 990–1992*. Cambridge, Massachusetts: Blackwell.

Tilly, Charles. 1992. Futures of European states. *Social Research* 59 (4): 705–717.

Tilly, Charles. 1994. Entanglements of European Cities and States. In *Cities and The Rise of States in Europe AD 1000 to 1800*, edited by Charles Tilly and Wim Blockmans, 1–27. Boulder, Colorado: Westview Press.

Tilly, Charles. 1998. Westphalia and China. Keynote address, Conference on "Westphalia and Beyond," Enschede, Netherlands, July 1998; available at Columbia International Affairs Online (CIAO) wwwc.cc.columbia.edu/sec/dlc/ciao/wps/sites/css.html.

Tilly, Charles. 1999. Power: Top Down and Bottom Up. *Journal of Political Philosophy* 7 (3): 330–352.

Tracy, James D. 1990. *Holland Under Habsburg Rule, 1506–1566: The Formation of a Body Politic*. Berkeley: University of California Press.

Treasure, G. R. R. 1966. *Seventeenth Century France*. London: Rivingtons.

Unger, Roberto M. 1987. *Plasticity into Power: Comparative-Historical Studies on the Institutional Conditions of Economic and Military Success*. Cambridge: Cambridge University Press.

Van der Veen, A. Maurits. 2001. The Evolution of Cooperation in Society: Transforming the Prisoner's Dilemma. Paper presented at the Workshop on "Agent-Based Modeling for Social Scientists," March, Harvard University.

Van Evera, Stephen. 1998. Offense, Defense, and the Causes of War. *International Security* 22 (4): 5–43.

Van Evera, Stephen. 1999. *Causes of War: Power and the Roots of Conflict*. Ithaca, New York: Cornell University Press.

Vasquez, John A. 1997. The Realist Paradigm and Degenerative Versus Progressive Research Programs: An Appraisal of Neotraditional Research on Waltz's Balancing Proposition. *American Political Science Review* 91 (4): 899–912.

Vasquez, John A. 2003. The New Debate on Balancing Power: A Reply to My Critics. In *Realism and the Balancing of Power: A New Debate*, edited by John A. Vasquez and Colin Elman, 87–113. Englewood Cliffs, New Jersey: Prentice-Hall.

Viner, Jacob. 1948. Power Versus Plenty as Objectives of Foreign Policy in the 17th and 18th Centuries. *World Politics* 1 (1): 1–29.

Wagner, Donald B. 1996. *Iron and Steel in Ancient China*. New York: E. J. Brill.

Wagner, R. Harrison. 1986. The Theory of Games and the Balance of Power. *World Politics* 38 (4): 546–576.

Walker, Richard. 1953. *The Multi-State System of Ancient China*. Westport, Connecticut: Greenwood Press.

Wallerstein, Immanuel. 1999a. The West, Capitalism, and the Modern World-System. In *China and Historical Capitalism: Genealogies of Sinological Knowledge*, edited by Gregory Blue and Timothy Brook, 10–56. Cambridge: Cambridge University Press.

Wallerstein, Immanuel. 1999b. States? Sovereignty? The Dilemmas of Capitalists in an Age of Transition. In *States and Sovereignty in the Global Economy*, edited by David A. Smith, Dorothy J. Solinger, and Steven C. Topik, 20–33. New York: Routledge.

Walt, Stephen M. 1987. *The Origins of Alliances*. Ithaca, New York: Cornell University Press.

Waltz, Kenneth. 1979. *Theory of International Politics*. Reading, Massachusetts: Addison-Wesley.

Waltz, Kenneth. 1986. Reflections on *Theory of International Politics*: A Response to My Critics. In *Neorealism and Its Critics*, edited by Robert O. Keohane, 322–345. New York: Columbia University Press.

Waltz, Kenneth. 1988. The Origins of War in Neorealist Theory. *Journal of Interdisciplinary History* 18 (4): 615–628.

Waltz, Kenneth. 1989. The Origins of War in Neorealist Theory. In *The Origin and Prevention of Major Wars*, edited by Robert I. Rotberg and Theodore K. Rabb, 39–52. Cambridge: Cambridge University Press.

Waltzer, Michael. 1977. *Just and Unjust Wars: A Moral Argument with Historical Illustrations*. New York: Basic Books.

Wang, Kevin, and James Lee Ray. 1994. Beginners and Winners: The Fate of Initiators of Interstate Wars Involving Great Powers Since 1495. *International Studies Quarterly* 38 (1): 139–154.

Wang, Xu. 1999. Mutual Empowerment of State and Society: Its Nature, Conditions, Mechanisms, and Limits. *Comparative Politics* 21 (2): 231–249.

Watkins, Frederick M. 1934. *The State as a Concept of Political Science*. New York: Harper and Brothers.

Watson, Adam. 1992. *The Evolution of International Society*. New York: Routledge.

Watson, Burton, translation with an introduction. 1963. *Hsün Tzu: Basic Writings*. New York: Columbia University Press.

Watson, Burton, translation with an introduction. 1964. *Han Fei Tzu: Basic Writings*. New York: Columbia University Press.

Watson, Burton, translation with a commentary. 1989. *The Tso chuan: Selections from China's Oldest Narrative History*. New York: Columbia University Press.

Weber, Max. 1958. Bureaucracy. In *From Max Weber: Essays in Sociology*, edited by H. H. Gerth and C. W. Mills, 196–244. London: Oxford University Press.

Weber, Max, translated by Frank H. Knight. 1982. *General Economic History*. New Brunswick, New Jersey: Transaction Books.

Weld, Susan. 1999. Chu Law in Action. In *Defining Chu: Image and Reality in Ancient China*, edited by Constance A. Cook and John S. Major, 77–97. Honolulu: University of Hawaii Press.

Wendt, Alexander. 1992. Anarchy Is What States Make of It: The Social Construction of Power Politics. *International Organization* 46 (2): 391–425.

Wendt, Alexander. 1999. *Social Theory of International Politics*. Cambridge: Cambridge University Press.

Williams, Michael C. 1996. Hobbes and International Relations: A Reconsideration. *International Organization* 50 (2): 213–236.

Williamson, Oliver E. 1985. *The Economic Institutions of Capitalism: Firms, Markets, Relational Contracting*. New York: Free Press.

Wohlforth, William C. 1999. The Stability of a Unipolar World. *International Security* 24 (1): 5–41.

Wohlforth, William C., Richard Little, Stuart Kaufman, David C. Kang, Charles Jones, Victoria Tin-bor Hui, Arthur Ecksten, Daniel H. Deudney, and William Brenner. 2005. Why Balancing Fails: Evidence from Eight International Systems. Unpublished manuscript, Dartmouth College.

Wolfer, Arnold. 1962. *Discord and Collaboration: Essays on International Politics*. Baltimore: Johns Hopkins University Press.

Wong, R. Bin. 1997. *China Transformed: Historical Change and the Limits of the European Experience*. Ithaca, New York: Cornell University Press.

Wong, R. Bin. 1999. The Political Economy of Agrarian Empire and Its Modern Legacy. In *China and Historical Capitalism: Genealogies of Sinological Knowledge*, edited by Gregory Blue and Timothy Brook, 210–245. Cambridge: Cambridge University Press.

Wootton, David. 1994. Introduction. In *Selected Political Writings: The Prince, Selections from the Discourses, Letter to Vettori*, by Niccolò Machiavelli, xi–xliv. Cambridge: Hackett.

Wu, Rongceng. 1995. Developmental Trends in the History of the Warring States Period and Qin Dynasty. In *Zhongguo lishishang de fenyuhe xueshu yantaohui lunwenji* (Collection of essays from the Seminar on Unification and Division in Chinese History), edited by editorial board, 45–56. Taipei: Lianjing chubanshe.

Xiao, Pan. 1990. *Xianqinshi* (Pre-Qin history). Taipei: Zhongwen Tushu.

Xie, Waiyang. 1995. *Zhongguo zaoqi guojia* (The early states in China). Hanzhou: Zhejiang renmin chubanshe.

Xin, Xiangyang. 1995. *Daguo zhuhou: Zhongguo zhongyang yu difang guanxi zhijie* (Great-power feudal lords: Central-local relations in China). Beijing: Zhongguo shehui chubanshe.

Xing, Yitian. 1987. *Qin-Han shi lunkao* (A discussion of the history of Qin and Han). Taipei: Dongda chubanshe.

Xu, Jinxiong. 1995. *Zhongguo Gudai Shehui* (Ancient Chinese society). Taipei: Taibei shangwu chubanshe.

Yang, Kuan, translated and edited with an introduction by Yu-ning Li. 1977. *Shang Yang's Reforms and State Control in China*. White Plains, New York: M. E. Sharpe.

Yang, Kuan. 1986. *Zhanguo Shi* (History of the Warring States). Taipei: Gufeng chubanshe.

Yang, Zihui, ed. 1996. *Zhongguo lidai renkou tongji ziliao yanjiu* (China historical population data and relevant studies). Beijing: Gaige chubanshe.

Yates, Robin D. S. 1980. The Mohists on Warfare: Technology, Techniques, and Justification. *Journal of the American Academy of Religion, Thematic Studies Supplement* 47 (3): 549–603.

Yates, Robin D. S. 1982. Siege Engines and Late Zhou Military Technology. In *Explorations in the History of Science and Technology in China*, edited by Guohao Li, Mengwen Zhang, and Tianqin Cao, 409–452. Shanghai: Shanghai Chinese Classics.

Yates, Robin D. S. 1987. Social Status in the Ch'in: Evidence from the Yun-meng Legal Documents. Part 1. Commoners. *Harvard Journal of Asiatic Studies* 47 (1): 197–237.

Ye, Daxiong. 1992. Xian Qin shiqi 'zhongguo' guannian de xingcheng yu fazhan (The formation and development of the concept of "China" in the pre-Qin period). Master's thesis, History Department, National Taiwan University.

Zacher, Mark W. 2001. The Territorial Integrity Norm: International Boundaries and the Use of Force. *International Organization* 55 (2): 215–250.

Zakaria, Fareed. 1998. *From Wealth to Power: The Unusual Origins of America's World Role*. Princeton, New Jersey: Princeton University Press.

Zakaria, Fareed. 1994. A Conversation with Lee Kuan Yew. *Foreign Affairs* 73 (2): 109–126.

Zakaria, Fareed. 1999 [1997]. The Rise of Illiberal Democracy. *Foreign Affairs* 76 (6): 22–43; reprinted in *The New Shape of World Politics*, Foreign Affairs Agenda, 242–258. New York: Foreign Affairs.

Zhang, Xiaosheng and Wenyan Liu. 1988. *Zhongguo Gudai Zhanzheng Tonglan* (An overview of wars in Ancient China). Beijing: Changzheng chubanshe.

"Zhongguo junshishi" editorial board. 1983–1991. *Zhongguo junshishi* (Chinese military history). vol. 1. *bingqi* (Military weapons). vol. 2. *binglue* (Military strategies). vol. 3. *bingzhi* (Military systems). vol. 4. *bingfa* (Art of war). vol. 5. *bingjia* (Schools of military thought). Beijing: Jiefangjun chubanshe (People's Liberation Army Press).

"Zhongguo lidai zhanzheng nianbiao" editorial board. 2003. *Zhongguo lidai zhanzheng nianbiao* (Chronology of wars in China through successive dynasties). Beijing: Jiefangjun chubanshe (People's Liberation Army Press).

Index